This is an annual. That is to say,
it is substantially revised each year, the
new edition appearing each November.
Those wishing to submit additions,
corrections, or suggestions for the
1994 edition should submit them prior
to March 1, 1993, using the form
provided in the back of this book.
(Forms reaching us after that date will,
unfortunately, have to wait for the
1995 edition.)

What Color Is Your Parachute?

Other Books by Richard N. Bolles

The Three Boxes of Life,
  And How To Get Out of Them

Where Do I Go From Here With My Life?
  (co-authored with John C. Crystal)

1993 Edition

What Color Is Your Parachute?

A Practical Manual
for
Job-Hunters
& Career-Changers

by

Richard Nelson Bolles

Ten Speed Press

The diagrams in chapters 3, 8, 9, 10 and 11 are by
Steven M. Johnson, author of *What The World Needs Now.*

Copyright © 1993, 1992, 1991, 1990, 1989, 1988, 1987, 1986, 1985, 1984,
1983, 1982, 1981, 1980, 1979, 1978, 1977, 1976, 1975, 1972, 1970
by Richard Nelson Bolles.

Library of Congress Catalog Card No. 84-649334
ISBN 0-89815-492-8, paper
ISBN 0-89815-506-1, cloth
Published by Ten Speed Press, P.O. Box 7123, Berkeley, California 94707

© Copyright 1981. United Feature Syndicate, Inc. Used by permission.

Type set by Haru Composition and Hannah Associates, San Francisco, California
Consolidated Printers, Inc., Berkeley, California
Printed in the United States of America

Contents

This is dedicated to the one I love
(my wife, Carol)

Preface

Yes, it's Hard Times indeed. Though not as *hard* as it was in the last century:

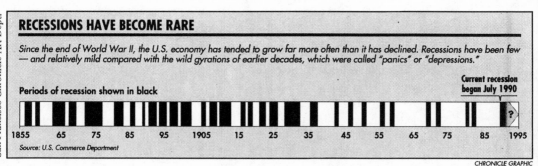

(The black lines are recessions, and the thicker the black, the longer the recession.)

Currently, the statistics are these. At any given moment during these Hard Times, typically,

35 out of every 100 unemployed persons have been out of work less than five weeks, thus far;

28 out of every 100 have been out of work between five and fourteen weeks, thus far;

13 out of every 100 have been out of work between fifteen and twenty-six weeks, thus far;

24 out of every 100 have been out of work twenty-seven weeks or longer; and/or have stopped looking altogether.[1]

Of course, these statistics are based on *a particular method of job-hunting*- - namely, the Neanderthal job-hunting system that is universally practiced in this country and elsewhere, which I describe in Chapter 3. Thus, these statistics should be prefaced with the remark: "*If* you go job-hunting the way *most* people do, this is how long your unemployment will likely last." And the statistics ought to end with: "If you find better ways of going about job-hunting, you may cut these figures down dramatically."[2]

1. Statistics based, in part, on the February 1992 issue of the *Monthly Labor Review*, published by the U.S. Department of Labor, Bureau of Labor Statistics; and, in part, on the figures for discouraged workers for that same time period; and, in part, on a paper by the late Bob Wegmann, entitled, "How Long Does Unemployment Last?"

2. This refers to the methods which I cover in Chapter 4, and describe in even more detail in Chapters 9, 10, and 11.

When we are out of work, we are usually told that it is the government that must take action, to 'jump-start' the economy, and create more jobs. But alas! Here in these belt-tightening '90s all the traditional spending programs that we counted on to save us in another day and age - - the 1930's for example - - are not available. And they are not available because everyone - - federal, state and local governments, banks, corporations, and individuals - - have all overspent during the '80s, and now must work off their debt, probably for several years, *before* any new or systemic remedies for unemployment can come into play.

The New Poverty

Because of the new 'belt-tightening' that is going on at workplaces throughout the U.S. during the '90s, it is becoming harder and harder to find a salary which will pay you what you got *'in the old days'* - - five years ago. Consequently, more and more people are being forced to live minimally, and do their own belt-tightening.

There are now 33.6 million people in the U.S. below the poverty line. Two million of these joined the rest just during the year 1990, due to their declining income. (In the U.S. currently, you are considered to be below the poverty line if you are a family of four and are making less than $13,921 annually.) Support for those living below the poverty line is decreasing, from both the Federal and State governments, due to the fact that these governments themselves are in dire financial straits. By 1991, forty States had cut or frozen benefits to families with children.

Nearly one out of every five workers in the U.S. is currently working part-time, many of them involuntarily - - they'd like to find full-time work, if they could. (The average work-week in the U.S. is now only 34.7 hours.)

Part-timers, on average, earn only 60% as much, per hour, as full-time workers, and are also less likely to have medical or pension benefits.

It is time we tried another way. Rather than waiting for the government, it's time for each individual to learn how to rescue themselves. An ancient proverb says: "Give me a fish, and I will eat for today; teach me to fish, and I will eat for the rest of my life." This book is an attempt to teach you how to fish, with respect to the most difficult task any of us faces in life: the job-hunt - - whether it be a hunt for the same thing you've always done, or for something new and different, in the way of a career.

The average person has to go job-hunting eight times in his or her life. This book is an attempt to *empower* you as job-hunter or career-changer so that no matter how many times you may have to go about this task during the rest of your life, you will know how to do it, and do it well.

Two profound changes happened with respect to this book in 1992. First of all, it was the book's very best year (no surprise, considering the economy). Over 25,000 job-hunters a month picked it up - - and not just in the U.S. and Canada, either. The book is being used in Eastern European countries, in Asia, and elsewhere.

Secondly, it was the year that I felt I simply had to rewrite the book from start to finish. I tried to preserve material from the *old book* that people have known and valued over the book's twenty-two-year history; but at the same time, the new realities of the '90s came crashing in, so I felt I had to rewrite it all, from scratch.

It's just about the same size as last year, but I rearranged the division between the body of the book and the appendices - - much of the stuff which used to be in the appendices, because it was optional, has now moved into the body of the book, because it is now part of the knowledge one needs, to survive in the '90s. Whereas this book had six chapters previously, with lots of optional appendices, it now has fourteen chapters and very little appendices.

It has been clear for some time that many readers do not tackle all the material in this book, all at once. And I am sure that will continue. Readers will not read Chapter 7, if they are not interested in moving. Readers will not read Chapter 6, if they have no interest in starting their own business, etc.

But, knowledge which you don't seem to need at all *this year,* may turn out to be knowledge you need very badly *next year.* So, I spent five months rewriting the whole book for the '90s, and I explained it all as carefully as I know how. I do want to emphasize, however, that the ideas discussed in this book are *not* my bright ideas, but are culled from the experience of *successful* job-hunters and career-changers -- thousands of them -- over the years.

And now, in closing this preface, my annual litany of heartfelt thanks. In order that this book could be written in the first place, endless travel and interviewing was conducted originally around the whole U.S. covering some 65,000 miles. Then, and since, I want to thank:

- The countless victims of our country's outdated, outmoded, and Neanderthal job-hunting apparatus, who shared with me their problems and difficulties, and finally their triumphs.
- Everyone who continues to take time to write and tell me how they used this book to effect meaningful changes in their life and work, and especially those who tell me *which* ideas in the book were particularly helpful to them.
- Those creative souls, who first pointed out to me what was wrong with this country's whole job-hunting and career-changing *system,* and gave me documentary evidence of the same - - in particular, Dick Lathrop, Sidney Fine, the late Bob Wegmann, Daniel Porot, Tom and Ellie Jackson, Howard Figler, Arthur Miller, Bernard Haldane, Nathan Azrin, Carol Christen, John Holland, Peter Drucker, and - - above all - - the late John Crystal, who gave me the framework, now preserved in Chapters 9, 10, and 11 in this book, of *What, Where, and How.* God bless you, John, in your heavenly rest.
- Bev Anderson, who has done the layout of this book *(and all my other written works)* year after year, since 1972. I love working with her; she is a delight.
- Haru Watanabe for the great care he gives to the typesetting each year.
- Phil Wood, my publisher, for his unfailing support in my work.
- His associates George Young, Hal Hershey, and Jackie Wan who each year help this book to get done and get done right.
- My office staff, who over the years have taken a great burden off my back, so that I might devote my time to research and writing.
- The Lord God, our Great Creator, who is the One who has given me the talents and the inspiration to write this book - - and the will to revise it each year.
- My dear ninety-year-old aunt, Sister Esther Mary, of the Community of the Transfiguration (Episcopal) in Glendale, Ohio, who has taught me from my youth up.
- And - - above all others - - my dear wife, Carol, for her wit, wisdom, encouragement, and love over the years. As my four

grown children, Stephen, Mark, Gary, and Sharon, and my 16-year-old stepdaughter, Serena, will attest, she is a *wonderful* woman. I am most blessed to be her husband.

Now, on with the book. My friend, I wish you good luck. I wish you persistence. I wish you success, not only with your job-hunt or career-change, but - - even more - - with your life.

Dick Bolles
P. O. Box 379
Walnut Creek, California 94597
July 26, 1992

A Grammar Footnote

I want to explain three points of grammar, in this book: pronouns, commas, and italics. My unorthodox use of them invariably offends unemployed English teachers so much that they write me to apply for a job as my editor.

To save us unnecessary correspondence, let me explain. Throughout this book, I often use the apparently plural pronoun "they," "them," or "their" with singular verbs or antecedents - - such as, "You must approach *someone* for a job and tell *them* what you can do." This sounds strange and even wrong to those who know English well. To be sure, we all know that there is another pronoun - - "you" - - that may be either singular or plural, but few of us realize that the pronoun "they," "them," or "their" was also once treated as both plural and singular in the English language. The latter usage changed, at a time in English history when agreement in number became more important than agreement as to sexual gender. Today, however, our priorities are shifting once again. Now, the distinguishing of sexual gender is considered by many to be more important than agreement in number.

The common artifices used for this new priority, such as "s/he," or "he/she," are tortuous and inelegant. Hence, Casey Miller and Kate Swift, in their classic *The Handbook of Nonsexist Writing*, argue that it is time to bring back the earlier usage of "they," "them," and "their" as both singular and plural - - just as "you" is/are. They further argue that this return to the earlier historical usage has already become quite common out on the street - - witness a typical sign by the ocean which reads "Anyone using this beach after 5 p.m. does so at their own risk." I have followed Casey and Kate's wise recommendation.

As for my commas, they are deliberately used according to my own rules - - rather than according to the rules of historic grammar (which I did learn - - I hastily add, to reassure my old Harvard English teachers, who despaired of me then and now). My own rules about commas are: write conversationally, and put in a comma wherever I would normally stop for a breath, were I speaking the same line.

The same conversational rule applies to my use of italics. I use italics wherever, were I speaking the sentence, I would put emphasis on that word or phrase. Rarely, I also use italics where there is a digression of thought, and I want to maintain the main thought and flow of the sentence.

*And I saw my ship
Carried on the great sea,
Safely, I thought,
Until suddenly I realized I was
In the belly of the great whale.*
Jonah

CHAPTER ONE

The Day That Jobs Began to Vanish

It was just another Recession--or so we thought--
The ninth since the end of World War II.
They seem to come and go,
With predictable regularity. So,
Sure, there were layoffs
Sometimes at the rate of over 2,000 a day; but then
There always were, in a Recession.
No cause for alarm. Layoffs
Are temporary, while business is
Bad. But when it improves, the workers
Would be called back. That's the way it always is,
And always had been,
And always would be,
For ever and ever. Amen.

But whoa! suddenly
We realized that something else was going on,
Before our very eyes.
This Recession was turning into a wicked
Thing, the longest on record
Since the Great Depression of the 1930s, and
Soon we heard,
Far beneath the surface of this Recession,
A profound shaking of the very ground
On which we stood; and we knew
We were experiencing a
Workquake.
Just like an earthquake,
Something of the magnitude that shook San Francisco
Back in '89,
When part of the Bay Bridge fell,
And buildings we had counted on,
Suddenly became unsafe,
Because huge earthplates moved
Far beneath the surface
Of the land.

Yes, this was something just like that:
A workquake,

A profound shaking of the whole marketplace,
  With businesses falling
    Crash, to the ground,
      And others standing, upright still,
        But needing shoring up
          With timbers made from Chapter 11,
            And many declared unsafe
              Except for fewer employees.

            Bewildered, many of us found
            We had no job; and layoffs
            Were permanent,
            We had to say
            The sweet goodbye,
          The bitter farewell,
        To life as we had known it
      Many jobs were dying, never to rise again.
        And we realized we were witnessing
      The Day That Jobs Began to Vanish.

    What were those two great workplates
      Beneath the surface of the market place,
    That were moving, and grinding
  And shaking
  Everything?
  One great workplate was debt,
Mountainous debt,
Incurred by almost *everyone*
In the '80s.

As a nation we had binged
Too much
  Throughout that expanding decade.
   Spending what we couldn't afford,
    Piling debt on debt.
     The federal government did it,
       Becoming the largest debtor nation in the world,
         Financial institutions did it,
           Costing the largest bailout in history,

Businesses did it,
Piling takeover upon takeover,
And junk bond upon junk bond,
Until, staggering under their burden of debt
Some of the biggest names we knew
Died.
Pan Am, Eastern Airlines, and others.
May they rest in Peace.
And, to our sorrow,
We individually also piled up debt,
Spending away our savings,
To buy all the necessities plus
Many things we did not *need*.
We only *wanted* them,
And that is not the same thing.

Anyway, here in the '90s,
All that debt, pressing down,
Beneath the surface of the workplace,
Moved, with crushing weight,
Against the other plate,
The other workplate,
Deep down there,
The plate called accountability.
People stopped spending,
For they could see
That you can only spend, so long,
What you do not have,
And then,
It's clearly time for accountability:
It's time
To pay the piper.
Consumer confidence plummeted,
The *public* was concerned -- ah,
Was it ever!
"There is a deep-seated concern
Out there,"
Said Alan Greenspan,
Chairman of the Federal Reserve,

"That I have not seen
In my lifetime." [1]

So now we are in the time
After the workquake, when
The government,
And banks,
And businesses
And individuals,
Have stopped expanding
Started playing down their debt,
And learning to *downsize*, to be
A leaner, meaner
Kind of economy,
A change announced when the temblor first hit,
That Day That Jobs Began to Vanish.

We will find work
In the new world
After the 'quake,
For the jobs will come back,
In greater number than ever before.
But
We may be doing
Something different,
And it may not pay as well
As the job we used to have;
The well-paying jobs
Are slowly disappearing
From our culture.
Still, we will find
Our way,
And we will learn
Not only how our bodies *can* survive,
But how our souls can prosper.

---

1. For further reading on this concern, the classic text is Donald L. Barlett and James B. Steele, *America: What Went Wrong?* Andrews & McMeel, publishers. 1992.

I've tried to be content
With my lot in life.
But, boy, I hate all this soot,
And seeing my sisters get out,
While I stay here, cleaning the hearth.
Come on, now, where
Is that glass slipper
You promised?

Cinderella

CHAPTER TWO

Are These
'Hard Times'?

Chapter 2

FOR THE UNEMPLOYED, IT'S ALWAYS 'HARD TIMES'

People generally think that if it isn't a Recession or Depression, it isn't Hard Times. That of course isn't true. A Recession is obviously a time that is hard. But, a Recession can be over, and it can still be Hard Times for many.

Is this present moment a Hard Time? The answer, of course, depends on whether you are unemployed, or employed but worried, or employed but secure. During typical Hard Times *(this 'snapshot' was taken 2/1/92):* 2 out of every 14 workers are unemployed *(to one degree or another),* 6 out of the 14 are employed but worried about losing their job, and 6 out of every 14 workers are employed and not worried about losing their job.

THE THREE CLASSES OF WORKERS CREATED BY HARD TIMES

SECURE	WORRIED	UNEMPLOYED
Those Who Have Jobs And Are Basically Not Worried About Losing Them	Those Who Have Jobs And ARE Worried About Losing Them	Those Who Have Lost Their Jobs In These Hard Times
(6 out of every 14 workers)	(6 out of every 14 workers)	(2 out of every 14 workers)

What conclusion you draw from these statistics, depends of course not only on what group you are in, but also on your basic nature. If you are sunnily optimistic, by nature, you will say, "Hey, these Hard Times aren't so bad; there are 12 people who have a job for every 2 who don't." If you are slightly pessimistic, by nature, you will say, "Hey, these truly are Hard Times; 8 out of every 14 workers either have lost their job or are worried about losing it." And if you are out of work you will say, "Hey, these Hard Times are awful. I'm one of some seventeen million people who want full-time jobs and can't find them." Seventeen million is a lot of people. There were only sixteen million who were out of work during the Great Depression of the 1930's.

HOW MANY PEOPLE ARE OUT OF WORK

The government claimed -- in the moment I highlighted above -- that there were 'only' eight million (8.9 million to be exact) out of work, not the seventeen million I just referred to. That's because the government *(whether it be Republican or Democrat)* has, over the years, evolved a very peculiar scheme for counting the unemployed. You and I, using our common sense, would suppose that at any given moment, the unemployed or almost-unemployed would include the following five groups:

THOSE WHO ARE ACTUALLY UNEMPLOYED IN HARD TIMES *A Typical Monthly Snapshot (taken 2/7/92)*				
New Workers Delaying Their Entry into the Job-seeking Group	Discouraged Workers Out of Work But Not Out Looking During the Last Four Weeks	Active Job-Seekers, Out of Work and Having Gone Job-hunting Sometime in Last Four Weeks	Partially Employed: Still Looking for a Full-time Job, but Meanwhile Holding Down Some Kind of Part-time Work	Prematurely Retired: Induced to Leave the Work-force With a Good 'Package' but Would Prefer to Keep on Working
166,000	1,300,000	8,900,000	6,700,000	Unknown
Total Who Are Actually Unemployed (or Only Partly-Employed) At Any Given Moment During Hard Times: 17,066,000				

This is what common sense tells us. But the government, with a logic known to them alone, counts only the third category (above) -- the 8,900,000 -- as unemployed. That leaves the unemployment figure, above, at only 7.1%, instead of the 13.5%

that the above diagram reveals.[1] But never mind what the government says. If you are out of work presently, or soon, you have much more company than you might think - - and obviously more than *they* think.[2]

HOW MANY WORKERS
ARE THINKING ABOUT
CHANGING CAREERS

Everyone would agree that it is Hard Times if seventeen million people are out of work or only partially employed. But there are even more people than that, who are out there looking for a new job, during these times.

That's because throughout modern history, people have gone looking for work due to two reasons. We may call these "outside forces" and "internal forces." The **outside forces** are the ones we all think of, when we are talking about unemployment: you find yourself thrown out of work due to somebody else's decision. This event is described in various ways. You are: laid off, or summarily dismissed, or fired, or 'canned', or terminated, or 'made redundant,' or whatever other euphemism our society can come up with. Your firing may be precipitated by: a "downsizing," or a restructuring, or your employer going out of business, or a personality conflict with your supervisor or boss, or some form of prejudice: age discrimination, racial discrimination, sex discrimination, and the like. In many cases, you are laid-off or fired totally without warning. You are *out of there*. It

---

1. *Harpers Magazine,* March 1992 issue, thinks this adds up to only 12.7% instead of 13.5% for the period indicated; but we're not disagreeing by much. Either figure is quite a bit larger than the 7.1% that the government claims.

2. The government's unemployment figures get criticized with regularity in the media. Cf. *Harper's Magazine,* in footnote 1; cf. also "Why Jobless Figures Can Be Bunk," a front page article in the *San Francisco Chronicle,* 4/3/92; also "America's Undercounted Unemployed," from the *New York Times,* summarized in *Manpower Argus,* March 1992. Articles also appear, though with less frequency, arguing in the government's defense that the unemployment statistics *overstate* the problem, since a number of those who claim to be unemployed are actually working, as part of *the underground economy* (people who work for cash, and never declare it to the government). I think that some of those who claim to be unemployed are actually working somehow somewhere, but I don't think it necessarily affords them a full-time living, nor do I think it makes a large statistical difference in the unemployment figures.

means nothing that you may have worked at that place for *years*, and have given that organization the best years of your life. You are 'history,' due to somebody else's decision, which is totally beyond your control. And very likely you will be depressed, or angry or even livid.[3]

On the other hand, none of this may happen to you. Your job may be as secure as can be; you could probably still have it for the next twenty years. Nonetheless, you are thinking about going job-hunting. And why? In this case, the answer is: **internal forces** -- things going on totally inside you. You're ready to chuck that job, even if the economy is in the dumps. You are tired of that job, bored, fed up, and hungry for something better in life -- something new, exciting, and challenging. Or, if your work has given you that -- in spades -- it may be that you're stressed, burnt out, exhausted, and hungry for something peaceful, calm, and secure. Either way, you're ready to go job-hunting, perhaps even to change careers. Of course everyone tells you you're crazy, and that this is precisely the wrong time to be making any such kind of move. But you don't care. Your internal time clock has just struck midnight.

---

3. Getting fired is no fun. I've been fired twice, myself, once when I was 22, and once when I was 41 years old. In the world of work today, you can get fired for 'screwing up' on the job OR you can get fired even when you're doing a simply excellent job. If your next employer asks *why* you were fired, it is sufficient if you merely say, "Usually, I get along well with everyone, but in this particular case the boss and I just didn't get along with each other. Difficult to say why." You don't need to say any more than that. For further reading, there are these:

Emily Koltnow and Lynne S. Dumas, *CONGRATULATIONS! You've Been Fired: Sound Advice for Women Who've Been Terminated, Pink-Slipped, Downsized, or Otherwise Unemployed.* Fawcett Columbine, published by Ballantine Books, 201 E. 50th St., New York, NY 10022.

Judith A. Dubin and Melanie R. Keveles, *Fired for Success: How to Turn Losing Your Job Into The Opportunity of a Lifetime!* Warner Books, Inc., 666 Fifth Ave., N.Y. N.Y. 10103. 1990.

Jill Jukes and Ruthan Rosenberg, *I've been fired, too! Coping with your husband's job loss.* Stoddart Publishing Co., Ltd., 34 Lesmill Rd., Toronto, Canada M3B 2T6. 1991.

Barry Gale and Linda Gale, *Stay or Leave: A Complete System for Deciding Whether to Remain at Your Job or Pack Your Traveling Bag.* HarperCollins, 10 East 53rd St., New York, NY 10022-5299. 1989.

Employment Law in the 50 States: A Reference for Employers. CUE/NAM, 1331 Pennsylvania Ave. NW, Suite 1500 - North Lobby, Washington, DC 20004-1703. 1987.

Richard Layard, *How To Beat Unemployment.* Oxford University Press, Walton St., Oxford, OX2 6DP, U.K. 1986.

If you feel this way, you have lots of company. In a survey conducted relatively recently *(in 1991),* it was found that 33% of all workers in the U.S. had thought seriously about chucking their jobs the previous year, and 14% actually did - - over a two year period. Given the fact that 118 million are working, *as I write,* that means 39 million of us toyed with the idea of seeking something better, and 16 million of us actually went through with it, during last year and the year before.

Adding this number to the unemployed, we get a figure of 33 million of us who are engrossed with the question of job-hunting or career-change, in this current age, and another 23 million who are edging into that area.

WHAT SKILLS ARE NEEDED TO SURVIVE IN HARD TIMES

It is clear that there are two basic skills you must master, if you are going to survive:

A. You need to know how to go about job-hunting in some original ways when jobs are scarce. *And,*

B. You need to know how to go about identifying and landing a new career, *without going back to school for retraining - - if possible.*

These are not *optional* skills which you can choose to pick up, or not, as you please. No, these are *necessary* skills - - crucial to your survival in this modern work-a-day world.

Ideally, you need to master these two survival skills *before* you land in the soup. It would be nice if our high schools and colleges taught these skills to you, before you had even embarked upon the rough seas of The Workplace. But no such luck. You will have to pick these survival skills up on your own. Sometimes - - *in fact, most times* - - right in the midst of the storm, internal or external, that you are in. That, of course, is why you are reading this book, isn't it? You have become acutely aware of the fact that you need these skills. Now.

And, my friend, since the average person does 6–8 job-hunts in his or her life, and three career changes, these are skills that you will need *for the rest of your life.*

WHAT GROUPS
NEED THESE SKILLS

From the above studies and statistics, we have already seen the beginning of a list of what groups need these skills. Let's flesh out that list now, and finish it off. Those of us who currently need job-hunting and career-changing skills are:

People who are new to the labor market
    High school students or graduates
    College students or graduates
    Former homemakers who now need or want to get a job
    Others
People who have gotten a degree and don't know what
to do with it
People who have been fired, laid-off, or made redundant;
especially:
    Workers in the automobile industry
    Workers in aerospace
    Workers in the airline industry
    Workers in banks and financial institutions
    Workers in communications
    Workers in the computer industry
    Workers in defense industries
    Workers in the entertainment industry
    Workers in government
    Workers in the newspaper industry
    Workers in the retail industry
    Workers in social services
    Workers in the travel industry
    A lot of other groups not mentioned above
People who have been induced to take early retirement,
before they wished to, and still want to work
People who have a job, but are worried they may lose it
People who have a job, but are fed up with it, or 'totally
stressed out'
People who like their job, but are totally 'stressed out'
People who are dying to 'switch'
People who want to make a career-change
People who want to go into business for themselves

People who have one kind of handicap or another, and consequently face possible prejudice in the job-hunt:

Those whose race, color, sexual orientation, ethnic background, or country of origin may be a problem with *some* employers

Those whose poor English may be a problem with *some* employers

Those whose body image may be a problem with *some* employers

Those whose lack of education may be a problem with *some* employers

Those who have too much education for *some* employers

Those whose age may be a problem with *some* employers

Those who are close to retirement, which may be a problem with *some* employers

Those with life-threatening diseases, such as AIDS, which may be a problem with *some* employers

Those who have a physical handicap that may be a problem for *some* employers

Those who have a mental or emotional handicap that may be a problem for *some* employers

Those who have a psychiatric history that may be a problem for *some* employers

Those who are in a major depression, which may be a problem with *some* employers

Those who have a prison record that may be a problem for *some* employers

Those whose lack of experience (in the job-market or in *their* industry) may be a problem for *some* employers

Those whose personality may be a problem for *some* employers

Ex-military

Ex-clergy or ordained

People from another city

People from another state

People from another country

People from another planet

Everyone who still has at least ten years ahead of
them in the workplace
A lot of other groups not mentioned above

All of us who are members of these groups need to master,
for the rest of our time in the world of work, the two basic
survival skills I mentioned above:

A. You need to know how to go about job-hunting in some
original ways when jobs are scarce, or nonexistent. *And,*

B. You need to know how to go about identifying and landing
a new career, *without going back to school for retraining - - if possible.*

UNDERSTAND
THERE ARE TWO KINDS
OF EMPLOYERS

You probably noticed, in this long list, how much I emphasized that if you have a so-called job-hunting *(or career- changing)*
handicap (age, sex, background, etc.) it is only a handicap *with
some employers*, didn't you? This leads us to a crucial job-hunting
principle, that you need to memorize before you even start out:

HOW TO THINK
ABOUT 'EMPLOYERS'

In approaching employers during a job-hunt it is
crucial to remember that there are two kinds of
employers out there:

• those who won't hire you because they will be put
off by whatever handicap you may have; AND

• those who will not be put off by your handicap, and
therefore will hire you, if you are qualified for the job.

During your job-hunt, you are not interested in the
former kind of employer, no matter how many of
them there are. You are only looking for those
employers who are not put off by your handicap, and
therefore will hire you if you can do the job.

UNDERSTAND WHAT A JOB IS

To understand how a person gets to be an employer, we must begin with a simple task: understanding what a job is. A simple illustration should help. Let's say that, for a number of years now, on your friends' birthdays you haven't sent them a store-bought greeting card. Instead, you have designed and drawn your own cards. Your friends love them. They tell you how pretty they are, and how witty they are, and how unusual they are. Your friends urge you to make more cards and sell them to the neighborhood. Since you don't have a job at the moment, you take their advice. You set out to design and draw a large number of such birthday cards. Then you go door to door, showing them to people, and asking them if they want to buy them. To your surprise, many of them say yes. In fact, soon you are making a very nice income by selling these cards door to door. You are also, however, exhausted. Drawing the cards all evening, and selling them all day, is just too much for you. You decide to get some help. You advertise for someone willing to go door to door, and out of all the prospects who show up in answer to your ad, you choose the best one; he or she is hired. You have an employee now. You have become an employer.

Whoa! Let's pause right there. What *makes* you an employer, in this story? Well, I think you see. You are an employer because you give up some of your **money**, in order to get someone else to give you some of their **time**. *Your money exchanged for their time.* That's what makes you an employer. OK, then what makes that other person an employee? Because of the reverse: they give up some of their time, in order to have some of your money. *Their time exchanged for your money.* That's what makes them an employee.

If we summarized it in a diagram, it would look like this:

	EMPLOYER	EMPLOYEE
HAS ▶	Money	X Skills Time
LACKS / NEEDS ▶	X Skills Someone's time	Money
WILLING TO MAKE THIS EXCHANGE: ▶	Money for Skills and time	Skills and time for Money

Granted, *many* other factors also enter in. e.g., the employee wants a feeling of contributing to this world, etc. But we want to keep this simple, for the time being.

Okay, on with our mythical story. Having given up some of your money to get this employee, you soon discover you are not left with less money. Magic! On the contrary, you have even more money than you did before you gave up some. And why? Because the person you hired is so helpful in going door to door, that twice as many cards are being sold as before. More income for you. More money to keep track of. Oops. You now recall how bad you are at keeping track of money, and balancing a checkbook. But it's becoming obvious that you need those skills, for your expanding business. What to do? Go back to school and learn how to do these things yourself? Takes too long. Nope, there's a better way. Hire a person who has those skills. So, you bring an accountant on board. Voila! You've just hired another employee.

So, you're a happy employer with two employees: everything seems to be going swimmingly, when suddenly Hard Times appear. The economy starts to turn down, consumers lose their confidence, their money is tighter, and they try to pinch pennies wherever they can. They decide to buy not so many of your cards, as before. Your income decreases. You come to the hard realization: you can only afford one employee now. You debate, and then decide to let the sales person go. Why not the accountant? Because you yourself can always go back to doing the door to door stuff, but you can't do accounting. You have no talent for it. So, the accountant stays, but you have to let the sales person go. The sales person is out of a job, and pounding the pavements. If this downcycle is happening just to your business, it's part of a typical business fluctuation called Hard Times. But if this is happening to a lot of people, it becomes a full-blown Recession.

That is the end of our story. We have just seen, graphically, how hiring and firing occur.

UNDERSTAND THE RULES
ABOUT HIRING AND FIRING

If you are not the boss in the above story, but rather the sales person, you will of course have some disappointed or bitter feelings about being let go. You might have expected the employer to show some loyalty to you, because you were the first hired, or because you were responsible for bringing in the money that made it possible to hire the accountant. If the accountant is a woman, and you are a man, you might feel you were let go because you weren't female. If the accountant is a man, and you are a woman, you might feel you were let go because you weren't male. Furthermore, you might feel anger at the customers who stopping buying the greeting cards. Or you might be in a deep mental depression over the fact that you have to go looking for work all over again, and you have a family to support.

Most of all, you might be dismayed at what this has shown you about the way in which the World of Work functions. This dismay comes about because most of us don't understand the nature of the world of work, until we bump our head or stub our toe on that nature. High school or college doesn't prepare us for this. Only in the hard school of life do we begin to slowly and painstakingly piece this information together. Eventually we realize there are twelve 'rules' in the world of work about Hiring and Firing. They are these:

1. Nobody owes you a job.

2. You have to fight to get a job. *("Fight" means "persevere," "use ingenuity," "compete.")*

3. You have to fight to keep a job. Loyalty, years of service, or personal friendship with the boss, do not in any way guarantee you a job at that place for the rest of your life.

4. You may quit anytime you want to.

5. Your employers may lay you off, or fire you, anytime they want to. They may do this because they have run out of money, and can't afford you any more. They may do this because they have to decrease the size of their business, or are going out of business. They may do this because they find your skills do not match the work that they need to have done. Or they may do this because they have a personality conflict with you.

6. You may quit without any warning or much notice at all to your employer, leaving them high and dry.

7. Your employers may fire you, or lay you off, without any warning or much notice at all to you, dumping you unceremoniously out on the street.

8. If you quit, you may do everything you can to help your employer find a suitable replacement, or you may do nothing.

9. If you are fired, your former employer may do everything in the world to help you find other employment, or may do nothing.

10. If *you* were the only one who was fired or let go, the other employees may promise they will fight to save your job, but you need to be prepared for the fact that when the chips are down, they may actually do nothing to help you. You will feel very alone.

11. As you look back, you may feel that your employers treated you very well, in accordance with their stated values - - or you may feel that your employers treated you very badly, in total contradiction of their stated values.

12. You remain a rare and unique individual, no matter how the world of work treats you. Your worth is not defined merely by your work, but by your spirit, your heart, and your compassion toward others.

If you are reading this before you are out of work, paste these on your mirror, and memorize them until you know them by heart. That way, there won't be any surprises for you, no matter how hard the times. You will be mentally prepared, for anything.

UNDERSTAND WHO WILL RESCUE YOU

Fairy tales have a wonderful power to help us understand life when we are young, or not so young. Remember *Beauty and the Beast*? But fairy tales about the world of work, when we have become adults, are not helpful. And what is *the* most popular fairy tale about the world of work? It is simply this: that if we ever are thrown out of work, or quit, someone out there will come to rescue us, come to our aid, steer us in the right direction, and hook us up with a proper job. Voila! Our troubles will be short-lived.

We are, of course, unclear about **who** that someone will be: the union, or the federal government, or the state, or private agencies, or newspapers -- but we believe it will be **someone**. Alas, when our time comes, and we are completely out of work, instead of someone coming to rescue us, there usually is only the sound of silence.

Many unemployed people have sat at home, waiting for God to prove that He loves them, by causing a job to just walk in the door. It does happen. But not often enough for you to ever count on it. The second rule of survival, especially in Hard Times, is this:

WHO WILL RESCUE YOU

No one else on earth cares as much about what happens to you, when you are unemployed, as you do. Therefore it is you who must take over the management of your own job-hunt or career-change, if it is to be successful.

No one else is going to be willing to lavish as much time on it, as you will.

No one else will be so persistent, as you will.

And if you decide to change careers, no one else will have so exact a picture of what kind of job you are looking for, as you will.

It is you who needs to learn, and master, for all the years to come, the process of creative job-hunting and effective career-change. You will need this knowledge desperately.

You may do it with support from others.
You may do it with coaching from others.
You may do it with God's help.
But, in the end, the one who must most immediately
rescue you, is

YOU...YOU...YOU.

UNDERSTAND HOW OFTEN
YOU WILL NEED RESCUING

Job-hunting is a repetitive activity. This isn't likely to be the
last time you're going to be doing this. Do remember that. Says
one job-hunter:

*"As a mid-level executive, I've lost my job two times in less than ten
years, and used* Parachute *both times to help me through the re-employ-
ment process. This book helped me through the roughest months of my
life."*

Twice in less than ten years is not remarkable. Jobs in this
country last an average of 4.2 years. Of course a particular job
you have may last longer than that -- especially as you grow
older. Nonetheless, surveys reveal that the number of times you
will have to go job-hunting during your lifetime will likely be
around eight. The time you spend on mastering your job-hunt
now will stand you in good stead the next time you go job-
hunting.

Do it well *this time* and you make life easier for yourself next
time. Throughout the rest of your life.

I saw, of course, the cliff,
I saw the turbulent ocean blue;
But everyone else was going that way,
So I thought that I would, too.

Larry Lemming

CHAPTER THREE

The Least Effective Job-Hunting Methods: Resumes, Agencies and Ads

Chapter 3

REJECTION SHOCK

When we are out of work, or have decided to go looking for a new job, we usually have no idea how to conduct our job-hunt. We only know that we dread it, before it even begins. And no wonder.

We *know* what lies ahead. We know we are going to have to approach one place after another, in one way or another. We know that we are going to get turned down, at a lot of those places. We know there is a lot of truth in my friend Tom Jackson's description of the typical job-hunt. In his *Guerrilla Tactics in the Job Market* he pictured it this way:

NO NO NO NO NO NO NO NO NO NO NO NO NO NO
NO NO NO NO NO NO NO NO NO NO NO NO NO NO
NO NO NO NO NO NO NO NO NO NO NO NO NO NO
NO NO NO NO NO NO NO NO NO NO NO NO NO YES

It's a difficult process to approach with any enthusiasm or joy. It looks like, it feels like, it smells like, nothing but a long process of rejection. And from the time we were kids in kindergarten we learned to *hate* rejection. At least most of us do. There are some people who seem to eat it up, and just thrive on it, who see it as a challenge, and delight to overcome it. But that's not true for most of us. Certainly, it's not true for me. Faced with rejection, I usually go into a corner and whimper a lot. Or jump into bed, curl into the fetal position, and turn the electric blanket up to nine.

Consider this paradox. All of our lives we are taught to hate being rejected. We learn at least fifty delicious ways to avoid rejection. We'll do anything to avoid being rejected, and I mean **anything**. The history of human dating, for example, is littered with such tactics as "I'll reject him (or her) before they have a chance to reject me." And then, along comes the job-hunt.

Eight times in our lifetime (on average) we have to go through this painful process. And, except at its very end, it is **nothing but** a process of rejection. The very thing we've spent our life trying to avoid.

There's got to be a better way. And, fortunately, there is. It's called 'the creative process of job-hunting' -- for want of a better name. It approaches every job-hunt as though it might be a career change, and it is explained at length in Chapters 9–11.

But first, we need to look at the job-hunting process that we normally fall into. The way that all of us were taught to go job-hunting, from our youth up. You know: resumes...classified ads...agencies...and the like. The job-hunting system that experts call 'Neanderthal.' Why? Well, consider this one example. In any typical city, there's an employer wandering around trying to find somebody with particular experience and skills, while at the same time there is in that city a job-hunter wandering around who has that experience and those skills; *and neither of them know how to find each other. That's* Neanderthal, believe me. If you are taking management of your own job-hunt, the first idea to get clear about, is that the job-hunting system in this country (and most countries of the world) is no system at all. (Say it again, Sam.)

OUR NEANDERTHAL JOB-HUNTING SYSTEM

This 'system' is composed of a number of different job-hunting methods. There are almost twenty of them. So, when you go job-hunting you sort of take your pick. *Naturally,* it would be helpful to know -- out of the twenty -- which ones are most effective, so that you could put your energy and your time into *those* methods. Lucky you. They've been studied a lot, over the years, and the findings can be summarized as follows:

The five most effective methods of finding a job *(according to various surveys, including one of ten million job-hunters)* turn out to be:

1. Applying directly to an employer, factory, or office in person (this leads to a job for 47 out of every 100 job-hunters who try it).

2. Asking friends for job-leads (this leads to a job for 34 out of every 100 job-hunters who try it).

3. Asking relatives for job-leads (this leads to a job for about 27 out of every 100 job-hunters who try it).

4. Using the placement office at the school or college that you once attended (this leads to a job for 21 out of every 100 job-hunters who try it).

5. And, in contrast to all of these, as I mentioned earlier, there is the creative approach to job-hunting - - *see Chapters 9–11* - - (which leads to a job for 86 out of every 100 job-hunters who try it).

Now, except for the last, none of these percentages are very inspiring, are they? But wait until you see the figures for the least effective.

The five least effective methods of finding a job are:

1. Using Computer Bank listings or 'registers' (this doesn't lead to a job for 96 out of every 100 job-hunters who try it).

2. Answering local newspaper ads (this doesn't lead to a job for between 76 to 95 out of every 100 job-hunters who try it - - *depending on the level sought; the higher the level, the less effective*).

3. Going to private employment agencies (this doesn't lead to a job for 76 to 95 out of every 100 job-hunters who try it - - *again, depending on the level sought*).

4. Answering ads in professional or trade journals within your field (this doesn't lead to a job for about 93 out of every 100 job-hunters who try it).

5. Mailing out resumes by the bushel (this doesn't lead to a job for 92 out of every 100 job-hunters who try it).

For those who like diagrams, I have summarized all of this on pages 28 and 29.

NOW HIRING

PERSONNEL

FRANKLY, THE FACT THAT YOU WANT TO WORK HERE IS A STRIKE AGAINST YOU RIGHT OFF.

GIVE EACH
THE TIME IT DESERVES

Now, if you're going to approach job-hunting through these traditional ways, no one should tell you to avoid any of these methods, even the five least effective. After all, answering ads in professional journals, for example, *has* paid off for seven lucky job-hunters out of every one hundred who tried it. You could be one of those lucky seven.

It does make sense, however, to suggest that you give each method the amount of time that its effectiveness deserves. For, after all, no matter how diligently you devote time to your job-hunt, you've only got a limited number of hours. It makes great sense to give each job-hunting method exactly the amount of time its effectiveness deserves. Applying directly to places of work -- *for example* -- is almost six times as effective as mailing out resumes; so, by this logic:

HOW TO ALLOT YOUR
JOB-HUNTING TIME

You should spend six times as many hours going directly, face to face, to places where you would like to work -- as you spend on mailing out resumes.

(This is because going directly to places where you would like to work is six times as effective in finding a job, as is sending out resumes.)

Extending this reasoning to all of the research listed above, we end up with the following:

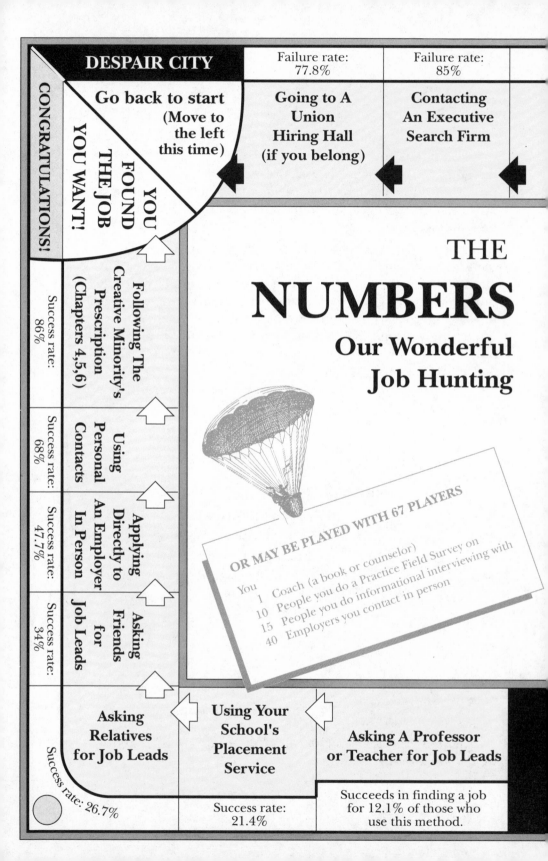

DESPAIR CITY

	Failure rate: 77.8%	Failure rate: 85%

Go back to start (Move to the left this time)

Going to A Union Hiring Hall (if you belong)

Contacting An Executive Search Firm

CONGRATULATIONS!

YOU FOUND THE JOB YOU WANT!

THE

NUMBERS

Our Wonderful Job Hunting

Following The Creative Minority's Prescription (Chapters 4,5,6)

Success rate: 86%

Using Personal Contacts

Success rate: 68%

Applying Directly to An Employer In Person

Success rate: 47.7%

Asking Friends for Job Leads

Success rate: 34%

OR MAY BE PLAYED WITH 67 PLAYERS

You
1 Coach (a book or counselor)
10 People you do a Practice Field Survey on
15 People you do informational interviewing with
40 Employers you contact in person

Asking Relatives for Job Leads

Success rate: 26.7%

Using Your School's Placement Service

Success rate: 21.4%

Asking A Professor or Teacher for Job Leads

Succeeds in finding a job for 12.1% of those who use this method.

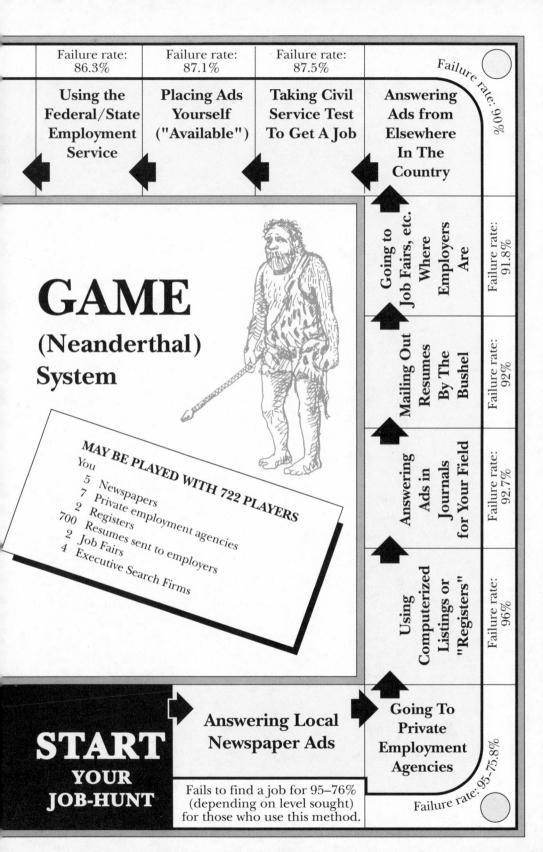

Failure rate: 86.3%	Failure rate: 87.1%	Failure rate: 87.5%	Failure rate: 90%
Using the Federal/State Employment Service	**Placing Ads Yourself ("Available")**	**Taking Civil Service Test To Get A Job**	**Answering Ads from Elsewhere In The Country**

GAME

(Neanderthal) System

MAY BE PLAYED WITH 722 PLAYERS

You
- 5 Newspapers
- 7 Private employment agencies
- 2 Registers
- 700 Resumes sent to employers
- 2 Job Fairs
- 4 Executive Search Firms

Going to Job Fairs, etc. Where Employers Are — Failure rate: 91.8%

Mailing Out Resumes By The Bushel — Failure rate: 92%

Answering Ads in Journals for Your Field — Failure rate: 92.7%

Using Computerized Listings or "Registers" — Failure rate: 96%

START YOUR JOB-HUNT

Answering Local Newspaper Ads

Going To Private Employment Agencies — Failure rate: 95–75.8%

Fails to find a job for 95–76% (depending on level sought) for those who use this method.

JOB-HUNTING METHODS TO SPEND THE MOST TIME ON

1. Knock on doors, at businesses, offices, factories, week after week. (47% effective)
2. Pump your friends and relatives continuously for every job-lead they may have heard of, at the place where they work, or elsewhere; and do this, week after week. (34%)
3. Use the placement office at the school or college you once attended, and return to check out their listings or leads at least every two weeks. (21%)
4. And, if these don't work, bite the bullet and do the creative approach to job-hunting (see Chapters 9-11) which is twice as much work but twice as effective as the methods listed above. (86%)

All in all, the job-hunt is like digging for gold; you put your energies where your efforts are most likely to pay off -- where the richest veins of gold are. That's what you *should* do. But what

> **lem·ming** \Ëlem-i⌃\n [Norw; akin to ON 1¯mr loon, L latrare to bark (1607) : any of several small short-tailed furry-footed rodents that are notable, in their European forms, for their recurrent mass migrations which often continue into the sea where vast numbers are drowned—**lem·ming·like**\-ÁlÙk\adj
>
> —Webster's

do we do, when it's our time to go job-hunting? With an instinct worthy of lemmings, we find ourselves:

SPENDING THE MOST TIME ON
THE LEAST EFFECTIVE METHODS

If you walk into almost any place of work, and ask the people there, "If you were to find yourself out of work in the coming year, what methods of job-hunting would you use?" you can bet what they're going to tell you. The big three: resumes, agencies, and help-wanted ads in newspapers. *Everybody* knows that!

But what's strange about those answers? Well, just this: every single one of the big three is found on the list of the five *least* effective methods of job-hunting, above. Not a one of them is on the list of the five most effective ways of finding a job.

So, if we are going to discuss the typical job-hunt, willy-nilly we are going to have to discuss the least effective methods of job-hunting. It's not a pretty sight.

Here's the picture. It's not that there aren't jobs out there. In even the worst of times, jobs fall vacant at an amazing rate. People retire, people get disabled, people get restless and switch jobs, etc. No, it isn't that there aren't jobs out there. It's that we have instinctively chosen the least effective ways of discovering those jobs. That, of course, is what makes our job-hunting *system* in this country (and elsewhere in the world) so Neanderthal.

But, if you're going to use these least effective methods of job-hunting, you might as well know how they work - - or how they *don't* work - - and, if you're determined to use them anyway, how you can make them be at their best.

OUR FAVORITE WAY OF AVOIDING
REJECTION: RESUMES

> **RÉ-SU-MÉ rez-ə-mā** n [F. *résumé* fr. pp. of *résumer* to resume, summarize] SUMMARY *specif:* a short account of one's career and qualifications prepared typically by an applicant for a position.   —Webster's

Yes, I know. You've heard - - since the day you were born - - that *the* way to go job-hunting is to prepare a decent resume *(or 'curriculum vitae')* and then send it out by the bushel baskets to every prospective employer you can think of, or find listed in your field in the local library. Blanket the country, if necessary - - the more, the merrier. So the mythology goes.

To help you, there are even organizations which will publish your resume (*along with a lot of other job-hunters'*) in a small booklet, and circulate it to employers. Forty-Plus Clubs do this, through their *Executive Manpower Directory*. So do some of the State Job Service/Employment Development Departments (*California, for example, has such a system, called PROMATCH, with 23 offices, which does this for experienced professionals*). It sounds as if *it couldn't hurt*, but do remember (if this sounds appealing to you) that you're in that booklet with a *lot* of other people.

My conversations with thousands of job-hunters, over the years, have convinced me that there is a passionate belief in resumes, whether distributed individually by you or in a booklet -- a belief that is out of all proportion to how often resumes in fact ever get anyone a job. I think this faith placed in resumes as *the premier job-hunting method* is a very misplaced faith. There are three reasons why I believe this:

1. Resumes have a lousy track record. A study of employers done a number of years ago discovered that there was one job-offer tendered and accepted, for every 1470 resumes that employers received, from job-hunters. Were such a study repeated today, I don't think the figures would have improved at all. In fact, quite the contrary, I believe the figures would be worse. Resumes have fallen into even greater disrepute among employers today, due to so many job-hunters lying about their qualifications -- *and being found out*. Employers do check resumes, these days. So how do the odds of one out of 1470 sound to you? Well, let me put it this way: would you take a plane flight if you knew that only one out of every 1470 planes ever made it to their destination? Then, why place so much faith in resumes, which are equally fragile?

2. If you are presently employed, you can lose your job by sending out a resume. We know someone this actually happened to. Let's call him Jim. Jim was the manager of a bank. He was happy where he was, but he also was looking down the road to think of where he might eventually go next. So, he sent out

one copy of his resume in answer to an ad from another bank, 'just to test the waters.' The employer to whom Jim sent that resume, however, was (unbeknownst to him) a friend of his current employer, so they talked, "Did you know one of your managers is looking for a new job?" Jim was called in and fired on the spot, despite his explanation that he was only looking way down the road. "You don't have the right attitude for working here," he was told. (They meant *loyalty until the death - - on* his *part, not theirs.*)[1]

3. Most of all, you can devastate your self-confidence by depending on resumes as your primary job-hunting strategy. Why? Because of the mythology about resumes that I alluded to, earlier, which causes a large number of job-hunters to believe that resumes *almost always* work, for everyone. Here's how that mythology gets fueled:

a) With at least nine million job-hunters out there hunting for a job during Hard Times, the odds are that *some* job-hunters will actually get an interview, and subsequently a job, *because* they sent out resumes.

b) But many, many more job-hunters do not get a job by means of a resume. In fact, an *incredible* number do not even get *one* invitation to an interview, in spite of sending out 800 or 900 resumes.

c) The ones who do get a job thereby, talk a lot about it; the ones who find that resumes didn't work for them, usually keep quiet about that. So, if you hear people discussing their experience with resumes, it's usually only those for whom it worked. Hence, the widespread impression that 'this is a method which works for almost everyone.'

---

1. By the way, speaking of hunting for a job while you are presently employed: *don't* use your present employer's stationery or envelopes for your resume, or send your resume from your employer's fax machine. Remember, that company's name appears at the top of every page when transmitted to a potential employer. The question this raises in the mind of the employer who *receives* your resume is: "This person is obviously using materials taken from that place without permission. If I were to hire this person, what materials or services would they take from *my* place, without asking?" Ethics *are* becoming more important in business and politics (or hadn't you noticed?). We know you don't want to get turned down just because your resume looks sloppy. Neither do you want to be turned down because your *resume ethics* look sloppy.

If you believe that, and you send out loads of resumes, and you don't even get a nibble, what are you going to think? It is not that another job-hunting method has been tried, and failed. It is that a method which you *think* works for almost everyone else, has failed for you. So you're going to think that something is wrong with *you*. Hence, plummeting self-esteem, and thence depression, emotional paralysis, and worse symptoms often follow. This has happened to tens of thousands of job-hunters. It has even happened to me. Don't let it happen to you. You have to get back to point #1, above: resumes have a lousy track record. If you decide to send out bushel baskets of them, and that doesn't get you a job, well - - that's how resumes are. They're just doing what they normally do: nothing. If you don't get even a nibble, that doesn't mean that anything's wrong with you. Something's desperately wrong with resumes…as a job-hunting technique.

So, to summarize: resumes will usually *fail* to get you a job, while they *succeed* in losing you your present job (if you have one), and your self-esteem. Don't let anyone tell you: "it can't do any harm to send out a lot of resumes." It can, it has, it does.

But, of course, you're probably going to send them out anyway. I think something of the Las Vegas gambler lives in us all: "Sure, they don't pay off very often; but maybe they'll pay off for me." *Oh, well.* In spite of all the evidence, old habits die hard. And, to be practical, if you're talking to some employer who is half-way across the country, you *may* need a resume. (Though oftentimes a long individual letter, summarizing the same stuff, is preferable - - since so many employers these days are highly allergic to resumes - - period - - and break out into a rash, if they even see one in their mail.)

But if, for one reason or another, you've decided to throw together a resume, you will want a few pointers:

RESUMES AND DATING

Beyond detailed instructions about how to put a resume together, it will help you immensely if you remember that resumes are a lot like dating. There is virtually no man who is liked by all the women he dates. There is virtually no woman who is liked by

all the men she dates. And so with resumes: some employers like resumes, others hate them. Some will like *your* resume; others won't. The only question that should concern you is: never mind if not all employers would like my resume -- will the employers I care about like it? And that is the $64,000 question.

I used to have a hobby of collecting resumes that had actually gotten someone an interview and, ultimately, a job. Being somewhat mischievous, I delighted in showing them to employers whom I knew. Many of them didn't like the winning resume at all. "That resume will never get anyone a job," they would say. Then, I would tell them, "Sorry, you're wrong. It already has. What you are saying is that it wouldn't get them a job *with you*."

The resume reproduced on the next page is an example of what I mean. *(You did want an example of what I mean, didn't you?)*

E.J. DYER   Street, City, Zip   Telephone No.

I SPEAK
THE LANGUAGE
OF
MEN
MACHINERY
AND
MANAGEMENT

...

OBJECTIVE: Sales of Heavy Equipment

QUALIFICATIONS * Knowledge of heavy equipment, its use and maintenance.

                * Ability to communicate with management and with men in the field.

                * Ability to favorably introduce change in the form of new
                  equipment or new ideas... the ability to sell.

EXPERIENCE   * Maintained, shipped, budgeted and set allocation priorities for
                  85 pieces of heavy equipment as head of a 500-man organization
Men and   (1975-1977).
Machinery
                * Constructed twelve field operation support complexes, employing
                  a 100-man crew and 19 pieces of heavy equipment (1965-1967).

                * Jack-hammer operator, heavy construction (summers 1956-1957-1958).

Management   * Planned, negotiated and executed large scale equipment purchases
                  on a nation to nation level (1972-1974).

Sales   * Achieved field customer acceptance of two major new computer-
                  based systems:
                  - Equipment inventory control and repair parts expedite system
                    (1968-1971)
                  - Decision makers' training system (1977-1979).
                * Proven leader ... repeatedly elected or appointed to senior posts.

EDUCATION   * B.A. Benedictine College, 1959. (Class President; Editor
                  Yearbook; "Who's Who in American Colleges").

                * Naval War College, 1975. (Class President; Graduated "With
                  Highest Distinction").

                * University of Maryland, 1973-1974. (Chinese Language).

                * Middle Level Management Training Course, 1967-1968
                  (Class Standing: 1 of 97).

PERSONAL   * Family: Sharon and our sons Jim (11), Andy (8) and Matt (5)
                  desire to locate in a Mountain State by 1982, however, in
                  the interim will consider a position elsewhere in or outside
                  the United States ... Health: Excellent ... Birthdate: December
                  9, 1937 ... Completing Military Service with the rank of
                  Lieutenant Colonel, U.S. Marine Corps.

SUMMARY   A seeker of challenge ... experienced, proven and confident of
                closing the sales for profit.

Jim Dyer, who had been in the Marines for twenty years, wanted a job as a salesman for heavy construction and mining equipment thousands of miles from where he was then living. He devised the resume you see, and had fifteen copies made. "I used," he said, "a grand total of seven before I got the job in the place I wanted!"

Like the employer who hired him, I loved this resume. Yet, when I've shown it to other employers, they have criticized it for using a picture, for being too long (or too short), etc., etc. In other words, had Jim sent his resume to *them*, they wouldn't have been impressed enough to invite him in for an interview.

So, don't believe anyone who tells you there's one right format for a resume, or one style that's guaranteed to win. It's still a gamble, where you're hoping that the employer(s) you like will also like your resume. Generally speaking, the most endearing quality needed in it, besides completeness, neatness and clarity, is that *you* shine through it all. One job-hunter, for example, found this unique *truthful* way of describing her period of job-hunting years:

"Job-Hunter (Self-Employed) January 1992–January 1993:
- Developed and executed all phases of marketing and advertising for product
- Targeted markets and identified the needs of diverse consumers
- Developed sales brochure
- Designed packaging, and upgraded visual appeal of product
- Scheduled and conducted oral presentations"

Thus, *she* shone through it all. Okay. Here endeth our two-minute crash course on resumes. If you decide you *do* want or need a resume, you will want more guidance than this. A number of books are listed in the footnote below.[2]

---

2. Richard Lathrop, *Who's Hiring Who?*, 12th Edition. Ten Speed Press, Box 7123, Berkeley, CA 94707. 1989, 1977, 1976, 1971, 1967, 1966, 1961, 1960, 1959. First-class, highly recommended. A simply excellent resource, best by a long shot on the subject of resumes (or qualifications brief, as Dick calls them). Used more often by our

The best of these, by a long shot, is Richard Lathrop's *Who's Hiring Who,* wherein he describes and recommends "a qualifications brief" - - an idea akin to that which John Crystal used to propose: that in approaching an employer you should think of offering him or her a written proposal of what you *will* do in the future, rather than "a resume" of what you did do in the past. Of course there are those who say, "No matter what you try to call it, it's still a resume in the end." Yana Parker, who has written the other most popular resume book (according to our mail) agrees, and has titled her book simply *The Damn Good Resume Guide.*

Resumes will be around as long as people go job-hunting, in spite of their terrible track-record. First of all, *sometimes* they work. Secondly, they *seem* like such a nice way to avoid rejection. Your name gets out there, and even if it doesn't lead to a job, at least you're not standing there in front of a would-be employer, staring into his or her face while you hear the bad news. With resumes, it's rejection all right. But it doesn't feel so...*personal.* I mean, there's so many *hundreds* of them that lead no where. And it offers a nice way out for those of us who are just afraid - - afraid to get out, afraid to go face-to-face, afraid to risk. Resumes are a nice way to kid ourselves, so that we *feel* we are

---

readers than any other book, besides *Parachute.*

David Swanson, *The Resume Solution; How To Write (and Use) A Resume That Gets Results.* JIST Works, Inc., 720 North Park Ave., Indianapolis, IN 46202-3431. 1991. This is a relatively new book on resumes, with tips not to be found in other books. It is very popular. (Dave has been on the staff of my workshops since 1978.)

Tom Jackson, *The Perfect Resume.* Anchor Press/Doubleday, Garden City, NY 11530. 1981. This is Tom's best-selling book, and with good reason.

Yana Parker, *The Damn Good Resume Guide.* New edition. Ten Speed Press, Box 7123, Berkeley, CA 94707. 1989, 1986, 1983. Describes how to write a functional resume. All new resumes in this new edition. Employers' comments upon resumes which actually got people jobs, are especially helpful. A very popular and useful book.

Yana Parker, *The Resume Catalog: 200 Damn Good Examples.* Ten Speed Press, Box 7123, Berkeley, CA 94707. 1988. The title says it all. A supplement to the book above.

Yana Parker, *Damn Good Self-Teaching Resume Templates.* Damn Good Resume Service, P.O. Box 3289, Berkeley, CA 94703. 1991. This is a computer disk, and manual, for both MAC and DOS computers. It is another supplement to the book above.

Donald Asher, *The Overnight Resume.* Ten Speed Press, P.O.Box 7123, Berkeley CA 94707. 1991.

There are more books on resumes than you can shake a stick at. If the above sampling is not enough for you, see your local bookstore.

doing something about our job-hunt, without actually risking *anything.*[3]

But, dear friend, real job-hunting *means* risk, by definition -- risk of rejection, face-to-face with employers. Remember the history of a job-hunt:

NO NO NO NO NO NO NO NO NO NO NO NO NO NO NO
NO NO NO NO NO NO NO NO NO NO NO NO NO NO NO
NO NO NO NO NO NO NO NO NO NO NO NO NO NO NO
NO NO NO NO NO NO NO NO NO NO NO NO NO NO YES

The good news (as Tom Jackson says) is that the more "NO"s you get out of the way, the closer you are to that "YES." Or hopefully two "YES"s, that you can choose between.

FRANK AND ERNEST *· by Bob Thaves*

© 1987 Newspaper Enterprise Association, Inc. Used by permission.

USING EMPLOYMENT AGENCIES

Left to our own devices, when we are unemployed, most of us will instinctively fall back upon three job-hunting strategies: resumes, employment agencies, and newspaper ads. Having dealt with the first, we turn now to the second of those strategies: agencies.

---

3. Except, of course, the paper, printing and postage…and your high hopes. Speaking of high hopes, there is a Catch-22 situation here. Every expert in the world will tell you that if you're going to send out resumes, send out as many as you possibly can. But, human nature being what it is, the more you send out, usually the higher your hopes get. Therefore, the more those hopes get dashed, when *even all those hundreds* don't get you a job. It's that old adage, 'The higher you go, the harder you fall.' Send out five copies of your resume, you don't care if they don't work; send out 800, *you care.*

Agencies seem like a wonderful idea, when you are unemployed. *My goodness, there's actually someone out there who can link employers looking for jobs with very-qualified me.* We all like to think that somewhere out there is just such a *switchboard,* where all the employers and all the job-hunters, in an area, can come to find each other.

Unhappily **no place** in this country has even a clue as to where all the jobs are. The best that *any place* can offer you is a kind of sampling, a sort of smorgasbord, if you will, of some of the jobs that are available, out there.

So, if you want a sampling, you will naturally want to visit an agency. Agencies are of several types: private, federal/state. and those retained by employers. Let's look at them in turn, beginning with the private agencies.

PRIVATE EMPLOYMENT AGENCIES

We need here a rundown in some methodical fashion:

Number: Nobody knows, since new ones are born, and old ones die, every week. The most *conservative* estimate is that there are more than 8,000 nationwide. In a typical small-sized city of some 75,000 inhabitants, you may find as many as 100 agencies, some of whom do nothing but, while others do employment business strictly as a small side-line. A *very* small side-line.

Types: Employment agencies are either for long-term work, or for temporary work. The latter are called 'temporary agencies.'

Specialization: Some agencies list all kinds of jobs. Most specialize. Typical specialties, among long-term as well as temporary agencies: accountants, office services, data processing, legal, insurance, sales/marketing, underwriting, industrial (assemblers, drivers, mechanics), construction, engineering, management/executives, financial, data processing, nannies (for young and old), and health care/dental/medical, *among others.* You can find them listed in the Yellow Pages of your local phone book, under such headings as *Employment Agencies; Employment Service – Government, Company, Fraternal, etc.; and Employment – Temporary.* If they specialize, their listing or their ads will usually indicate what their specialties are.

Fees: Employer or job-hunter may pay.[4] Be sure to ask which is the case. Most often, the fees are paid by employers. *Naturally,* you want agencies that make no charge to the job-hunter, if you can find them.

Loyalty: The first lesson to learn about agencies is that while they claim to represent employer and job-hunter equally, when push comes to shove (like, when the job listing they have doesn't quite match you) their loyalty will lie with those who pay the bills (which in most cases is the employer), and those who represent repeat business (again, employers). This means that some agencies may try to talk you into taking a job that doesn't fit you at all, just so they can get the employer's business (and fee).

Effectiveness: And now we come to the biggie: how well do agencies serve you, the unemployed job-hunter? Well, some time back, a spokesman for the Federal Trade Commission announced that the average placement rate for employment agencies was only 5% of those who walked in the door.[5] That means a 95% failure rate, right? *Tilt.* Incidentally, you should know that some agencies play games with their figures, so they can *claim* a high placement rate. They boast something like: "95% of all our

---

4. If you go to an agency where you, not the employer, are going to have to pay the fee, there are several things you should know. One is, the application form that you fill out is a legal contract. Be sure you understand all its implications. For example, with many agencies, if the contract states that you give them *exclusive* handling, and then you go out and find a job independently of them, you may still have to pay *them* a fee. Beware. Secondly, fees vary from state to state. Ask what it is, and if there's a limit. In New York, for example, a fee cannot exceed 60% of one month's salary, i.e., a $15,000-a-year job will cost you $750. The fee may be paid in weekly installments of 10% (e.g., $75 on a $750 total). In 80% of executives' cases, it is the employer who pays the fee. Thirdly, fees that you pay to find a job are usually tax deductible. But check it out with some tax expert beforehand, to see if that is the case, before you agree to the contract.

5. I was once at a meeting with a former head of an agency. Because he no longer worked there, he seemed like a good person to find out the truth from. So, I quoted this 5% success rate, to which he replied, "Oh no. That's not right. I'd say it was more like 1%."

"Let's put it this way — if you can find a village without an idiot, you've got yourself a job."

clients find jobs through our agency." The trick is in whom they consider to be clients. They don't mean all those who come through that door. No, no, no. They make this game work, by accepting as 'clients' only a small percentage of those who walk in the door. And whom might these be? You guessed it. The job-hunters that the agency thinks will be easiest to place. *Cute.* Of course they can place 95% of *them!*

Usefulness to career-changers: Very limited. Agency business is primarily a volume business, requiring rapid turnover of clientele, little time given to the individual job-hunter, with their primary focus on the most-marketable job-hunters, especially those on whom they can make a handsome fee. Career-changers, who have no previous track record in a particular industry or job, represent huge problems for agencies, which most of the time they are not willing to waste time on. Exception: *some* agencies are run by the most caring human beings in the world. If you are *lucky* enough to fall into *their* hands, you may get a lot of attention, even if you are new in the field where you are looking. This kind of care is most likely to be found at a new, or suddenly expanding agency, which needs names of job-hunters badly if it is ever to get employers to 'list' with them.

Recommendation: Agencies represent long-shot odds for you the job-hunter. They only know where a comparatively *few* jobs are, and none of them may fit you. Still, if you want to give a *proportionate* amount of time to them, this would be the advice of experts:

GOING TO PRIVATE AGENCIES

A study called *The Job Hunt: Job-Seeking Behavior of Unemployed Workers in a Local Economy* was made by A. Harvey Belitsky and Harold L. Sheppard some years ago. By studying blue-collar workers in West Virginia, they discovered that the greater the number of job-hunting avenues used by a job-hunter, the greater his or her job-finding success.

Therefore, it makes sense to use as many of these different job-hunting avenues as you can, but not spending more time on them than their track record warrants. In the case of employment agencies, that would mean one or two hours a week at most.

Now, to the other kind of employment agencies:

THE FEDERAL/STATE EMPLOYMENT SERVICE

Here's the rundown:

Name: Many job-hunters suppose that the local State employment office in their town or city is merely their own State's. But it is actually part of a nationwide Federal network, called "The United States Employment Service," or USES for short.

Number: There are about 2,000 USES offices, nationwide, and one-third of these call themselves "Job Service." The rest use other names: Employment Development Department, the State Unemployment Office, and so on. USES has seen its staff and budget, nationwide, greatly reduced over the past twenty years.

Services: Most State offices of USES not only serve entry-level workers, but also have services for professionals. Middle management and professionals have tended to avoid USES in the past, but that is now changing at least somewhat. About one-tenth of these offices offer job-search workshops, from time to time - - depending on the demand, and whether or not a counselor is available who knows how to teach such a workshop.

Out-of-State Jobs: Because it is part of a nationwide network, your local USES or Job Service office should have access to the Interstate Job Bank listings, which will tell you about job opportunities in other states or cities that may be of interest to you. The normal number of these listings runs around 6,000 at any one time; 98% of the USES offices have these listings on microfiche, and 20% of the offices *also* have a computer hookup. The listings are typically two weeks old before you see them, but many of them are for 'constant hires,' so that may not matter.

Openings: The most recent study revealed that about 7 million non-agricultural job vacancies were listed with USES during the year. That's for all fifty States.

Effectiveness: Ah, the bottom line again! Behind the impressive statistics, lies the all-important question: how much help are they going to be to you? Well, according to one study, USES placed only 13.7% of those who sought a job there. This means of course that they failed to find a job for 86.3% of the job-hunters who went there to find a job.[6] So, *if* you go there, *be realistic* about your chances of finding a job thereby. Your chances are 13 out of a 100. *Don't* put all your job-hunting eggs in this one basket.

---

6. Another study claimed that approximately 30% of those who search the job listings at USES find a job thereby. Many of these are only for temporary jobs, however. Still another survey revealed that 57% of those who found jobs at USES were not working at that job just 30 days later. This, of course, reduces the 30% claimed by the first study, to just 17%, after one month, which is pretty close to the 13.7% cited above.

AGENCIES RETAINED BY EMPLOYERS

When other types of agencies don't pay off, every job-hunter pricks up his or her ears upon hearing that there are actually firms which are retained by employers to find people for them. *Naturally,* these agencies/firms/organizations know about vacancies. They're being paid to *fill* them! Incidentally, the very existence of this thriving industry testifies to the fact that employers are as baffled by our country's Neanderthal job-hunting 'system' as we are. Employers don't know how to find decent employees, any more than job-hunters know how to find decent employers.

Small problem: are these firms looking for unemployed job-hunters? No, no, no. Unhappily (from the job-hunter's point of view) the mission these firms have been given by employers is *to hire away from other firms or employers,* workers who are already employed, and rising - - executives, salespeople, technicians, or whatever. *(In the old days, these firms searched only for executives, hence their now-outdated title.)*

Well, let's do our usual rundown:

Names: Executive search firms, executive recruiters, executive recruitment consultants, executive development specialists, management consultants, recruiters.

Nicknames: Headhunters, body snatchers, flesh peddlers, talent scouts.

Number: More than 2000 firms, with over 12,000 employees.

Volume of business: They have combined billings of more than two and a half billion dollars a year.

Number of vacancies handled by a firm: As a rule, each staff member can only handle 6 to 8 searches at a time; so, multiply number of staff that a firm has (if known) times 6. Majority of firms have 1 to 2 staff (hence, are handling 6 to 12 current openings); a few have 4 to 5 staff (24 to 30 openings are being searched for); and the largest have staffs handling 80 to 100 openings.

Not surprisingly, there are places that will sell you lists of such firms, for example:

1. *Directory of Executive Recruiters,* published by Consultant

News, Templeton Rd., Fitzwilliam, NH 03447. Published yearly. Lists several hundred firms and the industries served.

2. *Directory of Personnel Consultants by Specialization (Industry Grouping).* Published by the National Association of Personnel Consultants, Round House Square, 3133 Mt. Vernon Ave., Alexandria, VA 22305, 703-684-0180.

The question is: do you want these lists, i.e., are they going to do you any good?

Well, let's say you decide to send recruiters your resume (unsolicited -- they didn't ask you to send it, you just sent it uninvited). The average Executive Search firm will get as many as 1,000 such unsolicited resumes, or "broadcast letters," a week. Your chances of surviving? Well, *if* you currently make $75,000 or more per year, and *if* your resume and cover letter look *thoroughly* professional and well thought out, and *if* you send your resume to one of the larger executive search firms in this country, experts say you have a one in ten chance that they will contact you. On the other hand, the *first* to be eliminated will be those who a) are not presently on the level being looked for, or b) are not presently employed -- even if they *are* on that level, or c) are not presently rising in their firm. That's why many experts say to the unemployed, in general: *Forget it!*

I do think it is necessary, however, to point out that things are changing in the Recruiting field. For one thing, onetime employment agencies now prefer to call themselves Recruiters or Executive Search firms. *(Employment agencies typically have to operate under more stringent state or federal regulations, hence the appeal of a different, less supervised, genre such as Executive Search.)* Whatever they call themselves, these new Recruiters/old employment agencies now represent employers; but are hungry for the names of job-hunters, and in many cases will interview a job-hunter who comes into the office unannounced or mails them a resume. I have known so-called Recruiters in some of the smaller firms who truly extended themselves on behalf of very inexperienced job-hunters. So, were I job-hunting this year, I think I would get one of the aforementioned Directories, look up the firms that specialize in my particular kind of job or field, and go take a crack at them. As long as you don't put all your eggs or

"I'm hoping to find something in a meaningful, humanist, outreach kind of bag, with flexible hours, non-sexist bosses, and fabulous fringes."

hopes in this one basket, you really have nothing to lose --
except some stationery and stamps.[7]

AGENCIES SET UP BY EMPLOYERS

Everyone's dream is of a marketplace where employer and
job-hunter can come to meet face to face. It's like an agency,
except there's no job-order lying there on the desk. Instead,
there's a live hiring (or at least, interviewing) person on the
other side of the desk. Recruiters who come on campus, at some
colleges, seem to embody this dream. Also, 'job-fairs' set up by
business, industry, or private parties, embody the same dream.

People *do* find jobs from talking to recruiters, and people *do*
find jobs from going to job-fairs. But it should be an auxiliary
strategy, at best, since sometimes it leads nowhere. Here was one
job-hunter's experience with a job-fair:

---

7. Lucht, John, *Rites of Passage at $100,000+*. Viceroy Press (1-800-VICEROY, for order-
ing). Review by one of our readers: "This book describes in depth the methods of
headhunters, what to expect and how to deal with them on an on-going basis. Highly
recommended for anyone in middle-management or above..."

"I took the day off from work and drove 1½ hours to a job fair. The flyer for the fair claimed that __many__ companies would be participating, but when I got there I found only two, and the wait to speak to their representatives was about three hours. I didn't wait. My learning? Next time, I'll check out ahead of time, by phone, how many companies are there, before losing a day's pay over it."

Well, that finishes our examination of the first two favorite strategies for job-hunters who are out of work, or career-changers who are looking for new work: resumes, and agencies. Now we turn to the third and final strategy of most job-hunters: want ads.

WANT ADS
IN NEWSPAPERS

In a great many places these days, personnel experts will advise you to study the want ads in your newspaper daily and to study all of them, from A to Z - - because ads are alphabetized by job title - - and there are some very strange and unpredictable job titles floating around. They advise you that if you then see an ad for which you might qualify, even three-quarters, send off:

  a) your resume, OR
  b) your resume and a covering letter, OR
  c) just a covering letter which responds to the points raised in the ad

What you want to know, of course, is whether reading the want-ads is at all helpful to you in your job-hunt, or effective.

Let's do the rundown in the same methodical fashion that we used for agencies:

Where ads are found: In the business section, sports section, education section, or Sunday edition, of your local newspaper. Also, for management or financial job-hunters, in the *Wall Street Journal* (especially Tuesday's and Wednesday's editions).

Type of jobs advertised: Usually those which have a clear-cut title, well-defined specifications, and which the employer is having a hard time filling. If they can fill it by word-of-mouth, they don't advertise.

Number of resumes or other responses received by employer as a result of the ad: 20 to 1,000, and up.

Time it takes for the resumes or other responses to come in: 48 to 96 hours. Third day is usually the peak day, after ad is placed.

Number of resumes **not** screened out: Only 2 to 5 out of every 100 (normally) survive. In other words, 95 to 98 out of every 100 answers *are* screened out.

Why ads are run: People play all kinds of games with ads, besides looking for job-hunters; I have listed some of them in the next section. If, out of sheerest curiosity, you want further information I refer you to the chapter called "Blind Ad Man's Bluff" in David Noer's book, *How to Beat the Employment Game.*[8]

Effectiveness: Well, the odds are stacked against you just about as badly as when you send out your resume randomly. How badly? *(Better sit down.)* A study conducted in two "typical" cities - - one large, one small - - revealed, and I quote, that "85% of the employers in San Francisco, and 75% in Salt Lake City, did not hire any employees through want ads" during a typical year. Yes, that said *any* employees, *during the whole year.*[9]

Of course, you may be one who likes to cover all bets, since *some* employers do use want-ads to find employees, and if so, you will want to know how your answer to someone's ad can be the

---

8. Ten Speed Press, Box 7123, Berkeley, CA 94707. Or at your local library.

9. Olympus Research Corporation, *A Study to Test the Feasibility of Determining Whether Classified Ads in Daily Newspapers Are an Accurate Reflection of Local Labor Markets and of Significance to Employers and Job Seekers.* 1973. From: Olympus Research Corporation, 1670 East 1300 South, Salt Lake City, UT 84105.

one that gets through the Screening Process. (Let's be realistic: in spite of the overwhelming odds, answering ads *does* pay off for *some* job-hunters.) Most of the experts say, *if* you're going to play this game:

ANSWERING ADS

- Keep your answer brief. All you're trying to do, in answering the ad, is to be invited in for an interview. Period.
- Whether you get hired or not is the task of the interview, not the task of the answer you first send in.
- In answering, just quote the specifications that the ad asked for; nothing else. Then list what qualifications you have that exactly match each of those qualifications. That's the end of your answer.
- List your qualifications as a series of points, with maybe a 'bullet' (as it is called) in front of each -- as appears on this card.

ANSWERING ADS

• If there's a specification you don't meet (like, "experienced with motor boats"), you may wish at least to say something like "interested in motor boats." That is, if it's true.

• If there's anything else you're dying to tell them, save it for the interview. All they're looking for, among the answers they receive to their ad, is "who meets our specifications." They'll go on from there, with those that get invited in for an interview.

• Mail it in. Don't expect much. Remember, only 2 out 100 survive.

HOW TO ANSWER SALARY REQUESTS IN ADS

• If the ad requests, or even demands, that you state your salary requirements, beware. Employers often use this to screen out job-hunters who would otherwise qualify.

• Therefore, experts will give you contradictory advice here. Some say: ignore the request, don't even mention it. This leaves the employer free to think that maybe you just overlooked it.

• Other experts say: employers are not so easily fooled. Make some comment, at least, like: "I have enjoyed my career, because each new position has been increasingly challenging. I have been promoted

SALARY REQUESTS

regularly, with increasing authority, and commensurate increases in my salary."

- Still other experts say: Answer the request. But meet it head-on with a range, rather than a single salary figure. State a range, they say, of at least three to ten thousand dollars variation -- e.g., $15-20,000 -- and then add the words "depending on the nature and scope of my responsibilities," or words to that effect.

- The overarching rule is: if the ad doesn't mention salary, don't you either, in your response to that ad.

CHECKING YOUR RESPONSE BEFORE YOU MAIL IT

- You must make certain that the spelling in your letter (and resume if you include it) is absolutely errorless. Show it to at least two members of your family, or friends, or workmates, whom you know to be excellent spellers.

- If a spelling error is found, redo the entire letter. (White-Out is a no-no.)

- Check to make sure that the final sentence in your letter speaks about the next step, and that it leaves the control in your hands, not theirs. Not "I hope to hear from you," but "I look forward to hearing from you, and will call you next week to be sure you received this letter -- the mails being what they are."

YOUR RESPONSE

- Be sure to include your phone number, in case that's the way the employer prefers to contact you.
- Consider sending your response by Federal Express; until everyone is doing this (and they're not, yet) your response will stand out in the mind of the employer, or receptionist.

Some experts counsel other strategies - - *such as*, putting "Personal and Confidential" on your envelope; *and/or* mailing your letters so as to *arrive* in mid-week (that's Tuesday, Wednesday or Thursday); *and/or* following up with a phone call seven days later - - at either the beginning of the employer's workday, or near the end of it. The trouble is, some employers are weary of these strategies *(especially, putting "Personal and Confidential" on an envelope containing a resume)* and just grow irritated with people who use it. You don't want an employer irritated with you.

There is another strange strategy which often does work, however. It goes like this. Read your local newspaper every day, and make note of ads which you would like to respond to, except that you don't have all the credentials, qualifications or experience that the ad calls for. You may send your response in, anyway. But, because it falls short, it will usually be ignored.

Naturally, in time, the ad will stop running, so watch during succeeding weeks to see if that ad *starts running again*. It usually won't, because the employer found the person they were looking for. But if it *does* start running again, that's usually a sign that the employer couldn't find a person with the qualifications he or she was looking for. Now you have a chance to bargain.

Here's how one job-hunter reported her success with this strategy: *"The particular ad I answered the first time it ran required at least an associate degree, which I did not have. What I did have was almost ten years' experience in that particular field. When the ad reappeared a month later I sent a letter saying they obviously had not found* *what they were looking for in the way of a degree, so why not give me a chance; they already had my resume. Well, it worked. I got the interview, I made them an offer that was $6,000 less than they were going to pay a degreed person, but still a $6,000 increase for me, over my prior position. I got the job. Needless to say, everyone was happy. I have recommended this same procedure to three of my friends, and it worked for two out of three of them, also."*

THINGS TO BEWARE OF IN AD-LAND

If you think the only reason classified ads are run, is simply to find somebody for a job, you will get a rude education during your job-hunt. To save you from some of the traps laid for the unwary, here is a rundown of things you should watch out for when you are browsing in Ad-land.

Phrases Which Are Designed to Lure You In, But Conceal the Mundane Duties of That Job. Phrases like:

"Energetic self-starter wanted" (= You'll be working on commission)

"Good organizational skills" (= You'll be handling the filing)

"Make an investment in your future" (= This is a franchise or pyramid scheme)

"Much client contact" (= You handle the phone, or make 'cold calls' on clients)

"Planning and coordinating" (= You book the boss's travel arrangements)

"Opportunity of a lifetime" (= Nowhere else will you find such a low salary and so much work)

"Management training position" (= You'll be a salesperson with a wide territory)

"Varied, interesting travel" (= You'll be a salesperson with a wide territory)

Phone numbers in ads: many classified ads include the employers' phone number, because they want to see if they can *screen you out* without ever having to take the time to see you in person. It is in your best interest that you don't get screened out over the phone, but first get a chance to meet the employer face to face. Therefore, regarding whether or not to use the phone that the ad has *so helpfully* listed, most experts say, "don't use it, except to set up an appointment." Period. *("I can't talk right now. I'm calling from the office.")* They counsel that you should beware of saying more, lest you get screened out prematurely over the telephone. *Other experts, however,* think it is useful to use the phone number *if* it is a small company, and you can talk to the actual person you would be working for (*not* the personnel department). Certainly using the phone is helpful *if* you can use it just to get information about the job (without revealing your identity). But if you do reveal your identity, *and* the employer starts to *grill* you over the phone about your qualifications, you can be pretty sure the purpose of the phone number in the ad was indeed to allow them *to screen you out.* In such a case, politely resist the probing, thank them for their time, and gently hang up. Then send your resume in (it can't hurt), without ever mentioning that you were the one who talked to them on the phone. *If the employer actually invites you to send in your resume,* while still on the phone, be sure and thank them for their time, and then ask to be turned over to their secretary, so that from the latter you can get *the exact spelling* of this employer's name, title, and address. Then send a covering letter plus resume. In the covering letter you can say something like, "Thank you for our phone conversation, and thank you for encouraging me to send you my resume." In the remainder of the covering letter, then, highlight the parts of the phone interview that you want them to recall.

Blind Ads: *(no company name, just a box number).* These, according to most insiders, are *particularly* unrewarding to the job-hunter's time. But many job-hunters are skilled at answering them with just the information asked for, and they do get an interview, and sometimes a job, as a result. *However,* if by chance you are presently working, there is always the danger that this ad was placed by *your own* company unbeknownst to you. If that is the case, you can get fired on the spot - - just for answering it, as I mentioned earlier in our discussion of resumes. One way of protecting yourself: try giving the box number to the U.S. Post Office, and asking them for the company name. If it is a U.S. corporation, they *may* give it to you. Then again, they may not. Anyway, no harm trying.

Fake ads: *(which advertise positions that don't exist)* -- usually run by employment agencies or others, in order to lure you to write or come in, the better to fatten their "resume bank" for future clout with employers, or the better to be able to manipulate you with the old *"bait and switch"* scheme. Some agencies run ads for positions which *did* exist, again to lure you in, but they often use just a box number, so they'll *sound* like an employer and won't even disclose over the telephone that they are an employment agency. If you wonder how prevalent this is, you may draw what conclusions you will from the fact that in January of 1990 the Department of Consumer Affairs of the City of New York charged *50* Manhattan employment agencies with running deceptive ads that did not disclose they had been placed by employment agencies *(to do so is in violation of the New York City Consumer Protection Law).*

900 Phone-Number Ads: they promise you information about jobs, for a fee. They are usually listed in the Help Wanted sections of the newspapers. Their common denominator is a 900 area code phone number. They give no address, just the phone number. In 499 out of 500 cases, these are to be avoided like the plague. Their offer of help is *too good to be true.* (Read that again.) They will take your money, and offer nothing of value in return, except maybe some old and outdated ads.

Con men: some unscrupulous con men (and women), masquerading as employers, place ads solely in order to get your Social Security number, and the number of your driver's license, over the phone. With these two numbers alone, from you, they can often take you to the cleaners behind your back, with some of the con games they've invented. (Yes, you've got it right: they don't have any jobs to offer; they just want to do a job on you.) Legitimate employers *never* ask for such personal information, over the phone. *So, don't ever give your Social Security number and your driver's license number, over the phone, or in a letter, please -- except to State or Federal government agencies such as IRS, welfare, etc., or when you're dealing face-to-face with employers, banks, or hospitals.*

A SUMMARY OR DIGEST OF NEWSPAPER ADS

The idea of someone reading on your behalf the classified sections of a lot of newspapers in this country, and publishing a summary thereof on a weekly basis (or so), is not a new idea -- but it is certainly more popular in these (desperate) days than it used to be. There are two problems with such summaries: (1) How old the ads may be by the time you the subscriber read them. You'll recall from page 49 that most classified ads receive more than enough responses within 96 hours of the ad's first appearing. (2) How likely it is that an employer will wait for you to send in your response many days, or even weeks, later? This is something you must evaluate for yourself -- and weigh against the cost of the service.

If you decide that you do want this service, there are several places offering it. For example, the *Wall Street Journal* publishes a weekly compilation of "career-advancement positions" from its four regional editions. Available on some newsstands, or order from: National Business Employment Weekly, 420 Lexington Ave., New York, NY 10170, 1-212-808-6792. Each issue is $3.95. Also Militran, Inc., Box 490, Southeastern, PA 19299-0490, publishes a monthly summary of ads, called *Job Ads USA,* which they have culled from 100 newspapers a month. You can order it from them at the Pennsylvania address above.

ADS IN JOURNALS OR MAGAZINES

There is a list of such journals: see S. Norman Feingold and Glenda Ann Hansard-Winkler, *Where the Jobs Are: A Comprehensive Directory of 1200 Journals Listing Career Opportunities.* Garrett Park Press, Garrett Park, MD 20896. 1989. As you can tell by the title, this book lists more than 1200 journals, which all together describe (allegedly) over one million available jobs each year. The following list is only a sampling of some of these journals:

For Jobs Overseas: *International Employment Hotline,* a monthly newsletter which lists international employment opportunities. *International Employment Hotline,* Box 3030, Oakton, VA 22124.

For Jobs in Criminal Justice: The *NELS Monthly Bulletin,* National Employment Listing Service, Criminal Justice Center, Sam Houston State Univ., Huntsville, TX 77341, 1-409-294-1692. A nonprofit service providing information on current job opportunities in the criminal justice and social services fields.

For Jobs Outdoors: Environmental Opportunities, Box 670, Walpole, NH 03608, publishes a monthly listing of environmental jobs, internships, and positions-wanted notices under the same name. Each issue contains twenty-four to forty full-time positions in a variety of disciplines. The Association for Experiential Education, CU Box 249, Boulder, CO 80309, 1-303-492-1547, publishes a nationwide jobs clearinghouse list.

ADS IN 'REGISTERS'

As with ads in newspapers or journals, 'registers' are designed to be a place where employers can list vacancies. Unlike newspapers and journals, however, registers will also list job-hunters - - sometimes with a brief version of his or her resume. There is usually a charge to both job-hunter and employer. Here's a brief rundown on registers in general:

Types: Federal and private; general and specialized fields; listing either future projected openings, or present ones; listing employers' vacancies, or job-hunters' resumes (in brief), or both.

Cost to job-hunter: Ranges from free to $75 or more.

Effectiveness: A register may have as many as 13,000 job-hunters registered with it (if it is a private operation), and often as few as 500 openings from employers, at one time. You must figure out what the odds are for you as job-hunter of ever finding a job thereby *(statistics for some registers, are given below)*. Registers have always been an attractive idea to some job-hunters, because they seem to promise a place where job-hunter and employer can meet. Also the idea that the register *may* notify employers about you if your qualifications seem to even vaguely match the employer's job description, is mouthwatering. Alas and alack! 'tis often just a great illusion. *However,* were I job-hunting tomorrow, I'd probably list with one or two, myself - - *just in case.* But never never put any great trust in them, as far as actually producing a job for you is concerned. Here are a few examples of the registers out there:

Register for Teachers: *The NESC Jobs Newsletters* are published by the National Education Service Center, P.O. Box 1279, Dept. PB, Riverton, WY 82501, 1-307-856-0170. Between April and August, this weekly series of newsletters lists about 58,000 job openings annually. Each week's edition contains only new listings, none repeated. The newsletters are published year 'round, with fewer listings in the months August to April. You select one or more of fourteen different job categories, and receive listings of jobs in those categories only.

Register for Government Jobs: *Federal Career Opportunities,* published biweekly by Federal Research Service, Inc., 370 Maple Ave. W., Box 1059, Vienna, VA 22180, 1-703-281-0200. Each issue is 64 pages, and lists 3,200+ currently available federal jobs, in both the U.S. and overseas.

Register for Non-profit Organizations Doing Public or Community Service: ACCESS, Networking in the Public Interest, 50 Beacon St., 4th Floor, Boston, MA 02108, 1-617-720-5627. Fax #: 1-617-720-1318. It also has regional offices in D.C., Durham, NC, Chicago, and Berkeley. ACCESS is the first national clearinghouse of job opportunities for the country's 1.2 million non-profit organizations. Jobs range from entry level to Executive Director positions. This information is disseminated through three publications: (1) *Community Jobs: The Employment Newspaper*

For The Nonprofit Sector, 1601 Connecticut Ave., NW, Suite 600, Washington, DC 20009, which has a monthly section called *Opportunities in Nonprofit Organizations (ONPO); (2) Opportunities in Public Interest Law,* published three times a year with over 1000 positions listed; and (3) *Opportunities in State Government,* which also lists 1000 positions. Additionally, ACCESS will perform a Non-Profit Organization Search for you individually, for a fee, of non-profit organizations which fit your criteria. Write and ask them for their pamphlet: "Nonprofit Organization Search."

Registers in The Christian Church: Intercristo is a national Christian organization that lists over 30,000 jobs, covering hundreds of vocational categories within over 1,000 Christian organizations in the U.S. or overseas. Their service is called Christian Placement Network. In 1987, 13,000 people used the Christian Placement Network; one out of every twenty-five job-hunters who used this service found a job thereby. (That, of course, means twenty-four out of twenty-five didn't.) Their address is 19303 Fremont Ave. N., Seattle, WA 98133, and their toll-free phone number is 1-800-426-1342. Jeff Trautman, Executive Director.

Register for The Blind: Job Opportunities for the Blind, 1800 Johnson St., Baltimore, MD 21230, 1-301-659-9314, or 1-800-638-7518. Exists to inform blind applicants about positions that are open with public and private employers throughout the country. Maintains a computerized listing. Also, they have cassette instructions on everything for the blind job-seeker. Operated by the National Federation of the Blind in partnership with the U.S. Department of Labor.

One final word about registers: the very term "register" can be misleading. The vision: one central place where you can go, and find listed every vacancy in a particular field of endeavor. **But, sorry, Virginia; there ain't no such animal.** All you'll find by going to any of these places is A Selected List of some of the vacancies. A sampler or smorgasbord, if you will.

SHOULD YOU PLACE ADS YOURSELF?

Sometimes job-hunters try to make their availability known, by placing ads themselves in newspapers or journals.

Here's the rundown on that strategy:

Name of the ad section: *"Situations Wanted"* or *"Positions Wanted"* (by the job-hunter, that is).

Found in: *Wall Street Journal,* professional journals, and in trade association publications.

Cost: Varies, but typically runs around $20–25. During Hard Times, newspapers will often run free ads by job-hunters. The *Boston Globe* ran over 10,000 such ads in 1992; so have the *Sunday Gazette* in Schenectady, New York, and the *Blade-Citizen,* in Oceanside, California; so have others.

Effectiveness: Employers rarely read these ads, unless there is a concentrated campaign to get them to, as was the case with the *Boston Globe's* free ad offer.

Recommendation: **If you take odds seriously, you'd better forget it, unless of course your local newspaper has a campaign like the *Boston Globe's*. In which case, it couldn't hurt. If you are a professional of one sort or another, you *may* want to place an ad or two in professional journals appropriate to your field. Study other people's formats first, though, in those same journals. And be prepared for the fact that this is probably not going to lead anywhere.** With this, as with all the strategies in this chapter, the mischief is not in using the strategy. The mischief is in counting on it, or spending a great deal of time on it.

OTHER OFFBEAT METHODS

We have now finished our extensive overview of job-hunters' three favorite job-hunting methods: resumes, agencies, and ads. To these we must simply add that there are, of course some strange offbeat methods.

Mailing strange boxes to company presidents, with strange messages (or your resume) inside; using sandwich board signs and parading up and down in front of a company; sit-ins at a president's office, when you are simply determined to work for that company, association, or whatever. You name it, and if it's kooky, it's been tried. *Sometimes* (rarely) it *has* paid off. Kookiness is generally ill-advised, however. The $64,000 question every employer must weigh: if you're like this *before* you're hired, what will they have to live with *afterward*?

CONCLUSION

Well, Mr. or Ms. Job-Hunter, that just about covers the favorite job-hunting system of this country: resumes, agencies and ads.

The system which 'experts' call the Numbers Game.

If you send out that resume, or visit that agency, or scour those ads, and then find that it works for you, great! *Congratulations on your new job!*

But if it doesn't, you may be interested in the other plan -- you know, the one they had saved up for you, in case all of this didn't work? Small problem: with most of the personnel experts in our country, there is no other plan.

And that...is that.

*Pray, as though everything
depended on God;
then work, as though everything
depended on you.*

More Effective Ways of Job-Hunting

Chapter 4

RESUMES, AGENCIES AND ADS: WHY DON'T THEY WORK?

Well, of course, for *some* of you they have, or will. And if that's the case for you, you will probably write me *(if past mail is any indication)* telling me of your fabulous success with these methods that I have said don't work very well.

But that is not the problem at hand. I *know* they work... sometimes. The problem at hand is that they don't work often enough; and there are millions of you out there - - eight million, at least - - who faithfully send out resumes, visit agencies, and study newspaper ads, all in vain. You are still unemployed. It is you that I have a particular concern for. I want you not to take this personally. I want you to understand that the problem is not with you; the problem is with our Neanderthal job-hunting system, in this country.

I want to show you more effective job-hunting *(and career-changing)* methods, based on the experience of thousands of successful job-hunters, so that you can switch to these, and thus change your 'luck,' and your future. I want to give you some hope.

THE MYTHOLOGY: 'THERE ARE NO JOBS'

When we rest our job-hunt completely on resumes, agencies, and ads, and those methods don't work for us, you would suppose we would then say, "Well, obviously *these* methods don't work." But that is not what we say.

What we say is: "There are no jobs out there."

Our unspoken logic runs something like this: "I can't find any jobs using these methods; therefore, there must not be any jobs."

Wrong! *(We need a little Waylon Jennings' music here.)*

Suppose you moved to a big city, where you found a really nice apartment, but you decided you didn't want (or need) a telephone. And now let us suppose that someone over on the other side of that city is asked if you exist. They've never heard of you, so their first response is, "I dunno." Being resourceful, however, they go and look in the telephone book; they assume that *anyone* who lives in the big city *must* have a telephone. But when they look, there is no mention of you. They call information to ask if you have an unlisted number. Nope. So in this city, they conclude: you don't exist.

Now, you know what's wrong with their conclusion. You do exist! And, in that city! But you can see from this simple illustration that if someone can't find you through normal channels, it *does not mean* that you don't exist. It only means that he or she can't find you using those channels.

So it is with you and jobs, during hard times or easy. The fact that you can't find any jobs you want through the so-called 'normal job-hunt channels' -- resumes, agencies, and ads -- *doesn't* mean that the jobs don't exist.

It only means you can't find them -- using those methods.

THE JOBS *ARE* OUT THERE

Evidence #1: A Survey. There have been nine Recessions since World War II. They come around as regularly as clockwork, every few years. During one of them, the National Federation of Independent Business conducted a survey to discover how many vacancies there were among small businesses. They discovered there were one and a half million, right during that Recession. And that was just for *small* businesses, never mind *large* businesses.

That's why job experts will tell you that even during the hardest of times there are two million vacancies out there, at any given moment. Probably more.

Evidence #2: Logic. It's not hard to understand why the vacancies number two million. Let us start with the Great Depression of the '30s. Younger people's picture of that time is that everyone was out of work, and everyone was selling apples on street corners. It *was* a terrible time. But the picture is incorrect.

The unemployment rate at that time was between 25% and 37%. Even with the more pessimistic figure, the 37%, that means 63% of all workers at that time still had jobs. By the same token, even if the '90s ever had a tough economic time that reached the magnitude of the Great Depression, 79 million workers would still have their jobs. Among them, vacancies would inevitably develop. Workers would still get fed up and quit, never mind how hard the times -- and need to be replaced. Workers would still get fired for incompetence, and need to be replaced. Workers would still get disabled on the job, and for some time need to be replaced. Workers would still die before reaching their sixties, and need to be replaced. Workers would still retire, and need to be replaced. Out of 79 million workers still working *even in a Great Depression,* it's easy to see why two million vacancies would still develop. That's a vacancy rate of just 2.5% among active workers. With 118 million currently employed, a vacancy rate of 2.5% equals almost three million vacancies.

Evidence #3: Government Statistics: You will recall this diagram from Chapter 2:

THOSE WHO ARE ACTUALLY UNEMPLOYED IN HARD TIMES				
A Typical Monthly Snapshot (taken 2/7/92)				
New Workers Delaying Their Entry into the Job-seeking Group	Discouraged Workers Out of Work But Not Out Looking During the Last Four Weeks	Active Job-Seekers, Out of Work and Having Gone Job-hunting Sometime in Last Four Weeks	Partially Employed: Still Looking for a Full-time Job, but Meanwhile Holding Down Some Kind of Part-time Work	Prematurely Retired: Induced to Leave the Work-force With a Good 'Package' but Would Prefer to Keep on Working
166,000	1,300,000	8,900,000	6,700,000	Unknown

And you will recall that the government only recognizes category #3, the 8,900,000, as The Unemployed *at a particular moment.* (The moment here illustrated was shortly after the end of 1991, as you may recall.)

This raises the question, if this is the monthly figure, what's the yearly figure? How many did the government (and others) count as the Unemployed during the entire year, *(by the government's definition)*?

The answer, in a nutshell, turns out to be 25,000,000. That is, one out of every five workers in the U.S. was unemployed at some time during the year 1991, out of work, not by their own choice, at some point during the year.[1]

Okay, you do the arithmetic: 25,000,000 were unemployed, not by their own choice, sometime during the year 1991. By the beginning of 1992, 'only' 8,900,000 were still left, unemployed. *(But let's add to their number the 1,300,000 unemployed whom the government classifies as "discouraged.")* The total then is 10,200,000. This means that of the 25,000,000 who were unemployed sometime during the year, 'only' 10,200,000 were still unemployed going into 1992. On the dark side, that's still a *depressingly* large number. But, on the bright side, it means that:

15,000,000 of the unemployed found jobs, *even during the recessionary year of 1991*.

That works out to 1,250,000 job vacancies found and filled *each month* in 1991, by U.S. job-hunters.[2]

And since our earlier studies suggested there are two million vacancies each month, that means at least 750,000 vacancies went undiscovered and unfilled, *each month* in 1991.

Do remember that 1991 was a typical year for Hard Times. So, these same figures essentially hold true even as you are reading this. Indeed, if the times become easier, the total of the

---

1. For 1991 the Conference Board said this was the correct figure. The government claimed it was lower -- 17% -- though during a previous Hard Time, the government came up with the 20% figure also. One poll put the 1991 figure even higher: a Time/ CNN poll put it at 23% ("23% of American workers were unemployed, not by their own choice, at some time in 1991." Time, January 13, 1992)

2. Each month, on the first Friday of the month, the U.S. government reports the *net* gain in jobs the previous month. It is arrived at, by taking the total number of jobs one month, and subtracting the total number of jobs for the next month. Why this figure is in sharp contrast to the figure I have reported above is easily illustrated. Suppose in a given month 1,300,000 jobs were lost or eliminated, but in that same month some 1,250,000 vacancies got filled. That means 1,250,000 job-hunters found a job that month. However, the government will subtract 1,300,000 from 1,250,000 and report that the *net* figure for that month was 50,000 jobs lost, implying that *no* job-hunters found a job that month -- or, to be more blunt, that "there are no jobs out there."

number who found employment increases dramatically -- to your advantage.

These three evidences, cited above, explain why experts say "Of course, there are job vacancies out there -- even during the hardest of times."

If you can't find those jobs, that means you're using the wrong methods to look for them. But, we already told you that, in the previous chapter. So, let me put it another way:

> The major difference between successful and unsuc-
> cessful job-hunters is not some factor out there (such
> as a tight job-market), but the way they go about their
> job-hunt.

Now, this is very good news indeed -- to be told that your job-hunting success is dependent on *what you do*. That puts the power and control in *your* hands. If the hunt is not going well, you can change your job-hunting behavior. You can turn things around. You can *make* your job-hunt work. That way lies hope.

Were you at the complete mercy of what's going on *out there*, in the job-market, were your job-hunting success not the least bit affected by anything that *you* do, you would inevitably be reduced to complete despair.

True, you were and are at the mercy of forces outside yourself, *insofar as keeping or losing your job is concerned.*[3] But once you spring into action in your job-hunt, things are changed. You face the situation as potential victor, rather than victim, as empowered rather than powerless. Now, what you do and how you go about your job-hunt makes a difference. A *big* difference.

HOW TO IMPROVE YOUR
JOB-HUNTING SUCCESS

If you play tennis, and you wanted to learn how to improve your game, you would go talk to *good* tennis players, to learn

---

3. That's the whole point of the metaphor of 'workquakes,' which I explained in the first chapter.

how they do it. If you run, and wanted to improve your running, you would go talk to *good* runners, and learn how they do it. If you paint, and wanted to learn how to paint better, you would go study under *master* painters, to see how they do it.

It is the same with job-hunting. If you are job-hunting, and you want to learn how to do it better, you go talk to *successful* job-hunters, people who were out of work, and since then have found a job they really love.

SHORTCUT FOR NON-READERS

If you don't feel like finishing this book, then put it down, and go out there into the world, and talk to successful job-hunters among your neighbors, friends, relatives, and social groups: ask them how they did it, what they feel in retrospect they did wrong, what they feel in retrospect they did right, and so on. Then, go copy what the majority of them did.

If you don't want to go out and do all this interviewing, then read on. Over the years, thousands and thousands of successful job-hunters have shared with us what made their job-hunt work. This is our report to you of what strategies they used. There are ten of them.

THE FIRST WAY TO INCREASE YOUR JOB-HUNTING SUCCESS

Now, some of these 'secrets' for increasing your job-hunting success will sound remarkably silly, elementary and obvious to you. "Well, any fool would know *that!*" you will say to yourself. Unhappily that's not true. As is the case in other arenas of our life, when it is our time to go job-hunting we often overlook the obvious.

These *obvious* rules are what separate successful job-hunters from unsuccessful ones. Here's the first one:

BE PREPARED FOR A LONG JOB-HUNT

One job-hunter out of every three becomes an unsuccessful job-hunter, simply because they abandon their search before a job is found. Why? Because "I didn't think it was going to take this long."

Know this: the job-hunt in the U.S. (and many other countries) typically lasts from eight to twenty-three weeks -- or longer -- depending on the state of the economy, where you are, how old you are, and how high you are aiming.

Mentally prepare for your job-hunt to last longer than you think it will.

Don't count on the 'eight weeks.' Assume it is going to take the twenty-three weeks, at a minimum.

Don't give up! Jobs do not walk in the door while you're lying on the couch!

Persistence is the name of the game. Be gently, lovingly, stubbornly persistent.

For some reason, when we are unemployed we often shoot ourselves in the foot. I don't know exactly why, but without any rhyme or reason we often come up with some *unspoken* mental quotas in our head. It goes something like this: *this should take me 30 phone calls, 15 calls in person, and then I'll have a job.* We go about our job-hunt, fill those quotas, and then -- whether we have a job or not -- we give up. At least one out of every three of us does.

So let's begin with some realistic expectations. Successful job-hunters have kept records. This was one man's experience, which is fairly typical:

*107 places identified in his chosen geographical area
as "interesting"
126 phone calls placed to them
45 interviews conducted in person*

Another job-hunter, a woman in New Zealand, cited her experience:

"I have been job-hunting for the past twelve months. I'm now writing to tell you of my great success in finding a full-time job after my 205th job application. The job is a fulfillment of my lifetime ambition. I start this week and will be earning $20,384 a year."

These two job-hunters' records give you a realistic picture of how persistent a successful job-hunter *may* have to be. You need to keep up your job-hunt for as long as it takes.

Persistent also means being willing to go back to places that interested you, at least a couple of times in the following months, to see if by any chance their 'no vacancy' situation has changed.

Of course, there's no law that says the job-hunt has to take a long time. Sometimes lightning strikes. Here's another job-hunter's experience:

"After reading Parachute, and completing the homework, I wrote ONE letter to ONE corporation resulting in ONE fabulous job. From logo design to licensing to lesson plans, I was able to help a corporation establish its own on-site child care center. Amazing things happen when mind, heart, and soul are focused on the right task."

The conclusion of the matter, is this: the job-hunt is completely unpredictable, as to its length. *Your* task is to be mentally prepared for *whatever* it takes.

THE SECOND WAY TO INCREASE
YOUR JOB-HUNTING SUCCESS

SPEND MORE HOURS A WEEK
ON YOUR JOB-HUNT

Two-thirds of all job-hunters spend 5 hours or less on their job-hunt each week. Considering that the job-hunt may take 30 weeks or longer, you can see that what this adds up to: 150 hours of job-hunting, before their job-hunt is successful.

While it is true that some factors, such as how long a committee takes to make up their mind to hire you, are independent of the time you put in on your job-hunt, it makes sense to suggest that if a job-hunt takes 150 hours, spend more time on it, per week, and you should be able to shorten the number of weeks it takes for you to find employment.

Spend 20 hours a week, at least, on your job-hunt. 30 hours a week if you are desperate. This should cut down the number of weeks it takes you to find work, dramatically.

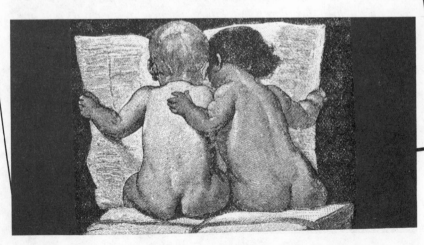

THE THIRD WAY TO INCREASE
YOUR JOB-HUNTING SUCCESS

GO VISIT THE PLACES WHERE YOU WOULD LIKE TO WORK

You must go face-to-face with employers, whenever possible.

"Face-to-face" means that you physically go to the places where you would like to work, rather than sending a piece of paper, such as a resume or covering letter.

"With employers" means that you try to see the boss, and not some in-between. Generally speaking you should try to avoid the personnel or human-resources department; only 15% of all organizations even have such departments, so with 85% of all companies, it's easy to talk to the boss.

Going face-to-face with employers leads to a job for 47 out of every one hundred people who try it.

There are, of course, companies where it is absolutely *impossible* to get in to see 'the boss,' i.e., the one who has the power to hire you. He or she is surrounded by a castle, with a moat, and eight large over-sized hungry alligators in the moat. You of course will hurl yourself against its ramparts a half-dozen times, anyway, furious that you can't get in to see that person. But, could I ask you a question: "*Why* do you want to work for a place like that?"

I mean, never mind that you're taking this *very personally.* Rejection, rejection, rejection, flashes on and off in your brain. But, haven't they *(by these actions)* told you something about themselves that is important information for you to have? And having gained that information, isn't it time for you to reassess *whether it's worth it?*

As for what to do about this step, if the companies or organizations that interest you, are far-away: see Chapter 7, *and* also use your contacts as much as you possibly can (see Chapter 12).

THE FOURTH WAY TO INCREASE
YOUR JOB-HUNTING SUCCESS

GO AFTER SMALL COMPANIES

Approach smaller businesses, companies, and organizations rather than large firms. Generally, small firms are much more likely to be expanding, but the 'big guys' are likely to be contracting. Since 1980, the 500 largest companies in the U.S. -- the 'Fortune 500' -- have *lost* a total of 3.9 million jobs. Since 1970, two out of every three new jobs have been created by organizations with one hundred or less employees. You therefore need to concentrate on every small firm in your town or city that is within commuting distance, that has one hundred or less employees. (I would start with those that have twenty or less employees, personally.) Small firms are easier to approach, the boss there is easier to talk to, and there are no forbidding personnel or human resources departments to screen you out.

Job-hunters who have no experience in job-hunting tend to make large organizations *'the measure of all things'* going on in the job-market. This is a very common, and very costly, mistake. Just because the Fortune 500 are downsizing, rather than expanding, does *not* mean 'there are no jobs out there.' It only means that large companies are *not* the place to go when times are Hard.

If there is expansion, it is likely to be among small companies which are on their way to becoming larger companies. Apple Computers, for example, started out in a garage.

That doesn't mean that *all* small companies are expanding. *Some* small companies are hit just as hard by Hard Times, as large companies are. But you keep going to small companies because somewhere among them *are* companies that are expanding. And your job is to find *those*, and then present your case.

THE FIFTH WAY TO INCREASE
YOUR JOB-HUNTING SUCCESS

SEE MORE EMPLOYERS
EACH WEEK

Job-hunters only visit six employers a month, on average; that's one reason why ten million job-hunters still can't find work. Job-hunters may need to see seventy employers or more, before they are through. You should determine to see at least two employers a day, one in the morning, one in the afternoon, every weekday, at a minimum, for as many months as your job-hunt may last.

THE SIXTH WAY TO INCREASE
YOUR JOB-HUNTING SUCCESS

USE EVERY CONTACT
YOU HAVE TO HELP YOU LOOK

It takes about seventy eyes and ears to find a job. Tell everyone you know that you are job-hunting and would appreciate their keeping their eyes and ears open. Ask your friends if they know of openings where they work. Ask your relatives if they know of openings where they work. Ask them if they know of openings where other members of their family work or where their friends work. Don't just tell them that you're 'looking for a job.' Tell them exactly what kind of a job you're looking for. The more specific you can be, the more they will be able to help you. Have as many other eyes and ears out there looking on your behalf, as possible.

If you happen to own a telephone answering machine, you might even consider putting this on that machine, as part of your opening message.

This leads to a job for 61 out of every one hundred job-hunters who use this approach.

However, I want to underline what is written on the card above. It is *not* sufficient to tell your friends, relatives, and working acquaintances, "Hey, I'm looking for a job. Let me know if you hear of *anything*." What does "anything" mean? Are you willing to take a job as a dishwasher in a local restaurant? Are you willing to work off a garbage truck? Are you willing to be a typist in a typing pool? Are you willing to sweep chimneys? All of these are honorable jobs for people who can do them with a sense of integrity and pride in their work. But do you really mean *anything*?

If you would enlist your friends, relatives, and working acquaintances to help you with your job-hunt, you've got to give them better information than *anything*. You've got to spell out specifically what kinds of work you're looking for, and what kinds of skills you like to use. Figure out whether you're best with People, or Things, or Information. It makes a difference. A big difference. Get as specific as you can *("I'm good with my hands," or "I like to help organize events and carry out planning to the last detail.")* You must know which are your best and most enjoyable skills.[4]

And, incidentally, since you never know *when* you may bump into someone who could lead you to a job, don't get *real sloppy* in your appearance while you are out of work. Be comparatively neat, clean, and nicely-dressed whenever you go out into the world -- even if it's just downtown, or out to the mall, for grocery shopping. You don't want any *contact* thinking, because of your sloppy dress, that you are 'on the skids.' No, no, no.

4. If you don't know how to describe in detail what you do best, then please see Chapter 9. Read it. Do it. It may seem to describe paper and pencil exercises that you only need if you are contemplating a career-change. But in actual fact, those exercises are useful to anyone who needs to describe what kind of work they are looking for, in more detail.

THE SEVENTH WAY TO INCREASE
YOUR JOB-HUNTING SUCCESS

HAVE A PLAN B

Don't expect that you will necessarily be able to find exactly the same kind of work as you have done in the past.

Take the job-label-from-your-past off yourself ("I am an auto-worker," etc.). Think of yourself instead as "a person who..."

Define some other line (or lines) of work that you could do, can do, and would enjoy doing, using the same skills and experiences.

Figure out what would make you different from nineteen other workers who can do the same thing.

You may be able to describe right off the top of your head some other kind of work that you like to do, and know you are good at; perhaps something you've done in your spare time *(like: make dresses, repair sailboats, etc.)* However, if you can't think of anything off the top of your head (or the tip of your tongue), and you want some help in figuring this out, then please read and do the exercises in Chapters 9 and 10, thoroughly.

THE EIGHTH WAY TO INCREASE
YOUR JOB-HUNTING SUCCESS

VISIT YOUR OLD SCHOOL

Visit the placement or career-planning office at the college or high school where you attended, or graduated.

21 out of every one hundred job-hunters who try this approach, end up finding a job because of it. Why are offices at schools so much more helpful than other placement agencies? Because they not only have listings of vacancies, but they also do something that normal agencies cannot do. They can put you in touch with other graduates of that school who now live in your town or city. In other words, they can give you **contacts** who may then be of great help to you -- as counselor, business contact, or potential employer.

Some job-hunters never think of going back to the college, community college, or high school that they once attended, to visit the placement/career-planning office there. Perhaps they don't even know it has one. Yet most of the 3,280 institutions of higher education in this country do, however informally.[5] So do many high schools, these days -- if they weren't hit by budget-cuts. In the placement or career-planning office there, look for bulletin board notices of jobs, vacancies, and even more importantly, look for lists of graduates who live in your geographical area. If you don't see that information, ask for it.

---

5. A directory listing many of these offices is published, and is available for perusal in most Placement Offices. It is called the *Directory of Career Planning and Placement Offices*, and is published by the College Placement Council, Inc., 62 Highland Ave., Bethlehem, PA 18017, 1-215-868-1421.

But what if your school is way far away, and you can't afford to go back there to peruse what they have by way of listings or contacts? If you are a hopeless romantic, you will have a vision of some kind of blissful cooperation existing *across the board* between, say, all colleges in the U.S. So that if you are a graduate of an East Coast college, and subsequently you move to California, and want help with career planning, you should in theory be able to walk into the placement office on any California campus, and be helped by that office (a non-altruistic service based on the likelihood that a graduate of that California campus is, at the same moment, walking into the placement office of your East Coast college; and thus, to coin a phrase, "one hand is washing another"). Some places do do this.

But, alas and alack, dear graduate, in *most* cases it doesn't work like that. You will be told, sometimes with genuine regret, that by official policy, this particular placement office on this particular campus is only allowed to aid its own students and alumni. And sometimes not even its own alumni. One Slight Ray of Hope: on a great many campuses, there are career counselors who think this policy is absolutely asinine, so if you walk into the Career Planning office on that campus, **are lucky enough to get one of Those Counselors**, and you don't mention whether or not you went to that college -- the counselor will never ask, and will proceed to help you just as though you were a real person.

This restriction (to their own students and graduates) is less likely to be found at community colleges than it is at four-year institutions. So if you run into a dead end, do try a community college near you.

THE NINTH WAY TO INCREASE
YOUR JOB-HUNTING SUCCESS

SETTLE ON MORE
THAN ONE 'TARGET'

What this means is that you don't 'put all your eggs in one basket' -- to coin a phrase. You don't decide to go after a job at just one factory, one government agency, one secretarial office, one volunteer organization, one library, one church, etc.

Years ago, it was entirely unnecessary to highlight this rule, since it was obvious to most people that *this way lies madness*. But of late, more and more job-hunters seem to be settling on one place as *"the ideal place where I would like to work,"* and having absolutely no plan B as to what they will do if that place obstinately refuses to hire them (as seems to be the case more often than not).

Don't do it. Have at least five target organizations or companies that you're going after.

Let me say it again. No matter how appetizing your *first choice* looks to you, no matter how much it makes your mouth water at the thought of working there, *you are committing job-hunting suicide* if you don't have some alternative targets. I mean, maybe you'll get that dream-come-true. But -- *big question* -- what are your plans if you don't? You've *got* to have other plans now -- not when that first target runs out of gas, three months from now. If you wait, you've wasted three months.

THE TENTH WAY TO INCREASE
YOUR JOB-HUNTING SUCCESS

TRY EVERY JOB-HUNTING METHOD THERE IS

There are seventeen different job-hunting *avenues.*
The average job-hunter uses less than two of them.
The greater the number that you use, the greater
the likelihood of your finding a job.

And what are the seventeen job-hunting avenues that consti-
tute our job-hunting system in this country (and most other
countries)? Well, we've already seen almost all of them, in this
chapter or the last; but let's tick them off again, with the most
effective first, and the least effective last. Here goes: using personal contacts, asking friends for job-leads, asking relatives for
job-leads, applying directly to an employer, using your school's
placement service, asking a professor or old teacher for job-
leads, going to a hiring hall (if you belong to a union), contacting agencies retained by employers *(executive search firms)*, using
the Federal/state employment service, placing ads yourself, taking civil service tests, answering ads from elsewhere in the country, mailing out resumes by the bushel, answering ads in journals
for your field, using computerized listings or registers, going to
private employment agencies, and looking at newspaper ads.

The track-record of *none* of these is very reassuring, and - - as
we have already seen - - the track-record of *some* of them is
dismal and depressing. *Nonetheless,* Sheppard and Belitsky in
their pioneering study, years ago, of the job-hunt, discovered
that the *more* of these methods a job-hunter used, the more
likely he or she was to find a job.[6]

---

6. The study was published by the W.E. Upjohn Institute for Employment Research,
under the title of *The Job Hunt: Job-Seeking Behavior of Unemployed Workers in a Local
Economy,* by Harvey Belitsky and Harold A. Sheppard.

For this reason, many personnel experts call the so-called job-hunting system of this country "The Numbers Game." You can guess where the term came from. It came from the world of gambling, where if you place sufficient bets on enough different numbers, one of them is more likely to pay off, for you. Same logic here.

If you don't like *the gambling* view of job-hunting, then try this:

> The essence of successful job-hunting is having alternatives. Alternative avenues of job-hunting. Alternative ways of describing what you do. Alternative ways of approaching employers. Alternative leads to jobs. Alternative 'target' organizations that you're going after. The problem with unsuccessful job-hunters is that often they pursue a plan that has no alternatives. You must not follow in their footsteps, if you want your job-hunt to be successful.

LIFESAVERS WHEN
NONE OF THIS IS WORKING

We have now covered the ten strategies that effective job-hunters use to find a job.

Now, naturally, you want to know what to do if you try all ten of these strategies, and you still don't have a job. *Whoa! You haven't had time to try all ten of those strategies; you just finished reading this chapter.*

But, of course, you want to look down the road - - just in case. Well, for your information (and curiosity) there are five possible lifesavers available to you. Here's what you do if you follow all the advice above, and you still aren't finding a job:

1. Check (down the road a piece) to be sure you really *are* doing all ten.
2. Go get a 'support group' to help you.
3. Play a game about making your job-hunt fail.
4. Play around with the idea of a major change in your location, workstyle, etc.

5. For a more systematic job-hunting system, go directly
to Chapters 9, 10, and 11; do not pass GO.

We'll look quickly at each lifesaver, now, in turn:

1. Check to be sure you really *are* doing all ten strategies.

Here's a convenient way to check yourself out, on this, once
your job-hunt is at least a couple of months old:

Strategy of Successful Job-Hunters	If You Did This, You Failed To Follow That Strategy
1. Being prepared to contact up to 200 places if necessary, *in person.*	1. You've decided to give up because "there are no jobs out there."
2. Spending 20-30 hours a week on your job-hunt.	2. You've spent only 5-10 hours a week, on your job-hunt, so far.
3. Going to visit places where you would like to work, and talking to actual employers -- people who have the power to hire you, there.	3. You sent cover letters and resumes to places, instead of going there in person; and if you did go there, you only talked to the personnel or human resource offices.
4. Going predominantly to visit small companies, with twenty or less employees, companies with names that probably nobody has ever heard of, even one hundred miles away.	4. You went to large companies, factories, universities, organizations, churches, agencies -- with names *everybody* in the country recognizes.
5. Going to see a minimum of two employers a day.	5. You have only contacted two employers a week, if that.
6 Asking at least 35 family members, relatives and friends to help you find what you are looking for, by telling them *exactly* what you are looking for.	6. You have only asked five friends and relatives to help you, and/or you failed to tell them in any detail what kind of work you can do.

7. Thinking out what other kinds of work you can do, and enjoy doing.

7. You've been looking for exactly the kind of work you used to do, and you haven't a clue about any kind of 'Plan B.'

8. Visiting the placement or career-planning office at your old college or high-school.

8. You haven't even thought about your old school.

9. Settling down on more than one 'target' organization that you're trying to get a job at.

9. You're resolutely going after *just one place.*

10. Using many different avenues of job-hunting.

10. You've settled just on looking at ads in the newspaper, or sending out resumes, etc. as your one job-hunting strategy.

Do remember that the above table is not a "smorgasbord," where - - out of the ten - - you choose two or three ideas that you like. You need to take *all ten* seriously.

As the old saying has it, "It is not that great ideas have been tried, and found inadequate; it is that they have been prejudged as inadequate, and never even tried."

> ## 2. Go get a 'support group' to help you.

The job-hunt is one of the loneliest experiences in all of life. Partly that is due to how we play it, when it's our turn to go job-hunting. We play it as a loner. *Me, myself, and I, are about to go job-hunting.*

If you've tried it that way, and you're getting really bogged down, it's time to rethink that strategy. You need somebody, or a bunch of somebodies, to cheer you on, cheer you up, serve as a sounding-board to bounce ideas off of, serve as a brainstorming group for identifying places, possible contacts, and so on. In the jargon of the day, this is called a support group. Who can serve this function, for you? Here's some suggestions:

a. Job-hunting groups that already exist in your city or town, such as "Forty Plus" clubs, "Experience Unlimited" groups, job-hunt classes at your local Federal/state employment offices, or at the local Chamber of Commerce, or at your local college or community college, or at your local Adult Education center, etc.[7] The likelihood that such help is available in your community increases dramatically for you if you are from certain groups held to be disadvantaged, such as low income, or welfare recipients, or youth, or displaced workers, etc. Ask around.

b. A job-hunting group that doesn't currently exist, but that you could help form with other unemployed people - - at your local church, synagogue or religious centre. (Often your priest, minister, rabbi or leader can put you in touch with such people.) Some enterprising job-hunters, unable to locate any group, have formed their own by running an ad in the local newspaper, near the "help wanted" listings. *"Am currently job-hunting, would like to meet weekly with other job-hunters for mutual support and encouragement."*

---

7. A sample listing of these kinds of places is to be found in the *National Business Employment Weekly,* on its pages called "Calendar of Career Events." It's available on some newsstands, or you can order an issue directly from: National Business Employment Weekly, 420 Lexington Ave., New York, NY 10170, 1-212-808-6792 or 800-JOB HUNT.

c. Your mate or partner, grandparent, brother or sister, or best friend. A loving 'taskmaster' is what you need. Someone who will make a regular weekly appointment to meet with you, check you out on what you've done that week, and be very stern wtih you if you've done little or nothing since you last met. You want understanding, sympathy, and discipline. If your mate, brother or sister, or best friend, can offer you all of these, run -- do not walk -- to enlist them immediately.

d. A local career counselor. I grant you that career counse- lors aren't usually thought of as 'a support group.' But many of them do have group sessions; and even by themselves they can be of inestimable support. If you can afford their services, and none of the above suggestions have worked, this is a good fall- back strategy. Before choosing such a counselor, however, *please* read Appendix A, in the back of this book, thoroughly. That appendix also tells you how to locate such counselors.

3. Play a game about making your job-hunt fail.

One of the first uses you can put this support person or group to, is to help you with the following 'game.'

HOW TO MAKE YOUR JOB-HUNT FAIL

If your job-hunt just isn't working, sit down with some friends, and play this mental game:

(1) Pretend you will be secretly paid a vast sum of money if you can *appear* to go about an effective job-hunt, but actually *ensure* that it will fail. You and your friends should then 'brainstorm' this, by listing all the ways you all can think of, to make sure your job-hunt would fail.

(2) Then *(this next step is the most important)* prioritize it so that the surest way to make the job-hunt fail is at the very top, etc. *(one man's surest factor was: "Sit at home.")*.

(3) In a second parallel column, then, list the exact opposite of each of those factors *(the opposite of 'Stay at home' is 'Get out of the house every day.')*. You will now have, in this second column, a list of what you must do to make your job-hunt succeed, with the factors listed *in their order of importance*. The game is over. Now, go do it. Follow that list of what you must do, to make your job-hunt succeed, and follow it in the exact order it is written.

> 4. Play around with the idea of a major change in
> your location, workstyle, etc.

Chapters 6 and 7 are devoted entirely to these ideas. Read, mark, learn, and inwardly digest those chapters.

If you're thinking about a major change in what you do for a living, i.e., a career-change, then turn to Chapters 9, 10, and 11 for detailed instructions on how to do that.

> 5. For a more systematic job-hunting system, go directly
> to Chapters 9, 10, and 11; do not pass GO.

As hinted earlier, there are two major 'families' of job-hunting strategies. The first is called 'The Numbers Game.' It is the Neanderthal job-hunting *system* that predominates in this country and most of the countries in the world. You've seen what the varying odds are, of finding a job through that family's methods, throughout the previous chapter.

The other job-hunting method is called the systematic approach to job-hunting. It's twice as much work, but it is also twice as effective as 'the Numbers Game.' According to careful records kept by the late John Crystal, and other counselors, it leads to a job for 86 out of every 100 job-hunters who faithfully try it.

Its essence is that it treats every job-hunt as though it might be a complete career-change.

It says, *For the most effective job-hunt, you have to know* what *your skills are, just as you would if you were making a complete career-change.*

It says, *For the most effective job-hunt, you have to know* where *you want to use those skills, just as you would if you were making a complete career-change.*

It says, *For the most effective job-hunt, you have to know how to find such work, just as you would if you were making a complete career-change.*

Therefore if you want to pursue this, it is to Chapters 9, 10 and 11 that you must turn, since those are the chapters which describe how to make a complete career-change. Those chapters also describe how to do a systematic approach to job-hunting, since -- by this view -- the two problems are one and the same.

CONCLUSION

These days, you may be out of work suddenly and without warning, at any moment, so you will be wise beyond your years if you are ready to go job-hunting, or make a career-change, at any time. Don't wait until the crisis is upon you before you start to think how you would go about it. Study the above methods of effective job-hunting, until you know them as well as your own name.

And do remember, job-hunting will be a repetitive activity throughout the rest of your life. Jobs in this country last *an average of* 4.2 years. As you grow older, a particular job will likely last longer than 4.2 years. But, over your lifetime, the number of times you will have to go job-hunting will likely be around eight. The time you spend mastering the job-hunt *now* will stand you in good stead the next time, as well.

Do the job-hunt well *this time* and you make life easier for yourself for as far down the road as your eyes can see.

What is success?
To laugh often and much;
To win the respect of intelligent people
*   and the affection of children;*
To earn the appreciation of honest critics
*   and endure the betrayal of false friends;*
To appreciate beauty;
To find the best in others;
To leave the world a bit better, whether by
*   a healthy child, a garden*
*   patch or a redeemed social condition;*
To know even one life has breathed
*   easier because you have lived;*
This is to have succeeded.

Ralph Waldo Emerson

CHAPTER FIVE

If It Looks Like It's Going To Be 'A Long Haul': How To Avoid Getting Depressed

Chapter 5

UNEMPLOYMENT AS
AN ENJOYABLE TIME

Strangely enough, many people enjoy unemployment, so long as it doesn't stretch on and on. For one thing, a number of people who *have* to work, would prefer not to. Finding themselves unemployed, they face a period in their lives where they can indulge their deepest wish without shame. Their family and friends cannot think they are lazy. Nor can anyone think they are shirking their duty. Everyone can see quite plainly that it is Hard Times, and they are *unemployed* through no fault of their own. And that is that.

They get to sleep late, or catch up on their reading, or go for long walks, or do whatever they have always dreamed they would do if they didn't *have* to work. Unemployment benefits or other sources of income keep them from starving. And, eventually the unemployment ends, and they go back to work, refreshed.

Since at least one out of every five workers in America is unemployed at *some* time during the year, you can bet that this prizing of *unemployment as vacation* is much more common than one would at first suppose.

Another group of people who find unemployment a welcome period in their lives are those who have always considered making a career-change, and now feel that they have the time -- while unemployed -- to give this idea the thought and attention that it deserves. For that reason, they too find unemployment a welcome time in their lives. While they were involved in a 9–5 job, it was hard to figure out what to do next, with their lives, But now they have just the time they need, to decide where to go next. And they don't have to be in any hurry.

If you are in either of the above groups, unemployment can be a relatively enjoyable time for you.

UNEMPLOYMENT AS
A DEPRESSING TIME

But then, there are the rest of us: the millions of us who don't like being out of work, and who find unemployment one of the most depressing times in our life.

There are three reasons why we find it so:

(1) It is the end of an era. For months, years, maybe decades, we were used to thinking of ourselves in terms of *that job* at *that place.* It gave our life its coherence, it gave us our daily routine, it gave us our identity. "Who are you?" *"Oh, I'm a foreman at the General Motors plant down the road."* But when we are laid-off or fired, that era comes to an end. What do we say now? "Who are you?" *"Well, I don't really know, any more."* That's depressing.

(2) It goes on too long. Most of us are good at doing difficult things, as long as we only have to do it for a short time. We can walk (quickly) through an area with a bad stench. We can put up with a three-day cold. We can stand to miss one meal. We can hold our breath for thirty seconds. We can run a hundred-yard dash. We can endure a bad relationship, as long as it doesn't last more than one week. But we don't like it when things go on too long. That starts to get us down.

This of course is our situation when we are unemployed. A period of unemployment that lasts only two weeks - - hey, *no problem!* But if it drags on and on and on, we get weary just thinking about it. "Enough, already," we cry. Yet, there is no end in sight. That's depressing.

(3) It makes us feel powerless. We like it when we can make a difference. In our household. In our neighborhood. In our community. At our workplace. We do something, something happens or changes, as a result. That makes us feel good. But we don't like it when we face the opposite situation. This is why unemployment is often about as welcome as a rattlesnake at a picnic. When we're out of a job, we try this. Sometimes it works like a charm. But other times, nothing happens. We try that. Nothing happens. We are still out of work. We still can't find a job. We still are unemployed. It goes on and on, and *nothing* we do seems to make any difference. We begin to feel absolutely powerless. That's depressing. *Very* depressing.

THE MEANING OF 'DEPRESSION'

The word 'depressing' or 'depression' is used, of course, in two different emotional senses: one by the unemployed, and the other by psychiatrists or therapists.

The latter mean by it, an emotional illness of uncertain origin and cure. If we are the victims of *this* kind of depression, it usually antedates our period of unemployment, and is something we have wrestled with for years. It may have a virulency like unto pneumonia, or be as low-grade as a cold. When it is as virulent as pneumonia, the emotional illness of depression is a burden that threatens to crush the soul, and many brave souls have endured this 'dark night of the soul' for years, with astounding courage - - though there are now medicines and treatments that can often hold it completely, or mostly, at bay. Anyone who is unemployed, and is feeling so depressed as to be suicidal, needs to get to a psychiatrist, therapist, or doctor, immediately, for help. *This is a medical emergency.*

Depression can be much milder, and in that form it is like a series of 'blue Mondays,' or it may be a gentle perpetual tinge of sadness that does not keep us from our feasts, but 'is just enough to appear as a death's-head at all our feasts.'[1]

---

de·pres·sion \di-Ëpresh-fln\ n (1): a state of feeling sad : DEJECTION (2): a psychoneurotic or psychotic disorder marked esp. by sadness, inactivity, difficulty in thinking and concentration, a significant increase or decrease in appetite and time spent sleeping, feelings of dejection and hopelessness, and sometimes suicidal tendencies (3): a reduction in activity, amount, quality, or force (4): a lowering of vitality or functional activity (5): a period of low general economic activity marked esp. by rising levels of unemployment. *Webster's*

---

1. The phrase is William Law's, who used it to describe token religion.

In whatever form, it is estimated by experts that some 10 million Americans experience depression sometime during the year.[2]

So much for the medical approach to depression. Now, when we are unemployed and we say, *"I feel depressed,"* we usually mean it in a somewhat different sense than doctors and psychiatrists do. It is not a medical diagnosis on our part; it is, rather, a metaphor, crying out for translation. When we are unemployed and say, "I'm depressed," we mean: *'I've got the blues.'* We mean: *'I feel sad.'* We mean: *'I'm not my usual self.'* We mean: *'I feel down, because it's hard to stay upbeat or optimistic in this situation.'* We mean: *"I'm depressed."* This feeling of being *depressed* is our emotional response to *that situation.* Once we have found a job, it lifts, and we start feeling happy and upbeat once again. So the question is, when your job-hunt is draggin', how do you avoid feeling blue, or feeling down?

HOW TO AVOID FEELING DEPRESSED
WHEN UNEMPLOYMENT DRAGS ON AND ON

Anyone who has a facile or glib answer to this problem, should be avoided like the plague. There is no universal guaranteed-to-work formula, believe me. Every person in this world is unique, and what works for one person, doesn't work for another. Especially, when we are dealing with the emotions.

But after talking to thousands of job-hunters, I do think there are five approaches you can take, that seem to banish, or at least lift, feelings of being depressed, for *most* job-hunters.

Those five approaches deal, in turn, with the: (1) physical; (2) emotional; (3) mental; (4) spiritual; and, finally, (5) activity - - during your time of unemployment. And they are not a kind of smorgasbord, from which you choose the one or two that you like best; you need to do all five, because *each* of the five *contributes* toward the feelings of depression. In this sense, depression is like a river, fed by these five tributaries.

---

2. For further reading, I refer you to: *The Good News About Depression,* by Mark S. Gold, M.D. Bantam Books, 666 Fifth Ave., New York, NY 10103. 1987. Let me repeat that depression is not a character failure, but often has a physical basis. If you cannot move yourself out of the depression by exercise, and activity, then you ought to get yourself to an experienced M.D. or therapist.

THE PHYSICAL REALM

Problem: you will likely feel depressed if you are short on your sleep, or your body is otherwise run-down.

The world never looks bright or happy to people who are *very short of sleep.*

The world never looks bright or happy to people who are *feeling depressed.*

It is therefore easy to confuse the two feeling-states. What you may imagine is depression may in fact be simply the feelings that come from sleep-deprivation. So, please don't take this matter lightly. It has been amazing to me, in the past, to see very-depressed job-hunters turn into happier, more upbeat people, just by catching up on their sleep. Turn off the TV by 10 o'clock, and *go to bed!* It may be difficult to do at first, but in time you'll like the new schedule. And, you'll feel better - - sometimes *much* better.

If you are trying to take this seriously, but are having trouble sleeping, the remedies are pretty well-known by now, but - - with my rich skills at overkill - - let me spell them out, anyway:

5 RULES FOR DEALING WITH SLEEP PROBLEMS

1. Try to keep regular hours, going to bed at the same time every night.

2. Go to bed before midnight, preferably by 11 p.m.

3. Avoid things that might keep you awake, such as caffeine, from dinner to bedtime. Reduce drinking to one drink, or none at all.

4. Use the bed only for sleeping or love-making.

5. If you lie awake for more than 30 minutes, get up and read, or meditate, until you get sleepy.

In addition to the sleep thing, there are other things that need to be done to keep yourself physically fit while unemployed. When I was myself out of work I found it important to:

• get regular exercise, involving a daily walk;

• drink plenty of water each day *(this seems silly, but it is often very important);*

• eliminate sugar as much as possible from the diet;[3]

• take supplementary vitamins daily *(no matter how often doctors and nutritionists will tell you that you already get plenty just from your daily food);*

• eat balanced meals *(don't pig out just on junk food in front of the telly);*

and all that other stuff that our mothers always told us to do.

Physical also means *physical space* around you, in your home or apartment -- which is important because it often mirrors how we feel about ourselves. If our physical environment looks like a disaster area, that in itself can make us depressed. If you've always vowed you wanted to learn to live neater, here is a simple way: each time you handle a *thing*, take it all the way to its destination; don't put it down, thinking that you will deal with it later. Do it now.

e.g., when you take clothes off, either put them in the clothes basket or hang them back up; don't just drop them on the floor.

e.g., when you finish eating, put the dishes where they are to be washed, and put the food back in the refrigerator.

---

3. The sugar/depression connection is a matter of speculation and controversy, but I believe it is an important truth, and were I feeling depressed the first thing I would eliminate from my diet would be sugar. See *Sugar Blues,* by William Duffy. Warner Books, Inc., 666 Fifth Ave., New York, NY 10103. 1975. (Available in your library or in health-food stores, if not elsewhere.)

e.g., if you get a screwdriver out, to fix a screw that's dropped out of something, when you're done, take the screwdriver all the way back to the tool chest or wherever its final destination is. Etc., etc., etc.

When things are put away in a timely fashion, neatness will start to appear in your physical environment; it will help lift your spirits immensely. Of course, if you were already keeping your place as neat as a pin, you will ignore this whole thing, and forget I ever mentioned a word, won't you?

THE EMOTIONS

> Problem: after you are 'let go', you will likely feel depressed if you are still carrying around a lot of anger, expressed or suppressed, about *what they did to you.*

Our instinctive first reaction to the fact that we were laid-off, fired, terminated, summarily dismissed, or made redundant -- especially *after all these years* - - is usually anger. Sometimes fierce, hot anger. Sometimes just a kind of dull, cold disillusionment about the workplace and how it treats people.

Need I mention that we would probably drop our anger quickly if it were relatively easy to find another job, doing basically the same thing at the same level of responsibility and at the same salary in the same town. But, given our Neanderthal job-hunting system, it is not. It is not easy to find such jobs even when they exist. Hence, much of the blame for our anger should lie at the door of this so-called job-hunting *'system'* - - which leaves us feeling devalued and discarded by our society for weeks, months, and sometimes years. Our anger is justified and understandable, in the beginning.

But if it keeps on and on, then that's another story. And if our anger is directed not against the job-hunting system in this country, but against our ex-employers, that's the beginning of trouble. I see this often, as people who have been let go discuss the place where they used to work: *'I'll never forgive them. They've ruined the rest of my life.'*

Of course, the only way our former employers can actually ruin the rest of our lives is if *we* help them out, by holding on to our anger forever. This *will* wreck the rest of our lives. I have seen it happen many many times in the lives of the unemployed.

We forget an ancient truth: that when anger becomes a burning fire within us, that fire gradually consumes not its object, but its host. Certainly it doesn't achieve its desired effect upon the objects of our anger. They are sleeping soundly, while it is we who are lying awake at night. No, anger consumes its host not its object, and it does this by giving birth within us to irritability, withdrawal, loneliness, broken relationships, divorce (often), and sometimes (rarely) suicide.

During this process, the anger very commonly segues into depression. It has struck me forcibly over the years that these two emotions often seem to be reverse sides of the same coin. It is as though *anger/depression* were an energy, which at first is directed outward toward others, but then like a boomerang eventually turns back against the self. This *feels* like depression, but it is born of the anger.

So, if you feel depressed as unemployment stretches on, it is helpful to consider the possibility that anger that may lie beneath that depression. Dealing with that anger often takes away the depressed feelings. People who have successfully done this, cite the following steps:

5 RULES FOR DEALING WITH ANGER

1. Your basic need is to let the past go, so that you may face the future with all your energies. Staying rooted in anger, keeps you rooted in the past, facing toward the past.

2. If you are angry about what has happened to you, face the anger openly and honestly. Talk about it, write a letter to yourself about it, but do not act it out in real life. Do not write to, or threaten, the objects of your anger. That way lies trouble of major dimensions.

3. Find a family member, or friends, or a therapist, with whom you can talk it out, instead.

4. If you have a lot of angry energy, so that you feel you'd like to punch someone, punch a pillow instead.

A big pillow. Or a mattress. Get the angry energy out of your system, harmlessly. Daily, if necessary.

5. If are a woman or man of faith, hand the anger over to God, and ask that Higher Power to help you set your face toward the future.

THE MENTAL

> Problem: you will likely feel depressed if you view this experience of being laid-off, and having to spend a long time finding a new job, as essentially a random, senseless and meaningless event in your life.

Let us begin here with a riddle:

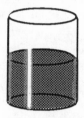 This is a glass containing fruit-juice. Is it half-empty, or is it half-full?

Most people have heard this riddle, but that doesn't mean it is well-understood. On its surface it seems to say that there are different ways of looking at a situation.

But that is not its major point. Its major point is that you *can change* how you view it. You can go from viewing it as *half-empty* to viewing it as *half-full.*

There is a habit of mind that is deadly, which is to spend much of our time each day, every day, brooding about what is *wrong.* What is wrong with people, what is wrong with our life, what is wrong with our situation, what is wrong with anything and everything. In our conversation with friends or family, we focus our attention on what we didn't like about the conversation...or *them.* In a movie or play, we focus on what we didn't like about it. When we travel, we focus on what we didn't like about each place we visited. This habit of mind focusses always on other people's failings, on what is not the way we want it to be, on what is (from our point of view) missing. It calls every glass, and every situation, *half-empty* - - focussing on what is lost, or never was. On the other hand, *half-full* focusses on what you have, on what still is, and is good. The first habit of mind leads to complaint and bitterness; the second habit of mind leads to gratitude and joy. If you would avoid getting depressed, it is *crucial* to look at how you think, and what you focus your attention on, all day long. It is crucial to avoid the deadly habit of mind alluded to, above. As Baltasar Gracián put it,[4] "Get used to the failings of your friends, family, and acquaintances...."

Depression arises, in part, from a sense of powerlessness. However, as the riddle reminds us, we *always* have power -- the power to change how we view a situation, and thus to alter that situation. Let me give an example.

At a medical symposium which I attended many years ago, a doctor was reviewing the puzzle of healing. Two patients, he said, of the same age and with the same medical history, would undergo the same operation. Yet, one would heal rapidly, while the other's healing was long delayed. Doctors had no idea why this was so. They set up a study at a major New York hospital, to see if they could identify what factors explained this difference.[5] Using a computer, they decided to compare *everything* about the patients who healed quickly, with those same factors -- or to be more exact, the *absence* of those same factors -- in the patients who healed slowly. And so they began to ask the computer their questions.

Were those who healed quickly characterized by *optimism,* while those who healed slowly were not? No, said the computer; that wasn't the answer.

Were those who healed quickly characterized by *some kind of religious faith,* while those who healed slowly were not? No, said the computer; that wasn't the answer.

And so it went.

What the answer finally turned out to be was this: those who healed quickly felt there was some meaning to every event that happened to them in their lives, even if they did not understand what that meaning was, at the present time; while those who healed slowly felt that most events which happened to them had no meaning; they were merely random or senseless. Hence, if both patients were being operated on for cancer, the one who

---

4. Baltasar Gracián, *The Art of Worldly Wisdom: A Pocket Oracle.* Doubleday/Currency, Publishers. 1992. Baltasar was a Spanish writer who lived in the 1600's.

5. I have, in the intervening years, tried to go back and identify that study, but have been basically unsuccessful in this search. I am left only with a clear memory of *the findings,* as they were reported by that doctor at the symposium.

viewed the cancer as having some meaning in the larger scheme of things, for their life, healed quickly; while the one who viewed the cancer as a senseless and meaningless interruption in their life, healed slowly. *Everything depended on how they viewed the situation.*

Surely you see how this applies to such events as being terminated. Being fired or terminated is rarely the outrageous, meaningless event that it at first seems to be. It may begin that way; but it does not end that way. You have the power to shape it, by how you choose to view it.

The last time I was fired, the firing occurred shortly before noon, and at 3 o'clock that same afternoon I had an appointment with my dentist, to have some drilling done. *'What a wonderful day this is turning out to be!'* I thought, with rich irony. Anyway, he was a wise man, on in years, and when I told him of my plight, he said some words I have never forgotten: "Someday," he said, "you will say this was the best thing that ever happened to you. I don't expect you to believe a word I am saying now, but wait and see. I have seen this happen in so many people's lives, that I know it will come true for you." Strangely enough, he turned out to be absolutely right. And he helped shape how I viewed that event. I now say, that firing was indeed the best thing that ever happened to me, for it caused me to rethink my whole life and what I wanted to contribute to the world. Thus, it proved to be a great blessing, as light was born out of the darkness of unemployment.

I now believe that every event in our lives has meaning, or can be given meaning, even though we don't always know what that meaning is, at the time. If this is how *you* view your life -- including the experience of being laid-off -- then that depression which arises from a sense of meaninglessness will not afflict you.

Spelling out more specifically what this means, we can state it in terms of our usual five rules (in this case, affirmations):[6]

---

6. The reference to the *loom*, which follows, comes by analogy to Sir Charles Sherrington's description of the brain: *"It is as if the Milky Way entered upon some cosmic dance. Swiftly the brain becomes an enchanted loom where millions of flashing shuttles weave a dissolving pattern, always a meaningful pattern though never an abiding one; a shifting harmony of subpatterns."*

5 RULES FOR DEALING WITH MEANINGLESSNESS

1. Your life is like a tapestry, being woven by God and history on an enchanted loom. Every bobble of the shuttle has meaning, every thread is important.

2. As a thread in that tapestry every event in your life has some meaning and purpose, for the larger pattern, even if you cannot see what this is, at the moment.

3. You will discover that meaning more quickly if you direct what thoughts you focus your mind on, during your time of unemployment.

4. To aid this, make a list of all the things you enjoy about your life, even while unemployed -- the simple pleasures: working with your hands, breathing fresh air, enjoying beautiful music, etc.

5. When you are having any dark times, sit down and write out stories. Stories about your life past, when you were most enjoying yourself. Write down what meaning you now see in those stories. This will increase your confidence that there is meaning in your present story, now unfolding.

To rule #4, above, we might add: conversation, cuddling, drives in the country, exercise, praying, helping others, singing, sitting in front of a fireplace, thinking, etc. If you need further help there are useful books you can take out of your library, or procure at your bookstore.[7]

---

7. Especially helpful is Barbara Ann Kipfer's *14,000 Things to Be Happy About.* Workman Publishing Company, 708 Broadway, New York, NY 10003. 1990.

THE SPIRITUAL

Problem: you will likely feel depressed if you believe in God, but feel that He[8] has somehow deserted you in this crisis.

There are about 6% of my readers who would probably prefer I omitted all mention of the spiritual, in a book on job-hunting. I am sensitive to those feelings, but if we are going to discuss depression, there is no way to omit it. According to Gallup Polls conducted since 1960, about 94% of the population in this country believe in *some* concept of God.[9] When they find themselves summarily dismissed from a job that they may have held for *years,* many find their faith in God a bulwark of strength that helps them through this very difficult period, daily.

Others, however, are often plunged into a depressing crisis of faith. The common form of the questioning, when it comes, is: *How could God let this happen to me, if He truly loved me?* Many of the unemployed decide from this that there must be no God, or

---

8. I know there are those, in our time, who do not like the male pronoun applied to God. I am very sensitive to sexist language, but here we are in a different realm. *All* language about God is metaphor, anyway, and because I grew up on the Old Testament (and the New), I myself prefer *this* metaphor, grounded as it is in some 4,000 years of usage. You can always alter it, in your mind, as you read, if you wish.

9. Reported in George Gallup's *The People's Religion: American Faith in the 90s.* Macmillan & Co. 1989. In addition to reporting that 94% of us believe in God, the Gallup polls also discovered that 90% of us pray, 88% of us believe God loves us, and 33% of us report we have had a life-changing religious experience; and these figures have remained pretty unvarying during the last thirty years of opinion polls conducted by the Gallup Organization.

at least not One who cares what happens to them. They conclude then that they must face the future resolutely alone, rely-
ing on their own strength, and their own strength alone, to
carry them through their period of unemployment.

Needless to say, this period is often far more difficult than
they had supposed it would be, and their resolution to bear it all
by themselves often flounders. They may find their own strength
inadequate for the task. They are left feeling very alone. Naturally, a feeling of despair, or depression follows, like the night
the day.

What are we to say to all this? What is the remedy when our
depression has - - even in part - - a spiritual origin? The remedy,
apart from discarding our faith, is obviously that we need to put
some energy into rethinking that faith on a higher level.

I said earlier that 94% of the people claim they have *some*
concept of God. But what unemployment, or any crisis, often
reveals is how poor and inadequate that concept is. It is inadequate because it holds God responsible for *everything*, and
makes no allowance for the free will and freedom of choice that
He has given to His creatures. The wonder is not that it breaks
down under the pain of unemployment, but that it didn't break
down sooner.

Well, then, to what higher concept might we press? Let's try
this: imagine that you have, in your dining room, a fine wooden
chair, which one day has its back broken off completely -- I
mean, into *smithereens* -- by someone in the house. You run
down the street, to call a carpenter who lives nearby. He comes
and examines the chair. He pronounces the back *unrepairable*.
"But," he says, "I think I could make a fine wooden stool out of
the remainder of the chair, for you." And so he spends much
time, shaping, polishing and sanding it, and fashioning out of
the former chair a fine stool, more resplendent than anything
you have ever dreamed. He inlays it with gold, and soon it is the
treasure of your house.

Let me underline a couple of key points in this parable. First
of all, the carpenter did not break the chair. Someone else did
that. But the carpenter came quickly, and with all his art and
powers, to see if he could not only repair it, but make of it
something even finer than it had been before. And, he labored
mightily, to that end.

And so, a higher concept of God holds that God does not create our unemployment or any of the calamities in our life -- *that* responsibility belongs to our fellow human beings. *They* are the ones who create our calamities. *But,* God -- like the carpenter -- comes quickly, with all His art and powers, to see if He can not only repair our life, but make of it something even finer than it had been before: not a physical thing, like the stool inlaid with gold, but a work on the spiritual level that corresponds to the stool, in splendor. And He labors mightily, within our mind and heart and spirit, toward that end.

If unemployment pushes us thus to rethink our faith, we should not only find our depression lifting, but also our self-esteem. Here are some helpful rules -- worth pasting up on your bathroom mirror:

5 RULES FOR DEALING WITH A SENSE OF ABANDONMENT

1. The 94% of us who believe in God usually need a larger conception of God, as we face each new crisis in our life. If you've got an old faith hanging in the closet of your mind, now would be a good time to take it out and dust it off.

2. Hold high the truth that God does not save us from hard times. Hard times come to believer and non-believer, alike.

3. On the other hand, God does not cause us to go into hard times (our fellow human beings do that).

4. But God is always in the middle of those times with us because He has promised to be with us, in all times. His role is that of Sustainer, Strengthener

and Rescuer. You should seek that Sustaining, that Strength, daily, even hourly, in prayer, especially when you get to feel that you just can't go on.

5. If you can't feel God's presence during hard times, that does not mean anything. Feelings many times fail to correspond to reality. We can be in a fog, as we say, that obscures our vision. Do not give such feelings more weight than they deserve.

To feel abandoned - - by God or man or woman - - while you are unemployed is *extremely* depressing. Everything you can do to avoid that feeling of being abandoned, will help you greatly in 'chasing away the blues'. You start with your faith in God, you continue on with the people around you: family, relatives, friends and acquaintances. If these last leave you feeling rather alone and unsupported, you should heed the advice in Chapter 4 about seeking, or forming, a support group with others who are unemployed.[10] If you can find no such group, and you feel you possess neither the wit nor the skill to start one yourself, then seek out whichever one of the established Twelve-Step groups there are in your community.[11] While strictly speaking they are designed to help you with personal growth, and job-hunting is never mentioned, they will at least keep you from feeling alone or unsupported in *life*, as you go about that hunt.

---

10. Such groups as *Experience Unlimited, Forty-Plus*, job-clubs, classes at your local Employment Office, or at your local Chamber of Commerce, etc.

11. AA (Alcoholics Anonymous), OA (Overeaters Anonymous), NA (Narcotics Anonymous), PA (Parents Anonymous - - for people who are having trouble being the kind of parents they want to be), GA (Gamblers Anonymous), and other similar groups are known collectively as 'Twelve-Step Groups.' They are usually wonderful about giving you a feeling of support. If you have trouble finding a particular 'Twelve-Step' Group that interests you, start by looking up Alcoholics Anonymous in the white pages of your telephone book, and ask them where you can find the other groups. They usually will know.

ACTIVITY

> Problem: you will likely feel depressed if you only have one goal for your time of unemployment.

Back in the days when you were working, suppose you decided to take a quick vacation with your spouse, or partner, or friend. You weren't quite sure what you wanted the vacation to accomplish for you. You thought that maybe you wanted to get a good rest, and not do a lick of work while you were at your vacation hideaway. On the other hand, you thought that maybe you wanted to catch up on some stuff at work that has been dogging you for weeks. You weren't sure. So, you took the work along, but determined you wouldn't feel guilty if you came back with it absolutely untouched.

Now that was going to be a rewarding vacation for you, as you knew even before you set out. Why? Because you had two alternative goals for the vacation, and *one* of them was bound to be achieved. *Either* you were going to get a good rest, *or* you were going to get some work accomplished. You couldn't lose.

Half of our misery *in our goal-driven lives* arises from our failure to thus have two alternative goals for a particular period. Again and again, we set only one goal. And then, if we fail to achieve it, as is so often the case, given the vagaries of human nature, we get depressed.

It is hardly a wonder, then, that when we get fired, sacked, terminated, or whatever, we approach unemployment in the same manner. We set ourselves only one goal for the period while we are unemployed: to find a *(meaningful)* job.

When we don't find a job -- *right away, at least* -- we get depressed. Real depressed. It is therefore important to face the activity problem here that may be contributing to that depression, and to fix it. How to fix it is obvious:

> You need to have more than one goal for your time of unemployment.

You need to define this period of unemployment in some such terms as this: *"My goals during this time of unemployment are: (1) to find a good job; and (2)...."* Aye, there's the rub; what should (2) be? (Or, not to be.)

The most important characteristic of this second goal must be that it is *achievable.* It does our self-esteem no good, after all, to have two goals if we then fail to achieve either one of them. The second one *must* be achievable.

Certain goals which might at first suggest themselves to us, are therefore disqualified by this consideration: for example, a goal like determining to use this period of unemployment to lose 40 pounds permanently. That *is* a nice, admirable goal, except we all know by now that diets often have a yo-yo effect -- down, up; off again, on again. Consequently, very iffy goals such as this may only increase your depressed feelings, when you can't find a job *and* you can't lose weight, either.

What kind of goals, then, *are* achievable? Studying successful job-hunters for some twenty or more years, it has become clear to me that there are several, which vary in appropriateness depending on how long you've been out of work. I'll summarize them accordingly.

You should take the time-divisions on the following file cards with a grain of salt. *Obviously,* if your money dictates that your job-hunt *has to* proceed much faster, then you will want to speed up all the time divisions on these cards, accordingly -- like, one month, two months, three months, and four months.

**IF YOU'VE BEEN OUT OF WORK
TWO MONTHS OR LESS**

Your goals for this time of unemployment are that you are going to use this time (1) to find a (meaningful) job; and (2) to work on what kind of person you are, and what kind of person you would like to be.

Take an inventory, first of all, of all that you have already: your skills (see Chapter 9), your knowledge (Chapter 10), your values, your worldly goods, your spiritual blessings, etc.

Then write out the kind of person you would like to be, and what you would like to do with your family, friends, etc. Write out a plan for starting to do this. Do a lot of meditating on what you have written, preferably outdoors amongst nature, or indoors with some of your favorite music playing.

Does *a person who has no job* still matter, in the larger scheme of things? That is the question which plagues many of us, when we have been out of work for anything up to two months. If that's the case with you, doubtless along about now you could stand some reassurance that you still matter as a person. Doing the paper-and-pen exercises mentioned on the file card, can contribute *immensely* toward that end.

> The truth is, who we are is more important than what we do. And who we are is: someone designed to be a blessing to this planet Earth.

> ### IF YOU'VE BEEN OUT OF WORK FOUR MONTHS OR MORE
>
> Your goals for this time of unemployment are to use this time (1) to find a (meaningful) job; and (2) volunteering to help others less fortunate than you are.
>
> It is important to preserve four weekdays (say, Monday, Tuesday, Thursday, Friday) for your job-hunt, but one weekday (say, Wednesday) can be given to the work of helping others who are less fortunate.
>
> You can volunteer your services:
> - at places which feed or give shelter to the homeless;
> - at places which give help to those afflicted with AIDS;
> - at places which help battered women or abused children;
> - at places which work with the disabled; and
> - at places which work with the elderly or the dying.

If you have been out of work for four months or more, you will likely be hungering for some way in which to reassure yourself that you are still making a meaningful contribution to society. Volunteering one day a week can accomplish this. According to the Bureau of Labor Statistics, at least one person out of five, 16 years or older, does some volunteer work, without pay, during a typical year. It doesn't matter whether you are employed or unemployed.

The crucial aspect of this second goal, is that it be work which puts you face-to-face with those who are in need, rather than doing administrative services at a desk or in an office. The latter is important, but it is not the kind of engagement that you most need at this juncture.

Your goal here is to avoid self-pity, and depression, by seeking greater compassion for those who are in need -- and particularly those who *(as the phrase has it)* are less fortunate than you.

Incidentally, if your own particular misfortunes are making you feel there is no one in the whole world who is as bad off as you are, believe me, there are *always* others less fortunate than you are. As the old saying puts it, *"I cried for a lack of shoes, until I saw a man who had no feet...."*[12]

If you need more ideas of places where you might volunteer your services than are listed on the file card above, I refer you to the footnote below.[13] One important word of caution here: do not get so engrossed in this secondary goal for your time of unemployment, that you forget/neglect your primary goal: that of finding a job. The rule is: four days a week on your primary goal - - job-hunting; one day a week on your secondary goal - - volunteering.[13] You should stick like glue to that kind of division of your time. Let nothing tempt you to give four days a week to the volunteering, and only one day a week to your job-hunt,

---

12. If you're *really* feeling sorry for yourself, the best restorative is to turn off the TV, and sit down and read stories of others who have had a lot to deal with on their plate, in life, but refused to be beaten down by adversity. Such books as:

Diane Cole's *After Great Pain: A New Life Emerges.* Summit Books. 1992.

Arnold R. Beisser's *Flying Without Wings: Personal Reflections on Being Disabled.* Doubleday, 666 Fifth Ave., New York, NY 10103. 1989. As one wise man said about his disability: "Every disabled person has the choice of either 'crying the blues' about their disability every day of their life, or realistically acknowledging what they have to do in order to have a successful, productive life." Beisser has ultimately opted for the latter, though it was not an easy battle, as this book reveals.

John Callahan's *Don't Worry, He Won't Get Far on Foot: The Autobiography of a Dangerous Man.* William Morrow & Co., Inc. 1989. John became a quadriplegic at the age of 21, due to an automobile accident. However, he has a wicked sense of humor, and so has become a famous cartoonist. This book is John's autobiography, and it is graphic, funny, touching, and irreverent. Arnold Beisser (above) wrote a most relevant passage in his book, apropos of such 'disabled humor' as John's: "The able-bodied person is likely to be appalled by 'disabled humor' and find nothing funny at all about it. But...tragedy and comedy are but two aspects of what is real, and whether we see the tragic or the humorous is a matter of perspective." John's perspective is clearly that he prefers to see the humorous amid the tragedy.

13. Your first resource is/are the Yellow Pages in your local telephone book. Look under "Social Service Organizations," "Handicapped & Disabled Services," etc. for ideas.

Your second resource is the volunteer bureau or the social services department in your town or nearby county seat. If neither of these exists, where you are, then your local churches or synagogues may know what facilities there are for helping those in need.

Your third resource is that of books, which you search for in your local library, and if nothing is there, in your local bookstore, and if nothing is there, you order by mail.

unless you have enough income to last for a long time, *and* the volunteering turns out to be the work you most love doing, in the whole world.

IF YOU'VE BEEN OUT OF WORK SIX MONTHS OR MORE

Your goals for this time of unemployment are to use this time (1) to find a (meaningful) job; and (2) to enroll at your local community college, or the adult education program in your town (if it has one) in order to learn something new.

This something new will be either:
- a subject that intrigues you, from past reading in newspapers or magazines; or
- a subject which upgrades your skills in your present (interrupted) career; or
- a subject which gives you skills or knowledge related to a possible new career that you are thinking about going into.

New titles keep appearing regularly, such as:

Volunteer USA: A comprehensive guide to worthy causes that need you—from AIDS to the environment to illiteracy—where to find them, and how you can help, by Andrew Carroll. Fawcett Columbine Books, Ballantine Books, New York, NY. 1991.

For our Canadian readers there is:

Directory of Volunteer Opportunities, edited by Ellen Shenk. Career Information Centre, University of Waterloo, Waterloo, Ontario, N2L 3G1 Canada. 1986.

For our older readers there is:

Volunteerism and Older Adults, by Mary K. Kouri. ABC-CLIO, Inc., 130 Cremona Dr., P.O. Box 1911, Santa Barbara, CA 93116-1911. 1990.

You may also want to look at books about social service careers - - *if* they list places where you would be working directly with those in need, rather than doing administrative, legislative, or managerial work. Such books include:

Good Works: A Guide to Careers in Social Change, 4th ed., edited by Jessica Cowan, Preface by Ralph Nader. Barricade Books Inc., Publisher, 61 Fourth Ave., New York, NY 10003; distributed by Publishers Group West, 4065 Hollis, Emeryville, CA 94608. 1991. It has a topical index, a geographical index, and an alphabetical index.

In a poll reported in *USA Today*,[14] where people were asked what they would do if they won one million dollars, 20% of them said they would go back to school. So, apparently this is a very common wish. It often gets lost, however, in the time-pressures we are under, when holding down a full-time job.

But, during this current period of unemployment, you are not holding down a full-time job, so now is a wonderful time to go back to school, and fulfill that longtime wish. Attending school is also a great way to keep your mind occupied with something other than your current misfortune.

One important word of caution here, as earlier: do not get so engrossed in this secondary goal for your time of unemployment, that you forget/neglect your primary goal, that of finding a job. The rule is the same as earlier: four days a week on goal #1 - - job-hunting; one day a week on goal #2 - - attending a class or two. Let nothing tempt you to give four days a week to school, and only one day a week to your job-hunt, unless you have enough income to last for the duration *and* you have decided this would be a good time to go back to school and get retrained for a new career. If that is the case, first read Chapters 9 and 10 very carefully, *please.*

Otherwise, your *main* goal for this period - - finding meaning-ful, paid work - - still requires the lion's share of your time, no matter *how long* you've been out of work. As far as your second goal is concerned, here, it should be a class, or two at the most, that you are dealing with, at this juncture. Agreed? Okay. If there is a nearby campus, go visit it, get their catalog, and see what they offer. If you can't afford the big college or university, look at a community college or local adult education program in your community.

If money is a problem, you should *always* talk to the Financial Aid office on the campus that interests you, to see what accom-modations they can make to the fact that you are unemployed.[15]

If you are living out in the middle of *nowhere*, and there isn't any kind of adult education facility for a hundred miles around,

---

14. (7/25/89).

15. Also see (*Bear's Guide to*) *Finding Money for College*, by John Bear. Ten Speed Press, Box 7123, Berkeley, CA 94707. 1992, revised.

you may want to consider a correspondence course *(now frequently called 'off-campus study program')* from some college that offers one.[16] (Even if you live in a metropolis, you may like this idea, though since the job-hunt is so often a lonely enterprise, I myself would elect to go sit in a classroom with other people. *Anything* you can do to make the job-hunt period of your life less lonely, is to be prized.)

IF YOU'VE BEEN OUT OF WORK EIGHT MONTHS OR MORE

Okay, this is beginning to drag on forever. You still want two goals for this period of unemployment, but now after eight months you're thinking they should be equal goals, rather than a primary and a secondary one.

The first remains the same as always, to find meaningful work, doing what you've done before. But the second goal is now equal: to consider some things you've never tried before: moving, starting your own business, etc. And that's what the next chapter is all about.

---

16. The best books, by a long shot, about how to find a good correspondence course, are John Bear's. There is *Bear's Guide to Earning College Degrees Non-Traditionally,* 1992, available directly from the author, John Bear, P.O. Box 826, Benicia, CA 94510. 1-800-835-8535. Cost: $23. And/or the shorter version of it, John Bear's *College Degrees by Mail.* Ten Speed Press, Box 7123, Berkeley, CA 94707. 1991. $12.95. John's books deal with taking courses, as well as getting degrees. He covers *everything,* including schools overseas that offer correspondence degrees to Americans and Canadians, how to get a degree while in prison, and other subjects nobody but John would think of.

SUMMARY

When it looks like your job-hunt is going to stretch on for quite some time, you need to figure out how to avoid getting depressed. 'The blues,' sadness, discouragement, dejection, apathy, or feelings of being 'down,' all add up to the same thing: "I'm depressed."

Unemployment depression *(or, as some have called it, 'recession depression')* is like a kind of phantom octopus, which has five tentacles: physical, emotional, mental, spiritual, and activity. If you would ward off feelings of depression, you must tackle all five, rather than just hacking away at one or two causes of it. As we know from studying thousands of job-hunters, the physical contribution toward depression, is the state of being very tired, and out of shape. The emotional source of depression is stored-up anger. The mental source is the idea of meaninglessness. The spiritual source of depression resides in feelings of abandonment. And the activity side of our being contributes to our depression when we have only one goal, and that one goal is getting completely frustrated.

You tackle depression while you are out of work by staying physically fit, and rested, by getting the anger out of your system, by believing in the meaning of every event, by strengthening whatever relationship you have with God, and by setting at least two goals for your period of unemployment, only one of which should be that of finding meaningful work.

I do want to reiterate, however, that if you attack depression on all five fronts and it doesn't yield, you should immediately get yourself to a doctor or therapist, for further help. There are drugs and medicines, much as you may hate the idea, and there is also psychotherapy. The major point I'm making is that you should fight against accepting depression as though it were an inevitable and permanent part of your life. It isn't.

On the other hand, it will not do to view depression simply as a dark intruder into your life. When it arises in response to a crisis, like finding yourself unemployed, *and only then,* it often is a messenger bearing a gift. The gift is the announcement that the old center, around which your life used to revolve, is no longer sufficient. The depression is often a feeling of having abandoned the old center, but not yet finding the new. It's like an astronaut's journey from circling one planet to another. It's while you're *out there,* in-between, that you feel depressed.

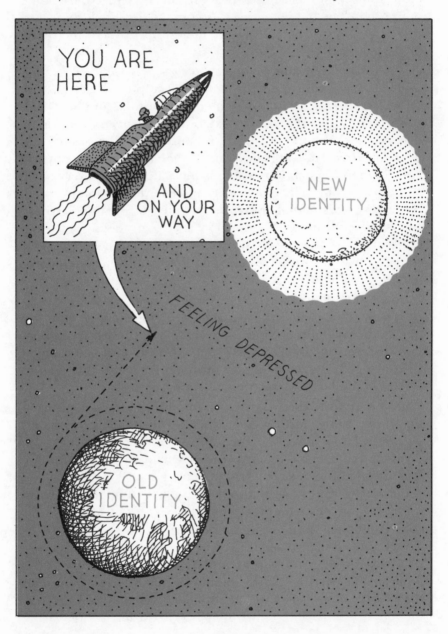

Hence, the depression is a wake-up call to your soul, telling you not just to stay out there, in the ozone. It is time to move on, time to look for a new destination, and find a new center, time to rethink your lifestyle, the way you typically do things, the goals you want to achieve, and the values (like honesty) that you want your life to enshrine.

You can use unemployment well, face the future rather than the past, and so, rebuild your life - - *if* you reject any picture you may have of yourself as passive, pitiable martyr, and opt instead for a picture of yourself as one who is actively at work, re-building your life, on new and stronger foundations.[17]

Every human drama - - even *unemployment* - - is ultimately a drama about the survival of the spirit. Even in an unpredictable life. Even in a life that you wish were otherwise. You can be joyful in your daily living, even after considering all the facts. Your spirit *will* survive, and life can be even more triumphant than before.

---

17. Chapters 9, 10, and 11 are designed to help you do just that.

Two roads diverged in a yellow wood,
And sorry I could not travel both
And be one traveler, long I stood
And looked down one as far as I could
To where it bent in the undergrowth;

Then took the other, as just as fair,
And having perhaps the better claim,
Because it was grassy and wanted wear;
Though as for that the passing there
Had worn them really about the same,

And both that morning equally lay
In leaves no step had trodden black.
Oh, I kept the first for another day!
Yet knowing how way leads on to way,
I doubted if I should ever come back.

I shall be telling this with a sigh
Somewhere ages and ages hence:
Two roads diverged in a wood, and I—
I took the one less traveled by,
And that has made all the difference.

Robert Frost (1874–1963) [1]

---

1. The title of this poem is "The Road Not Taken," from *The Poetry of Robert Frost,* edited by Edward Connery Lathem. Copyright 1916, © 1969 by Holt, Rinehart & Winston. Copyright 1944 by Robert Frost. Henry Holt and Company, Publisher. Used with permission. Incidentally, Scotty Peck's modern classic, *The Road Less Traveled,* takes its title from this poem.

CHAPTER SIX

Trying Something New: Working at Home, Starting Your Own Business, etc.

Chapter 6

WORKING AT HOME

Sure, you've thought about it, a million times. Hasn't everyone? Every time you're tied up in traffic going to or from work. You've toyed with the idea of not having to go to an office or other place of business, but of running your own business, out of your own home, making your own product or selling your own services, being your own boss, and keeping all the profits for yourself.

Great idea! *But,* nothing's ever come of it. Until now. Now, you're at a crossroads. You're out of work, or you're fed up with your job, and you're thinking to yourself: *Maybe it's now, or never. Maybe I ought to just* do *it.*

Three hundred years ago, nearly everybody did it. They worked at home or on their farm. Then the industrial revolution came; and the idea of working *away from* home became normal. But now we've come full circle. The idea of working at home is finding new life, mainly due to congestion on the highways.

Statistics

Surveys indicate that currently 26.7 million people (nearly a quarter of the work force) do at least some work out of their homes. 6.7 million work full-time at home while the remaining 20 million are part-time. Many of the latter are women. Nearly two million people began working from home for the first time, in 1991.

It is doubtless an idea that will continue to grow in popularity, as the U.S. moves more and more, in its metropolitan areas, toward national gridlock. Experts predict that in twenty years congestion on our nation's freeways will be four times as bad as it is today, while congestion on non-freeways will be twice as bad as it is today.[2] *Doesn't that thrill ya?* The idea of working at home is looking more and more attractive by the minute. Don't call it *working at home.* Just call it 'the world's fastest commute.'

Not everyone who works at home is in business for themselves. Some people have been able to talk their boss into letting them do at least *some* of their work at home; in other cases their boss has *asked* them to work at home, connected to their offices by computer-network telephone lines. These people are, accordingly, called *'telecommuters'*-- a term coined by Jack Nilles in 1973.[3]

Statistics

The number of telecommuters, who work for someone else, but at home, is greatly in dispute. Some put the figure at 100,000. Others at 3,000,000. Telecommuters usually put in at least *some* time at the office or place of work each week; typically they work at home between 2 to 4½ days a week.

GOING INTO BUSINESS
FOR YOURSELF

You, of course, are most likely *not* thinking about working at home *for someone else.* You are thinking about working at home *for yourself,* like the 23.7 million, plus, who already do that, or the estimated 25 million additional workers who are *thinking* about it.

Sure you can do it, as long as you are aware of the problems. The two major problems of home-based businesses, according to experts, are that on average home-based workers only earn 70% of what their full-time office-based equals do. And it's often difficult to maintain the balance between business and family

---

2. According to the F.H.C. (Federal Highway Commission), reported in Zero Population Growth Fact Sheet, June, 1989.

3. If you want to read further about this idea, see Brad Schepp, *The Telecommuter's Handbook: How to Work for a Salary—Without Ever Leaving the House.* Pharos Books: A Scripps Howard Company, 200 Park Ave., New York, NY 10166. 1990. It describes the jobs best suited for telecommuting, names and addresses of more than 100 companies that allow employees to work at home, pros and cons of telecommuting for both employee and employer.

time. Sometimes the *family* time gets short-changed, while in other cases the demands of family (particularly with small children) may become so interruptive, that the *business* gets short-changed. So, you do need to investigate thoroughly *how* you go about doing this *well*.[4]

How easy will it be for you to start a business at home? Much depends on the nature of the business, and how radical a departure it represents, from what you have been doing. For example, it will be relatively easy to make the transition to a home-based operation, if you are already (or want to be) a professional: a business expert, writer, consultant, craftsperson, or the like, where the part of your work that requires you to interact with others can be done through the mail, computers, fax machines, modems, cellular telephones, 'call-forwarding,'[5] or voice/electronic mail.

If that's the case, you could in fact work *anywhere* in the world. I mean, wherever your preferred environment in the whole world is -- whether that be out in nature, or at your favorite vacation spot, or skiing chalet, or elsewhere. Think about it. If the idea grows on you, set about exploring it.[6]

---

4. Books to help you do this, include:

Barbara Brabec, *Homemade Money: The Definitive Guide to Success in a Home Business.* 3rd ed. Betterway Publications, Inc., White Hall, VA 22987. 1989, 1986, 1984. A very fine book, with an A-to-Z business section, and a most helpful summary of which states have laws regulating (or prohibiting) certain home-based businesses; it is updated regularly. Barbara also publishes a newsletter, *National Home Business Report.* If you wish more information, you can ask for her catalog, by writing to National Home Business Network, P.O. Box 2137, Naperville, IL 60567.

Lynie Arden, *The Work-at-Home Sourcebook.* 3rd ed. Live Oak Publications, P.O. Box 2193, Boulder, CO 80306. 1990.

Paul and Sarah Edwards, *Working from Home: Everything You Need to Know about Living and Working under the Same Roof.* J. P. Tarcher, Inc., 5858 Wilshire Blvd., Los Angeles, CA 90036. 1985. Now revised and expanded. 436 pages. Has a long section on computerizing your home business, and on telecommunicating.

Homeworking Mothers, a quarterly newsletter for women who want to start their own businesses and work from their homes. Mother's Home Business Network, Box 423, East Meadow, NY 11554.

Frank and Sharon Barnett, *Working Together: Entrepreneurial Couples.* Ten Speed Press, P.O. Box 7123, Berkeley, CA 94707. 1989.

5. This is the technology where people call your one fixed telephone number, and then get automatically forwarded to wherever you have told the phone company you currently are.

Upon reflection, however, you *may* decide you don't want something *quite* that exotic. You just want to start working out of your own home, or apartment. Trouble is, you're not sure exactly where to start. In other words, you haven't a clue as to what kind of business you'd like to run. That's why you're reading this book. Okay, let's dig in.

Reprinted with special permission of King Features Syndicate, Inc.

DREAMS OF MOBILITY, UP OR DOWN

The first thing you ought to look at are your dreams. What have you always dreamed about doing? Since childhood? Since last week? Now is the time to dust off those dreams.

And please don't pay any attention, for now, to whether those dreams represent *a step up* for you in life, or not. Who cares? Your dreams are yours. *It may be* you're dreaming of doing something more ambitious than anything you've ever done before. But then again, you may be dreaming about doing something that's less ambitious than what you have been doing in the past. Maybe you want a simpler life.

---

6. Jeffrey Maltzman, *Jobs in Paradise: The Definitive Guide to Exotic Jobs Everywhere.* Perennial Library, HarperCollins, 10 East 53rd St., New York, NY 10022. 1990. Describes jobs at lakes, rivers, coasts and beaches, snow and skiing, tropical islands, mountains, deserts, and so forth. You will probably not want to look so much at the *jobs* described here, as at the *categories,* to help you think out just what *kind* of place you might like to be a telecommuter from. As a place to *start* some informational interviewing, this is a great book -- *if* you're interested in working exactly where you'd also like to spend your leisure time.

You may have been dreaming of earning *more* money. But then again, you may have been dreaming of doing work that you really love, even if it means a lesser salary or income than you have been accustomed to. Don't *judge* your dreams, and don't let anyone else judge them either.

You of course are not alone in this world, with your dreams. There is a community, of which you are a part. You need to take that community seriously. For example, if you aren't living all by yourself, you need to sit down with your partner or spouse and ask what the implications are *for them* if you try this new thing. Will it require all your joint savings? Will they have to give up things? If so, what? Are they willing to make those sacrifices? And so on.

But you do *not* need to pay attention to what well-meaning acquaintances, around the border of your life, may say about your proposed venture. Every adventurer since Noah has had friends who confidently said, "It'll never work."

The latest self-help book for pessimists.

It is up to you to do your research thoroughly, weigh the risks, count the cost, get counsel from those intimately involved with you, and then if you decide you want to do it (whatever *it* is), go ahead and try -- no matter what your acquaintances say. You only have one life here on this earth, and that life (under God) is *yours* to say how it will be spent, or not spent.

HOW TO CHOOSE YOUR OWN HOME BUSINESS

In the absence of any specific dreams you've had, there are two ways to proceed. One is to start with *you,* and ask what kind of work *you* would most like to do. This is the preferred *way to go.* It takes your life seriously, as sacred and unique. It involves exploring for what purposes were you put here on earth, and what are your unique talents and gifts? *However,* it takes some work and some hard thinking. And not everyone is up to it. If you are (and I hope you are) then it will be necessary for you eventually to read and *do* all the stuff that is described at length in Chapters 9, 10, and 11. When you are done, the work you will have chosen in this fashion will be work that you love to do. And that's *everything!*

The other way, for those who want a quicker and easier approach, is to start with *the job-market,* and ask what the market needs. If you want to begin with this question, rather than with the issue of your own desires, you need to look around your own community, and ask yourself what services or products do people seem to need the most? Or what service or product already offered in the community could stand a lot of *improving?* You may not *love* work chosen in this manner, but this approach focuses on money and *expected profitability* -- that's why many people like to start at this end.

Needless to say, if you are an Episcopalian/Anglican or if you just like *the middle road* on general principles, you *can* go *both ways:* start with *your* needs and wishes, and *also* start with what the market needs, and then see *where they intersect.*[7]

---

7. There is a parallel, but not identical, concept in the Epilogue, page 370.

WHAT DO PEOPLE NEED?

If you begin with market needs, a theme which your research will quickly uncover is the great need for services and products that cater to families where both husband and wife work. This is a large category, since over 21.5 million mothers are currently in the work force. You may also want to target single parents, and singles, because the theme in all cases is the same: products and services which save time. Mark my fat words: that's the underlying theme to 90% of the businesses that are *out there* these days.

Among the ideas that you might consider are: offering home deliveries of local restaurants' dinners, or home delivery of grocery orders from any downtown supermarket. Evening delivery services of laundry, etc. Daytime or evening office cleaning services and/or home cleaning services. Home repairs, especially in the evening or on weekends, of TVs, radios, audio systems, laundries, dishwashers, etc. Lawn care. Care for the elderly in their own homes. Childcare in their own homes. Pickup and delivery of things (even personal stuff, like cleaning) at the office. Automobile care or repair services, with pickup and delivery. Offering short-term business consultancy in various fields. Other successful businesses these days deal with leisure activities.

These are just *samples,* to whet your appetite. Many, many additional ideas are listed in the resources listed in the footnote below.[8] Go browse them in your local library, or at your local bookstore.

---

8. Jay Conrad Levinson, *555 Ways to Earn Extra Money: The ultimate idea book for supplementing your income.* Revised for the '90s. Henry Holt and Company, Inc., 115 W. 18th St., New York, NY 10011. 1991. Ideas for people who are artistic, or oriented toward people, or things, or ideas.

Entrepreneur Magazine's *184 Businesses Anyone Can Start and Make a Lot of Money.* 2nd ed., Bantam Books, 666 Fifth Ave., New York, NY 10103. 1990. Ideas related to Personal Services, Business Services, Food, Retail, Sports and Entertainment, Automotive Businesses, Publishing, and miscellaneous.

Sharon Kahn and The Philip Lief Group, *101 Best Businesses to Start.* Doubleday, a division of Bantam Doubleday Dell Publishing Group, Inc., 666 Fifth Ave., New York, NY 10103. 1988. The categories here are the same as above, plus Healthcare and Fitness, Household Services, Real Estate, Sales and Marketing, and Travel.

If you find no needs within your own community, you may want to broaden your search, to ask what is needed in the country as a whole -- or the world. After all, mail order businesses can be started *small* at home, and catalogs can be sent *anywhere*. If this interests you, read up on the subject,[9] and for heaven's sake, go talk to other mail order people (for names, just look at the catalogs you're already receiving).

LOOK BEFORE YOU LEAP, LOOK BEFORE YOU LEAP

No matter what idea you pick, the most basic problem you will have to deal with is your own understandable anxiety about launching yourself into this brand new world. *"I'm thinking about doing what?"*

There is comfort to be derived, however, from knowing the four rules of life about trying something new. They are:

1. Throughout your life, you are always free to try something new, provided it is honest, and does not hurt other people, or make other people pay the cost for your adventure.

2. There is always some risk, in trying something new. Your job is not to avoid risk -- there is no way to do that -- but to make sure ahead of time that the risks are *manageable*.

3. You find this out before you start, by first talking to others who have already done what you are thinking of doing; then you evaluate whether or not you still want to go ahead and try it.

4. If you do, go ahead. But have a Plan B, already laid out, *before you start,* as to what you will do if it doesn't work out; i.e., know where you are going to go, next.

Paul and Sarah Edwards, *The Best Home Businesses for the 90s: The Inside Information You Need to Know to Select a Home-based Business That's Right For You.* Jeremy P. Tarcher, Inc., 5858 Wilshire Blvd., Suite 200, Los Angeles, CA 90036. 1991. The book profiles 70 top businesses (in their view).

9. Cecil C. Hoge, Sr., *Mail Order Moonlighting.* Ten Speed Press, Box 7123, Berkeley, CA 94707. 1988.

These rules always apply, no matter where you are in your life: just starting out, already employed, unemployed, in mid-life, recovering after a crisis or accident, facing retirement, or whatever. They apply regardless of your circumstances.

WHEN IS A RISK MANAGEABLE?

The concept of 'manageable' risk, above, is very important, but difficult to define. It is very much a matter of personal disposition. Only you can say, in a given situation, whether the risks are manageable or not. Hence it is you who must do the research, to find out the risks ahead of time, and then to weigh those risks. In doing that weighing, the key questions are: *what's the worst possible outcome?* And: *what would I do, if that were to happen?*

"I don't have a parachute of any color."

Because that *may* indeed happen, you MUST have a 'Plan B' -- by which I mean your next move -- mapped out, in outline form, before you even start this one. Don't wait until you're in a crisis, before you even think about what you're going to do next. *Puh-leaze!* Write it out, now. *This is what I'm going to go to do, if this doesn't work out:*

THE RISKS OF STARTING YOUR OWN BUSINESS

If you investigate the risks of starting your own business, the first thing you will come across are some *intimidating* statistics. At least, at first sight. Actually, hidden in them is not just bad news, but also some good news.

Statistics

Currently, 10.2 million people -- or one out of every 12 people in the work force -- have started their own business. *But,* at least 65% of all new businesses fail within their first five years of operation -- that's more than one out of every two. A well-known statistic, and the only debate you'll get on it from experts is whether or not the figure is *too low.* So, if you want to go into business for yourself, there's a great risk that it's going to go belly-up[10] *early on.* That is, as they say, the bad news.

The good news is that *if* you survive this early-on period, things start to look up. The risk decreases. There are two evidences for saying this.

First, only about 25% of new businesses fail *in any given year;* so, taking it on just a year-to-year basis, you have a 75% chance of *not* going belly-up *that* year.[11] Secondly, there are about 28 *old* businesses in this country, for every new business that starts up. So, the national bankruptcy/failure rate -- taking *all* businesses into account -- is *much* lower than most people think. In one year recently, out of each 10,000 businesses in this country, only 120 failed.[12] That means that 9,880 out of each 10,000 businesses survived.

---

10. If any of my readers outside the U.S. do not understand the slang phrase "belly-up," other more familiar synonyms would be: bankrupt, out of business, kaput.

11. These figures are from David Birch's *Job Creation in America.* The Free Press, 866 Third Ave., New York, NY 10022. 1987. David is an excellent researcher, and knows more about small businesses than anyone else in the country that I know of; I recommend this book, highly. It describes at length where the new jobs are coming from, and how our smallest companies put the most people to work.

12. 1986, the most recent year for which I have statistics.

What these statistics add up to, is that *if* you can make it through the first few years in your home business, you'll probably survive thereafter. That leaves the BIG question: how do you survive those first few difficult years? The answer is: *Research. Homework. Interviewing people.*

Now, that doesn't mean just: go *talk* to them. There has to be a purpose to your talking. You're trying to find out something. That *something* can be summarized in the following formula:

A, MINUS B, EQUALS C

It is *mindboggling* to discover how many people start a new business, at home or elsewhere, without ever going to talk to other people, who have started up the same kind of business. One job-hunter told me she started a homemade candle business, without ever talking to anyone else who had tried a similar endeavor. Her business went belly-up within a year and a half.

She concluded: no one should go into such a business.

I concluded: she hadn't done her homework, before she started.

Here, then, are the rules for the homework you *must* do, before starting your own home business - - or any kind of new venture. Please *memorize* them:

$$A - B = C$$

1. You write out exactly what kind of business you are thinking about starting.

2. You identify towns or cities that are at least twenty-five miles away, and you try to get their phone books, addresses of their Chambers of Commerce, etc.

3. By using the phone book and the Chambers, you try to identify names of three businesses in those towns, that are identical or similar to the business you are thinking of starting. You journey to that town or city, and talk to the founder/owner of same.

4. When you talk to them, you ask them what pitfalls or obstacles they ran into. You ask them how they overcame them. You ask them what skills or

knowledges do they think are necessary to running this kind of business successfully. You make a list of the latter. When you've finished talking to all three owners, you put together a list of the skills and knowledges they agreed on, as necessary to running the business. We'll call this list "A."

5. Back home you sit down and inventory your own skills and knowledges, perhaps using Chapters 9 and 10 in this book. We'll call this list "B."

6. Finally, you subtract "B" from "A," and this results in a list we will call "C." That's the list of the skills or knowledges you don't have, but must find -- either by taking courses, or by getting volunteers with those skills, or by hiring someone with those skills.

Why twenty-five miles away? Well, actually, that's a minimum. You want to interview businesses which, *if they were in the same town* with you, would be your rival. And if they were in the same town with you, wouldn't likely tell you how to get started. After all, they're not going to train you just so you can then take business away from them.

But, when a guy, a gal, or a business is twenty-five miles away -- even better, fifty miles away -- you're not as likely to be perceived as a rival, and therefore they're much more likely to tell you what you want to know about their own experience, and how *they* got started, and where the landmines are hidden.

Doubtless at this point you would like an example of this whole process. Okay. Our job-hunter is a woman who has been making harps for some employer, but now is thinking about going into business for herself, not only *making* harps at home, but also *designing* harps, with the aid of a computer. After interviewing several home-based harpmakers and harp designers, and finishing her own self-assessment, her chart of $A - B = C$ came out looking like this:

A − B = C

Skills and Knowledges Needed to Run This Kind of Business Successfully	Skills and Knowledges Which I Have	Skills and Knowledges Needed, Which I Do Not Have, and Which I Will Therefore Have to Get Someone to Volunteer, or I Will Have to Go Out and Hire
Precision-working with tools and instruments	Precision-working with tools and instruments	
Planning and directing an entire project	Planning and directing an entire project	
Programming computers, inventing programs that solve physical problems		Programming computers, inventing programs that solve physical problems
Problem solving: evaluating why a particular design or process isn't working.	Problem solving: evaluating why a particular design or process isn't working.	
Being self-motivated, resourceful, patient, and persevering, accurate, methodical, and thorough	Being self-motivated, resourceful, patient, and persevering, accurate, methodical and thorough	
Thorough knowledge of: Principles of electronics	*Thorough knowledge of:*	*Thorough knowledge of:* Principles of electronics
Physics of strings	Physics of strings	
Principles of vibration	Principles of vibration	
Properties of woods	Properties of woods	
Computer programming		Computer programming
Accounting		Accounting

If she decides to try her hand at becoming an independent harpmaker and harp designer, she now knows what she needs but lacks: *computer programming, knowledge of the principles of electronics, and accounting.* Column **C.** These she must either go to school to acquire for herself, OR enlist from some friends of hers in those fields, on a volunteer basis, OR go out and hire, part-time.

Now, let us suppose you've done this homework. What next?

PUTTING THIS HOMEWORK TO USE

First, you decide if you still want to start your own business, and if so, how? If you're out of work, your major problem will be finding the start-up money. If you aren't out of work, you will need to debate the wisdom of quitting your job before you start up the new company, or business. And what do the experts say, here? In a word, they say, if you have a job, *don't* quit it. Better by far to move *gradually* into self-employment, doing it as a moonlighting activity first of all, while you are still holding down that regular job somewhere else. That way, you can test out your new enterprise, as you would test a floorboard in an old run-down house, stepping on it cautiously without at first putting your full weight on it, to see whether or not it will support you.[13]

Secondly, you get whatever help you need. If your investigation revealed that it takes good accounting practices in order to turn a profit, and you don't know a thing about accounting, you go out and hire a (part-time) accountant *immediately* - - or, if you absolutely have no money, you talk an accountant friend of yours into giving you some volunteer time, for a while.

Well, that's it. That's our overview of the general kind of homework that you *must* do, before starting something new. That's what separates successful home businesses from unsuccessful ones. Now, let us turn and look at the seven most common problems that people run into, when trying to do this interviewing and research.

---

13. See Philip Holland, *How to Start a Business without Quitting Your Job: The Moonlight Entrepreneur's Guide.* Ten Speed Press, P. O. Box 7123, Berkeley, CA 94707. 1992.

WHEN YOU NEED A SECOND JOB
TO HELP MAKE ENDS MEET,
AT HOME OR OTHERWISE

Research
Problem

#1

> ### Statistics
>
> Currently, the number of people having two careers, businesses, or jobs *(one or both of them part-time)* is at least 50% higher than it was ten years ago. This year one out of every 16 workers, will be holding down two or more jobs. That comes to 7.5 million people.

Surveys reveal that half of these 7.5 million people are *not* holding down two jobs because they love to work. They are holding down two jobs because they can't make ends meet, otherwise. It is the hard '90s, an era of decreased standards of living, decreased expectations, decreased income, and lower salaries. Twenty years ago, when things got tight, the solution was to have your spouse go to work. Now, in the '90s, when most spouses are *already* working, the only solution left, is for you to take on a second, part-time, job.

You may decide, in such a case, that your best shot at a second job consists in working at night or on weekends for someone else. So, you'll call up your brother, or your uncle, or your best friend, and see if they have any suggestions, or know of any part-time vacancies. If they don't, then you'll probably want to go back to Chapter 4 - - which applies to finding a part-time job, as much as it does to finding a full-time job - - and follow its advice.

On the other hand you may decide that if you're going to start a(nother) part-time job, you want it to be out of your home; and in that case, all of the steps listed previously about inventing your own business apply as much to a part-time business as they do to full-time ones. I will only remind you: do your homework, thoroughly, *before* you dive in. You might as well find a second job that you truly enjoy, and *not* just one that brings in money, but bores you out of your skull.[14]

---

14. Sad footnote: as you will find out when you do your investigation, many of the part-time jobs that pay really well *are* boring beyond belief. Nobody wants such jobs. That's *why* employers pay such big bucks - - to get someone to take the job. Bridge toll-takers (in some States) are an example of this.

FREE-LANCING, OR
CONTRACTING OUT
YOUR SERVICES

Many people don't have to *invent* a business, when they decide to work out of their home They already know what they
want to do. They've been doing it for years, full-time, for someone else. Now they want to do it on their own. We call this *free-
lancing* or *contracting out your services.*

Free-lancing has its own peculiar set of circumstances, namely,
you are in a very real sense a perpetual job-hunter -- *always*
seeking new clients, which is to say, new employers. I call them
employers, because they *pay* you for the work you are doing.
The only difference between this and a full-time job is that here
the contract is limited. But if you free-lance, you will have to continually beat the bushes for new clients -- that is, short-term
employers.

Of course, the dream of most free-lancers is that some day
you will be so well known, and so in demand, that clients will be
literally beating down your doors, and you will be able to stop

Research
Problem
2

this endless job-hunting for employer/clients. But that only happens to a privileged few, and your realistic self knows that.

The greater likelihood is that you will *always* have to beat the bushes for employers/clients. It may get easier as you get better at it, but it will probably be the one aspect of your work that you will cordially dislike. If you're going to go this route, you'll probably have to learn to *like* it - - at least grudgingly.

If you hate it, if you avoid it like the plague until there's literally no bread on the table, you're probably going to find *free-lancing* is just a glamorous synonym for *'starving.'* I know *many* free-lancers to whom this has happened, and it happened precisely because they couldn't stomach going out to beat the bushes for clients. If that's true for you, *hire* somebody part-time, who is willing to do this for you - - who, in fact, 'eats it up.'

As for the rest of A – B = C, do the same kind of interviewing before you start out, as I have advised throughout. Talk to people who have been free-lancers, until you know the name of every pitfall and obstacle.

Where do you find such people? Well, free-lancers are *every-where*. Independent screenwriters, copywriters, artists, song-writers, photographers, illustrators, interior designers, video people, film people, consultants, and therapists, are only *some* examples of the type of people who must free-lance, in the very nature of their job.[15] Go talk to them, even if they're not free-lancing in the same business you have in mind; you will still learn much from their experience.

WHEN YOU'VE THOUGHT OF A BUSINESS OR CAREER THAT NO ONE'S EVER HEARD OF, BEFORE

Research Problem #3

No matter how inventive you are, you're probably *not* going to invent a job that *no one* has ever heard of, before. You're only going to invent a job that *most* people have never heard of, before. But the likelihood is *great* that someone, somewhere, in this world of endless creativity, has already put together the kind of job you're dreaming about. Your task: to find her, or him, and interview them thoroughly. And then...well, you know the drill: A – B = C.

---

15. For books to help you with your particular specialty, see such catalogs as that of Writer's Digest Books/North Light Books, 1507 Dana Ave., Cincinnati, OH 45207.

But suppose, in spite of all your contacts, the phone book, Chambers of Commerce, and the like, you can't find such a person? It's possible. In which case, what you're going to have to figure out is who is doing something *close* to what you're dreaming of doing. Then go interview *that* person.

This is, incidentally, how you put together any career that has three or more diverse parts to it (say, your favorite three subjects in college or high school). No matter what business you dream up, no matter how kooky it seems, or how many conflicting parts it seems to have, you *never* need conclude that there is no one who can instruct you out of their own experience, in the pitfalls of starting that business or career.

WHEN NO ONE HAS DONE WHAT YOU WANT TO DO

You can always find someone who has done something that at least approximates what you want to do. The rules are:

1. Break down your projected business or career into its parts.

2. Then take any two of those parts at a time. See what kind of person that describes.

3. Find out the names of such persons, preferably two or more.

4. Go see, phone, write, him or her; you will learn a great deal, that is relevant to your dream.

5. They, in turn, may be able to give you a lead to someone whose business is even closer to what it is you want to do. And then you can go interview them. And so on, and so forth.

For example, let's suppose your dream is -- here we take a ridiculous case -- to use computers to monitor the growth of plants at the South Pole. And suppose you can't find anybody who's ever done such a thing. The way to tackle this seemingly insurmountable problem, is to break the proposed business down into its parts, which -- in this case -- are: *computers, plants,* and *the Arctic.*

Then you try combining any two parts, together, to define the person or persons you need to talk to. In this case, that would mean finding someone who's *used computers with plants here in the States,* or someone who's *used computers at the Arctic,* or someone who has *worked with plants at the Arctic,* etc. You go talk to them, and along the way you may discover there *is* someone who has used computers to monitor the growth of plants at the South Pole. Then again, you may not. In any event, you will learn most of the pitfalls that wait for you, by hearing the experience of those who are in *parallel* businesses or careers.

Thus, it is *always* possible -- with a little blood, sweat and imagination -- to find out what $A - B = C$ is, for the business you're trying to invent.

WHEN YOU'VE INVENTED
SOMETHING --
OR WOULD LIKE TO

Research
Problem

4

If you are inclined toward invention or tinkering, you might want to start by improving on an idea that's already *out there.* Start with something you like, such as bicycles. You might experiment with making -- let us say -- a folding-bicycle. Or, if you like to go to the beach, and your skills run to sewing, you might think about making and selling beach towels with weights sewn in the corners, against windy days.

If you've already invented something, and it's been sitting in your drawer, or the garage, but you've never attempted to duplicate or manufacture it before, now might be a good time to try. Think out very carefully just how you are going to get it manufactured, advertised, and marketed, etc. There are firms out there which claim to specialize in promoting inventions such as yours, for a fee. However, according to the Federal Trade Commission, in a study of 30,000 people who paid such promoters, not a single inventor ever made a profit after giving their invention to such firms.[16] If you want to gamble some of your hard-earned money on such firms, consider whether you might better drop it at the tables in Las Vegas. I think the odds are *better* there.

You're much better off, *of course,* doing your own research as to how one gets an invention marketed. Through the copyright office, and your library, locate other inventors, and ask if they were successful in marketing their own invention. When you find those who were, pick their brains for everything they're worth. Of course one of the first things they're going to tell you is to go get your invention copyrighted or trademarked or patented.[17]

WHEN YOU WANT TWO
DIFFERENT HOME BUSINESSES
AT THE SAME TIME

When you've finished your investigation/research/homework, one of the things you may discover is that you don't want to start up just one home business; you want to start up two -- both part-time, *of course.* Perhaps *variety* is your middle name. You were born to be a *two-career-at-the-same-time* person. Or, perhaps you're just starving. You started your other home business *ages* ago; and now you need to start up a second one, as well, if you're going to survive, financially.

In any event, the advice is the same as it is for one business. For each of the businesses you propose, you need to go interview people who have already done this, to find out A – B = C. You may also want to talk to people who have juggled two (or more) careers, at the same time. Since it may be difficult for

Research
Problem

#5

---

16. *San Francisco Chronicle,* 1/26/91.

17. Richard C. Levy, *The Inventor's Desktop Companion: A Guide to Successfully Marketing and Protecting Your Ideas.* Visible Ink Press, a division of Gale Research Inc., 835 Penobscot Bldg., Detroit, MI 48226-4094. 1991. From securing a patent for it, to selling it, a very complete compendium.

    Fred Grisson and David Pressman, *The Inventor's Notebook.* Nolo Press, 950 Parker St., Berkeley, CA 94710. 1989. A manual to help you keep records about your invention.

you to find the names of such people, you should know about Jay Conrad Levinson. He was in just such a situation, and has written a book about his choices -- and his philosophy -- called *Earning Money Without A Job.* If you can't find people in your town or city who have gone this route, then you will profit by reading his experience.[18] As you will see there, you put together a two-career life by figuring out *what* two careers you want to do, and then deciding how much time you will allot to each.

WHEN THE BUSINESS IS TOO LARGE FOR THE HOUSE: DREAMS AND FRANCHISES

Research Problem

#6

Your dream may be to do something that's too big for the house. You *know* you're gonna have to go rent a place, or sell your home and buy some acreage. For example, *I want a horse ranch, where I can raise and sell horses.* Or *I want to run a bed-and-breakfast place.*[19] Stuff like that. If so, you'd better go talk to other people who have already done that. Pick their brains for everything they're worth.

If you don't have a dream, but you still want your own business - - and you don't *mind* if it's too big for the house - - then you may want to think about a franchise. Though some of them can be done from your home,[20] the majority require an outside site.

Franchises exist because some people want to have their own business, but don't want to go through the agony of starting it up. They want to *buy in* on an already established business, and they have the money in their savings with which to do that (or they know where they can get a bank loan). Fortunately for them, there are more than 2,100 franchised businesses operating in this country, with more than 478,000 outlets, employing more than 6 million people. Your library or bookstore will have books that list many of these.[21]

---

18. Jay Conrad Levinson, *Earning Money without a Job*. Revised for the '90s. Henry Holt and Company, Inc., 115 W. 18th St., New York, NY 10011. 1991. The first part of this excellent book is devoted to his story, and his idea of "modular economics" - - putting together several small jobs, rather than one big one. The second part of the book is devoted to actual businesses that can thus be put together.

19. Barbara Notarius and Gail Sforza Brewer, *Open Your Own Bed & Breakfast*. John Wiley & Sons, Inc., Business/Law/General Books Division, 605 Third Ave., New York, NY 10158-0012. 1987.

20. Lynie Arden, *Franchises You Can Run from Home,* John Wiley & Sons, Professional and Trade Division, 605 Third Ave., New York, NY 10158-0012. 1990.

21. *Franchise Opportunities,* 22nd ed. Sterling Publishing Co., Inc., 387 Park Ave. S., New York, NY 10016. 1991. This is a reprint of the 22nd edition of *Franchise Opportunities Handbook,* issued by the U.S. Government Printing Office. An immensely thorough book, together with a good introductory section about how to investigate a franchise.

Erwin J. Keup, *Franchise Bible: A Comprehensive Guide*. The Oasis Press®/PSI Research, 300 N. Valley Dr., Grants Pass, OR 97526. 1990. Mr. Keup is a lawyer who has specialized in franchise law and franchise consulting for the past 32 years. He covers 'buying an existing business,' as well as franchises. Also, if you have a successful business already, he discusses the pros and cons of turning it into a franchise.

Ray Bard and Sheila Henderson, *Own Your Own Franchise: Everything You Need to Know about the Best Opportunities in America*. A Stonesong Press Book, Addison-Wesley Publishing Co., Inc., Route 128, Reading, MA 01876. 1987.

Robert Laurance Perry, *The 50 Best Low-Investment, High-Profit Franchises*. Prentice-Hall, Business & Professional Division, A division of Simon & Schuster, Englewood Cliffs, NJ 07632. 1990. Since there is a disturbing trend in franchises these days toward higher and higher start-up fees, up in the $150,000 category or higher, Perry attempts to list ones which people can afford; most of them are less than $20,000, some less than $5,000.

Constance Jones, *The 220 Best Franchises to Buy*. Philip Lief Group, 319 E. 52nd St., New York, NY 10022. 1987. A sourcebook for evaluating the best franchise opportunities.

Overall, the failure rate for franchises is less than 4%.[22] You want to keep in mind that some *types* of franchises have a failure rate greater than that. The ten *riskiest* small businesses, according to experts, are local laundries and dry cleaners, used car dealerships, gas stations, local trucking firms, restaurants, infant clothing stores, bakeries, machine shops, grocery or meat stores, and car washes -- though I'm sure there will be some new nominees for this list, by the time you read this. *Risky* doesn't mean you can't make them succeed. It only means the odds are greater than they would be with other small businesses.

You want to keep in mind also that some individual franchises are *terrible* -- and that includes well-known names. They charge too much for you to *get on board,* and often they don't do the advertising or other commitments that they promised they would.

There isn't a franchising book that doesn't warn you eighteen times to go talk to people who have *already* bought that same franchise, before you ever decide to go with them. And I mean *several* people, not just one. Most experts also warn you to go talk to *other* franchises in the same field, not just the kind you're thinking about signing up with. Maybe there's something better, that such research will uncover.

If you are drawn to the idea of a franchise, because you are in a hurry, and you don't want to do any homework first, *'cause it's just too much trouble,* you will deserve what you get, believe me. That way lies madness.

22. Ray Bard and Sheila Henderson, *Own Your Own Franchise,* page 1.

WHEN YOU WANT TO FIND
FUNDING THROUGH A GRANT

When you decide to set up a business at home, it may be that you want to do something that doesn't have any direct customers or clients -- like, research. Or it may be something that requires a hefty financial investment, up front, and you don't have it -- nor can you get it. As you may have already discovered, many banks, in the '90s, are adopting new tough postures against making loans to people they would gladly have lent to, in the '80s.

Research
Problem
#7

So the idea of a grant may sound appealing to you. Either a foundation grant or a government grant. How, you ask, can I find such a grant? Well, it isn't going to be easy, and you may, after much work, strike out. So, you'd better have a 'Plan B' ready, or to use a baseball metaphor, you'd better have a pitcher warming up in the bullpen.

But if you want to give this a shot, you go about trying to find a grant basically the same way you look for a job. There are some rules, as Matthew Lesko points out:[23]

1. If it is a government grant you seek, look at state and local governments as well as the Federal.

2. The money may not be where logic would suggest it should be. For example, the Department of Labor funds doctoral dissertations, the Department of Agriculture funds teenage entrepreneurs, and the like.

3. Talk to the people at the agency who are in charge of dispersing the grant funds.

4. When you have located an appropriate agency for what you want to do, ask to see a copy of a successful application (under the Freedom of Information Act).

5. If they make clear that they will not give you a large amount, ask for a small amount for a year; and use that year as a chance for them to get to know you.

To get you started with funding possibilities, consult your library (or your banker) for one of the directories of grants

23. Matthew Lesko, *Getting Yours: The Complete Guide to Government Money.* Viking Penguin Inc., 40 W. 23rd St., New York, NY 10010. 1987.

already given: such as the *Annual Register of Grant Support,* published by Reed Reference Publishing, 121 Chanlon Rd., New Providence, NJ 07974. The directory or register covers 3,000 current grant programs, and has four helpful indexes.

Women who are thinking of starting their own business can get counseling over the phone, from the American Women's Economic Development Corporation (AWED), Monday through Friday, between 9 a.m. and 5 p.m. Eastern time, at a cost of $10 for up to ten minutes. The hotline offers an expert in the area in which the caller needs help. Longer counseling, up to one and a half hours, is also offered, at a cost of $35. If calling from New York City, Alaska, or Hawaii, call 1-212-688-1900. If calling from any other area, call 1-800-222-AWED. Both services may be charged to major credit cards.

Non-profit organizations, seeking grants, can obtain assistance from The Foundation Center, 79 Fifth Ave., New York, NY 10003, an independent, nonprofit organization offering assistance in locating grants *to non-profit organizations, only.* It publishes *The Foundation Directory,* which lists over 8,000 U.S. foundations, whose grants accounted en toto for 92% of all U.S. dollars awarded in three typical years. There are four reference collections operated by the Center, in New York, Washington, DC, Cleveland, and San Francisco. There are also dozens of co-operating collections nationwide. For information on locations nearest you, call 1-800-424-9836.

THE KEY TO SUCCEEDING
AT SOMETHING NEW

That ends our look at the various problems you may need to deal with, during your research. Now, in general, if you want to try something new in your life, you should try it - - subject to the rules I mentioned in this chapter. Don't let anyone tell you, and certainly don't *ever* tell yourself, that trying something new is a privilege open only to other people, not to you.

You know the kind of dialogue with yourself that I'm talking about: *"Well, I know others could do this, but I can't, because..."* and then you name some real or imagined handicap. Such as: I have held too many jobs before; I am overqualified; I am too inexperienced; I am too old; I am too shy; I've only worked for large organizations; I've only worked for small organizations; I've only worked for volunteer organizations; I've only worked at home; I'm a woman; I am gay; I belong to an ethnic minority; I'm a recent immigrant; I am too much of a generalist; I am too much of a specialist; I have a police or prison record; I have a psychiatric history; I didn't get good enough grades in school; I have a physical or mental disability; I have a chronic illness; I have AIDS; I live in too urban an area; I live in too rural an area; I live in too small a town; I live where too many people are; I have no skills; I have no money; etc., etc.

If you *are* feeling especially inhibited from doing this new thing you're thinking about, I would like to tell you one simple fact: *every* job-hunter or career-changer in the world is handicapped. The only question is: what is your handicap, and how much does it show?[24]

If you doubt this - - that every job-hunter is handicapped in *some* way - - sit down and think a minute. There are, let us say, 13,000 truly different skills that human beings possess. We have discovered over the years that the average job-hunter has 700 skills. That's a lot, but it still means that there are 12,300 things each of us *can't* do. Believe me, we're *all* handicapped. Sit down

---

24. For those with clear disabilities, I refer you to a companion booklet to *Parachute* entitled, *Job-Hunting Tips for the So-Called Handicapped or People Who Have Disabilities*, Ten Speed Press, Box 7123, Berkeley CA 94707. 1991. To save yourself some money, see if your library has it, first.

and put Mozart on your stereo or CD player, when you're searching for some humility.

Yet, in spite of having the same handicaps you have, thousands of people have successfully done any new thing that you can think of. If *they* did, so can *you*. The key: believing that you can, and doing your homework *thoroughly* ahead of time, to find out what the risks are, and if they are manageable.

The homework, as I have said throughout this chapter, is crucial. People fail, not because they have handicaps, but because they didn't do their homework. It's as simple as that. Most business failures could have been avoided. See the resources listed below.[25]

---

25. There are a lot of them. You should browse these in your local library, or bookstore, to see which ones look interesting and helpful, for your particular case. Then borrow them, or purchase them, and read them *thoroughly*. The business you save will be your own:

Michael Madden, ed., *Small Business Start-Up Index*. Updated annually. Gale Research, Inc., P.O. Box 33477, Detroit, MI 48232-5477. Current practical information on starting specific types of small businesses. See your local library.

William A. Cohen, *The Entrepreneur and Small Business Problem Solver: An Encyclopedic Reference and Guide*, 2nd ed. John Wiley & Sons, 605 Third Ave., N.Y., NY 10158-0012. It is, indeed, encyclopedic, covering almost every kind of problem you can think of.

William J. Stolze, *Startup: An Entrepreneur's Guide to Launching & Managing a New Venture*. Rock Beach Press, 1255 University Ave., Rochester, NY 14607. 1989.

Ted Nicholas, *How to Form Your Own Corporation without a Lawyer for Under $50.00. Complete with Tear-Out Forms, Certificate of Incorporation, Minutes, By-Laws*. Enterprise Publishing Co., Inc., 1000 Oakfield Lane, Wilmington, DE 19810. 1973.

Bernard Kamoroff, *Small-Time Operator*. Bell Springs Publishing, P.O. Box 640, Laytonville, CA 95454. 1988. How to start your own small business, keep your books, pay your taxes, and stay out of trouble.

Leigh and Sureleigh Silliphant, *Making $70,000+ a Year As a Self-Employed Manufacturer's Representative*. Ten Speed Press, Box 7123, Berkeley, CA 94707. 1988.

Jay Conrad Levinson, *Guerrilla Marketing Attack: New Strategies, Tactics, and Weapons for Winning Big Profits for Your Small Business*. Houghton Mifflin Co., 2 Park St., Boston, MA 02108. 1989.

Jay Conrad Levinson, *Guerrilla Marketing: Secrets for Making Big Profits from Your Small Business*. Waldentapes, Box 1084, Stamford, CT 06904. 1985. Listen & Learn Cassettes, ISBN 0-681-30739-0.

Starting a Small Business in Ontario. Ministry of Industry, Trade, and Technology, Small Business Branch, 7th Floor, Hearst Block, 900 Bay St., Toronto, Ontario M7A 9Z9, Canada.

Godfrey Golzen, *Working for Yourself*. Kogan Page Ltd., 120 Pentonville Rd., London Nl 9JN. 1987. How to start a business, raise capital, etc.

CONCLUSION:
ALWAYS HAVE A 'PLAN B'

Whatever new thing you decide to try in this chapter, AL-WAYS have a Plan B: *"I'm going to try out this new venture, but my Plan B is that if after a certain number of months it doesn't look like I'm going to make it, then I'm going to* _____ (fill in the blank carefully, with a *detailed* alternative plan)." *Don't* say to yourself, 'Well, I'll wait, and if it doesn't pan out, *then* I'll think about what I'm going to do next.'

No, no, my friend. The condition of trying something new in your life, *particularly if you have others depending on you,* is that - - before you even start - - you have your Plan B *all in place, and ready to go.*

You wouldn't start out on a long car trip across the country, without a spare. Don't start any other life trip without one, either.

I decided not to wait a long time,
To wait for the mercies of God;
I simply took a broom in my hand,
And started sweeping.

> A Russian Jew, an aeronautical
> engineer, upon emigrating
> to Israel.

CHAPTER SEVEN

Trying Something New: Moving

Chapter 7

WHEN YOU WANT
TO PULL UP STAKES,
MOVE, AND RELOCATE

> "When times are bad Americans have always picked up and
> tried to find prosperity somewhere else. This time, it may
> be tougher than ever; no areas are booming, and the reces-
> sion has touched nearly every industry and job level." *Where
> the Jobs Are: The Best Places to Look*, in *Newsweek*, 1/20/92

However, people don't have to wait until times are bad, before they relocate. Surveys reveal that the average American
moves eleven times between birth and death. Sometimes that's
within the same town.[1] But sometimes it's to a faraway place.

There are two reasons, above all else, why people relocate:

(1) You find yourself stuck in some miserable city that you
hate every day you are there. Finally it just gets too much. You
decide you can't stay there any longer. You only have one life to
live, on this earth, and you want to spend the rest of it in a place
you really enjoy. This can happen when you're twenty, forty, or
sixty. Listed in the footnote on the next page are some very
helpful books, to help you find a place you could really love.[2]
The best of these, by a long shot, is Richard Boyer and David
Savageau's *Places Rated Almanac*.

(2) You just can't find any work, or any decent well-paying
work, anyway, where you presently live. It seems to you that
every job is filled, numbered, and has a waiting list besides.

---

1. While I was growing up in Teaneck, New Jersey, my parents could only afford to
rent, and when rents changed, we moved. Between the time I was five and eighteen
years old, we moved seven times, within the same town. This is a typical experience for
many urban dwellers who rent.

You've *got* to move. But how do you figure out, ahead of time, where to move to? There are several strategies which people use:

a) You know exactly where to move. There's a town or city where you have family or friends. You decide to move *there,* because you will have their support and help. Or there's some city or area where you've always *dreamed* of being able to live. *Now's the time.* You're confident you'll be able to find a job there, somehow, somewhere, once you get there.

---

2. Richard Boyer and David Savageau, *Places Rated Almanac: Your Guide to Finding the Best Places to Live in America.* Rand McNally & Co., Box 7600, Chicago, IL 60680. 1989. A marvelous book. Immensely helpful for anyone weighing where to move next. All 333 metropolitan areas are ranked and compared for living costs, job outlook, crime, health, transportation, education, the arts, recreation, and climate. Has numerous helpful diagrams, charts and maps, showing (for example) earthquake risk areas, tornado and hurricane risk areas, the snowiest areas, the stormiest areas, the driest areas, and so on. Don't leave home without it.

David Savageau, *Retirement Places Rated.* Prentice-Hall Press, a division of Simon & Schuster, Inc., 15 Columbus Circle, New York, NY 10023. 1990. Although purportedly about retirement, it is useful information for anyone. Compares 151 top geographical areas in the U.S.

G. Scott Thomas, *The Rating Guide to Life in America's Small Cities.* Prometheus Books, 700 E. Amherst St., Buffalo, NY 14215. 1990. Compares 219 small cities in areas of climate, economics, education, health care, housing, public safety, transportation, proximity to urban centers, sophistication, and diversions.

Jill Andresky Fraser, *The Best U.S. Cities for Working Women.* Plume Books, New American Library, 1633 Broadway, New York, NY 10019. 1986.

b) You have no idea where to move to, but your first consideration is that it be a place you could love; if you can figure out where *that* is, you're pretty confident you'll be able to find a job there, somehow, somewhere.

c) You have no idea where to move to, but your first consideration is that it should offer jobs for someone who does whatever it is you do, and that it should pay a decent wage; you're pretty sure that you'll get used to living there, after you settle in.

We'll begin with this last alternative, first.

Choosing A Place
By Whether or Not It Has Jobs

If jobs are the first thing on your mind, you have two ways to go. One is to move where the unemployment rate is low for *all* jobs. Your local Federal/State employment office can usually give you the current statistics about all 50 States. You look for the States with the lowest unemployment rate. Currently, as I write, these are Nebraska, Hawaii, North and South Dakota, Arizona, and Utah. They are followed by Iowa, Colorado, Kansas, Minnesota, Wisconsin, and Nevada. Then you pick one or more metropolitan areas in those States, and write to their Chambers of Commerce (pick up your phone and ask Information for their phone numbers, in each city). You ask those Chambers for all the information they have in writing about businesses which deal with your trade or specialty, and you ask that these lists be sent to you.

Send them a thank-you note *the day* the stuff arrives, *please.* You may need to contact them again later, perhaps when you're actually in the area, and it will help you a lot if they can say, *"Oh yes, you're that nice person who sent us a thank-you note when we sent you our materials. First thank-you note we've gotten in three years."* Chances are, they will bend over *backwards* to help you.

Your other strategy for choosing a place by whether or not it has jobs, is to find out what places in the country (if any) have a particular need for your kind of skills. This is hard to do in the case of some kinds of jobs -- like that of a writer, say, but easier to do if you are a craftsperson or practice a particular trade. In the latter case, you would go to your local library, and ask the

librarian to help you find a trade association directory, or directories. You would then look up the association that deals with
your occupation, and jot down the address of their national
headquarters. Then write or phone them and ask if they know
where the demand is greatest, in that industry, nationwide. If
their answer turns out to be 'several places,' then you can fall
back on such books as Richard Boyer and David Savageau's
Places Rated Almanac, to decide which of those is your first choice,
which is your second, etc.

Choosing A Place
By Whether or Not You Love It There

To look forward, toward finding a place you will love, *when
you don't even know its name,* it is helpful if you first look back.
You may not know the *name* of the place you'd like to move to,
but you sure know its *description.* It's tucked away in the recesses
of your mind, and all you need to do now is *tease* it out.

This is the way you do that: most of us have lived in a number
of places, over our lifespan thus far. We remember those places
well. Mostly, we remember what we *didn't* like about them. The
mind tends to *warn* us of things to avoid in the future, by saving
its memories in negative rather than in positive form. Never
mind. Make a list of such. List *any* factor, for *any* city where you
have ever lived, that you *didn't* like. It might come out looking
something like this:

Places Where I Have Lived	Things I Didn't Like About Those Places	
Milwaukee	Bad winters	
Teaneck	Poor newspaper	
Chicago	No symphony	
Lido Beach	Lots of crime	
Cambridge	Traffic congestion	
New York	Expensive housing	
Palisades Park	Not enough sunny days	
San Francisco	Cold summers	
Passaic	Too much air polution	

Now, what's the third column for? Well, actually, there's both a third *and* a fourth column. Ignoring the first column, on the previous page, this is how the rest of it goes:

Final Column,
For One Person

Things I Didn't Like About Those Places	The Opposite	Items in the Column to The Left, Ranked in Order of Importance to Me
Bad winters	Mild winters	1. Lots of sunny days
Poor newspaper	Good newspaper	2. Mild winters
No symphony	Symphony concerts	3. Low crime rate
Lots of crime	Low crime rate	4. Good newspaper
Traffic congestion	Little congestion	5. Symphony concerts
Expensive housing	Affordable housing	6. Affordable housing
Not enough sunny days	Lots of sunny days	7. Low air pollution
Too much air polution	Low air pollution	8. Little traffic congestion

If, at this point, you think of some things about places where you have lived, that you *did* like, and you don't see them in the Final Column above, you can always add them now, putting them *into* the list wherever each belongs, as determined by your own personal values and priorities.

Now, what do you do if you have a spouse or partner, and you want to take *their* desires into account, as well as your own, in choosing a place to move to? You have them go through the same process, above, and end up with their own Final Column, as above. Then you list the two columns, yours and your partner's, side by side, and integrate them into a final Final Column, in the manner shown on the next page:

Final Column,
For Two People

My Items, Ranked in Order of Importance to Me	My Partner's Items, Ranked in Order of Importance to Them	Our Two Lists Integrated, In Order
1. Lots of sunny days 2. Mild winters 3. Low crime rate 4. Good newspaper 5. Symphony concerts 6. Affordable housing 7. Low air pollution 8. Little traffic congestion	A. Low crime rate B. Little congestion C. Near water D. Near skiing E. Good library F. Good schools G. Lots of sunny days H. Place for a garden	A. Low crime rate 1. Lots of sunny days B. Little traffic congestion 2. Mild winters C. Near water 3. * D. Near skiing 4. Good newspaper E. Good library 5. Symphony F. Good schools 6. Affordable housing G. * 7. Low air pollution H. Place for a garden 8. *

Factors are omitted from final list, if they have already been used.

Now you have your *description* of a town or towns you could *love.* All you lack are their *names.* To obtain those, you show the Final Column (whether for one person or two people) to *all* your friends, and ask them what towns or cities they know of, that fit *this* description. Ask them for details, as to *why* they think so. Do this for a week, with everyone you meet, that you know at all well.

Incidentally, if there seem to be contradictory factors on your list, there is usually an answer anyway. For example, in the case of the Final Column above, the answer to: "lots of sunny days," "mild winters," and "near skiing" is *Palm Springs, California,* among others. There's *always* an answer. Just ask enough people.

When you have a decent list, cross off any towns or cities that you, or your partner, *hate(s)* on sight. Look up the remainder in such books as Richard Boyer and David Savageau's *Places Rated Almanac.* Cross off, yet again, any that you decide you don't like. And as for those that are left, write away to those towns or cities for as much information about them as their Chambers of Commerce can give you. When you are done, rank them in order, as to which city/town looks the most appealing, which the next most, and which is third. You want three names, because if your first choice doesn't pan out, for some reason, you want a backup, and then a backup to that backup.

Now, how do you go about finding out about *jobs* in your chosen city/town? If it has a local newspaper, *subscribe,* while you still live where you are now. Read the whole paper, each day it arrives. Look particularly for: news of companies that are *expanding,* news of *promotions* or *transfers* (that create vacancies *down below* in 'the company store'), and the like.

If you can get the phone company, or someone you know there, to send you their phone book, particularly the Yellow Pages, by all means get it. When you're ready to go visit that town or city *in person,* line up contacts and interviews *ahead of time,* before you go there. If you have trouble connecting with someone, see if that town has any church, synagogue, or national organization that you belong to where you presently are. Write, tell them of your local affiliation, and ask for their help in finding the person you're looking to connect with.

If you have a spouse or partner, who works, they should be doing the same kind of research, and setting up the same kinds of interviews, as you are.

When you get there, in addition to interviewing about jobs, you will want to explore (of course) the issues of apartment vs. house, of rental vs. buying, and the like. Back home again, you will want to weigh what you have learned, and weigh whether or not it will be easy to sell your present home, if you own one -- or are on your way toward owning one.

> # What To Do
> # When You Can't Get There,
> # To Visit or Interview

If your finances are tight, it may just be impossible for you to go there, at least in the forseeable future. In which case you do your best to research the place from a distance, as described above. When that research seems completed, you should have discovered some organizations that, at a distance, look like "possibles." Then, since you can't go there, you will want to contact them by mail.

However, you will want to research each organization that you are going to approach by mail, so that you know *who* to address the letter to, by name. That letter will carry a lot more weight if you can mention, in it, the name of *a mutual friend.*

Toward that end, it is important that you have identified people in that city or town as your *contacts.* If you went to college, find out if any graduates of that same college live in that city or town. (Contact the alumni office of your college, and ask.) Also any church, synagogue, or national organization you belong to, that has a presence there - - as mentioned above. Any relatives of friends of yours (ask your friends locally, if they know of anyone who lives in that city or town).

Use these names *if* they know the employer to whom you are writing, because *generally speaking* your letter to employers in that faraway city will receive much more favorable attention *if* you mention some mutual friend, than would be the case if you merely wrote as a total stranger.[3]

Should you also enclose a resume? Professional opinions vary widely. *Everything* depends on the nature of the resume, and the nature of the person you are sending it to. With some employers I know, a resume is *death.* It will *ensure* that your letter is

---

3. Unless - - the job-hunter's nightmare - - your mutual "friend"/contact has *misrepresented* how close he or she is to your target employer, and as a matter of fact said employer can't stand the sight of this "mutual friend." *It has happened.* It is to die. Asking a question beforehand, of the "mutual friend," like "How *well* do you know him - - or her?" may help avoid this.

merely tossed aside. Other employers like to see one. Just to play it safe, I think a well-composed letter summarizing all you would say in a resume, may be your best bet.

WHEN YOU WANT TO MOVE 'TO THE COUNTRY'

If you are living in a very urban area, and your idea of *paradise* is to move at last to the country, you will find that one of the side benefits is that life out in the country is usually cheaper than in metropolitan areas - - which you probably already know. However, if you want to consider this option, I advise you to investigate the subject *very* thoroughly. Fortunately, there are a number of resources to help you.[4]

---

4. They include:

John F. Edwards, *Starting Fresh: How to Plan for a Simpler, Happier, and More Fulfilling New Life in the Country.* Prima Publishing & Communications, P. O Box 1260SF, Rocklin, CA 95677.

Frank Levering and Wanda Urbanska, *Simple Living.* Viking Penguin, 375 Hudson St., New York, NY 10014. 1992.

William L. Seavey, ed., *The Eden Seeker's Guide.* Loompanics Unlimited, P. O. Box 1197, Port Townsend, WA 98368. 1989. What kinds of places offer optimum quality of life. The author also has a business called Relocation Research, a clearinghouse of hard-to-acquire information about places in the hinterlands, with consulting also offered: Relocation Research, P. O Box 1122, Sierra Madre, CA 91025, 1-818-568-8484.

Frank Kirkpatrick, *How to Find and Buy Your Business in the Country.* Storey Communications, Inc., Pownal, VT 05261. 1985. How to find a simpler life-style, away from the hustle and bustle of the city.

Marilyn and Tom Ross, *Country Bound!™ Trade Your Business Suit Blues For Blue Jean Dreams™.* Communication Creativity, P. O. Box 909, 425 Cedar St., Buena Vista, CO 81211. 1992.

WHEN YOU WANT TO WORK OVERSEAS

On the other hand, if you've always wanted to live and work overseas, then that too is a dream you might want to explore. Though, in these turbulent times overseas, you might want to re-examine the dream. Of course, given such events as the 1992 L.A. riots here at home, maybe life can be turbulent *anywhere.*

Regarding overseas work: many people assume you find an overseas job by packing a bag, buying a ticket and passing out resumes once you reach your foreign destination. No, no, no. Work-permit requirements and high unemployment make finding jobs at foreign destinations often difficult, and sometimes impossible.

For example, if you were to study employment classifieds in, say, a newspaper from London, England, you would at first sight think you had found some grand opportunities for yourself. *Unfortunately,* these are in most cases job opportunities open only to British nationals or citizens of EEC nations. What is true in England is true elsewhere. Your U.S. citizenship will actually preclude you from working in a foreign country - - even Canada - - unless your employer can prove that a local national is unavailable to take the job, and thus secure a work permit for *you.*

Your wisest approach to overseas employment is to conduct your job-hunt for an overseas job while you are still here in the U.S. How do you go about it? Well, first of all, research the country or countries that interest you, as to living conditions, conditions of employment, etc. Talk to everyone you possibly can who has in fact been overseas, most especially to those country or countries. A nearby large university will probably have such faculty or students *(ask).* Companies in your city which have overseas branches *(your library should be able to tell you which they are)* should be able to lead you to people also - - possibly to the names and addresses of personnel who are still "over there" to whom you can write for the information you are seeking. Alternatively, try asking every single person you meet for the next week (at the supermarket checkout, at your work, at home, at church, or synagogue, etc.) if they know someone who used to live overseas and now lives here in your city or town. You may be amazed at how many normal-looking people are actually world travelers. By doing research with such people, you will learn a great deal. Find out what they liked and didn't like, about the country which interests you.[5] Find out what they know about the conditions for working over there.

Next, you need to research what kinds of job possibilities exist in that country. Every *successful* overseas search starts with *some* sources of information on "who's hiring now." *Which* sources you access, and how you make use of them, will greatly affect your chances of landing an overseas assignment.

What do I mean? Well, for openers, beware of such sources as employment agencies that promise to find you an overseas job for an advance fee. This is always a scam. This fleecing industry

---

5. As for the general facts about living overseas, books get outdated very fast; but currently the live ones are:

Dale Chambers, *Passport to Overseas Employment: 100,000 Job Opportunities Abroad.* Arco Books, Simon & Schuster, Inc., 200 Old Tappan Rd., Old Tappan, NJ 07675. 1990. Deals with overseas study programs, international careers, temporary employment, airlines and cruises, embassies and consulates, United Nations, and volunteer programs.

Howard Schuman, *Making It Abroad -- The International Job Hunting Guide.* John Wiley & Sons, 605 Third Ave., New York, NY 10158-0012. 1988.

Joy Mullett and Lois Darley, *Careers for People Who Love to Travel.* Arco Books, 200 Old Tappan Rd., Old Tappan, NJ 07675. 1986.

Curtis W. Casewit, *How to Get a Job Overseas.* Arco Publishing, Inc., 200 Old Tappan Rd., Old Tappan, NJ 07675. 1984.

Susan Griffith, *Work Your Way Around the World.* Writer's Digest Books/North Light Books, 1507 Dana Ave., Cincinnati, OH 45207. 1989.

Susan Griffith and Sharon Legg, *The Au Pair & Nanny's Guide to Working Abroad.* Writer's Digest Books/North Light Books, 1507 Dana Ave., Cincinnati, OH 45207. 1989.

Mary Green and Stanley Gillmar, *How to Be an Importer and Pay for Your World Travel.* Ten Speed Press, Box 7123, Berkeley, CA 94707.

For teachers wishing to work overseas, the Department of Defense publishes a pamphlet, with application, entitled *Overseas Employment Opportunities for Educators.* Write to U.S. Department of Defense Dependent Schools, Recruitment and Assignments Section, Hoffman Bldg. I, 2461 Eisenhower Ave., Alexandria, VA 22331-1100, for the pamphlet/application.

Your library should also have books such as Juvenal Angel, *Dictionary of American Firms Operating in Foreign Countries* (World Trade Academy Press).

And to research overseas public companies which sell stock in this country, the Securities Exchange Commission will have their Form 6-K, which they filed in order to be able to sell that stock.

If you want more books about overseas work (or study), write to WorldWise Books, P.O. Box 3030, Oakton, VA 22124, and/or Writer's Digest Books, 1507 Dana Ave., Cincinnati, OH 45207, and ask for their catalogs.

has flourished for years, with a few individuals often running scores of companies under an assortment of names. Such companies regularly go out of business or file for bankruptcy *once they've fleeced enough suckers.* Beware. If you patronize them, you will be out your fee, and have nothing to show for it.

Beware also of directories advertised in newspapers, etc. as *listing overseas employers.* Many, though not all, of these job listings are out of date and tend to report on "who *was* hiring" rather than "who is hiring *now.*"

You can still make effective use of any such directory by taking care that *if* you contact an organization listed therein, you include a cover letter which requests that your resume be kept on file 'for further consideration *if there are no current openings.*' As I have emphasized elsewhere in this book, pure dumb luck - - which means, having your name in 'the right place at the right time' - - plays a crucial role in finding most jobs. Since you can't get *over there,* at the moment, you will have to rely more heavily on resumes here than I would normally advise, to keep your name in the right place. In the case of overseas employment, the more employers who have your resume, the better.

Rather than the kind of resources mentioned above, I think your best bet for job leads are authoritative directories such as those listed below.[6] Also, in your job-search do not forget that

---

6. *International Employment Hotline,* Box 3030, Oakton, VA 22124. Published monthly since 1980, this newsletter provides job-search advice and names and addresses of employers currently hiring for international work in government, nonprofit organizations, and private companies. They also have other titles on overseas work, which you can ask them about. Incidentally, do *not* confuse this reputable firm with International Employment Hotline in Amsterdam, Holland, or London; there is *no* connection whatsoever.

The Fischer Report and *Manlink.* Group Fischer, 110 Newport Center Drive, Suite 150, Newport Beach, CA 92660. You can write to them and ask for their pamphlet "Group Fischer Information Services," which describes their programs and package, whose cost is expensive, from the point of view of a *poor* job-hunter. The *best* sentences in their pamphlet: "If you are looking for a job, you should understand that no one can get you a job except you. You will be hired because you are in the right place, at the right time, with the right skills...The ONLY services that anyone can render you in your job search are: 1) Information, 2) Introduction, 3) Advice. No employment agency, employment service, job listing service, membership organization (excluding unions), recruiting or executive search firms, or any publication can do more. How this is done is what makes the difference." Amen, brother.

the U.S. Government is a heavy overseas employer. Understandably, in the post-USSR world, with the end of the cold war, there are numerous cutbacks going on overseas. Nonetheless, this possibility is still well worth exploring. *How* you explore it, is described in the book listed below.[7]

One final word about hunting for an overseas job: above all, be patient. The search for an overseas job takes *more* time than looking for a job in this country. Don't expect to be in an exotic foreign capital within 90 days. Perseverance is the key.

WHEN YOU RUN INTO A STONEWALL

If you run into an absolute stonewall in your search for an overseas job, there are two backup strategies for you to consider. The first is to seek an international internship. How you do this is described below.[8] The second strategy begins with the fact that many companies operating in this country, both domestic and foreign-owned, *have branches overseas.* Thus, *sometimes* your ticket to getting overseas may be to start working here in the U.S. for such a company, hoping they will eventually send you overseas. It *does* happen. And if it happens, they will likely take care of the visa and work-permit red tape, pick up your travel bill, and provide other helpful benefits. Unfortunately, however, you can't *count* on their ever sending you overseas. In other

---

7. Will Cantrell and Francine Modderno, *How to Find an Overseas Job with the U.S. Government.* Worldwise Books, P.O. Box 3030, Oakton, VA 22124. 1992. Comprehensive guide to finding work with the organization that hires the greatest number of Americans abroad. In-depth job descriptions and application procedures are provided for over 17 individual government agencies, along with information on how to complete the government's standard application for employment (SF-171), and how to prepare for and pass the Foreign Service exam. Highly recommended.

8. Will Cantrell and Francine Modderno, *International Internships and Volunteer Programs.* Worldwise Books, P.O. Box 3030, Oakton, VA 22124. 1992. Up-to-date information on programs serving as 'stepping-stones' to international careers, for both students and professionals. Positions include salaried and volunteer opportunities, both abroad and also here in the U.S.

Arthur Frommer, *New World of Travel 1992: A Guide to Alternative Vacations in America and throughout the World,* 5th ed. A Frommer Book, published by Prentice-Hall Trade Division, One Gulf+Western Plaza, New York, NY 10023. 1991. Revised annually. A wonderful book by a great guy, on opportunities for travel here and abroad.

words, it's a big fat gamble. *You* have to decide whether you're willing to take it, or not.

If you decide it is worth it, you'll find the names of such organizations by going to your local library and asking the reference librarian to help you find such directories as these: *Principal International Businesses,* published by Dun's Marketing Service; *International Directory of Corporate Affiliations,* published by Corporate Affiliations Information Services, of the National Register Publishing Company; and *International Organizations, revised annually,* published by Gale Research Inc.

Lastly, contact every friend you have who already lives overseas -- even if it's not in the country that is your target. Ask for their counsel, advice, help, and prayers. They went before you; hopefully they can now be your guide, and door-opener.

At my present job,
the only enjoyment is breakfast,
morning break,
lunch,
afternoon break,
4:30,
and payday.
Most of the time my body is there
but my mind is in the past
shooting buffalo with Jim Bridger,
riding with Butch and Sundance,
flying with Red Baron in his Fokker Tri-plane
or anything that offers escape.
I can't wait until tomorrow so I
can have breakfast at McDonalds,
and after that
everything is downhill.

A worker in New Jersey

CHAPTER EIGHT

How to Choose
Or Change
A Career

Chapter 8

The basic question you always have to ask yourself, about your job, is: "Is this *really* what I want to do for the rest of my life?"

"*Same career, change of career, same career...change of...*"

The answer often is "No," -- for millions and millions of workers. And maybe for you. This doesn't necessarily mean that you made a big fat mistake in ever taking your current job (though that happens often enough, Heaven knows).

But even if it *was* a good choice, it is a law of life that jobs can alter profoundly in a day and a night. Your workplace comes under stringent budget cuts. Or your supervisor moves on, leaving you working for a jerk. Whatever. The job which was a perfect match for you just a year ago, is now your living nightmare.

"Is this *really* what I want to do for the rest of my life?" Millions say "No," for another reason. And that is because, as we grow older, we come to want different things out of our work. When we are very young, work is largely a matter of how to find bread to eat, and clothes to wear, and a roof over our head. But as we move through the various stages of our life, our work becomes increasingly a matter *also* of how our soul lives out its dreams.

WHAT DO YOU CALL YOUR WORK?

We see this change in what we want from our job, mirrored in the different terms we use for our work - - at different periods in our lifetime. When we are very young, we refer to our work as a job. It means we do something for someone else, and get paid for doing it. *"I have a job over at the supermarket."*

Then, as we get a little older, we start referring to our work as an occupation. This is reflected in the fact that we begin to think of ourselves in terms of a general job-title. I don't mean an *organizational*-title, such as "Controller," or "Business Manager" or "Accounts Receivable Department," which you might be given at a particular workplace. I mean a more general descriptor, a title which points to what *skills* you use - - such as *accountant.* This general *job*-title stays with us even when we change jobs. Thus you may stay *an accountant, or teacher, or carpenter,* over a number of years, even though you hold down four different jobs, at four completely different workplaces during that time.

When we grow tired of being in our present occupation, we not only change jobs - - we also change our occupation. One would think this would be called *an occupation change,* but in our culture it is most commonly called instead, a career-change - - particularly if the change *appears* to be dramatic (e.g., from high-school teacher to factory-worker, or vice versa). Thus, we have slid into a new term for our work, since we are now implicitly describing it as a career. (The average person, incidentally, has three different careers during their lifetime.)

And, finally, if our soul realizes its dreams, and we end up doing the work we really feel we were *born* to do, then we speak of our work as a vocation, or calling. Which we often attribute to

God - - working out His purpose in us. Vocation refers to work which is the justification for our having been given life, and put on this earth. It is work as the deepest fulfillment of our being.

It is this life-long search for, and journey toward, *meaning*, that lies beneath all the *surface* changes we make in our jobs, occupations, job-titles, and careers during our lifetime. We want our work - - increasingly - - to reflect who we most truly are.

So, if you are thinking about making some change in the work you have been doing, you've worked your way up from *job,* and *occupation* to *career.* You're looking at a *career-change.*[1]

CAREER-CHANGE ISN'T JUST 'A MID-LIFE THING'

According to popular mythology, career-change typically doesn't happen to people until they reach so-called 'mid-life' - - a time when many are thought to sit down and take stock of where their lives are going. Because of this mythology, many experts think that the remainder of the 1990's will see a lot more 'mid-life career-change,' since this is the decade when a whopping number - - this country's 76 million 'baby boomers' - - are entering mid-life.

Well, many people in mid-life *do* consider career-change. It is a logical time to sit down and figure out what quality of life you

1. The word career remains a very fuzzy word in the English language, but there are three principal senses in which it is used. It is used, first of all, to mean *work* in contrast to *learning* or *leisure.* Thus when clothing ads speak of "a career outfit," they are referring to clothes which are worn primarily at work, rather than during learning-activities or leisure-activities. It is used, secondly, to sum up *a person's whole life in the world of work.* Thus when people say of someone at the end of their life, "He or she had a brilliant career," they are not referring to a particular occupation, but to *all* the occupations this person ever held, and all the work this person ever did. Thirdly, in its most common sense, as I indicated above, it is used·as a synonym for the word *occupation* or *job* - - particularly where that occupation or job offers opportunity for promotion and advancement, toward the top. (This *movement toward a goal* is its most primitive meaning, as it dates from the origin of the word. *Career* comes from the Latin *carrus,* referring to a race-track where horses compete in an effort to win a race.) *From the article on "Careers" in* Collier's Encyclopedia, *written by the author. Copyright © 1991 by Macmillan Educational Company.*

want, and how you can take more time 'to smell the roses.'[2]

But mid-life is *not* the only time career-change is undertaken. In the most recent year surveyed, 1986, it was discovered that 5.3 million workers changed careers that year, *voluntarily;* in 7 out of 10 cases their income went up. 1.3 million workers changed careers *involuntarily,* because of what happened to them in the economy; in 7 out of 10 cases, their income went down, mostly - - I think - - because our schools don't teach people how to change careers, and they weren't prepared for it. And, to round out the 1986 statistics, 3.4 million workers changed careers for a mixture of voluntary and involuntary reasons (such as needing to go from part-time to full-time work, etc.). So, this added up to 10 million workers, who changed careers that year.

However, *only one million,* out of the ten, were in mid-life. And so, the moral of this tale is that career-change is *not* merely a 'mid-life' phenomenon. People can and do change careers at any and every age. And so can you. Whether you're twenty-two. Or forty. Or sixty-five.

WHY ARE YOU UNHAPPY WITH WHAT YOU HAVE BEEN DOING?

All intelligent forward movement depends upon first looking back. It is not enough simply to tell ourselves, "I'm unhappy." Unless we know *why* we're unhappy, we're liable to 'jump out of the frying pan into the fire.'

So, *'where does it hurt?'* You know that's the first thing your mother, father or guardian used to ask you, when you were injured. The same question applies to unhappiness at work. If you're unhappy enough to be thinking about changing careers, you ought first to figure out just where 'it is hurting.'

---

2. The following resources deal with career-change at mid-life:

Paula I. Robbins, *Successful Midlife Career Change: Self-Understanding and Strategies for Action.* AMACOM, 135 W. 50th St., New York, NY 10020. Very thorough, very helpful. The best book dealing with this problem.

Betsy Jaffe, Ed.D., *Altered Ambitions: What's Next in Your Life? Winning Strategies to Reshape Your Career.* Donald I. Fine, Inc., 19 W. 21st St., New York, NY 10010. 1991.

Godfrey Golzen and Philip Plumbley, *Changing Your Job After 35.* Kogan Page Ltd., 120 Pentonville Rd., London N1 9JN. 1988.

Jack Falvey, *What's Next? Career Strategies After 35.* Williamson Publishing, Charlotte, VT 05445. 1987.

It's going to be in one of eight areas, because *every* job, occupation, or career has eight distinct parts to it. The first five of these are defined by the career, or employer, and the last three by the employee.

Let's begin with the parts that are defined by the career, or the employer:

(1) You may be unhappy about the workplace, or physical setting, that is required by your present career. The workplace is defined by such factors as whether or not it is indoors or outdoors; whether it is physically attractive or not; whether it has windows that can be opened, or not; whether it has a time clock, where employees have to punch in and punch out, or not; whether or not workers are heavily supervised, with the the tasks being heavily *prescribed;* etc., etc.; and/or

(2) You may be unhappy about the stated goal, outcome, or product required by your present career, for example, if it produces military weapons, or despoils the environment; and/or

(3) You may be unhappy about the assigned tasks, that your present career requires you to do, as when you're required to shuffle paper when you'd rather deal with people; and/or

(4) You may be unhappy about the kinds of tools or instruments, that you have to use in your present career, as when you have to drive a truck, but you'd rather be using a computer; and

(5) Of course, you may be unhappy about the salary, commission or other form of pay, plus additional benefits, tangible or intangible (such as medical plan, vacation with pay, or a prestigious *organizational*-title, etc.) that is available in your present career. Bound up with this, also, you may be unhappy about any lack of hope for advancement and promotion, or the absence of any *career ladder* in this career.

In addition to -- or instead of -- these five job-conditions defined by your career or employer, you may be unhappy about the three parts of the job that *you,* as employee, are asked to contribute:

(6) **Your time.** You may feel this career requires too much of your time, leaving none for your family or your leisure; or you may feel that the time is being badly wasted on truly asinine tasks.

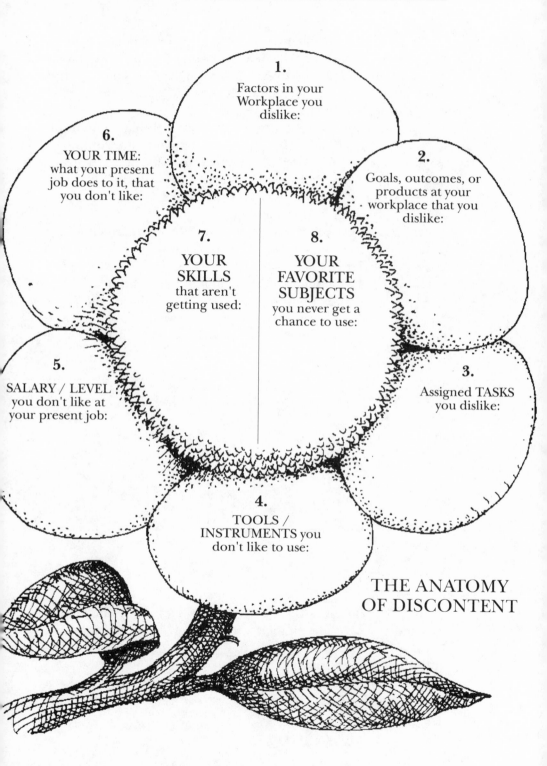

1.
Factors in your
Workplace you
dislike:

6.
YOUR TIME:
what your present
job does to it, that
you don't like:

2.
Goals, outcomes, or
products at your
workplace that you
dislike:

7.
YOUR
SKILLS
that aren't
getting used:

8.
YOUR
FAVORITE
SUBJECTS
you never get a
chance to use:

5.
SALARY / LEVEL
you don't like at
your present job:

3.
Assigned TASKS
you dislike:

4.
TOOLS /
INSTRUMENTS you
don't like to use:

THE ANATOMY
OF DISCONTENT

(7) **Your talents or skills,** with people, information, or things. You may feel that the skills you most enjoy using, either with information, people, or things, just aren't getting used in this career. You're shuffling paper when you'd rather be dealing with people, for example.

(8) **Your fields of knowledge.** You may feel that you have to work with subject matter in this career that you have zero interest in; and that you never get a chance to work in the fields of knowledge that have been your favorites, all your life long -- or since last month. You're working with legal briefs when your preferred knowledge is gardening.

Those are the eight parts of a job, and the eight arenas where your unhappiness surely lies. Knowing in *which* of the eight it lies, will help you make a much better career choice coming up. Do some hard thinking and meditation at this point, *please.*

And if your unhappiness is in more than one of the eight arenas, then list the arenas of your unhappiness *in order of importance* to you -- out there, on a piece of paper, and not just in your head.

ARLO & JANIS reprinted by permission of NEA, Inc.

'I STILL DON'T UNDERSTAND THE EIGHT PARTS'

Well, let's illustrate the eight parts of a job, with an occupation most people are familiar with, namely that of a waiter or waitress at a restaurant: (1) there *the workplace* is the restaurant, an indoor place (usually) with lots of supervision; (2) *the stated goal* is to wait on customers, keep them happy, and make a profit for the restaurant owners; (3) *the tasks assigned* the waiter or waitress may include: to clean and set tables; to bring the customers a menu, water, and bread; to take their orders; to hand the orders in to the kitchen; to serve the orders, when ready; to stay alert to any additional service the customers may require; to bring them their check when done; and to clear off and set the table again; (4) *the tools* furnished the waiter or waitress are: the uniform (if there is one), cleaning rags, silverware, napkins, plates, menus, food, checks, pen or pencil, and perhaps a calculator; (5) *the salary* is whatever the boss and waiter/waitress agree upon, plus tips, of course; (6) *the time* involved is whatever number of hours there are on the worker's shift; (7) *the talents or skills* needed are: *punctuality* - - being able to get to work on time; *taking instructions* from both boss and customer; *advising* (customers on what is good on the menu, if they ask); *empathy* (conveying warmth); *memory* (remembering who ordered what); *finger-dexterity* (being skillful at handling dishes); *copying* (prices onto the check); *computing* (the total on the check); and *problem-solving* (when problems arise, with the customer); (8) *the fields of knowledge* needed include: *food* (what the items on the menu mean); *mathematics* (addition, and subtraction, at least); *machine operation* (knowing how to operate a cash register and/or calculator).

WHAT IS 'THE ESSENCE' OF CAREER-CHANGE?

Career-change can be a change in many of the eight areas listed above - - sometimes *all* eight. But *in its essence* it is a change in *two* areas, above all. Those areas are: the skills you want to use, and the fields of knowledge you want to use them in.

Memorize these simple equations:

1. Skills ≈ general job-titles.   Job-titles ≈ skills.

2. Knowledges ≈ field.   Field ≈ knowledges.

To expand on these equations, a little, remember that a general job-title is *not* the same thing as an organizational-title. A general job-title refers to *skills* - - such as *teacher, mechanic, accountant,* etc. Okay, now: if you start with a general job-title that you like, then *that* title determines what skills you will get a chance to use. On the other hand, if you reverse that process, and begin by determining what skills you would like to use, they then *point to* a general job-title. Or, to *several organizational*-titles, at particular workplaces. Incidentally, note that in the equations above we use *correspond to* (≈) instead of the *equals* (=) sign. Skills ≈ job-titles.   Job-titles ≈ skills.

In the case of equation #2, above, if you choose your field first, then that field determines what knowledges you need to use or acquire. On the other hand, if you reverse that process, and begin by determining what knowledges you are most at home in, and enjoy - - *gardening, airplanes, antiques, travel, religion, psychology, etc.* - - they then *point to* a field. Knowledges ≈ field.   Field ≈ knowledges.

So, the essence of a career-change is that you change one or both of these: your general job-title, and the field you operate in: what skills you use, and where you use them.

If you change just the field, but not your general job-title, then this is a mini-career-change (**A** to **B** in the diagram on the next page). If you change your general job-title, but not your field, this is more of a genuine career-change (**A** to **C** in the diagram). However, if you change *both* the general job-title *and* the field, then we say this is a *dramatic* career-change (**A** to **D** in the diagram).

By permission of Johnny Hart and Creators Syndicate, Inc.

Types of Career Change Visualized

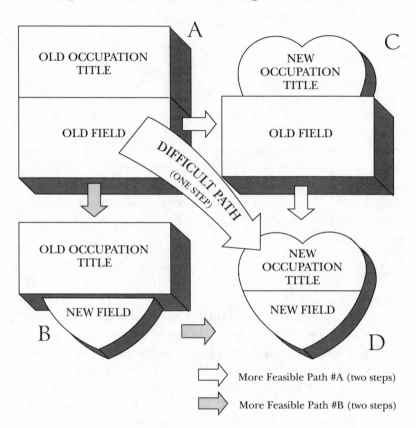

More Feasible Path #A (two steps)

More Feasible Path #B (two steps)

To illustrate, let's say you're an accountant, and you work for a television station. If you move to a new field, but keep the same general job-title, (**A** to **B**) then you might, let us say, become an accountant with a medical firm. If you keep the same field, but move to a new general job-title (**A** to **C**), you might become a reporter at that television station. And if you change both title and field (**A** to **D**), you might become a reporter for a medical journal. So, the profoundest career-change would, in this case, be that of moving from being an accountant at a television station, to a reporter for a medical journal. Both the general job-title and field have changed.

Note, in the diagram above, that were you to pursue this

profoundest career-change (A to D), there are three ways you can move into your new career - - gradually or abruptly, in steps or all at once - - as shown by the arrows.

SO, HOW DO YOU GO ABOUT IT?

When people change careers, voluntarily or involuntarily, it is widely assumed that there is only *one* way to go about it: go back to school, for retraining. With this approach, you look at the diagram above, and you see that career-change involves a field and a general job-title - - so you *choose* a field or general job-title - - often on the basis of very little knowledge - - and then go major in that field at some nearby college.

This is the way that 98% of all career-choice or career-change is done. But there are several problems with this approach to career-change.

● Problem #1: you don't know enough about what you're choosing, if you *begin* with the field or the general job-title. How can you? The number of careers open to you is truly bewildering. You have at least 12,860 different occupations or careers to choose between in the U.S., and they have some 8,000 alternative job-titles, for a total of approximately 20,000 that you can choose between. A description of all these 20,000 occupations is to be found in the *Dictionary of Occupational Titles,* familiarly known as the *D.O.T.,* published by the U.S. Department of Labor's Bureau of Labor Statistics.[3] It is easy to find, since it is in virtually every public library. It is not so easy to use.

Read it, and get depressed. Most people find the list of careers, contained in the *D.O.T.,* absolutely overwhelming. Trying to choose between 20,000 of anything, is almost humanly impossible. That's why, as it's turned out, ninety per cent of the work force of 120 million workers in this country are employed in just 300 job-titles.

In fact, half of the work force is employed in just 50 job-titles. These are: automobile mechanics, carpenters, electricians, light- or heavy-truck drivers, construction laborers, welders & cutters,

---

3. The D.O.T. is updated periodically - - most recently in 1991, with the previous revision 1977, supplemented in 1982, 1986, and 1987.

groundskeepers & gardeners, electrical and electronic engineers, freight, stock, and material movers or handlers, guards and police, production occupations supervisors, farmers, commodities sales representatives, laborers, lawyers, farm workers, stockhandlers & baggers, insurance sales, janitors & cleaners, managers & administrators, supervisors & proprietors, machine operators, teachers - - university, college, secondary and elementary school, stock & inventory clerks, accountants & auditors, underwriters and other financial officers, secretaries, receptionists, childcare workers, registered nurses, typists, bookkeepers, textile sewing machine operators, nursing aides, orderlies & attendants, hairdressers & cosmetologists, waiters & waitresses, maids and housemen, cashiers, general office clerks, administrative support occupations, sales workers, computer operators, miscellaneous food preparation occupations, production inspectors, checkers & examiners, cooks, real estate sales, and assemblers.

You'll notice a lot of these don't require you to go back to school for retraining. On the other hand, even for those that do, if none of these 50 interest you, then the point is moot.

● Problem #2: Just because you pick a field that *sounds* attractive, and go get a degree in that field, *doesn't* mean you get to use your favorite skills or your favorite knowledges. You may *think* you will, but once you are done with your education, and once you have found a job in that field, you may discover that *none* of your favorite skills and knowledges are called for. *Oops!* Thus, your new career may turn out to be just as unfulfilling as your old career. You will be just as miserable, only in a different environment. (This will remind some people of jumping into a second marriage without having first taken time to learn the lessons from the first).

● Problem #3: Many times, if you enroll in a particular degree program, you spend *a lot of time* learning knowledges and skills you really already have. I once spent a weekend with a group of graduate students in Spokane, Washington, who asked me to help them identify the skills and fields of knowledge they already possessed; when they saw how parallel these were to what they allegedly were trying to pick up in graduate school, they turned *just a little* bitter about the degree they were pursuing. Why study to acquire what you already possess?

● Last Problem (#4): One logical answer to the question immediately above, might run something like this: *"Well, I put in time studying stuff I already know because the degree-program requires it. And I put up with that asinine requirement, because - - after all - - the degree will help me make this career-change, by making me much more marketable."* Small problem: You *think* that *if* you get this degree, you will be much more *marketable* and able to command a higher salary - - but unfortunately there is no guarantee, *whatsoever,* that this is true. Every year thousands and thousands of people finish a degree program, and then find out they *still* cannot find a job. The degree does *not* come with a job automatically attached. I cannot tell you how many letters I have received from dejected adult-graduates, 22 years of age, 30 years of age, 40 years of age, who lament that their new degree *(bought with blood, sweat and tears)* hasn't improved their chances of finding a job in a new career *one iota!* In their letters, they are unemployed, a year later, or hired only for a pittance, often in occupations totally unrelated to their hard-won degree. They feel they were lied to, by our culture, and they are depressed, and crestfallen, and very bitter. I could quote some of those letters here, but then *you* would be depressed. Anyway, there is an unwitting irony in the phrase, "Getting a job by degrees."

The moral here is: don't assume that the only way to make a career-change is by going back to school. That takes a lot of your time, a lot of your money, and doesn't do *a thing* to guarantee you a job in your new career. It *can't* be the only way.

OKAY, WHAT'S 'THE OTHER WAY'? (THERE MUST BE ONE)

The other way - - the creative way - - involves forgetting about going back to school, at least for the time being, and forget about *starting with* a field and a general job-title.

Start instead by doing some hard homework on yourself, beginning with an inventory of the skills and knowledges you already have, and determine which of these are your *favorites.* Then let those *point to* a new career, whose name you discover through some investigation, interviews, and research. This alternative approach looks like this, and will be the subject of our next three chapters:

The Creative Process of Career Change

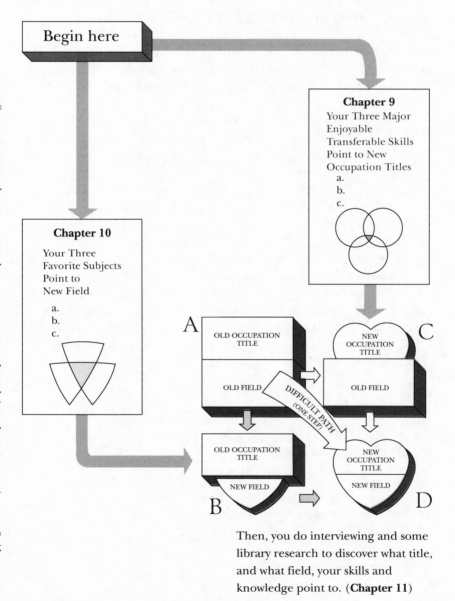

Begin here

Chapter 9
Your Three Major Enjoyable Transferable Skills Point to New Occupation Titles
a.
b.
c.

Chapter 10
Your Three Favorite Subjects Point to New Field
a.
b.
c.

A

OLD OCCUPATION TITLE

OLD FIELD

NEW OCCUPATION TITLE

OLD FIELD

C

DIFFICULT PATH (ONE STEP)

OLD OCCUPATION TITLE

NEW FIELD

NEW OCCUPATION TITLE

NEW FIELD

B

D

Then, you do interviewing and some library research to discover what title, and what field, your skills and knowledge point to. (**Chapter 11**)

LET'S NOT BE SILLY: *SOMETIMES* SCHOOL IS NECESSARY

It is claimed by experts that one-third of all careers require less than twelve years of schooling;[4] one-third of all careers require at least a high school degree; and one-third of all careers require a college degree, or beyond. So, two-thirds of all careers *don't* require you to go back to school. *But,* one-third do. Therefore, when you finish the process described above - - that is, when you have finished doing the work in Chapters 9, 10, and 11 - - it may turn out that you *do* need some further schooling, for the career you eventually decide upon. But then again, it may not.

Example: if after inventorying your skills and knowledges, and doing your own research, you discover that you want to move from being a typist to being a surgeon, this *will* require going back to school.

Example: if after inventorying your skills and knowledges, and doing your own research, you discover that you want to move from being a sales manager to being an author, this may not require going back to school at all.

The point is, with the creative approach to career-change, you make this decision *after* some thoughtful homework on yourself, and after some careful investigation - - and not on whim or impulse. What do I mean by *whim and impulse?* Once, I overheard two college students talking, in Central Park in New York City. We'll call them Jim and Fred. In half a minute of conversation they perfectly illustrated *whim and impulse:*

Jim: Hey, what are you majoring in?
Fred: Physics.
Jim: Physics? Man, you shouldn't major in physics.
Computer science is the thing these days.
Fred: Naw, I like physics.
Jim: Man, physics doesn't pay much.

---

4. *The Guide to Basic Skills Jobs, Vol. 1.* RPM Press, Inc., Verndale, MN 56481. 1986. A catalog of viable jobs for individuals with only basic work skills. This volume identifies 5,000 major occupations within the U.S. economy which require no more than an eighth-grade level of education, and no more than one year of specific vocational preparation. Immensely useful book.

Fred: Really? What does?
Jim: Computer science. You should switch to computer
science.
Fred: Okay, I'll look into it tomorrow.

You see my point. Huge life-decisions often are made in the
whim of a moment. Indeed, this is the way altogether-too-many
career choices are made. No wonder, surveys of worker dissatis-
faction find that up to 80%, or four out of every five workers,
are dissatisfied with some important aspects of their careers. *It's
not a pretty picture.*

This is why it is so important for you to do your homework,
identifying your favorite and strongest skills, before you choose
a career, change a career, or go out to pound the pavement.
The conversation, above, illustrates another point:

> You have got to know what it is you want, or else someone
> is going to sell you a bill of goods somewhere along the
> line that can do irreparable damage to your self-esteem,
> your sense of worth, and your stewardship of the talents
> that God gave you.

The alternative to *whim and impulse* is *planning,* and *hard
thinking* and *work.* For the lazy, this is not good news. But as you
grow older, and hopefully wiser, most of us begin to see the
merit of this kind of homework. For one thing, your chances of
finding a truly *satisfying* new career, increase sevenfold thereby.

AN OUTLINE OF THE
PLANNING, HARD THINKING
AND WORK

The creative approach to career-change always has homework with three parts, that you must tackle. They come in the
form of three questions:

1. **WHAT?** This has to do with your skills or talents. You
need to inventory and identify what skills you have that you
most enjoy using. Skills like the ones I referred to, in the waiter/
waitress illustration earlier. The experts call these transferable

skills, because they are transferable to any field/career that you choose, regardless of where you first picked them up, or even if you've had them since you were born. The full question here is *what are the skills you most enjoy using?*

2. **WHERE?** This has to do with the fields of knowledge you have already acquired, and enjoy using. Fields create job environments. Think of yourself as a flower. You know that a flower which blooms in the desert will not do well at 10,000 feet up -- and vice versa. Every flower has an environment where it does best. So do you. Your favorite knowledges help create the environment in which you thrive the most, and do your most effective work. The full question here is *where do you most want to use those skills?*

3. **HOW?** This has to do with putting a name to the skills and the knowledges, by finding out what job-titles and fields they point to. *And,* the names of organizations (in your preferred geographical area) which have such jobs to offer. *And,* the names of the people or person there who actually has the power to hire you. The full question here is *how do you find such jobs, that use these skills and these fields of knowledge?*

You may think of these three as like unto a cart, horse, and road. If you only do your homework on the WHAT, you will be like a cart without any horse to pull it. It just stands helplessly beside the road.

'WHAT' furnishes you with the cart; 'WHERE' furnishes the horse to pull it; and 'HOW' furnishes the road along which your cart and horse travel, to your chosen destination.

In this book, the next chapter, Chapter 9, is devoted to *what.* Chapter 10 is devoted to *where.* And Chapter 11 is devoted to *how.*

IS THIS THE RIGHT TIME
TO CHANGE CAREERS?

Whenever we are unhappy in our present job or career, we usually can hear two voices raging back and forth within our mind:

Is this what you want to do for the rest of your life?

"No."

Then what are you going to do about it?

"I don't know. Perhaps this just isn't the right time."

And so the dialogue goes -- while in our inmost spirit we know that waiting for 'the right time' is *often* just another name for *procrastination.*

Friend, there will probably never be *a right time.* Conditions will always be *difficult.* Obstacles will always be *in your way,* which you must overcome. It will always be a challenge, if you decide to launch out into the deep and mysterious destiny to which you feel called, by the dreams of your soul.

Yet a time comes in each of our lives when we *know* we simply *must* accept that challenge. When we know we must go do what we really want to do with our life. -- no matter how hard the times, and no matter how difficult the struggle may be. We know that there is always a chance that we may not succeed at it. But we know we will never feel we have really lived our life, until we at least *try.*

And, in some ways, it is a journey in which we cannot fail. Even if we are not able to *pull it off,* in any way that the world calls 'successful,' we know we will at the very least be a better man or woman, for having tried. There is something about *adversity* and *challenge* that tests and refines *character,* even as the fire tempers steel. A challenge toward growth and change -- willingly accepted -- can often bring out the very best in us.

If nothing else, it brings *clarity of vision.* As the late Sylvia Sims,[5] the legendary singer, once said about adversity, "I'm down

---

5. Born in *1918,* died in *1992.*

A Word to Procrastinators

If two weeks have gone by, and you just haven't gone on to *do* Chapters 9, and 10, then - - I hate to tell you this - - you're going to have to get someone to help you. Choose a helper for your job-hunt - - a friend rather than family, if possible. A *tough* friend. You know, *taskmaster.* Ask them if they're willing to help you. Assuming they say yes, put down in *both* your appointment books a regular *weekly* date when you will guarantee to meet with them, and they will guarantee to meet with you, check you out on what you've done already, and be very stern with you if you've done little or nothing since last week's meeting. Tell them that it is at least a 20,000-hour, $200,000 project. It's also responsible, concerned, committed Stewardship of the talents God gave you.

Where did we get 20,000 hours? Well, a forty-hour-a-week job, done for fifty weeks a year, adds up to 2,000 hours annually. So, how long are you going to be doing this new career that you are looking for? How many years do you plan to stay in the world of work? Ten years? That means 20,000 hours. Twenty years? That's 40,000 hours. So, it's at least a 20,000-hour project.

Why $200,000? Well, figure it out for yourself. If you earned, let us say, at least $10 an hour in your new career, that *times* 20,000 hours adds up to $200,000. If by chance you were to earn $20 an hour, that would be $400,000.

So, in working through Chapters 9, 10, and 11, you're working on a 20,000 hour, $200,000 project, at least. It's *worth* giving the time to, believe me.

And if you don't have the self-discipline to stick at it, it's worth enlisting a friend to help you.

If you have no friend who will help you, then you're probably going to want to think about professional help. Read, study, memorize, Appendix A in the back of this book. Go talk to several career-counselors. Choose the one you like best, and *get on with it.*

You've only one life to live, my friend. And every day is precious.

to the bottom of my sound, but I'm up to the clearest understanding of my life."

Is this the time? Only you can know. Only you can tell yourself, if that time *has* come for you to try. But if it has, then the
one thing I can tell you is that it will involve some hard
thinking...and work, on your part. Figuring out what your skills
and talents are, that the good Lord has given you, and which of
these you most love to use. Figuring out where you want to use
those skills. And doing the research necessary to find the career,
and the job. In other words: *doing* Chapters 9, 10, and 11. But,
oh! the rewards.

SHOULD I DO THIS HOMEWORK
EVEN IF I'M NOT THINKING ABOUT
CHANGING CAREERS?

Oh yes. As one worker wrote me, "I like my present job a lot.
Still, the skills inventory you have people do in your book is
something I do every two or three years. Each time I do it, I find
out more specific things about what I do well. This information
tells me what to watch for in the world - - what kind of tasks I can
volunteer for and do very well at. I know more about the *kind* of
thing I want to be, do, be surrounded by. I am now sensitized
and ready to recognize them when they swim by."

*W*ork is Love made visible.
And if you can't work with love but only with distaste,
It is better that you should leave your work
and sit at the gate of the temple and
take alms of the people who work with joy.

Kahlil Gibran, *The Prophet*

CHAPTER NINE

The Systematic Approach To The Job-Hunt and Career-Change:

PART I

What
Skills Do You Most Enjoy Using?

Chapter 9

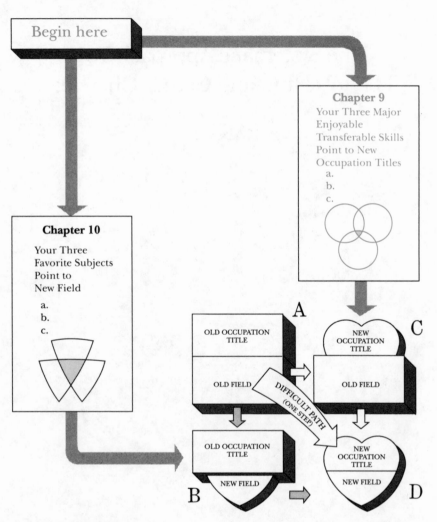

Begin here

Chapter 9
Your Three Major
Enjoyable
Transferable Skills
Point to New
Occupation Titles
a.
b.
c.

Chapter 10

Your Three
Favorite Subjects
Point to
New Field

a.
b.
c.

OLD OCCUPATION
TITLE

OLD FIELD

A

NEW
OCCUPATION
TITLE

OLD FIELD

C

DIFFICULT PATH
(ONE STEP)

OLD OCCUPATION
TITLE

NEW FIELD

B

NEW
OCCUPATION
TITLE

NEW FIELD

D

The Creative Process of Career Change

Then, you do interviewing and some library research to discover what title, and what field, your skills and knowledge point to. (**Chapter 11**)

Skills

THE MOST MISUNDERSTOOD WORD IN THE WORLD OF WORK

You begin the creative approach to career-change by identifying your skills. Problem is, many people just *freeze* when they hear the word 'skills.' It begins early: "I haven't really got any skills," high school graduates say. It continues with college students: "I've spent four years in college, studying my (head) off; I haven't had time to pick up any skills." And it lasts through the middle years, especially when a person is thinking of changing his or her career: "I want to change careers, but all my skills are in my old career." All of this self-put-down about one's own 'skills' is very common - - and stems from a total misunderstanding of what the word means. A misunderstanding that is shared, we might add, by altogether too many employers, human resource departments, and other so-called 'vocational experts.'

By seeking to understand the word, at this very outset, you will automatically put yourself way ahead of most job-hunters, unfortunately. I say *'Unfortunately'* because *all* job-hunters and career-changers need to understand *skills*. Once you gain a better understanding of the word, I hope you will share it with others.

A CRASH COURSE ON SKILLS

Here are the ten most important truths you need to keep in mind about skills:

1. Skills are the most basic unit - - the atoms - - of whatever career you may choose. When you ask yourself what you have to offer to an employer, there are many answers you might come up with, but the most basic answer is: skills. You can see this from this diagram:

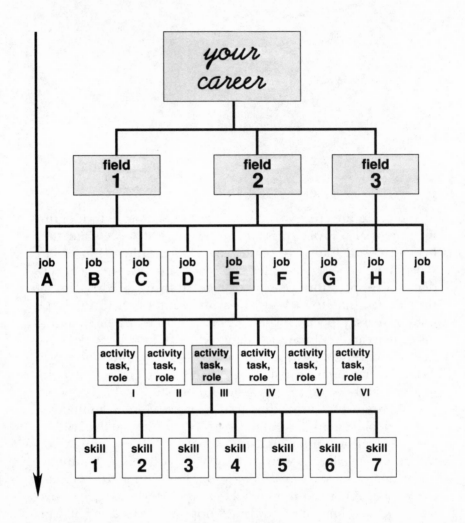

2. Skills are **transferable,** from one career to another. Skills are the one thing that all jobs, and all careers, have in common. Thus skills serve as a bridge from one job to another, or one career to another. Once you have demonstrated or mastered a skill in one career, you can easily *transfer* it to another career, and use it there. To put this another way: your new career will demand that you have certain skills - - with *Things* or *People* or *Data/Information*. With this creative approach, you choose your new career precisely because it requires the skills you already have. The skills that are your favorites. You simply *transfer* them.

3. The essence of career-change is not so much the mastering of *new* skills, as it is the rearrangement of *old* skills into new *priorities,* and hence new *patterns.* It is most akin to the rearranging of *building blocks* that we used to do, as a child:

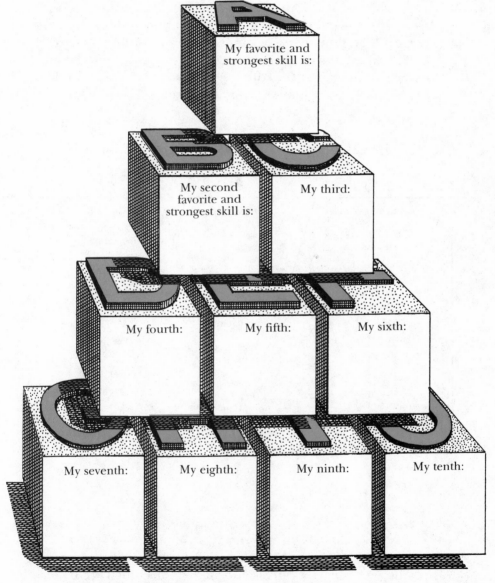

My favorite and strongest skill is:

My second favorite and strongest skill is:

My third:

My fourth:

My fifth:

My sixth:

My seventh:

My eighth:

My ninth:

My tenth:

Change this arrangement, and you change your career.

4. There are many skills, but basically they break down into three *families,* according to the object upon which the skill *acts.* The three families are determined by whether or not the skills are being used with **Data** (**Information**), or **People** or **Things**.

5. Within each family, there are *simple* skills, and there are *more complex* skills. If these are listed - - within each family - - in a vertical hierarchy that is arranged in order of increasing complexity, where the simpler skills are at the bottom, and the more complex ones are at the top, the three families come out looking like inverted pyramids, as shown here:

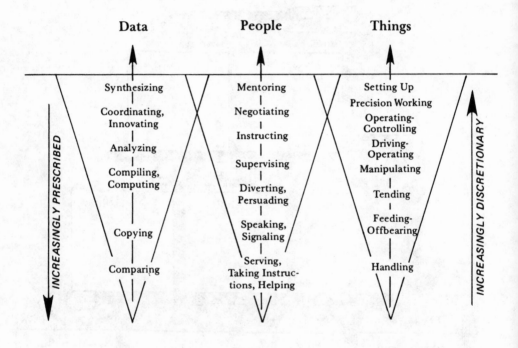

6. Typically, each skill - - as you go up the inverted pyramids - - involves most or all of those skills which are listed below it. This means that if you can do a skill that is, let us say, mid-way up the pyramid, you can also do all the skills which are beneath it in the pyramid-diagram. Those *simpler* skills are necessary in

order to do the higher skill. (This is not *always* true, but it *is* true most of the time.) To see the truth of this point, study this detailed explanation of the skills which workers have with *People.*[1]

WORKING WITH PEOPLE
Increasing Levels of Skill
Beginning With
The Most Elementary Definition

TAKING INSTRUCTIONS--HELPING

Attends to the work assignment, instructions, or orders of supervisor. No immediate response or verbal exchange is required unless clarification of instruction is needed.

SERVING

Attends to the needs or requests of people or animals, or to the expressed or implicit wishes of people. Immediate response is involved.

EXCHANGING INFORMATION

Talks to, converses with, and/or signals people to convey or obtain information, or to clarify and work out details of an assignment, within the framework of well-established procedures.

COACHING

Befriends and encourages individuals on a personal, caring basis by approximating a peer- or family-type relationship either in a one-to-one or small group situation, and gives instruction, advice, and personal assistance concerning activities of daily living, the use of various institutional services, and participation in groups.

PERSUADING

Influences others in favor of a product, service, or point of view by talks or demonstrations.

DIVERTING   Amuses others.

continued

---

1 You will note that this *People* list differs not only from the previous pictorial, but also from the skills lists found later in this chapter. This particular list of definitions is taken from the third edition (1965) of the *Dictionary of Occupational Titles,* Vol. II, pp. 649–50, as modified and adapted by Dr. Sidney A. Fine. You can find similar lists for *Data* and *Things* at your public library, in the 1991 revised fourth edition of the D.O.T., on pp. 1005–1006, in vol. II.

CONSULTING

Serves as a source of technical information and gives such information or provides ideas to define, clarify, enlarge upon, or sharpen procedures, capabilities, or product specifications.

INSTRUCTING

Teaches subject matter to others, or trains others, including animals, through explanation, demonstration, practice, and test.

TREATING

Acts on or interacts with individuals or small groups of people or animals who need help (as in sickness) to carry out specialized therapeutic or adjustment procedures. Systematically observes results of treatment within the framework of total personal behavior because unique individual reactions to prescriptions (chemical, behavioral, physician's) may not fall within the range of prediction. Motivates, supports, and instructs individuals to accept or cooperate with therapeutic adjustment procedures, when necessary.

SUPERVISING

Determines and/or interprets work procedure for a group of workers, assigns specific duties to them (particularly those which are prescribed), maintains harmonious relations among them, evaluates performance (both prescribed and discretionary), and promotes efficiency and other organizational values. Makes decisions on procedural and technical levels.

NEGOTIATING

Exchange ideas, information, and opinions with others on a formal basis to formulate policies and programs on an initiating basis (e.g., contracts) and/or arrives at resolutions of problems growing out of administration of existing policies and programs, usually after a bargaining process.

MENTORING

Deals with individuals in terms of their overall life adjustment behavior in order to advise, counsel, and/or guide them with regard to problems that may be resolved by legal, scientific, clinical, spiritual and/or other professional principles. Advises clients on implications of diagnostic or similar categories, courses of action open to deal with a problem, and merits of one strategy over another.

7. Simpler skills can be, and usually are, heavily prescribed (by the employer) as to how they get used on the job. More complex skills demand more discretion be left in the worker's hands.

8. You should always claim the *highest* skill you legitimately can, on each pyramid. Of course, left to your own devices, and in keeping with the modest nature for which you are doubtless known far and wide, you will be *tempted* to check off your skills as being down near the bottom of the inverted pyramids - - "just to be on the safe side." No, no, no. The *higher* the skills you have, the more you will be given discretion in your new career to carve out the job the way you want to - - so that it truly fits you. The lower the skill you claim, the more you will have to *'fit in'* - - following the instructions of your supervisor and doing exactly what you are told.

9. The higher the level of skills that you can honestly and legitimately claim for yourself, on the basis of your past performance, the less likely it is that the jobs which use such skills will be advertised through normal channels. Not for you the way of classified ads, resumes, and agencies. No, you *must* follow the unorthodox, creative, methods described in Chapters 11 and 12, if you are going to uncover the jobs where you will be allowed and encouraged to use your highest skills, in this new career of yours.

10. The harder it is for you to uncover an opportunity in this new career, and the more you approach favorite workplaces rather than just those with known vacancies, the less competition you will face for whatever jobs you uncover. And, in fact, even if there is no vacancy there, if they like you well enough, they may be willing to create for you a job that does not presently exist. It is amazing how many times this happens in the world of work. (The reason it does is that they have been *thinking* about creating such a job, but they never got around to doing it until they saw you. Then they decided they didn't want to let you get away, since *good employees are as hard to find as are good employers.*) In such a case, you will be competing with no one, since you will be the sole applicant for that newly created job.

And now, the paradoxical moral of this crash course about skills: The higher a skill level you legitimately claim, with *People* and/or *Things* and/or *Data*, the more likely you are to find a job in your new career. Just the opposite of what the typical career-changer starts out believing.

"...and give me good abstract-reasoning ability, interpersonal skills, cultural perspective, linguistic comprehension, and a high sociodynamic potential."

NOW, WHAT HAVE WE HERE?

If you are not familiar with *skills,* you will of course want to see a list of them, *now.* Following is a sampler. The way in which this list is typically used by career-changers is to put a check-mark in front of each skill that: a) you believe you have; b) you enjoy doing; and c) you believe you do well:

A List of 250 Skills as Verbs

achieving	detailing	handling	meeting	raising	studying
acting	detecting	having	memorizing	reading	summarizing
adapting	determining	responsibility	mentoring	realizing	supervising
addressing	developing	heading	modeling	reasoning	supplying
administering	devising	helping	monitoring	receiving	symbolizing
advising	diagnosing	hypothesizing	motivating	recommending	synergizing
analyzing	digging	identifying	navigating	reconciling	synthesizing
anticipating	directing	illustrating	negotiating	recording	systematizing
arbitrating	discovering	imagining	observing	recruiting	taking
arranging	dispensing	implementing	obtaining	reducing	taking
ascertaining	displaying	improving	offering	referring	instructions
assembling	disproving	improvising	operating	rehabilitating	talking
assessing	dissecting	increasing	ordering	relating	teaching
attaining	distributing	influencing	organizing	remembering	team-building
auditing	diverting	informing	originating	rendering	telling
budgeting	dramatizing	initiating	overseeing	repairing	tending
building	drawing	innovating	painting	reporting	testing and
calculating	driving	inspecting	perceiving	representing	proving
charting	editing	inspiring	performing	researching	training
checking	eliminating	installing	persuading	resolving	transcribing
classifying	empathizing	instituting	photographing	responding	translating
coaching	enforcing	instructing	piloting	restoring	traveling
collecting	establishing	integrating	planning	retrieving	treating
communicating	estimating	interpreting	playing	reviewing	trouble-
compiling	evaluating	interviewing	predicting	risking	shooting
completing	examining	intuiting	preparing	scheduling	tutoring
composing	expanding	inventing	prescribing	selecting	typing
computing	experimenting	inventorying	presenting	selling	umpiring
conceptualizing	explaining	investigating	printing	sensing	understanding
conducting	expressing	judging	problem	separating	understudying
conserving	extracting	keeping	solving	serving	undertaking
consolidating	filing	leading	processing	setting	unifying
constructing	financing	learning	producing	setting-up	uniting
controlling	fixing	lecturing	programming	sewing	upgrading
coordinating	following	lifting	projecting	shaping	using
coping	formulating	listening	promoting	sharing	utilizing
counseling	founding	logging	proof-reading	showing	verbalizing
creating	gathering	maintaining	protecting	singing	washing
deciding	generating	making	providing	sketching	weighing
defining	getting	managing	publicizing	solving	winning
delivering	giving	manipulating	purchasing	sorting	working
designing	guiding	mediating	questioning	speaking	writing

FLESHING OUT THE VERBS

Once you have checked these off, choose your ten *favorites*. (You can of course choose more, if you wish, and then narrow them down to ten, at the end.)

You will need, then, to *flesh these out,* with at least one story for each verb. This is necessary because *you* need to see each chosen skill in its fullness, and a mere verb isn't sufficient for that. You should never choose a new career merely on the basis of ten words.

Also, down the line, when you are in an actual job-interview, you do not want to just *claim* you have a skill. You want to *prove* you have the skill you are claiming. What your story says, for each skill, is that you *can* do it, because you *did* do it. Each story that you write should follow a predictable pattern, as shown here:

Column I	II	III	IV	V
Your Goal: What You Wanted To Accomplish	Some Kind of Hurdle or Restraint You Faced	What You Did Step by Step *(Use your verb, plus other verbs)*	Description of the Result *(What you accomplished)*	Any Measure or Quantities To Prove Your Achievement

The story should describe some past achievement of yours, where you used this skill *(verb)* successfully. It doesn't matter how old or young you were at the time, nor where you did it. It can be at work, or on vacation, or wherever. Having chosen which achievement you wish to describe, you will then need to follow the outline in columns I–V, above.

Here is a specific example, so you can see how it is to be done. This story was written by a career-changer, to illustrate the skill-verb *designing*. He chose an achievement of his, from one summer's vacation:

I.) **Your goal: what you wanted to accomplish:** *"I wanted to be able to take a summer trip with my marriage partner and four children."*

II.) Some kind of hurdle, obstacle or constraint that you faced (self-imposed or otherwise): *"I had a very limited budget, and could not afford to put my family up, in motels."*

III.) A description of what you did, step by step (how you set about to ultimately achieve your goal, above, in spite of this hurdle or constraint): *"I decided to rig our station wagon as a camper. First I went to the library to get some books on campers. I read those books. Next I designed a plan of what I had to build, to outfit the*

inside of the station wagon, as well as topside. Then I went and purchased the necessary wood. On weekends, over a period of six weeks, I..." etc., etc.

IV.) A description of the outcome or result: *"When we went on our summer trip, we were able to be on the road for four weeks, and we stayed within our budget, since we didn't have to stay at motels."*

V.) Any measurable/quantifiable statement of that outcome, that you can think of: *"As a result of doing this, I saved $1200 on motel bills, during our summer vacation."*

When you have thus written at least one story for each of your top ten favorite skills, arrange them in order of your favorite skill first, next favorite next, next favorite, etc. This will be helped if you write each story on a separate sheet of paper. Then you need only shuffle the sheets of paper, until your favorite skill is on top, the least favorite is on the bottom, etc. Then you should *number* the sheets of paper, 1–10.

WHY DO YOU NEED TO THUS PRIORITIZE YOUR TOP TEN FAVORITE SKILLS?

Because, *anytime* you have gathered information - - about yourself, or about the world out there - - it is *crucial* that you prioritize it. Unprioritized, you have ten things (let us say), and it is not clear which you could let drop, if you had to, and which you would want to hang on to, at all costs.

This is particularly true of skills. You *must* prioritize them. As I mentioned previously, every full-fledged career-change requires that you *rearrange* the 'building blocks' of your skills, into a new order of priority. The priority is *everything*. It will ultimately help determine *what* career you choose.

Also, down the line, this prioritizing will help you to better describe yourself during a job-interview. Instead of saying, in effect, "I have some skills," you will be prepared to say, whenever you need to, "This is my greatest strength or talent, this is my next greatest, etc."

Hence the absolute importance, once you have fleshed out your skills, of putting them in order of importance or priority to you. If you skip over this step, you are essentially committing job-hunting suicide.

A prioritizing grid appears on pages 222–23.

SKILLS BROKEN DOWN
INTO FAMILIES

If you do not like the list of *Skills As Verbs,* above, because it fails to divide the skills into those with *Data, People,* and *Things,* then here is a different list, laid out as *mock typewriter keys* (we call them *skills keys*) which does thus divide the skills. You may find this more useful than the preceding list (most career-changers do), and you can perform the same exercise with it, checking off the ones you truly enjoy, then fleshing them out with a story:

My transferable skills dealing with

THINGS

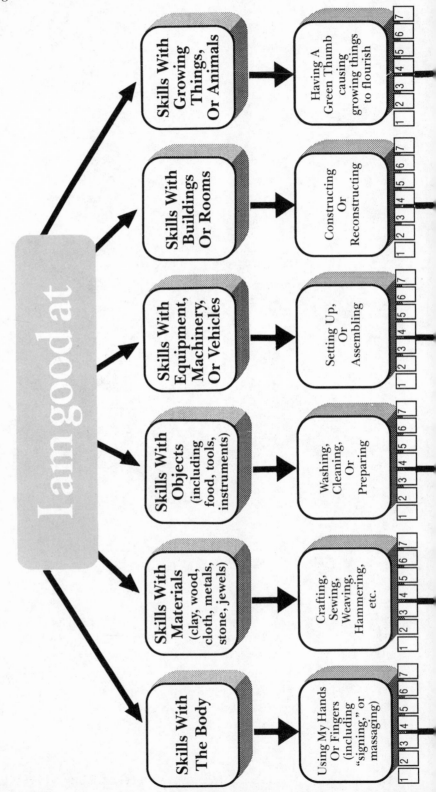

I am good at

Skills With Growing Things, Or Animals → Having A Green Thumb causing growing things to flourish | 1 2 3 4 5 6 7

Skills With Buildings Or Rooms → Constructing Or Reconstructing | 1 2 3 4 5 6 7

Skills With Equipment, Machinery, Or Vehicles → Setting Up, Or Assembling | 1 2 3 4 5 6 7

Skills With Objects (including food, tools, instruments) → Washing, Cleaning, Or Preparing | 1 2 3 4 5 6 7

Skills With Materials (clay, wood, cloth, metals, stone, jewels) → Crafting, Sewing, Weaving, Hammering, etc. | 1 2 3 4 5 6 7

Skills With The Body → Using My Hands Or Fingers (including "signing," or massaging) | 1 2 3 4 5 6 7

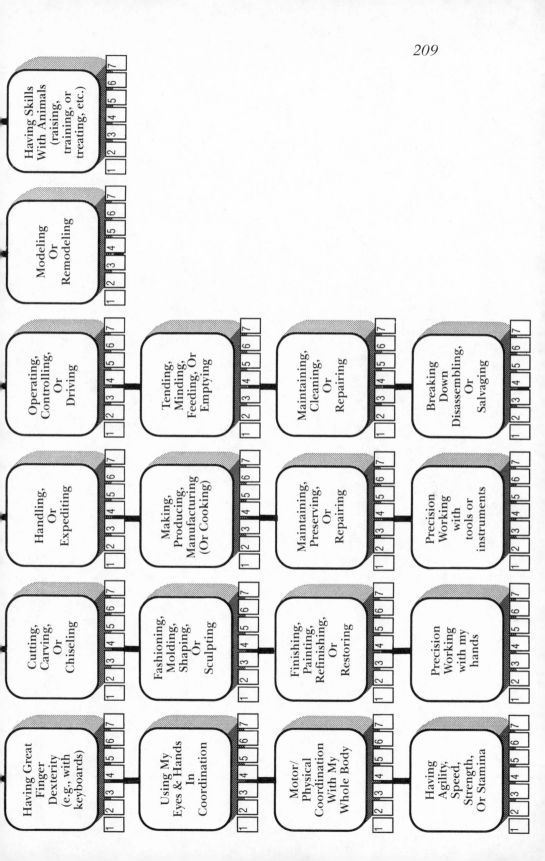

My transferable skills dealing with

PEOPLE

I am good at

With Individuals one at a time

With Groups, Organizations, or the masses

Taking Instructions, Serving, Or Helping

1 2 3 4 5 6 7

Diagnosing, Treating, Or Healing

1 2 3 4 5 6 7

Communicating Effectively to a group or a multitude

1 2 3 4 5 6 7

Playing Games, or a particular game, Leading Others in recreation or exercise

1 2 3 4 5 6 7

Managing, Supervising, Or Running (a business, fund drive, etc.)

1 2 3 4 5 6 7

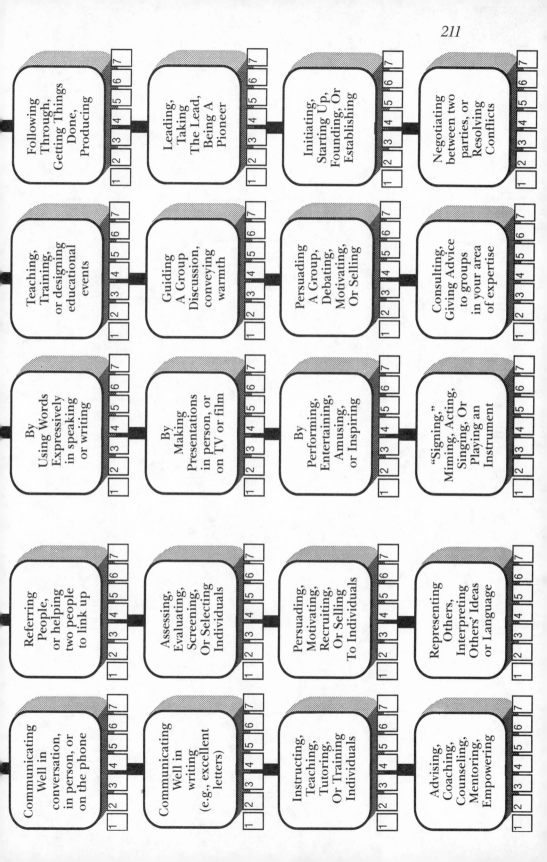

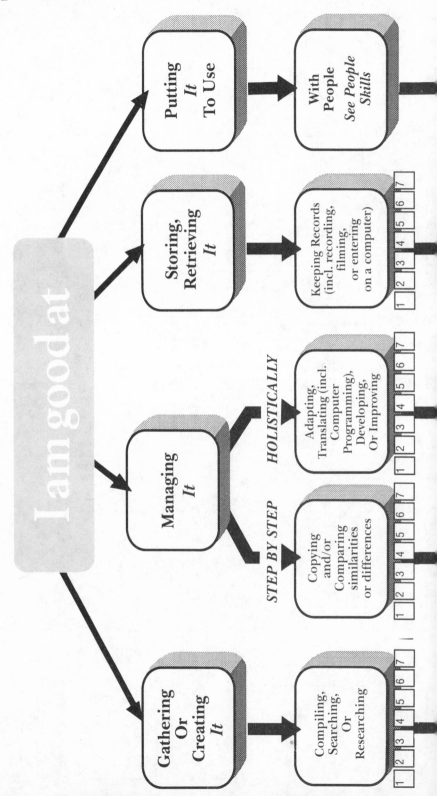

212

My transferable skills dealing with

INFORMATION, DATA, AND IDEAS

I am good at

Putting
It
To Use

With
People
See People Skills

Storing,
Retrieving
It

Keeping Records
(incl. recording,
filming,
or entering
on a computer)

1 2 3 4 5 6 7

Managing
It

HOLISTICALLY

Adapting,
Translating (incl.
Computer
Programming),
Developing,
Or Improving

1 2 3 4 5 6 7

STEP BY STEP

Copying
and/or
Comparing
similarities
or differences

1 2 3 4 5 6 7

Gathering
Or
Creating
It

Compiling,
Searching,
Or
Researching

1 2 3 4 5 6 7

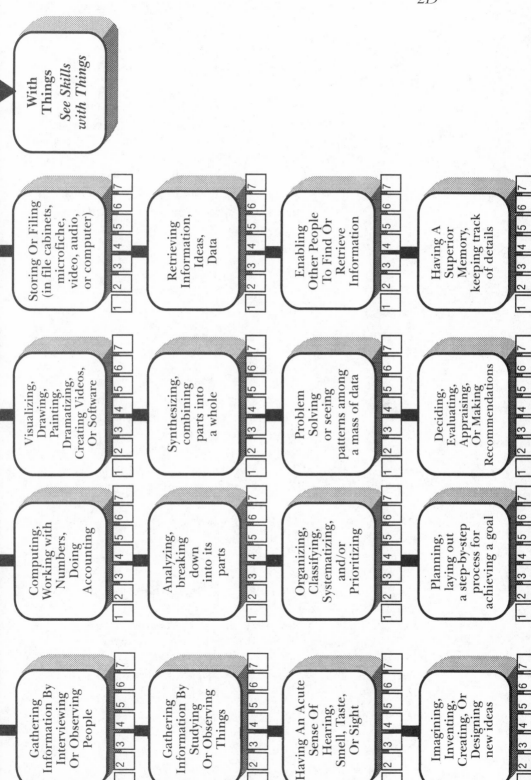

With Things
See Skills with Things

Gathering Information By Interviewing Or Observing People
1 2 3 4 5 6 7

Gathering Information By Studying Or Observing Things
1 2 3 4 5 6 7

Having An Acute Sense Of Hearing, Smell, Taste, Or Sight
1 2 3 4 5 6 7

Imagining, Inventing, Creating, Or Designing new ideas
1 2 3 4 5 6 7

Computing, Working with Numbers, Doing Accounting
1 2 3 4 5 6 7

Analyzing, breaking down into its parts
1 2 3 4 5 6 7

Organizing, Classifying, Systematizing, and/or Prioritizing
1 2 3 4 5 6 7

Planning, laying out a step-by-step process for achieving a goal
1 2 3 4 5 6 7

Visualizing, Drawing, Painting, Dramatizing, Creating Videos, Or Software
1 2 3 4 5 6 7

Synthesizing, combining parts into a whole
1 2 3 4 5 6 7

Problem Solving or seeing patterns among a mass of data
1 2 3 4 5 6 7

Deciding, Evaluating, Appraising, Or Making Recommendations
1 2 3 4 5 6 7

Storing Or Filing (in file cabinets, microfiche, video, audio, or computer)
1 2 3 4 5 6 7

Retrieving Information, Ideas, Data
1 2 3 4 5 6 7

Enabling Other People To Find Or Retrieve Information
1 2 3 4 5 6 7

Having A Superior Memory, keeping track of details
1 2 3 4 5 6 7

"I WOULDN'T RECOGNIZE MY SKILLS IF THEY CAME UP AND SHOOK HANDS WITH ME"

If you feel that a list of skills - - whether verbs, or *skills keys* - - just leaves you feeling baffled, because you haven't the foggiest notion what your skills are, then there are two alternative approaches - - which offer a more detailed and thorough method of identifying your skills. What they both have in common is that instead of working from skills to stories, they work from stories to skills. Here are the steps in this more detailed skill-identification process. I commend them to you. Were I myself changing careers tomorrow, this is the process I would prefer for my own life.

GATHER YOUR STORIES

Plan A

A. Write a detailed *unstructured* mini-autobiography of your entire life. An informal summary for your eyes only - - *who cares about your spelling or grammar?* - - of where you've ever been, and what you've ever done, where you were ever working, and what you did there (not in terms of job titles - - *forget them* - - but in terms of what you feel you accomplished there).

B. Describe your spare time, in each place where you lived. What did you do? What did you most enjoy doing? Any hobbies? Avocations? Great. Were there any activities in your work that paralleled the kinds of things you enjoyed doing in your leisure?

C. Concentrate both on the things you have done, and also on the particular characteristics of your surroundings that were important to you, and that you really enjoyed: green grass, the theater, tennis, warm climate, skiing, or whatever.

D. Sift later. For now, put down anything that helped you to enjoy a particular moment or period of your life. Keep your eye constantly on: *enjoyable*. It's not *always* a guide to what you should be putting down, but it sure is more reliable than any other key that people have come up with.

E. Don't be afraid if at times it sounds, to your modest ears, like boasting. Who's going to see this document besides you, God, and any loved one that you choose to show it to? So, let it rip. Just be *sure* to back up your elation and sense of pride with concrete examples, and figures.

F. Don't try to make this mini-autobiography very structured. You can bounce back and forth in time, if that's more congruent with *your* way of doing things.

G. When your mini-autobiography is all done, you may have a small book - - it can run 30 pages or more. *(My, you've done a lot of living, haven't you?)* Now, you have something to search, looking for evidences of your skills.

Plan B

If you don't like writing an *unstructured* mini-autobiography, you can write a structured *outline* of one, instead, using the Memory Net, which follows. It is faster than writing the biography, since the Net only takes three hours at most - - even allowing for heavy thinking. *(Remember a job-hunt takes up to nineteen weeks - - or more; what's three hours?)*

The Net is on the next two pages. The first three columns are alternative ways of establishing *pegs* on which to hang your memories. You can use five-year periods of your life (Column 1), *or* jobs you have held (Column 2), *or* places you have lived (Column 3). *Naturally,* you can use alternative *pegs* if you wish: people who were influential in your life at various times, schools you attended, etc., etc.

As you continue across the Memory Net, after Column 3, you should fill out Columns 4, 6, and 8 first *(Activities)*. Then go back and fill in Columns 5, 7, and 9 *(Accomplishments)*. The Activities are more general, and easier to recall. The Accomplishments are more specific, and can use some memory-jogging - - which the *Activities* furnish. In all the columns, put down just a few words, to jog your memory, rather than attempting a more detailed description, *at this time.*

Once you have the Memory Net all filled in, or your mini-autobiography all written, you are ready to go on to the next step in this detailed skill-identification.

Memory

	Column 1	Column 2	Column 3	Column 4	Column 5

Jogging Your Memory

Leisure

In Terms of Five-Year Periods	In Terms of Jobs You Have Held	In Terms of Places You Have Lived	Activities	Accomplishments
e.g. 1988–1992				
1983–1987				
1978–1982				
1973–1977				
1968–1972				
1963–1967				
1958–1962				
1953–1957				
1948–1952				
1943–1947				
1938–1942				
1933–1937				

Net

Column 6	Column 7	Column 8	Column 9
Learning		**Labor**	
Activities	Accomplishments	Activities	Accomplishments

SELECT ONE OF YOUR
FAVORITE ACCOMPLISHMENTS

Now, look over your mini-autobiography, or your Memory Net, and select *one* accomplishment, about a time when you were truly enjoying yourself, and felt you achieved something. If you are using the Memory Net, study columns 5, 7, and 9 in particular. The most useful stories will be those that fit, or can be *fleshed out* to fit, the outline we have already seen:

Column I	II	III	IV	V
Your Goal: What You Wanted To Accomplish	Some Kind of Hurdle or Restraint You Faced	What You Did Step by Step *(Use your verb, plus other verbs)*	Description of the Result *(What you accomplished)*	Any Measure or Quantities To Prove Your Achievement

Whether you pick a story/achievement from early in your life, or from a more recent time, doesn't matter. Whether it is an achievement in your work-life, or your leisure-life, or your learning-life, again, doesn't matter.

Flesh out the story, so that it follows the outline above. Be especially sure that you describe what kind of *data,* or *things,* were involved in your pulling-off your achievement. And also, what kind of *people* you did it with. Number the story, at the top of the page: this is *Story/Achievement #1.*

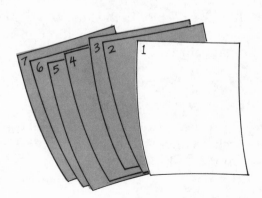

ANALYZE THE STORY
USING THE 'SKILLS KEYS'
DIAGRAM

Once you have the first story/achievement written - - it should probably be less than a page - - go to the *skills keys* diagram, found on pages 208–13. On each page, there, work down each column vertically. Ask yourself, as you look at each *key*, "Did I use this skill *in this story?*" If you decide you probably did, color in the little box that is right under that key. Since this is your Story/Achievement #1, it is the #1 little box that you color in. I suggest you use a red pen, pencil, or crayon, to do this coloring.

Keep going down each vertical column, in turn, on each of the *skills keys* pages. Color in box #1, immediately below each key, *only if* you feel you used that skill *in this story.* When you are done with all the *skills keys,* for Things, People, and Information, you have finished with Story/Achievement #1.

PICK ANOTHER
STORY

Now, it is time to take a second sheet of paper, label it "Story/ Achievement #2," and look over your mini-autobiography, or your Memory Net, once again. Choose, if possible, an entirely different story/achievement from another time in your life, or another arena *(work/leisure/learning)* that is different from that of the first story.

Once you have selected this story, write it out in detail, following the same procedures as you did with Story/Achievement #1. Back to the *skills keys,* then, back to the same question - - different box - - "Did I use this skill *in this story* (#2)?" If the answer is "Yes," or even "I think so," color in the little box right under that *key,* that has the number 2 in it. Continue through all the *keys* in the same fashion as before.

AND ANOTHER,
AND ANOTHER

Repeat the same process five more times, until you have been through Story/Achievement #7, and the little boxes under each *skill key* that are numbered 7.

STUDY THE SKILLS KEYS, NOW

You will want to ask yourself five questions, as you study the *skills keys* pages, with their red-filled-in little boxes.

1) Which skills are *most* colored-in -- those on the Things page, or those on the People page, or those on the Data page?

2) Do I see any *patterns* -- where the same skills *popped up* again and again, in most of my stories? (Experts call this *the irresistibility* of skills -- some skills, in each of us, *insist* on getting used.)

3) Which of the three families of skills are my personal favorites -- regardless of whether the little boxes are colored-in under them, or not? Is my strong-suit with Things, or People, or Data? And if the answer is *More than one,* in what order of priority?

4) Looking at all the *skills keys* pages, which are my ten favorite skills, regardless of which *family* they belong to?

5) Are they the *skills keys* that got the most little boxes colored-in under them, or does my intuition tell me I chose bad stories, and my really favorite skills include some that are not well colored-in? (If so, write some new stories, that demonstrate you have these skills, which are your favorites.)

PRIORITIZE, PRIORITIZE

Take your ten favorite skills, and put them in absolute order of importance to you. You can do this prioritizing either by guess and by gosh, *or* you can use the prioritizing grid on the following pages.

How to Prioritize Your Lists of Anything

Here is a method for taking ten items, and figuring out which one is most important to you, which is next most important, etc.

• Insert the items to be prioritized, in any order, in Section A. Then compare two items at a time, circling the one you prefer -- between the two -- in Section B. Which one is more important to you? State the question any way you want to: In the case of geographical factors, you might ask, "If I were being offered two jobs, one in an area that had factor #1, but not factor #2; the other in an area that had factor #2, but not factor #1, all other things being equal, which job would I take?" *Circle it.* Then go on to the next pair, etc.

• When you are all done, count up the number of times each number got circled, all told. Enter these totals on the TIMES line in Section C. Then notice the number of times each item was circled ("Times" = "Times Circled"). This determines the item's ranking. Most circled = #1, next most circled = #2, etc. Enter this ranking on the RANK line in Section C. If two items are circled the same number of times, look back in Section B to see -- when those two were compared there -- which one you preferred. Give that one an extra half point. List the items, now in their proper rank, in Section D.

Each time you use this grid, make a photocopy of it, and fill in the photocopy rather than the original. If you don't want to do that, and you have a personal computer that is an IBM or IBM-compatible, there is a computer program on a 5.25-inch disk that prints this Grid for you. You can order it, for a $5.00 check made out to Ron Grossman, 9 Union Sq., Suite 212, Southbury, CT 06488.)

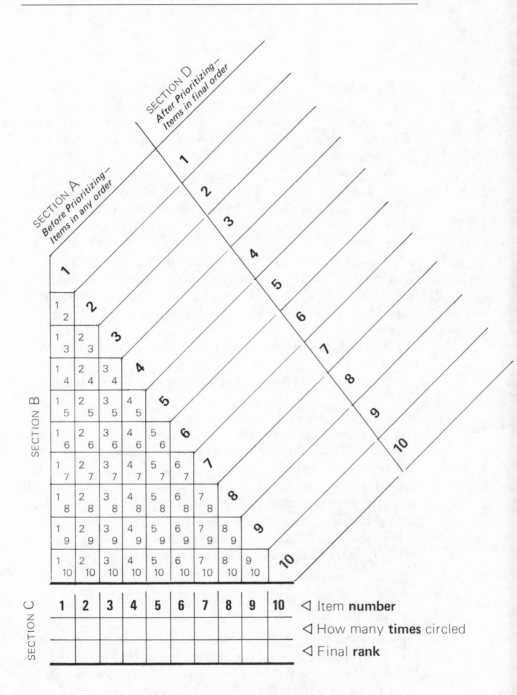

SECTION D
After Prioritizing—
Items in final order

SECTION A
Before Prioritizing—
Items in any order

SECTION B

SECTION C

◁ Item **number**

◁ How many **times** circled

◁ Final **rank**

Prioritizing Grid
for 10 Items

'FLESH OUT'
YOUR TOP TEN

Now, you need to *flesh out* your skill-description, for each of your ten favorites. Currently, each one is only *one word*. One word is a good place to begin, but a poor place to end. In the end, you want to be able to describe what you do in more than just one word.

"I'm good at *organizing*" doesn't tell us much. Organizing what? People, as at a party? Nuts and bolts, as on a workbench? Or lots of information, on a computer? Those are three entirely different skills. The one word "organizing" doesn't tell us which one is *yours*.

So, *please* go back over the skills you identified as your ten favorites, and make sure that each one-word definition gets *fleshed out* with an object -- some kind of Data/Information, or some kind of People, or some kind of Thing. Add an adverb or adjective, too.

Why adjectives? Well, "I'm good at analyzing (people with marital problems) *painstakingly, by asking them a lot of questions*," and "I'm good at analyzing (people with marital problems) *in a flash, by intuition*," are two *entirely different* skills. The difference between them is spelled out not in the verb, but in the adjectival or adverbial phrase there at the end. When you are face-to-face with an employer, and you are trying to explain what makes you different from nineteen other people who can basically do the same thing that you can do, it is the adjective or adverb that will save you. So, try expanding each definition of your ten favorite skills as much as you can, in the fashion I have just described.

When you are done, enter the *full* description of each skill on a larger diagram, as shown on the next page.

THE 'STYLE' WITH WHICH
YOU USE YOUR SKILLS

Now, one final task in your skill-identification. You will notice on the diagram that there is a space at the bottom called 'My Style of Doing Them.' This serves as a kind of *catch-basin* for what people traditionally call *Traits*. Traits are *not* functional/transferable skills -- though they are often confused with them -- but are, rather, the *style* with which we do *some* skills. For

Verb   *Modifying Phrase*   *Object*

In order to do
my favorite tasks
I need to be using my
favorite Functional/Transferable

SKILLS
What I Like to Do With.

T H I N G S   O R   P E O P L E   O R   I N F O R M A T I O N / I D E A S

1. Writing, particularly with humor, for people who need to know more information about one of my favorite fields of interest/knowledge   INFORMATION
2. Crafting, with precision, wooden objects of my own design   THINGS
3. Precision working with my own tools and instruments to do woodcrafting THINGS
4. Planning and directing an entire activity (physical project), bringing it to completion, with great attention to the last detail   INFORMATION
5. Inventing solutions to problems in the physical world, by creating new technologies   IDEAS
6. Programming computers, particularly with programs that solve particular problems in the physical world   IDEAS
7. Laying out a step-by-step process for achieving the implementation of a design of my own devising   IDEAS
8. Evaluating why a particular design or process in the physical world isn't working   INFORMATION
9. Teaching a group of people who need to know more information about one of my favorite fields of interest/knowledge   INFORMATION
10. Starting, initiating new physical projects involved with design, problem-solving, and the employment of electronics   IDEAS

My Style of Doing Them:

I am a person who is self-motivated, takes lots of initiative, is resourceful and creative, patient and persevering despite obstacles. I enjoy a challenge, maintain neatness and order in my workplace, am accurate, methodical, thorough, particularly with details, and achievement oriented.

example, if people say that you are *dynamic,* they mean *when making presentations,* or they mean *when leading meetings,* or they mean *has boundless energy in accomplishing the day's tasks.* They do not necessarily mean you are dynamic while *reading* or dynamic while *eating* or -- well, you get the point. Traits tend to be the *style* with which you do *some* skills.

You need to list your traits. Later on, when you are face-to-face with an employer, they will be useful as you try to describe what makes you different from nineteen other people who can do the same thing that you do.

Try checking them off on the following list, and then, when you are done, choose the ten you like the best about yourself, and add them as you see on the diagram above.

Style with Which I Do These Skills

● I am VERY:

- ☐ Accurate
- ☐ Achievement-oriented
- ☐ Adaptable
- ☐ Adept
- ☐ Adept at having fun
- ☐ Adventuresome
- ☐ Alert
- ☐ Appreciative
- ☐ Assertive
- ☐ Astute
- ☐ Authoritative
- ☐ Calm
- ☐ Cautious
- ☐ Charismatic
- ☐ Competent
- ☐ Consistent
- ☐ Contagious in my enthusiasm
- ☐ Cooperative
- ☐ Courageous
- ☐ Creative
- ☐ Decisive
- ☐ Deliberate
- ☐ Dependable/have dependability
- ☐ Diligent
- ☐ Diplomatic
- ☐ Discreet

- ☐ Driving
- ☐ Dynamic
- ☐ Extremely economical
- ☐ Effective
- ☐ Energetic
- ☐ Enthusiastic
- ☐ Exceptional
- ☐ Exhaustive
- ☐ Experienced
- ☐ Expert
- ☐ Firm
- ☐ Flexible
- ☐ Humanly oriented
- ☐ Impulsive
- ☐ Independent
- ☐ Innovative
- ☐ Knowledgeable
- ☐ Loyal
- ☐ Methodical
- ☐ Objective
- ☐ Open-minded
- ☐ Outgoing
- ☐ Outstanding
- ☐ Patient
- ☐ Penetrating
- ☐ Perceptive
- ☐ Persevering
- ☐ Persistent

- ☐ Pioneering
- ☐ Practical
- ☐ Professional
- ☐ Protective
- ☐ Punctual
- ☐ Quick/work quickly
- ☐ Rational
- ☐ Realistic
- ☐ Reliable
- ☐ Repeatedly
- ☐ Resourceful
- ☐ Responsible
- ☐ Responsive
- ☐ Safeguarding
- ☐ Self-motivated
- ☐ Self-reliant
- ☐ Sensitive
- ☐ Sophisticated, very sophisticated
- ☐ Strong
- ☐ Supportive
- ☐ Tactful
- ☐ Thorough
- ☐ Unique
- ☐ Unusual
- ☐ Versatile
- ☐ Vigorous

● I am a person who:

With respect to execution of a task, and achievement
☐ Takes initiative
☐ Is able to handle a great variety of tasks and responsibilities simultaneously and efficiently
☐ Takes risks
☐   Takes calculated risks
☐ Is expert at getting things done

With respect to time, and achievement
☐ Consistently tackles tasks ahead of time
☐ Is adept at finding ways to speed up a task
☐ Gets the most done in the shortest time
☐ Expedites the task at hand
☐ Meets deadlines
☐   Delivers on promises on time
☐   Brings projects in on time and within budget

With respect to working conditions
☐ Maintains order and neatness in my workspace
☐ Is attendant to details
☐ Has a high tolerance of repetition and/or monotonous routines
☐ Likes planning and directing an entire activity
☐ Demonstrates mastery
☐ Promotes change
☐ Works well under pressure and still improvises
☐ Enjoys a challenge
☐ Loves working outdoors
☐ Loves to travel
☐ Has an unusually good grasp of . . .
☐ Is good at responding to emergencies
☐ Has the courage of his or her convictions

Voila! You have finished your skill-identification.[2]

---

2. If you want a more detailed form of skill-identification, using the pictorial of a *flower,* I refer you to my workbook, *How To Create A Picture of Your Ideal Job,* which is available from Ten Speed Press, P.O. Box 7123, Berkeley, CA 94707, 1-510-845-8414. This workbook also has an extended list of *synonyms* for the verbs that were laid out on the skills keys, earlier in this chapter - - in case you want different ways of saying the same thing.

*S*ow a thought and you reap a deed,
sow a deed and you reap a habit,
sow a habit and you reap a character,
sow a character and you reap a destiny.

Charles Reade (1814–64)

CHAPTER TEN

The Systematic Approach To The Job-Hunt and Career-Change:

PART II

Where

Do You Want To Use Your Skills?

Chapter 10

WHERE, OH WHERE

Once you've figured out *What* your favorite skills are, you must then solve the question: *Where* do I want to use these skills? Of course, you may feel that *Where* is of no personal importance to you. You feel you could be happy anywhere just as long as you were using your favorite skills. Almost no organization in the country is to be ruled out. You're ready to go charging out there and look at them all. *Lots of luck! You'll need it.* There are 5,708,000 organizations, hence 5,708,000 job-markets, out there for you to go look at. We'll see you again in about 43 years.

No, no, no. You have to **cut the territory down.** You have to find some way to narrow down the list of organizations that you will need to weigh, consider, go visit, or research. Otherwise your job-hunting and career-changing territory will be just too big.

THE LANGUAGE OF A WORKPLACE

You cut the territory down, in this fashion, by doing some homework on the question of *Where* do you want to use your skills. *Where* is not complicated. It is primarily a matter of the *language* used, at the workplace - - along with a few other considerations, as we shall see.

Language? Let me explain: suppose you had a dream, one night, where you found yourself working at a fast-food place which had twelve other employees - - none of whom spoke any language except Portuguese. All the customers, also, spoke nothing but Portuguese. And, in this dream, you spoke nothing but English. You can imagine how difficult it was, in the dream, for you to enjoy that job.

As this dream makes clear, the language spoken at your workplace is crucial. Except that, language is not merely a question of whether employees speak English or Portuguese. There are other languages at work. Let us take a job-title I once chose myself, that of *secretary*, and see how this truth works out.

If you work as a legal secretary, the language is that of Legal procedures. Therefore, Law is the language you have to live with, all day long, at that workplace.

If you work as a secretary at a gardening store, the language is that of Gardens and such. Therefore, Gardening is the language you have to live with, all day long, at that workplace.

If you work as a secretary at an airline, the language is that of Airlines procedures. Therefore, Airlines is the language you have to live with, all day long, at that workplace.

If you work as a secretary at a church, the language is that of Church procedures. Therefore, Religion is the language you have to live with, all day long, at that workplace.

If you work as a secretary in a photographic laboratory, the language is that of Photographic procedures. Therefore, Photography is the language you have to live with, all day long, at that workplace.

If you work as a secretary at a bank, the language is that of Banking procedures. Therefore, Banking is the language you have to live with, all day long, at that workplace.

If you work as a secretary at a chemical plant, the language is that of Chemicals manufacturing. Therefore, Chemistry is the language you have to live with, all day long, at that workplace.

If you work as a secretary for the Federal government, the language is that of Government procedures. Therefore, Government is the language you have to live with, all day long, at that workplace.

Now, you may think these *languages* are *Fields,* and so they are. But the significance of a field is that it is the language which you have to listen to, speak, and work in, all day long. And it might as well be one you delight in. Indeed, if you would be truly happy in a new career, it had better be a *Field*/*language*/*subject* that is your absolute favorite. Or - - since more than one language is typically spoken at a particular workplace - - it had better be "*subjects* (plural) that are your favorites."

LEAVE A LANGUAGE,
CHANGE A CAREER

So, what happens if you've come to the place in your life where you don't *enjoy* the language that is spoken at your workplace, all day long? Well, of course, you have to change your field. Voila! We're talking *career-change.*

There are three reasons, at least, why this may happen:

1. You have some favorite subjects, and the language spoken at your workplace isn't one of them. For example, *gardening* may be one of your favorite subjects, but you work at a place where *legal procedures* is the language you have to listen to, and speak, all day long. If you *never* hear about another *brief, tort,* or *court-case,* you will be a happy person. You'd like to work at a place where the language of *gardening* is what you get to listen to, all day long. Voila! You're ready for a career-change.

2. You've decided that among all your favorite subjects, there is one that has become increasingly important to you, and you want to work at a place where you can use that language. For example, you're finding that your faith is more and more important to you, and you'd like to work at a place where the language of *faith, religion,* or *theology,* is what you get to listen to, all day long. You're ready for a career-change.

3. You've decided that you don't like the *values* which go along with *the* language spoken at your workplace all day long. For example, suppose you like to do *welding,* and you are working at a place that makes arms for the military. You may find the language spoken there -- that of *arms* or *fighting* -- objectionable, on moral grounds. You're ready for a career-change. Another example: you're a CFO -- chief financial officer -- for a large firm. You're *ordered* to 'sign off' on a project that is going to bilk taxpayers out of millions of dollars. I said earlier that more than one language is typically spoken at a workplace. Here, the languages are three: *accounting,* and *government (grants)* and *fraudery.*[1] You find the latter objectionable, on moral grounds. You'd like to work at a place where the language of *fraudery* is never again spoken. You're ready for a job-change, and probably a career-change.

---

1. There's no such word, but language is to play with.

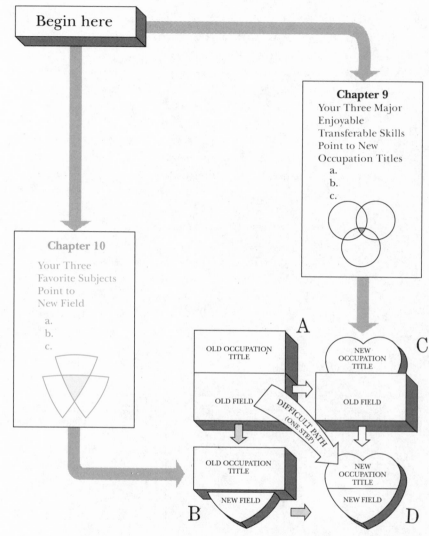

Begin here

Chapter 9
Your Three Major
Enjoyable
Transferable Skills
Point to New
Occupation Titles
a.
b.
c.

Chapter 10
Your Three
Favorite Subjects
Point to
New Field

a.
b.
c.

OLD OCCUPATION TITLE

OLD FIELD

NEW OCCUPATION TITLE

OLD FIELD

DIFFICULT PATH (ONE STEP)

A

C

OLD OCCUPATION TITLE

NEW FIELD

NEW OCCUPATION TITLE

NEW FIELD

B

D

Then, you do interviewing and some library research
to discover what title, and what field, your skills and
knowledge point to. **(Chapter 11)**

It is not sufficient merely to know *What* your favorite skills are - -
which you discovered in the last chapter. You must press on to
this next step in your systematic career-change: *Where* do you
want to use these skills? And the *Where* is defined by the lan-
guage/subjects/field you would most like to be able to speak,
and listen to, and work with, all day long, at your workplace.

Please note, that by approaching the question of *Where* in terms of what *you* want, rather than 'what's available,' you are setting yourself apart from the vast majority of career-changers in this country, and around the world. *They* try to solve the *Where* question by asking what careers look *up and coming,* or by asking where is *the most opportunity.* It is a career-changer mentality that is comparable to the *want-ad* mentality of the average job-hunter, who lets vacancies determine *Where.*

Letting *what's available,* or *opportunities,* or careers which are *up and coming,* or *vacancies* determine *Where* you go, is manifestly a recipe for unhappiness. A survey of the Federal/state employment service, for example, found that 57% of those who found jobs at USES were not working at that job just 30 days later. Many people are equally miserable in the new careers they choose on the basis of articles, advice, and whimsy, such as: "Hot Careers of the '90s."

57% of those who found jobs at USES were not working at that job just 30 days later, *because* they used the first ten or twenty days *on the job* to screen out the job. By doing the exercises in this chapter, you are choosing a better way, by far. Essentially, you are *screening out* careers *before* you commit to them.

PEANUTS reprinted by permission of UFS, Inc.

"THAT MUCH I DO KNOW"

As this old expression implies, there are a lot of things we know *something* about. That is what we begin with, in identifying our favorite subjects. True, you can identify as one of your favorites a subject that, at the present, you know *absolutely nothing about.* And then go learn about that subject at a nearby adult education center, or community college, or college.

But, it is much better to start by asking what are the subjects that:

a) You already know quite a bit about; *and*

b) You love.

It could be *astronomy,* or it could be *movies,* or *psychology,* or *whatever.*

It does *not* need to be only subjects that you have *mastered.* It does not even need to be subjects you studied in school. It is sufficient that you picked up a working knowledge of the subject, and who cares how or where? As the late John Crystal used to say, it doesn't matter whether you learned it in college, or sitting at the end of a log. If it's one of your favorite subjects, that's sufficient.

For example, you may know quite a bit about antiques, and *antiques* are one of your favorite subjects. Yet, you never studied it in school. You picked up a knowledge of antiques by going around to antique stores, and asking lots of questions. And you supplemented this by reading a few books on the subject, and you subscribe to an antiques magazine. That's enough, for you to put a checkmark in front of *antiques,* on the list below. Your knowledge could even be less than that.

Settle it in your mind: the issue is, *what* language do you want to be speaking, and listening to, and working with, all day at work? *How* you picked up that language, or your degree of *mastery* of that language, is irrelevant - - *unless you want to work at a level in that field that demands and requires mastery.*

FIRST, REMEMBER;
THEN, EVALUATE

Let's catalog where you might have learned about your favorite subjects. There are *at least* seven possible places:

1. In high school
2. In a college of any kind
3. In a seminar or workshop
4. At work, during an apprenticeship or internship
5. In your leisure, by reading, etc.
6. By video or computer program, correspondence school, etc.
7. By trial and error, while you were experimenting with something, or doing something

One way to approach this issue of *what are your favorite subjects?* is to use the table on the next page, and simply make a list of all the things you've ever studied or learned or learned about, in *each* of the seven places mentioned above.

I said, "All the things" -- not just *your favorites*. We have found, over the years, that career-changers need to cast a wider net than just *their favorites,* at first. The reason for this, is that trying to do two things at once -- *remember* and *evaluate* -- seems to short-circuit one's memory-banks. Separating the two tasks is much more productive. First, *remember.* Then, *evaluate.*

During the *remembering* phase, you may want to look back at your Memory Net, pages 216–217, and see what subjects come to mind as you look over all the notes you've jotted down, there.

IF YOU JUST CAN'T REMEMBER, TO SAVE YOUR LIFE

If you're not having much luck coming up with the names of the subjects you studied in these seven arenas, then you will of course want a list. Unfortunately, there is no list in the world that could possibly cover all the subjects that you might know something about. We will have to settle for A Sampler only.

In using this list, the same admonition as set forth above applies here: "First, *remember.* Then, *evaluate.*" Go through the list a first time, and check off any subject that you know *anything* about. Do remember that the list is A Sampler. It's just a bunch of pegs on which to hang your memories. Be *sure* and jot down any other subjects you know something about, as they occur to you, which are not on that list.

Subjects I Learned About in High School	Subjects I Learned About in Any Kind of College	Subjects I Learned About at a Seminar / Workshop	Subjects I Learned About in Apprenticeship or Internship	Subjects I Learned About in My Leisure (Reading, etc.)	Subjects I Learned About by a Computer or Video Program	Subjects I Learned About by Trial and Error Doing It Myself

A Sampler
of
Subjects I Know *Something* About

General Fields

- [ ] History
- [ ] Biology
- [ ] Physics
- [ ] Chemistry
- [ ] Geometry
- [ ] Astronomy
- [ ] Geography
- [ ] Knowledge of foreign countries
  (which one/s?)
- [ ] Spanish or some other language
  (which one/s?)
- [ ] Psychology
  - [ ] The way the brain works

The Arts
  - [ ] Principles of art
  - [ ] Cinema
  - [ ] Musical knowledge and taste
  - [ ] Drawing
  - [ ] Graphic arts
  - [ ] Art materials
  - [ ] Music appreciation
  - [ ] Photography
  - [ ] Broadcasting
  - [ ] Woodcuts, engravings, lithographs
  - [ ] Paintings, drawings, silk screens
  - [ ] How to make videos
  - [ ] Music (what kinds?)
  - [ ] Principles of recording
- [ ] Sociology
- [ ] Linguistics or languages
- [ ] Communication
  - [ ] Human nature's need for symbols
  - [ ] The use and meaning of words
  - [ ] Numbers or statistics
  - [ ] Instructional principles and techniques
  - [ ] Speed reading

How to Create Visuals
  - [ ] Designs
  - [ ] Blueprints
  - [ ] Wall-charts
  - [ ] Schematics

How To Produce
- ☐ Procedures
- ☐ Guidebooks
- ☐ Manuals
- ☐ Newsletters

Particular How-To's

- ☐ How to run a particular machine (which one/s?)
- ☐ How to drive an automobile
- ☐ How to sew
- ☐ Carpentry
- ☐ Plumbing
- ☐ Painting
- ☐ Electrical work
- ☐ Household repairs
- ☐ Typing or 'keyboarding'
- ☐ How to operate a computer
- ☐ How computers work
- ☐ Computer programming
- ☐ Knowledge of a particular program
- ☐ Design engineering
- ☐ Interior decorating
- ☐ Knowledge of antiques
- ☐ Knowledge of gardening
- ☐ Horticulture
- ☐ Car repairs
- ☐ How to play a musical instrument (which one/s?)
- ☐ Principles of comparison shopping

Kinds of Personal Problems People Have That I Know Something About, and Know How To Deal With

Economic/Planning Problems for Individuals
- ☐ Identifying and finding meaningful work
- ☐ Job-hunting, career-change, unemployment, being fired or laid off
- ☐ Work satisfaction
- ☐ Life/work planning
- ☐ Personal economics
    - ☐ Financial planning
    - ☐ Budgeting
- ☐ Financial planning and management
- ☐ How to do taxes

Educational Problems
- ☐ Illiteracy, educational needs
- ☐ Performance problems, appraisal

Health Problems
- [ ] Physical fitness
- [ ] Physical handicaps
- [ ] Principles of outdoor survival
- [ ] Weight control
- [ ] Low energy
- [ ] Sleep disorders
- [ ] Principles of behavioral modification
- [ ] Mental/emotional/psychosomatic illness
  - [ ] Depression
  - [ ] Psychiatric hospitalization
  - [ ] Stress
  - [ ] Various kinds of mental/emotional problems
- [ ] Holistic health
- [ ] Self-healing, psychic healing
- [ ] Nutritional problems
- [ ] Addictions
  - [ ] Drug problems
  - [ ] Alcoholism
  - [ ] Smoking
- [ ] Principles of preventative health care
- [ ] Dealing with hypertension
- [ ] Allergies
- [ ] Pain control
- [ ] Dealing with people in terminal illness

Relationship Problems
- [ ] Relationships
- [ ] Personal insight, therapy
- [ ] Sexual education, sexual problems
- [ ] Sexual dysfunction
- [ ] Marriage problems
- [ ] Pregnancy and childbirth
- [ ] Parenting
- [ ] Discipline problems, self-discipline
- [ ] Physical abuse, rape, sexual harassment
- [ ] Divorce
- [ ] Death and grief

Religious/Value Problems
- [ ] Spiritual principles
- [ ] Values identification
- [ ] The nature of religion or religions (which ones?)
- [ ] Philosophy of religion
- [ ] Philosophical problems
- [ ] Ethics
- [ ] Life after death
- [ ] Psychic phenomena

**Kinds of Organizational Problems
I Know Quite a Bit About and
Know How to Deal With**

With People
- ☐ Manpower requirements analysis and planning
- ☐ Personnel administration
- ☐ Recruiting
- ☐ Industry in-house training
- ☐ Principles of group dynamics
- ☐ The *how-to* of customer relations and service
- ☐ Performance specifications

With Finances
- ☐ Accounting
- ☐ Bookkeeping
- ☐ Financial records
- ☐ Fiscal analysis, controls, reductions, and programming
- ☐ Statistical analyses

With Organization Planning
- ☐ Principles of planning and management
- ☐ Systems analysis
- ☐ Data analysis studies
- ☐ Industrial applications
- ☐ Government contracts
- ☐ Merchandising
- ☐ Marketing/sales
- ☐ Packaging
- ☐ Distribution
- ☐ Policy development
- ☐ R & D program and project management
- ☐ How a volunteer organization works

CROSS OUT, PRIORITIZE, REVIEW

When you are done checking off subjects on this list, well -- you know the drill. Cross off *any* subjects you checked, which are not your favorites (clue: you couldn't stand working at a place where *this* was the language you had to listen to, all day long).

You *may* want to copy the survivors on a separate piece of paper, so you can see them clearly. What you need to do next is to look at all the subjects that are checked, but *not* crossed off, and, by guess and by gosh, circle your ten favorites. Don't sit and agonize about this. Just quickly circle the ten that your instincts tell you are your favorites. Go back later, to review, meditate, ponder, and agonize, if you wish.

When you are pretty well satisfied with the ten, you will then need to prioritize these in exact order, using the prioritizing grid on pages 222–23, so that you end up with your absolutely favorite subject in the number one position, your next favorite in the number two, etc.

It is always wise, at that point, to review your list, and ask yourself, "Do I *really* want this subject to be one of the languages of my new career, or not?" example: you may know how to play the trumpet, and this may have come up as number two or three on your prioritized list of favorite subjects. *But,* you know in your heart you don't *really* want to talk about trumpets all day. Or do you? Only you can say. What you want to be certain to do, at this point, is *choose* your three *favorite* subjects - - ones which:

a) You know something about; *and*

b) Are among your top ten favorite subjects; *and*

c) You would like to have as a language you get to listen to, speak, and deal with, at your workplace.

WHAT ELSE DETERMINES *Where?*

It is, of course, obvious that there *are* other factors - - besides your *favorite subjects* - - which will determine *Where* you want to use your skills. Let's look at some of them. Check off one or more of your preferences in each of the following categories:

The Kind of Place I'd Like to Work

I would prefer to work for an organization that
- ☐ Produces information
- ☐ Invents/produces/sells a product
- ☐ Serves people

And one which is
- ☐ Outdoors
- ☐ Indoors
- ☐ A place with 5 or less employees
- ☐ A place with 20 or less employees
- ☐ A place with 100 or less employees

- ☐ A large corporation
- ☐ A place in a large city
- ☐ A place in the suburbs
- ☐ A place in the country
- ☐ In a particular part of this country *(see Chapter 7)*
- ☐ A profit-making firm
- ☐ A non-profit firm or organization
- ☐ A service organization
- ☐ An old organization
- ☐ A new organization
- ☐ A place which is 'going and growing'
- ☐ An organization with lots of problems
- ☐ My own business *(see Chapter 6)*

I Would Like To Work at a Place That Deals With, Or at Least, Has:

Growing Things
- ☐ Trees, bushes, landscaping stuff
- ☐ Flowers, plants
- ☐ Garden tools
- ☐ Crops
- ☐ Ploughs
- ☐ Threshing machines, reapers, harvesters

Materials
- ☐ Paper
- ☐ Woods, plywood, etc.
- ☐ Pottery, pewter
- ☐ Bronze, brass, or aluminum
- ☐ Textiles, cloth, felt, hides, synthetics

Clothing
- ☐ Sewing machines
- ☐ Patterns, safety pins, buttons, zippers
- ☐ Dyes
- ☐ Shoes
- ☐ Ski clothes, swimming suits

Shelter
- ☐ Tents
- ☐ Trailers
- ☐ Apartments, condos, houses
- ☐ Carpenter's tools
- ☐ Paints, wall coverings, carpeting

- ☐ Heating elements, furnaces, air-conditioners, fans
- ☐ Security devices, alarm systems, fire extinguishers, fire alarms
- ☐ Furniture
- ☐ Household items, furniture, kitchen items
- ☐ Washing machines, dryers
- ☐ Kitchen appliances, refrigerators, microwaves, ovens, dishwashers, compactors
- ☐ Cosmetics
- ☐ Tools, power tools

Food
- ☐ Meats
- ☐ Breads and other baked goods
- ☐ Health foods
- ☐ Vitamins
- ☐ Dairy equipment
- ☐ Winemaking equipment

Health Equipment or Materials
- ☐ Medicines, vaccines, thermometers
- ☐ Anesthetics
- ☐ Dental equipment
- ☐ X-ray machines
- ☐ False parts of the human body, hearing aids
- ☐ Spectacles, glasses, contact lenses
- ☐ Gym Equipment

Transportation
Land
- ☐ Roads
- ☐ Bicycles, motorcycles, mopeds
- ☐ Automobiles
- ☐ Trains

Air
- ☐ Gliders
- ☐ Balloons
- ☐ Airplanes
- ☐ Parachutes

Water
- ☐ Rivers, streams, canals
- ☐ Lakes, oceans
- ☐ Boats, steamships, sailboats, canoes, kayaks

Amusement
- ☐ Amusement parks, game parks, aquatic parks
- ☐ Toys
- ☐ Cards, board games, checkers, chess, Monopoly, etc.
- ☐ Kites
- ☐ Musical instruments
     Specify:

Sports equipment
- ☐ Fishing rods, fishhooks, bait
- ☐ Skis, lodges

Manufactured Stuff
- ☐ Office supplies: pens, pencils, desks, tables
- ☐ Computers, typewriters
- ☐ Copying machines, fax machines, printers, printing presses
- ☐ Walkie-talkies, telephones, cellular phones, voice mail, answering machines
- ☐ Tools
- ☐ Clocks
- ☐ Telescopes
- ☐ Microscopes
- ☐ Electrical and electronics equipment
- ☐ Calculators
- ☐ Adding machines
- ☐ Cash registers
- ☐ Money
- ☐ Laser beams
- ☐ Educational materials: easels, projectors, flipcharts, etc.

If I Have To Find Information Someone Else Has Already Gathered, I Prefer to Read or Gather It From:
- ☐ Newspapers
- ☐ Magazines
- ☐ Computers
- ☐ Computer printouts
- ☐ Books
- ☐ Catalogs
- ☐ Handbooks
- ☐ Records, files
- ☐ Trade or professional literature
- ☐ Videotapes
- ☐ Audiotapes
- ☐ Interviewing others, in person or by phone
- ☐ Seminars, learning from trainers
- ☐ Courses, learning from teachers

If It Is My Job to Go Gather the Information, Which Nobody Else Has, I Would Like to Participate In
- ☐ Investigations
- ☐ Surveys or polls
- ☐ Research projects, research and development projects, project reports
- ☐ Data analysis studies
- ☐ None of the above

> ## Kinds of Co-workers I Would Prefer
> ## To Have, in My New Career

I prefer to work with the following kinds of co-workers, colleagues, bosses, or subordinates:
- ☐ Men primarily
- ☐ Women primarily
- ☐ Both sexes
- ☐ Heterosexuals
- ☐ Homosexuals
- ☐ All people regardless of sexual orientation
- ☐ People of all ages
- ☐ Adolescents or young people
- ☐ College students
- ☐ Young adults
- ☐ People in their thirties
- ☐ The middle-aged
- ☐ The elderly
- ☐ The retired
- ☐ People of a particular cultural background:
- ☐ People of a particular economic background:
- ☐ People of a particular social background:
- ☐ People of a particular educational background:
- ☐ People of a particular philosophy or religious belief:
- ☐ Certain kinds of workers (blue-collar, white-collar, executives, or whatever):
- ☐ People in a particular place (the Armed Forces, prison, etc.):
- ☐ All people regardless of background
- ☐ People who are easy to work with:
- ☐ People who are difficult to work with

> ## Kinds of People I Prefer To Try To
> ## Help, or Serve, in My New Career

- ☐ Men
- ☐ Women
- ☐ Individuals
- ☐ Groups of eight or less
- ☐ Groups larger than eight
- ☐ Babies
- ☐ School-age children
- ☐ Adolescents or young people
- ☐ College students

☐ Young adults
☐ People in their thirties
☐ The middle-aged
☐ The elderly
☐ The retired
☐ All people regardless of age
☐ Heterosexuals
☐ Homosexuals
☐ All people regardless of sex
☐ People of a particular social background:
☐ People of a particular educational background:
☐ People of a particular philosophy or religious belief:
☐ Certain kinds of workers (blue-collar, white-collar, executives, or whatever):
☐ People who are poor:
☐ People who are easy to work with:
☐ People who are difficult to work with:
☐ People in a particular place (the Armed Forces, prison, etc.)

My Primary Goals In This New Career Are

☐ To do work which brings more information/truth into the world.
☐ To do work which brings more beauty into the world.
☐ To do work which brings more justice, truth, and ethical behavior into the world.
☐ To serve or help those who are in need.
☐ To have an impact, to cause change.
☐ To influence people and gain a response.
☐ To impress people with my going the second mile, in meeting their needs.
☐ To begin a new business, or do some project from start to finish.
☐ To be in charge of whatever it is that I am doing, so that I get to be *the* decision-maker.
☐ To develop or build something, where there was nothing.
☐ To have a vision of what something could be, and help that vision to come true.
☐ To fix something that is broken,
☐ To improve something or make it better.
☐ To do something that no one has done before.
☐ To do something that everyone says couldn't be done.
☐ To combat some force/influence/pervasive trend, persevere and prevail.
☐ To master some technique, or field.

□ To excel and be the best at whatever it is I do.
□ To be in the spotlight, gain recognition, and be known.
□ To make it into a higher echelon than I currently am, in terms of reputation, and/or prestige, and/or membership, and/or salary.[2]

At This Salary or Level

□ Salary and level I would like to have, at a minimum:
□ Salary and level I would like eventually to reach, if I can:

ON THE LAST DAY
OF YOUR LIFE

In case the lists, preceding, haven't captured all your dreams, here's a catch-basin, to make sure you do catch anything that got left out:

*"Oh, darn, and just as I was beginning
to take charge of my life."*

---

2. I am indebted to my friend, Arthur Miller, for suggesting many of these goals. His pioneering work with respect to goals is enshrined in his book, *The Truth About You*, by Arthur F. Miller and Ralph T. Mattson; available from Ten Speed Press, Box 7123, Berkeley, CA 94707.

ON THE LAST DAY OF MY LIFE

Spend as much time as necessary writing an article entitled "Before I die, I want to..." (And then list all the things you would like to do, before you die.) Confess them on a piece of paper now, and maybe you can begin to make them happen.

As you get involved with this exercise, you may notice that it is impossible to keep your focus only on your proposed new career. You will find some dreams creeping in concerning your leisure or your lifelong learning, of places you want to visit, and experiences you want to have that are not on-the-job. Don't omit these. Be just as detailed as you can be.

GET THE PICTURE?

It is useful, when you are done with all the foregoing exercises, to summarize the results on a pictorial. Having tried many pictorials over the years, career-changers have generally preferred a *flower* picture. You may, too. If you want it, here it is:[3]

---

3. A more elaborate picture of the Flower diagram, together with the skills keys used in Chapter 9, is available as a poster you can write on, from Ten Speed Press, Box 7123, Berkeley, CA 94707. They also have a more elaborate process than the one discussed in Chapters 9, 10, and 11, here, available from them as a workbook. It is called "How to Create A Picture of Your Ideal Job," and you can order it directly from them.

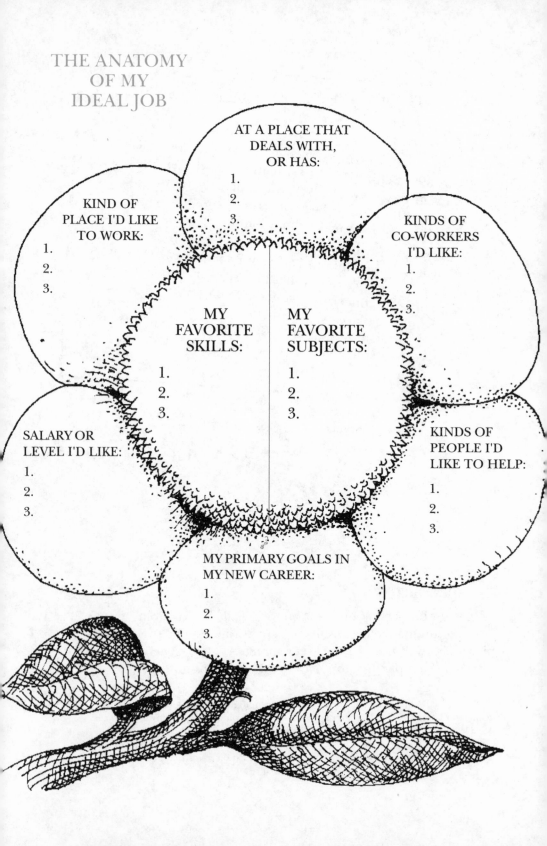

THE ANATOMY
OF MY
IDEAL JOB

AT A PLACE THAT
DEALS WITH,
OR HAS:
1.
2.
3.

KIND OF
PLACE I'D LIKE
TO WORK:
1.
2.
3.

KINDS OF
CO-WORKERS
I'D LIKE:
1.
2.
3.

MY
FAVORITE
SKILLS:
1.
2.
3.

MY
FAVORITE
SUBJECTS:
1.
2.
3.

SALARY OR
LEVEL I'D LIKE:
1.
2.
3.

KINDS OF
PEOPLE I'D
LIKE TO HELP:
1.
2.
3.

MY PRIMARY GOALS IN
MY NEW CAREER:
1.
2.
3.

IN CONCLUSION

As you look over this completed *flower* picture, the beginnings of an idea may be forming in your head, as to what your new career might be. Fine. Only one warning: Please *don't* say to yourself, at this point: "Well, this is what I'm dying to be able to do, but I *know* there is no job in the world like that, that *I* would be able to get."

You don't know any such thing. You need to do your (re)search first (next chapter). Of course, it's possible that at the end of that search, you may not be able to find *all* that you want, down to the last detail. But why not aim for it, and then settle for less *if and when* you find that you simply have to? Until then, you may be surprised at what you are able to turn up.

Sometimes, of course, the *implementation* of vocational dreams will have to be taken in stages. One man we know of, who had been a senior executive with a publishing company, found himself not enjoying retirement, after age 65. In fact, he was bored to death. He contacted a business acquaintance, who said apologetically, "We just don't have anything open that matches or requires your abilities; right now all we need is someone in our mail room." The 65-year-old executive said, "I'll take that job!" He did, and over the ensuing years steadily advanced once again, to just the job he wanted: as a senior executive, where he utilized all his prized skills, for some time. He retired, for the second time, at the age of 85.

It is amazing how often people do get their dreams, whether in stages or directly. The more you don't *cut* the dream down, because of what you *think* you know about *the real world,* the more likely you are to find what you are looking for. If you decide to just pursue half your dream, you will hunt for it with only half a heart. If you decide to pursue all of your dream, you will hunt for it with all your heart.

Having done all the hard work in this chapter, you are well on your way.

*You can judge your age
by the amount of pain you feel
when you come in contact with
a new idea.*

John Nuveen

*Students spend four or more years
learning how to dig data out of the library
and other sources, but it rarely occurs
to them that they should also apply some of
the same new-found research skill to their
own benefit - - to looking up information
on companies, types of professions, sections
of the country that might interest them.*

Professor Albert Shapero
*The late William H. Davis Professor
of The American Free Enterprise System
at Ohio State University*

CHAPTER ELEVEN

The Systematic Approach To
The Job-Hunt and Career-Change:

PART III

How

Do You Go About
Finding Such A Job?

Chapter 11

WHAT DO YOU NEED TO KNOW, NOW?

You know your favorite skills and favorite subjects. Now, you're going to be gathering information about places where you would like to be hired. In order to get to that point, there are four questions you need answers to -- each of which, in turn, further narrows down the territory for your job-search:

QUESTION #1

What are the names of jobs or careers that would give me a chance to use my most enjoyable skills, in a field that is based on my favorite subjects?

QUESTION #2

What kinds of organizations would and/or do employ people in these careers?

QUESTION #3

Among the kinds of organizations uncovered in the previous question, what are the names of the organizations that I particularly like?

QUESTION #4

Among the organizations that I particularly like, what needs do they have or what outcomes are they trying to produce, that my skills and knowledge could help with?

The Creative Process of Career Change

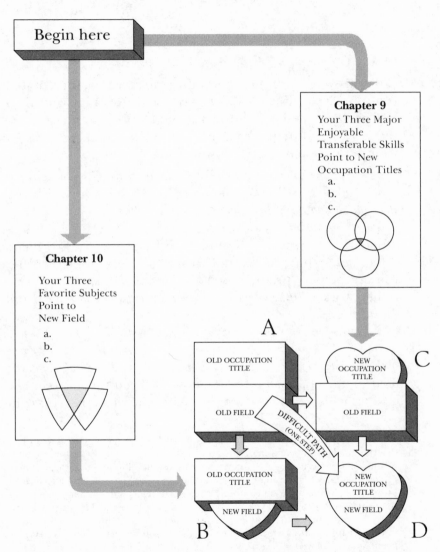

Then, you do interviewing and some library research to discover what title, and what field, your skills and knowledge point to.

And now, to the first question, above: What are **the names of jobs or careers** that would give you a chance to use your most enjoyable skills, in a field based on your favorite subjects?

WHAT CAREERS DO YOUR FAVORITE SKILLS AND SUBJECTS POINT TO?

This is where you take the information you gathered about your favorite skills, and your favorite subjects/languages/fields, in Chapters 9 and 10, and make some sense out of it all. Look them over, and then take a sheet of blank paper, and write out your hunches about the following four choices:

1. Thus far, what's your hunch about the type of job or career you think might interest you the most, in terms of broad fields: do you think it might be something in Agriculture, or something in Manufacturing, or something in Information/Services/Helping people? To put it another way, do you have a hunch you'd rather work primarily with *growing* things; or would you rather work primarily where you are helping produce, sell, or service *things;* or would you rather work primarily with *information* or with *helping* people directly?[1]

2. Thus far, what type of job or career interests you the most, in terms of your favorite skills: a career which works primarily with Things, or with Information/Data/Ideas, or with People? In almost any career field there is opportunity to choose between these three. Let's take agriculture as an example. Within agriculture, you could

---

1. What the dominant economy is in this country at any one time, should never be the determining factor in choosing your career. If you want to be a blacksmith, you should be one, even if there were only three left in the country. But, it is of historical interest to note that careers and career patterns in the U.S. have changed dramatically during this century. There was a time, around the turn of the century, when the majority of the work force -- that is, over 50% of all workers -- were employed in agriculture. Then, by mid-century, that had changed, and the majority of workers were employed in manufacturing. Today, that has changed again, and the majority of workers in this country are employed in careers which deal with information, and/or render services to people. Consequently, though many individuals still choose a career in manufacturing or even in agriculture, it is the services/information sector that is growing the most rapidly today, and therefore creating the most job opportunities. Hence, the common statement that the U.S. has become "The Information Society."

be driving tractors and other farm machinery - - and thus working primarily with things; or you could be gathering statistics about crop growth for some state agency - - and thus working primarily with information/data; or you could be teaching agriculture in a college classroom, and thus working primarily with people and ideas. Almost all careers break down into these three sub-divisions. So regardless of what field you eventually choose, you will have to make a further decision about where you want to work *within* that field. It is your favorite skills that will give you the clue. Look them over now, and see what you think. You can always *refine* your choice, or even *change* it, later.

3. *Thus far, what type of job or career interests you the most, in terms of your favorite subjects?* As I pointed out at length in Chapter 10, every job or career requires you to know a bit - - sometimes *quite* a bit - - about *something*. Various jobs or careers require you to know something about: health, or construction, or law, or computers, or buildings, or art, or the Japanese, or oceanography, or physics, or psychology, or the human body, or religion, or building materials, or cars, or gardening, or sports, or drama, or almost any subject you can name. It is, therefore, important for you to look over the *prioritized* list of your favorite subjects, at this point, to see which subjects/fields/languages you would *like* to be working *in,* and *with,* all day, at work. Jot the top three down, on the piece of paper, as possible fields.

4. *Thus far, what type of job or career interests you the most, in terms of **career families?*** This part of your research would be maddening, not to say impossible, if you had to study all 20,000 job-titles that exist in this, and many other, countries. Fortunately, they have been reduced to 19 'families' or 'clusters,' laid out by the federal government.[2] Read the list below and see if any of these *grab* you. If not, later research will uncover ones which do.

CAREER OR OCCUPATIONAL FAMILIES [3]

1. Executive, Administrative, and Managerial Occupations
2. Engineers, Surveyors, and Architects
3. Natural Scientists and Mathematicians
4. Social Scientists, Social Workers, Religious Workers, and Lawyers
5. Teachers, Counselors, Librarians and Archivists
6. Health Diagnosing and Treating Practitioners
7. Registered Nurses, Pharmacists, Dieticians, Therapists, and Physician Assistants
8. Health Technologists and Technicians
9. Writers, Artists, and Entertainers
10. Technologists and Technicians, Except Health
11. Marketing and Sales Occupations
12. Administrative Support Occupations, Including Clerical
13. Service Occupations
14. Agricultural, Forestry, and Fishing Occupations
15. Mechanics and Repairers
16. Construction and Extractive Occupations
17. Production Occupations
18. Transportation and Material Moving Occupations
19. Handlers, Equipment Cleaners, Helpers, and Laborers

Okay, now that you have your four *hunches* written down on a sheet of paper, flesh these hunches out a little, by going to some reference books to see what they can tell you.[4]

---

2. Through the U.S. Department of Labor, Bureau of Labor Statistics, (published in the *Occupational Outlook Handbook,* available in any library).

SUGGESTED JOBS
OR CAREERS

If you browse through some of these reference *books,* you will probably find the journey mildly frustrating, because you don't quite know how to use them. So you think to yourself, *"You know, maybe people would be of more help to me than books."*

Okay, go talk to your family and friends for ideas about your ideal career. Before you do that, take those lists you compiled in Chapters 9 and 10, and from those lists, copy your three favorite transferable skills and your three favorite subjects onto one piece of paper.

During the following week, show this list to all your family and friends, and ask them what jobs or careers come to mind,

---

3. If you wish a more detailed explanation of these families, you can order *Matching Yourself With the World of Work, 1986 edition,* reprinted from the *Occupational Outlook Quarterly, Fall 1986,* from the Superintendent of Documents, U.S. Government Printing Office, Washington D.C. 20402. It describes types of job characteristics for each family, in the form of an extended table, that you can compare to your skills and interests.

4. For further information in the library about careers which may interest you, see:

Dictionary of Occupational Titles (DOT), 4th ed., revised 1991. *In two volumes.* Supt. of Documents, U.S. Govt. Printing Office, Washington, DC 20402. A catalog of the 12,860 occupations known to exist in the U.S. at present. It has an alphabetical index, by occupations. It is also available in an exact reprint from JIST Works, Inc., 720 North Park Ave., Indianapolis, IN 46202-3431. This is a very useful, though difficult, book. If you want to plumb its depths, I would recommend **strongly** that you *first* use Holland's Self-Directed Search, and thence *his* Dictionary *(both are explained more fully on page 263)* to tell you which occupations to go seeking in the DOT.

Occupational Outlook Handbook, 90–91. Bureau of Labor Statistics, available from Supt. of Documents, U.S. Govt. Printing Office, Washington, DC 20402. 225 occupations organized by interest and job title. This has also been published commercially under the title, *America's Top 300 Jobs,* by JIST Works, Inc., 720 N. Park Ave., Indianapolis, IN 46202-3431. 1990. The latter has some helpful indices and supplemental material.

Selected Characteristics of Occupations Defined in the Dictionary of Occupational Titles. U.S. Dept. of Labor, Employment and Training Admin., available from Supt. of Documents, U.S. Govt. Printing Office, Washington, DC 20402.

Job Selection Workbook, for use with Guide for Occupational Exploration. U.S. Employment Service, Employment and Training Admin., available from Supt. of Documents, U.S. Govt. Printing Office, Washington, DC 20402. 1979.

William E. Hopke, ed., *Encyclopedia of Careers and Vocational Guidance,* 8th ed. 4 volumes. Garrett Park Press, Box 190, Garrett Park, MD 20896. 1990.

There are also *numerous* books in most libraries, and certainly in most bookstores, on various groups of careers. You will find titles like Ten Speed Press' *Offbeat Careers: The Directory of Unusual Work,* career books on the health fields, etc., etc.

that they think might use such skills; and what fields come to mind, that comprise your favorite subjects. Family and friends can sometimes come up with some *great* suggestions.

You may also want to go visit strangers, to get their perspective and suggestions. These would be specific strangers, indicated by your skills and subjects.

Let's take an illustration, to see how you do that. Suppose you discovered from your exercises in Chapters 9 and 10 that:

(a) at the top of your list of favorite skills, is the fact that you are skilled in advising, mentoring, and counseling people, particularly in one-to-one situations;

(b) at the top of your list of favorite subjects, is some knowledge of psychiatry, which you *love* to use;

(c) next on your list of favorite subjects is carpentry;

(d) third on your list of favorite subjects are plants -- the kind that grow in gardens.

Now, how do go about finding out what career will unify and use all of these? It comes down, of course, to a simpler question: *who do you go see,* for information?

To figure that out, you mentally translate each of the skills, and each of the favorite subjects you have, into a corresponding person. In this particular case, Counseling = a counselor, psychiatry = a psychiatrist, carpentry = a carpenter, plants = a gardener.

Next, you ask yourself which of these persons is most likely to have the largest overview. This is often, but not always, the same as asking: who took the longest to get their training? The particular answer here: the psychiatrist.

In the place where you presently are, then, plan to go see a psychiatrist (pay them for fifteen minutes of their time, if there is no other way) or go see the head of the psychiatry department at the nearest college or university, and ask them: *Do you have any idea how to put all the above together in a job? And if you don't, who might?* Keep going until you find someone who knows the answer.

In this particular case (this is from an actual career-changer's experience), you will eventually be told: "Yes, it can all be put together. There is a branch of psychiatry that uses plants to help heal people. You can use all your skills and interests. You can even use your carpentry to build planters for those plants."

And that's the way it works.

That's how you put together three or four of *anything* into one unified job or career.

ANOTHER METHOD FOR TURNING UP NAMES OF INTERESTING JOBS OR CAREERS

If the above method isn't turning up enough ideas about an ideal job or ideal career, there is an alternative approach to all of this, called the RIASEC theory, that was invented by John L. Holland, which you should certainly try.

In John's system, all jobs, careers, skills, and personality types are divided into six clusters or families, rather than the nineteen we saw above. To get a quick fix on which of these six *families* of careers you are *attracted to,* try this exercise:

R for "Realistic"

I for "Investigative"

People who have athletic or mechanical ability, prefer to work with objects, machines, tools, plants, or animals, or to be outdoors.

People who like to observe, learn, investigate, analyze, evaluate, or solve problems.

The Party

People who like to work with data, have clerical or numerical ability, carrying things out in detail or following through on others's instructions.

People who have artistic, innovating or intuitional abilities, and like to work in unstructured situations, using their imagination or creativity.

C for "Conventional"

A for "Artistic"

People who like to work with people -- influencing, persuading or performing or leading or managing for organizational goals or for economic gain.

People who like to work with people-- to inform, enlighten. help, train, develop, or cure them, or are skilled with words.

E for "Enterprising"

S for "Social"

On the previous page is an aerial view of a room in which a *two-day* party is taking place. At this party, people with the same or similar interests have (for some reason) all gathered in the same corner of the room. It is a six-sided room, and all six corners are filled with babbling people. What they are babbling about, I have made clear by each corner. Now, the questions:

(1) Which corner of the room would you instinctively be drawn to, as the group of people you would most *enjoy* being with for the longest time? (Leave aside any question of shyness, or whether you would have to talk with them.)

Write the *letter* for that corner here:

(2) After fifteen minutes, everyone in the corner you have chosen leaves for another party crosstown, except you. Of the groups *that still remain* now, which corner or group would you be drawn to the most, as the people you would most *enjoy* being with for the longest time?

Write the letter for that corner here:

(3) After fifteen minutes, this group too leaves for another party, except you. Of the corners, and groups, which remain now, which one would you most enjoy being with for the longest time?

Write the letter for that corner here:

These three letters, in the order in which you wrote them, form what is known as your 'Holland code' - - such as 'S I A.'[5]

But this is only *a quick fix* on your 'code.' In order to be more detailed and precise, you should take the following steps:

1. Get your hands on a copy of John L. Holland's instrument called 'The Self-Directed Search (SDS).'[6] You can order an SDS Specimen Set for $6.95, which includes the SDS, Form R,[7] a brief *Occupations Finder* and a booklet 'You and Your Career,' from the publisher, Psychological Assessment Resources, Inc., Box 998, Odessa, FL 33556, (1-800-331-TEST, or in Florida 1-813-968-3003). This is a self-marking test, which takes about 15–25 minutes. You score it yourself, and it will tell you *exactly* what your 'Holland code' is.[8]

2. You then want to look up *what* jobs or careers match your 'code.' The brief *Occupations Finder,* that is included in the Specimen Set, will *not* do. Instead, buy, borrow, or go to your local library for the Dictionary of Holland Occupational Codes: A Comprehensive Cross-Index of Holland's RIASEC Codes with 12,000 DOT Occupations, by John L. Holland and Gary D. Gottfredson. 1989. 2nd ed., revised and expanded. If you can't find it *anywhere,* it is available from the same publisher, listed above, but it costs $31. This immensely helpful book, if you are working with Holland's system, gives a comprehensive list of occupations which your 'code' suggests, plus the DOT number for each of 12,860 occupations. You are thus able to go from this *Dictionary* to the DOT, and look up more detailed information on any occupation that looks interesting to you here. So, look up your 'code' here in the *Dictionary of Holland Occupational*

---

5. John Holland developed this more than twenty years ago, and has continually updated it since then. It has been used by more than 10 million people, thus far.

6. If you want a different approach to Holland's 'codes,' there is also *Your Career: Choices, Chances, Changes* by David C. Borchard, John J. Kelly, and Nancy-Pat K. Weaver. Kendall/Hunt Publishing Company, Dubuque, Iowa. 1992. Fifth Edition. Pages 64–104 deal with Holland exercises.

7. There is a Form E, for those with below-average reading skills, or for young people; there are also Canadian editions, in either English or French.

8. Holland codes are useful for other purposes than identifying interesting jobs or careers. They can also be used for choosing one's major in college, and for choosing one's leisure activities.

If you are just starting college, and are puzzled about what to major in, you may want to get your hands on the *College Majors Finder.* It helps identify the college majors that match your Holland 'code.' Over 900 college majors are listed. Psychological Assessment Resources, Inc., Box 998, Odessa, FL 33556.

If you want to choose leisure activities that are the *opposite* of the skills you use all week long at work, see: *The Leisure Activities Finder: For Use with the Self-Directed Search and the Vocational Preference Inventory.* 1990. Psychological Assessment Resources, Inc., Box 998, Odessa, FL 33556. This takes your Holland Code and relates it to leisure activities. We recommend, however, that instead of taking your *favorite* corner, e.g., 'S,' you go *across the hexagon* (as in the Party exercise, p. 261) -- which in this example, would be 'R,' and look up *those* leisure activities. The reason for this advice, is that leisure is best when it is an *alternating rhythm* to the stuff you do, and the skills you use, when you are at work.

The background theory for Holland's 'codes' is carefully explained in:

John L. Holland, *Making Vocational Choices. A Theory of Vocational Personalities and Work Environments,* 2nd ed. Prentice-Hall, Inc., Sylvan Ave., Englewood Cliffs, NJ 07632. 1985. You can order it from Psychological Assessment Resources, Inc., Box 998, Odessa, FL 33556, (1-800-331-TEST, or in Florida 1-813-968-3003). $19.95.

Codes, and from among all the occupations you find there, with that 'code,' jot down on a piece of paper ten or fifteen that *really* look interesting, to you. Ones that you want to explore further.

3. The next thing you need to do is further research in reference books, regarding this list of the ten or fifteen careers that look interesting to you, and match your 'code.' That research can best be done in the U.S. Government's Dictionary of Occupational Titles (DOT), and it is to that mammoth volume (actually two volumes) you should turn at your local public or college library. Holland's *Dictionary* is cross-referenced to the DOT, so you should have no difficulty knowing *what* to look up. The DOT will then tell you, *in detail,* about those ten or fifteen careers you're trying to find out more about. On your list of ten or fifteen, *cross out* any that no longer interest you, after looking them up here in the DOT. This will leave you with less than fifteen to go investigate with personal interviews.[9]

HOW YOU GO ABOUT FINDING ANSWERS TO ALL YOUR QUESTIONS: WRITTEN STUFF AND PEOPLE

From the above, we see the rhythm of this research beginning to unfold. It goes like this:

Reference books: You read, until you need some information that no book seems to have.

People: Then you go talk to people until you have found out what you needed to know.

Reference books: Back then to do some more reading, until you need some information that no book seems to have.

People: Then you go talk to people until you have found out what you needed to know. Etc., etc.

WHERE TO FIND THE MOST DEPENDABLE INFORMATION

In this endlessly changing world, where *'someone keeps moving the goal-posts,'* the most dependable and up-to-date information will usually be found from talking to people. However, as you

---

9. If, by chance, none of the fifteen survive step 3, then go back to Holland's dictionary and choose fifteen new ones.

have already seen, you *will* need to do some reading, also.

Here's why:

People you seek information from will *usually* treat you with a warm welcome, *provided*...

a. *provided* that you know what questions you are trying to find answers to; *and*

b. *provided* the answers can't easily be found in the library -- either in printed materials (reference books, magazines, journals), microfiche, or whatever; or in any printed materials that *this place* may have, for distribution. Be sure to go pick those up *first,* before you take up someone's valuable time, unnecessarily.

c. *provided* that when it is time for you to approach people, you approach first of all those people whose business it is to give out information to the public. I am thinking of such people as librarians, receptionists, public relations officers, the front desk in personnel offices, and the like; *and*

d. *provided* that if you approach some organization, you approach those in lesser authority first, to find out everything that *they* know, *before* you approach anyone higher up in the same organization.

Ask Me Only What I Alone Know

The principle here is that you approach people for the information they alone know. If some of their subordinates know this information, don't waste the time of the senior person. Get it from their subordinates.[10]

If the information you are seeking exists in print, and is easily found, don't bother the subordinates, either.

People with jobs are busy people. When you, in effect, expect them to do your research for you, they will be turned off to you.

---

10. Incidentally, visiting a senior person in an organization unannounced ("I just happened to be in the neighborhood") is universally perceived as the conduct of an amateur. If you would like to be seen as a professional,

a) make an appointment; *and*

b) state at that time what amount of time you will need (eighteen minutes, *max*); *and*

c) state at that time what it is that you are trying to find out. (Someone other than the person you are trying to see may actually be the one who has the information you are looking for. Often the aide/assistant/secretary/receptionist can tell you over the phone who that is, thus saving you from a fool's chase.)

The reason you do research in reference books, *first,* comes from courtesy, kindness, thoughtfulness, consideration, and all those other qualities so difficult to find these days. But which *you* want to be known for, in your job-search, believe me.

WHAT KIND OF BOOKS SHOULD YOU GO TO?

Depends on what you're trying to find out. Most of the reference books you want, will be found in your local libraries *(that's plural):* the public library, your local community college library, university library, business library, and so forth.

If you are clear about what information you're looking for, there are two ways to proceed:

1. Walk right up to the helpful librarian, in any of the above, and tell him or her what you're trying to find out. Ask them what directories, or other reference book(s), they think would help. If necessary, ask them to help you find them.

2. If there's no librarian available, or at least no *helpful* librarian, there are *(mercifully)* indexes (indices) to all the directories likely to have the stuff you're trying to find out. Names of those directories to directories are:

• Klein's *Guide to American Directories;* and

• *Directories in Print, 1993,* 10th ed., Gale Research, Inc., P.O. Box 33477, Detroit, MI 48232-5477, which contains over 15,000 current listings of directories, indexed by title or key word or subject (over 3,500 subject headings).

You are of course curious to know what kinds of books these directories, or the librarian, will point you to. Accordingly, there is a sampler of the ones job-hunters and career-changers have found most useful, at the beginning of Appendix B.

WHAT KINDS OF PEOPLE SHOULD YOU GO SEE?

If you as job-hunter or career-changer go to see people - - for *any* purpose, during your job-search - - this is automatically called *interviewing.* The word has a broader meaning than most people give to it.

The Three Types of Interviews

The late John Crystal, back in 1972, when he was working with retirees from the State Department, first came up with this insight - - after observing successful job-hunters and career-changers. He contended that there are actually three types of *interviews* that successful job-hunters should do: first, interviewing just for practice and pleasure; secondly, interviewing in order to find out the information you are looking for; and, finally, interviewing with employers, to secure a job.[11]

People who followed John's advice, in this regard, had an 86% success rate in finding a job - - moreover, not just any job, but *the* job they were looking for.

So, in more recent years, these three stages have been put into the form of a diagram, and given a name - - PIE - - by the job-hunting expert in Europe, Daniel Porot. This has helped thousands of job-hunters and career-changers in Europe understand what is involved in a successful job-hunt and career-change, so I want to lay it out, here - - with Daniel's kind permission:

The Three Stages of Interviewing
If You Would Change
Your Career

---

11. John also was the inventor of WHAT, WHERE and HOW - - which I have used as the basic framework for Chapters 9, 10, and 11, here.

Initial:	Pleasure **P**	Information **I**	Employment **E**
Kind of Interview	Practice Field Survey	Informational Interviewing or Researching	Employment Interview or Hiring Interview
Purpose	To Get Used to Talking with People to Enjoy It; To "Penetrate" Networks	To Find Out If You'd Like a Job, Before You Go Trying to Get It	To Get Hired for the Work You Have Decided You Would Most Like to Do
How You Go to the Interview	You Can Take Somebody with You	By Yourself or You Can Take Somebody with You	By Yourself
Who You Talk To	Anyone Who Shares Your Enthusiasm About a (for You) Non-Job-Related Subject	A Worker Who Is Doing the Actual Work You Are Thinking About Doing	An Employer Who Has the Power to Hire You for the Job You Have Decided You Would Most Like to Do
How Long a Time You Ask For	10 Minutes (and DON'T run over -- asking to see them at 11:50 may help keep you honest, since most employers have lunch appointments at noon)	Ditto	
What You Ask Them	Any Curiosity You Have About Your Shared Interest or Enthusiasm	Any Questions You Have About This Job or This Kind of Work	You Tell Them What It Is You Like About Their Organization and What Kind of Work You Are Looking For.

Initial:	Pleasure **P**	Information **I**	Employment **E**
What You Ask Them *(continued)*	If Nothing Occurs to You, Ask: 1. How did you start, with this hobby, interest, etc.? 2. What excites or interests you the most about it? 3. What do you find is the thing you like the least about it? 4. Who else do you know of who shares this interest, hobby or enthusiasm, or could tell me more about my curiosity? a. Can I go and see them? b. May I mention that it was you who suggested I see them? c. May I say that you recommended them? ***Get their name and address***	If Nothing Occurs to You, Ask: 1. How did you get interested in this work and how did you get hired? 2. What excites or interests you the most about it? 3. What do you find is the thing you like the least about it? 4. Who else do you know of who does this kind of work, or similar work but with this difference: _____? 5. What kinds of challenges or problems do you have to deal with in this job? 6. What skills do you need in order to meet those challenges or problems? ***Get their name and address***	You tell them the kinds of challenges you like to deal with. What skills you have to deal with those challenges. What experience you have had in dealing with those challenges in the past.
AFTERWARD: That Same Night	SEND A THANK YOU NOTE	SEND A THANK YOU NOTE	SEND A THANK YOU NOTE

Since understanding *interviewing* is so crucial to the success of your job-hunt and career-change, I will explain each of these three kinds of interviewing, in detail: **P** and **I** in the remainder of this chapter, then **E** in Chapter 12, following.

ooooooooooooooooooooooooooooooooooooooooooooooooo

THE **P** IN PIE

ooooooooooooooooooooooooooooooooooooooooooooooooo

WARMING-UP WITH PRACTICE
JUST FOR PLEASURE

Effective interviewing for your job-search involves your doing a kind of warm-up, first - - just as people do before they undertake physical exercise. John Crystal named this warm-up "The Practice Field Survey." Daniel Porot calls it **P** for *pleasure* - - that is, interviewing for pleasure. Of course, it could equally well be **P** for *practice.*

Whatever its name, the purpose of this first kind of interviewing is simply to get you comfortable about going out and talking to people *one-on-one.* This is achieved by having you choose a topic - - *any* topic - - that is a pleasure for you to talk about with other people. And by encouraging you to make it a topic that has *nothing* to do with any present or future career of yours. Kinds of topics that work best, for the purposes of this exercise, are:

• a hobby you *love,* such as skiing, bridge playing, exercise, computers, etc.

• any leisure-time enthusiasm of yours, such as a movie you just saw, that you liked a lot

• a long-time curiosity, such as how do they predict the weather, or what do policemen do

• an aspect of the town or city you live in, such as a new shopping mall that just opened

• an issue you feel strongly about, such as the homeless, AIDS sufferers, ecology, peace, health, etc.

WHO TO GO VISIT
(or Whom to go Visit)

As you can see from the first part of Daniel's diagram, you want to go talk to someone who is as enthusiastic about your chosen topic, as you are. It should be someone you don't already know, but otherwise, there are no rules. Use the Yellow Pages, ask around among your friends, *who do you know that loves to talk about this topic?* It's relatively easy to find the kind of person you're looking for.

You love to talk about skiing? *Try a ski-clothes store, or a skiing instructor.* You love to talk about writing? *Try a professor on a nearby college campus, who teaches English.* You love to talk about physical exercise? *Try a trainer, or someone who teaches physical therapy.*

Once you've identified this potential Sharer-of-Your-Enthusiasm, you go talk with them. You can do this with or without an appointment - - though it is often better if it is spontaneous, rather than planned long before.

When you meet them, you ask for *ten minutes of their time.* Period. Stop. Exclamation point. And you watch your wrist-watch *like a hawk,* to be sure you stay no longer. Only stay longer, if they *beg* you to.[12]

Once they've agreed to give you ten minutes, you ask them whatever questions are on your mind about the topic you have chosen. It is crucial that this topic, as described above, be one which you *love* to talk with other people, about. Absent that kind of enthusiasm, this exercise will be *a bomb.*

ARE YOU HAVING FUN?
HAS SHYNESS YIELDED TO LOVE?

The test of whether or not you are doing this correctly, is how much *fun* you are having. *And,* how much you are forgetting all about your inborn shyness - - if you are at all shy about talking to people.

---

12. And I mean *beg.* A polite, "Oh do you have to go?" should be understood for what it is: politeness. Your response should be, "Yes, I promised to only take ten minutes of your time, and I want to keep to my word." This will almost always leave a *very* favorable impression behind you.

The wonderful gift from this kind of interviewing is that it helps those of us who are shy, even *Terminally* shy, to get over it.[13] The learning is: shyness always loses its power and its painful self-consciousness -- *if* and *when* you are talking about something *you love.*

For example, if you love gardens,[14] you will forget all about your shyness when you're talking to someone else about gardens and flowers. *"You ever been to Buchart Gardens?"*

If you love movies, you'll forget all about your shyness when you're talking to someone else about movies. *"I just hated that scene where they...."*

If you love computers, then you will forget all about your shyness when you're talking to someone else about computers. *"Do you work on a Mac or an MS-DOS machine?"*

Enthusiasm

Throughout the job-hunt (and career-change) the key to interviewing is not found in memorizing a dozen rules about what you're *supposed* to do.

No, the key is just this one thing: now and always, be *sure* you are talking about something you feel *passionate about.*[15] Enthusiasm is the key -- to *enjoying* interviewing, and conducting *effective* interviews, that open doors for you.

That's why it is important that it be your *favorite* skills and your *favorite* subjects, that you are here exploring and pursuing (Chapters 9 and 10).

This not only leads to job-satisfaction, down the line, but it makes interviewing *fun,* right now. *Fun* is the key, and the acid test. So, you may discuss anything and ask any questions which come to your mind, just as long as you're having fun talking to this person about the *enthusiasm* you have chosen.

---

13. Job-hunters often imagine that books like this are written by very aggressive, *take charge* kind of people. Not true. I, for example, am painfully shy; always have been. Unless, of course, I'm talking about a subject *I love.* The same will be true of many of you.

14. *Puh-leeze* don't drop me a line telling me that "grammatically you can't *love* gardens, movies, computers, etc.; you can only love *people.*" We know what I mean.

15. This is what the late Joseph Campbell used to call 'your bliss.'

It's usually easy to figure out what to talk about. But, of course, you want to know what to do if it *isn't*.

Well, if nothing occurs to you, the following questions have proved to be good conversation starters to thousands of job-hunters and career-changers before you. I have put a little short-hand in front of each of them, to help you memorize the list, if you desire.[16]

- (How) How did you get involved with/become inter-ested in this? (*"This"* is the hobby, curiosity, aspect, issue, or enthusiasm, that you are very interested in.)
- (+) What do you like the most about it?
- (–) What do you like the least about it?
- (Who?) Who else would you suggest I go talk to that shares the same interest?
- (William) Can I use your name?
- (Tell) May I tell them you recommended that I talk to them?
- (Phoned) Then, choosing one person off the list of sev-eral names they may have given you, you say, Well, I think I will begin by going to talk to this person. Would you be willing to call ahead, so they will know who I am when I go over there?

These questions are recommended, because they are the same questions you can later use well, when you're gathering information *for real*. The rationale for each of these questions is as follows:

(How): helps you find out how people get into jobs and careers.

(+): helps you find out what's good about a particular job or career.

(–): helps you find out what's bad about a particular job or career.

(Who?): helps you get leads on other people to go see.

---

16. Some of you, on reading these questions, will think to yourself, *Hey, I thought we should be exploring some non-job-related interest?* True. That means: an interest that isn't related to any job or career that *you* are considering. But your visits will almost always involve questions about someone else's job.

(William): helps you get in the door to see the other people.

(Tell): helps you to get recommendations, which further eases the opening of the door.

(Phoned): helps you to get an appointment, which further eases the opening of the door.

TAKE SOMEONE WITH YOU

If you need some support when you first go out to try this *Pleasurable Practice,* it's perfectly okay to take someone with you -- at *this* stage of the job-hunt. Your best friend, a fellow career-changer, your mother, whoever. It's perfectly okay to take someone, *at this stage,* because you're *not* interviewing for a job. You're just trying to get at ease in talking to people *about a mutual enthusiasm.*

If you're so shy you are tongue-tied in going to see people, the someone you take along with you should be one who is more outgoing than you feel you are. At the practice interview, let them take the lead in the conversation, while you watch to see how they do it. Then on the second or third interview, *you* take the lead, and let them follow.

Alone or with someone, keep at this, until you feel very much at ease in talking with people and asking them questions about things you are curious about. It may take your seeing four people. It may take ten. Or twenty. You'll know.

When you feel comfortable doing this, and it's easy to talk to people about topics in which you take great pleasure, then you are ready for the second phase of interviewing:

ooooooooooooooooooooooooooooooooooooooooooooooooc

THE   IN PIE

ooooooooooooooooooooooooooooooooooooooooooooooooo

THE REAL THING: RESEARCHING OR 'INFORMATIONAL INTERVIEWING'

The **I,** as you may or may not recall, stands for *Information.* This is *Interviewing for Information,* or Informational interviewing.

Having gotten Practice in interviewing, you now settle down to your basic task: career-change. You need to find out what jobs or careers *match* your *favorite skills* and *favorite subjects,* that you identified in Chapters 9 and 10.

All the confidence you picked up during the P phase of interviewing, will stand you in good stead, as you now go into Informational interviewing.

You are still working on the first question, remember?

QUESTION #1

What are the names of jobs or careers that would give me a chance to use my most enjoyable skills, in a field that is based on my favorite subjects?

"WE'RE OFF TO SEE THE WORKERS…"

Earlier in this chapter, whether through your Holland 'code,' or through interviewing of friends and family, or from studying the DOT, you came up with the names of ten or fifteen careers - - maybe less - - that look *real interesting,* on paper. Question is: are they really that interesting *in actual fact*? Time to go see **the** workers who actually do that kind of work. *They'll* be able to tell you. You'll find out 'from the horse's mouth' whether these jobs are as attractive to you, as they look on paper.

Do remember, it is not *employers* you want to see *at this point* in your research -- unless they are the ones who are doing the work that interests you. It is *workers* you want to see, at this point. Go back and look at Daniel Porot's chart, and you will see: **P** = fun people; **I** = workers; and **E** = employers.

During the **P**ractice phase of interviewing, you go see people who share your enthusiasm for something; during the **I**nformational phase of interviewing, you go see workers who are doing work you think you might like to do; and during the **E**mployment phase of interviewing, you go see employers who have the power to hire you for the job you want. Don't get them mixed up, *please.* See the box on the next page.

WHAT DO YOU WANT THE WORKERS TO TELL YOU?

When you find workers doing work you think you might like to do, you ask them *the same* four things we saw earlier, during the Practice Field Survey:

1. How did you get into this work?
2. What do you like the most about it?
3. What do you like the least about it?
4. And, where else could I find people who do this kind of work? (*Or,* if you have discovered from this interview that this kind of job definitely turns you *off,* then you ask them for ideas as to who you could go talk to about the *other* kinds of work your friends/family suggested to you.) Then, either way, you go visit the people they suggest.

You should always ask them for more than one name, so that if you run into a dead end at any point, you can easily go back and visit the other people they suggested.

In effect, what you are doing here is trying on jobs to see if they fit you. It is exactly analogous to your going to a clothing store and trying on different suits (or dresses) that you see in their window. Except instead of suits, it is jobs you are trying on.

Deception

There is no honest, open-hearted *technique* that cannot be twisted by those with clever, devious hearts, into some kind of *trick*.

This has happened in the past, with Informational interviewing, and visits to employers. Of course, you will object immediately that, so far as you understand it, Informational interviewers shouldn't be visiting employers -- just, *workers*. Quite so.

But *some* job-hunters in the past have thought, "Wouldn't this be a great *trick* to use on employers -- asking them for some of their time, claiming you need *information*, and then hitting them up for a job?" In case *you*, even for a moment, are tempted to follow in their footsteps, let me gently inform you that employers universally resent such deception, and have in the past usually thrown the liar out of their offices.

One employer told me he said to such a trickster: "You came to see me to ask for some information. And I gladly gave you my time. But now, it is apparent, you really want a job here, and think you found a 'trick' that would open the door here. Let me tell you something: on the basis of what I have just seen of your style of doing things, I wouldn't hire you, if you were the last person in the world. I know this Informational interviewing process well -- I've read *Parachute* -- but by turning it into a *trick,* you give the whole process a bad name, and make life difficult for every job-hunter who comes after you." *Ouch!*

In this Age of Rudeness, Lies, and Manipulation, *you* will want, above all else, to stay a beacon of integrity, truth, and kindness. *That's* the kind of employee employers are *dying* to find.

The quota for those who practice deception is already filled.

And why? Well, the suits that look terrific in the window don't always look so terrific when you see them on you. They don't hang quite right, etc., etc. Likewise, the jobs that look so terrific in the books or in your imagination don't always look so terrific when you see them up close, in all their true reality. You're looking for one that looks terrific in the window, *and* on you.

LOOK FOR THE EXCEPTIONS
TO THE RULES

In trying to go into a new field, or career, look for the exceptions to the rules about what it takes to get into that field. People might *tell* you the rule is:

"In order to do this work, you have to have a master's degree and ten years' experience at it."

But, if you aren't willing to go the long route, you will want to search for the exception: "Yes, but do you know of anyone in the field who got into it *without* that master's degree, and ten years' experience? And where might I find him or her? And if you don't know of any such person, who might know?" Keep asking this sort of question.

Throughout Informational interviewing, one person's word should rarely be taken as *gospel.* There are people out there who will tell you something that absolutely *isn't* so, with every conviction in their being -- because they *think* it's true. Sincerity they have, one hundred percent. Accuracy is something else again. You will need to check and cross-check any information that people tell you or that you read in books (even this one).

Believe me, there are exceptions to almost *every* rule, except where there are rigid examinations one must take, as in medicine or law. Yet, even here, you can get *close* to the profession *without* such exams, as in para-medical, or para-legal, work.

Throughout your Informational interviewing, don't assume anything ("But I just assumed that…") Question *all* assumptions, no matter how many people told you that 'this is the way things are.'

Be careful. Be thorough. Be persistent. This is your life you're working on, and your future. Make it glorious. Whatever it takes, find out the name of your ideal job -- or jobs.

THE OTHER QUESTIONS
FOR INFORMATIONAL INTERVIEWING

As you go about talking to actual workers, you will not only be discovering information about potential careers. You will also, inevitably, be discovering the answers to the other three questions you need to find answers to:

QUESTION #2

What kinds of organizations would and/or do employ people in these careers?

QUESTION #3

Among the kinds of organizations uncovered in the previous question, what are the names of the organizations that I particularly like?

QUESTION #4

Among the organizations that I particularly like, what needs do they have or what outcomes are they trying to produce, that my skills and knowledge could help with?

For, although we can logically separate these questions on paper, in the actual interviewing they are all intertwined. When workers tell you about jobs or careers, *of course* they will also tell you about *kinds* of organizations, and actual names of organizations, that have such jobs - - including what's good or bad about the place where *they* work.

Kinds of organizations is an important question. Don't try to leap over it. For example, suppose you want to be a teacher, in your new career. We turn, then, to our question: what kinds of organizations have such jobs? The answer is not, as you might at first suppose: *"just schools."* No, no, my friend, not just schools. There are countless other *kinds* of organizations and agencies out there which have a teaching arm, and therefore employ teachers. For example, corporate training and educational departments, workshop sponsors, foundations, private research firms, educational consultants, teachers' associations, professional and trade societies, military bases, state and local councils on higher education, fire and police training academies, and so on, and so forth. You want to discover all such places. Your local town or city librarian can be a great help.

'*Kinds* of places' means many things, such as:

- places that would employ you full-time;
- places that would employ you part-time (maybe you'll end up deciding to hold down two or even three part-time jobs, which altogether would add up to one full-time job, in order to give yourself more variety);
- places which you yourself would start up, if you want to be your own boss;
- places that are for profit;
- places that are nonprofit;
- places that take temporary workers, on assignment for one project at a time;
- places that take consultants, one project at a time;
- places that operate with volunteers, etc.

If you *don't* discover *kinds* of places, first, before you get down to actual names, you will automatically be missing many names of organizations that would have been useful to know about. So, stay with these three questions as long as you need to. Since the average job-hunt may last five or six months, you've got the time, believe me. You want to find everything that is in the deck of cards called *Where My New Career Is To Be Found.* Remember, Confucius says: "Never choose a card, except from a full deck."[17]

KEEP CUTTING
THE TERRITORY DOWN:
YOUR 'SEARCH STATEMENT'

As you undoubtedly realize by now, the more you can cut the territory down, the easier it will be to conduct your job-search. Here is where you will want to use some of the other exercises you did in Chapter 10 and elsewhere, as you *refine* and *narrow down* your 'search statement.'

Geography *(Chapter 7)*, for one, can save you from saying, "I'm looking for the names of organizations which hire welders." Taken on its face, that statement could include the whole country - - which is much too broad. But if you've decided you really want to live and work in, let us say, the San Jose area of California, then this cuts your job-search area down to a more manageable size. Now your *search statement* reads: "I'm looking for the names of organizations in the San Jose area which hire welders."

Again, if in Chapter 10, you told yourself that you wanted to work for an organization with fifty or less employees, then you add this to your *search statement*. Thus you further cut the territory down. Your *search statement* now reads: "I'm looking for the names of organizations having fifty or less employees which hire welders, in the San Jose area."

Again, let us say that in Chapter 10, you told yourself you want to work for an organization which works with, or produces, *wheels,* then you add this to your *search statement:* "I'm looking for the names of organizations in the San Jose area, which produce wheels, hire welders, and have fifty or less employees." Now, you're talking! That's a manageable area in which to do your job-search!

HOW DO YOU FIND OUT AN ORGANIZATION'S PROBLEMS OR NEEDS?

Once you've identified organizations *(plural, not singular)* you'd really like to work for, you use every friend you have to find someone who works there. Then you ask them in detail about what's making that workplace thrive, or what's giving that workplace *trouble.*

Also, many job-hunters and career-changers have found that a useful way to explore organizations is to sign up with some

---

17. A very helpful resource during this phase of informational interviewing is *JOB HUNTER'S SOURCEBOOK: Where to find employment leads and other job search resources,* edited by Michelle LeCompte, and published by Gale Research, Inc., Box 33477, Detroit, MI 48232-5477. 1991. See your local library. It is an invaluable resource which tells how to find sources of information and job-leads for a whole variety of occupations. Somebody did their homework.

temporary agency, as mentioned in an earlier chapter. Temporary agencies, in the old days, were solely for clerical workers and secretarial help. But the field has seen an explosion of services in recent years -- according to the Bureau of Labor Statistics, temporary or part-time workers now number over 35 million in number, and represent 29% of the total civilian labor force -- and now there are temporary agencies (at least in the larger cities) for many different occupations. See your local phone book, under 'Temporary Agencies.' The advantage to you of temporary work is that if there is an agency which loans out people with your particular skills and expertise, you get a chance to visit a number of different organizations over a period of several weeks, and see each one from the inside. Not so coincidentally, a number of employers now use temporary agencies as a way for *them* to shop for permanent employees. Both of you get a chance to look at each other, without any long-range commitment.

Another useful way to explore a field, is volunteer work. Because you offer your services *without pay* for a set period of time, it's relatively easy to talk them into letting you work there for a while. Thus you get a chance to know them from the inside. Not so coincidentally, if you decide you would really like to work there permanently, they've had a chance to see you in action, and when you are about to end your volunteer time there, *may* want to hire you permanently. I say *may*. Don't be mad if they simply say, "Thanks very much for helping us out." You've still learned a lot, that will stand you in good stead, in the future.

WHAT IF I GET OFFERED A JOB ALONG THE WAY, WHILE I'M STILL ONLY GATHERING INFORMATION

You probably won't. During this information gathering, you're *not* talking primarily to employers. You're talking to workers. *"Oh, I forgot that."* Understandable.

Nonetheless, an occasional employer *may* stray across your path during all this Informational interviewing. And that employer *may* be so impressed with the carefulness you're showing, in going about your career-change and job-search, that they want to hire you, on the spot. So, it's possible that you might get offered a job while you're still doing your information gathering. Not *likely*, but *possible*. And if that happens, what should you say?

Why, of course, you simply tell them what you're doing. You tell them that the average job-hunter tries to screen a job after they take it. But you are doing what you are *sure* this employer would do if they were in your situation: you are examining careers, fields, industries, jobs, organizations before you decide where you can do your best and most effective work.

And you tell them that during this part of your Informational interviewing, it is premature for you to be thinking about accepting their job offer; you don't know yet where you can be most effective, until you've finished your research.

But, in concluding, you add something along these lines: "Of course, I'm tickled pink that you would want me to be working here. I'm sure you understand, however, that until I've finished my survey and am clearer about where my skills could best be used, I just can't say Yes or No to your kind invitation. But, when I've finished my personal survey, I'll be glad to get back to you about this, as this seems to me to be the kind of place I'd like to work in, and the kind of people I'd like to work with."

You don't walk through any opened doors yet; but neither do you slam them shut.

A SUMMARY FOR THOSE WHO LIKE SUMMARIES

This has been a chapter filled with many ideas. Your head is swimming. You want to recall the central theme of all this research. Okay, here it is:

> Job-hunting is a two-way street. For the time being, whether the places you are interested in, happen to have a vacancy, or happen to *want* you, is irrelevant.
>
> In this dance of life, called the job-hunt, you get first choice: you get to decide first of all whether or not *you* want *them*.
>
> Only after you have decided that, is it appropriate to ask if they also want you.

You're a bunch of jackasses. You work your rear ends off in a trivial course that no one will ever care about again. You're not willing to spend time researching a company that you're interested in working for. Why don't you decide who you want to work for and go after them?

Professor Albert Shapero (again)
The late William H. Davis Professor of The American Free Enterprise System at Ohio State University

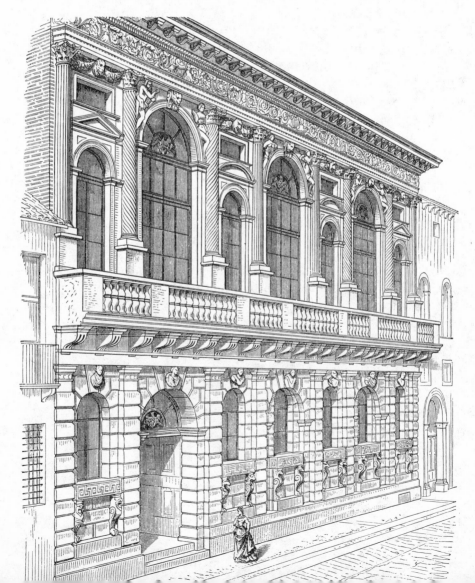

CHAPTER TWELVE

Securing the Interview

How

Do You Find The
Person Who Has The Power
To Hire You For
The Job That You Want?

Chapter 12

Okay, so you've found a place -- better yet, *places* -- where you'd *love* to work. But the person you'd have to see, in order to get hired there, is in an office with a ring of fire around it, three knights in full-armor guarding it, in a castle with fifty-foot walls, surrounded by a wide moat whose deep waters are filled with hungry alligators. And you want to know how to get in there for a job-interview. Right?

Well, it isn't as difficult as it might at first seem. There is a way.

THE  IN PIE

E, as you recall if you read the previous chapter, stands for Interviewing for **E**mployment. Job-interviews are terrifying to a lot of people -- turning the knees to jelly, and causing the palms to sweat. There are two problems: one is even getting in to *see* the person–who–has–the–power–to–hire–you. That's a biggie. The other is persuading them to hire you, once they do agree to see you. That's even more difficult.

Interviewing. *Yuk!*

HOW TO BE AN INTERVIEWING VETERAN

However, most of us make it more difficult for ourselves than it needs to be, because we wait until it's time for the job-interview, before we even think about *how do you do interviewing?* We're rusty. Out of practice. Out of shape. And so, we crash and burn right in front of the prospective employer we care the most about.

But -- as we saw in the previous chapter -- successful job-hunters and career-changers avoid this humiliation by only facing employers after they have been doing interviews *throughout their whole job-hunt.* They realize there are actually three types of *interviews* one must do, in the job-hunt. Early on, in your job-hunt, you tackle interviewing whose purpose is merely that of Practice and pleasure; in the middle of your job-hunt, you tackle interviewing whose purpose is to dig up Information you need about careers, organizations, and employers; and then toward the end of your job-hunt, you approach *employers* for the first time, to see about Employment, or getting hired there -- but by then you're *an interviewing veteran.* Voila! P- I -E is the key.

That's the way to tackle it. Most job-hunters, of course, don't.

Half Our 'Ills' In Life Are Self-Inflicted.

This is a hard truth for me to write about, and hard for each of us to take to heart in our own lives.

However, here it is: when we have a problem, life often shows us the solution, but we duck it because it involves *work,* and we wait instead for magic -- which never comes. And so, the problem remains.

We like then to pretend to ourselves that some mysterious outside influence -- life, the labor market, the government, an uncaring society -- is *doing this* to us. But by refusing to adopt the solution life has shown us, it is actually we who are doing it to ourselves.

We are like prisoners in a cell where the jailor is gone and the door is open. But we still just sit there, claiming we are a prisoner still.

To apply this to our present problem: the P–I–E method *will* solve the terror of *interviewing,* on which our job-hunt depends. But most of us duck doing the P–I–E method because it involves *work,* and we hope instead for magic -- which never comes. And so, interviewing continues to terrify us.

TRAVELS WITH FARLEY by Phil Frank © 1982 Field Enterprises, Inc. Courtesy of Field Newspaper Syndicate

If you would be wise beyond your years, my friend, go back and read *and do* Chapter 11. That's how you defang interviewing of all its terrors.

Then you are fully ready to tackle the two problems we are about to discuss: getting in to *see* the person–who–has–the–power–to–hire–you (which is the subject of *this* chapter). And persuading them to hire you, once they do agree to see you (which we deal with in the next).

THE FIRST CRUCIAL QUESTION: HOW LARGE IS THE ORGANIZATION?

All techniques or strategies for securing an interview fall into two groups, *depending* on whether the organization you are trying to approach is a relatively large organization, *or* is one which has twenty-five or less employees.

Most discussions of job-interviewing *assume* you are approaching a large organization - - you know, the ones where you need a floor-plan of the building, and an alphabetical directory of the staff. There *are* huge problems in approaching such giants for a job-interview - - not the least of which is that they are doing more layoffs than hiring, here in the '90s.

But two-thirds of all new openings are found in small organizations.

And, with a small organization, there is no Personnel or Human Resources Department to screen you out.

With a small organization, you don't need to wait until there's a *known* vacancy, because they rarely advertise vacancies even when there is one. You just go there and ask if they need someone.

With a small organization, if it's growing, there is a greater likelihood that they will be willing to create a new position for you, *if they think you are too good to let you slip out of their grasp.*

With a small organization, there's no problem in identifying the person–who–has–the–power–to–hire–you. It's *the boss.* Everyone there knows who it is. They can point to his or her office door, easily.

With a small organization, you do not need to approach them through the mail; you can go in to see the boss. And if, by chance, he or she is well protected from intruders, it is relatively easy to figure out how to get around *that.* Contacts are the answer, as we shall see.

All this adds up to the fact that if figuring out how–to–get–in–for–a–job–interview is a big problem for you, the solution is for you to target small organizations *exclusively.*

After you've figured out, as in the previous chapter, what your ideal job looks like, and where the workplaces are that have such jobs, in your chosen geographical area, then you collect the names and addresses of those workplaces with 25 or less employees, and go after them. Look particularly for small organizations that are *established* or *growing.*

THE FOUR WAYS TO APPROACH LARGE ORGANIZATIONS FOR AN INTERVIEW

In securing job-interviews, it's the large organizations that are the problem - - the ones, as I mentioned above, where you need a floor-plan of the building, and an alphabetical directory of the staff. The ones where you can't even figure out *who* is the person–who–has–the–power–to–hire–you, much less get in to see them.

There is a way, as I will make clear.

But most job-hunters *don't* even *try* to find out *who* is the person–who–has–the–power–to–hire–you. They tend to approach each large organization in a general, haphazard, scatter-shot fashion. And their methods of approach break down into four. I will list them in order of *decreasing* effectiveness. You will notice, of course, that many job-hunters use these approaches with small organizations, as well as large:

1. *The Most Effective.* Using your personal acquaintances or **contacts,** you find out *who* at that organization has the power to hire you for the position you have in mind - - in a way I shall describe a little later.

Then you use your contacts to help you secure an appointment there, with that person–who–has–the–power–to–hire–you.

Using this direct approach, you will probably never see a job application, at least until after you are hired.

When used with a number of organizations, and not just one, this method has an 86% effectiveness rate, for getting an interview and, subsequently, a job.

2. *The Next Most Effective.* You go face-to-face at that organization, to seek a job, without any introductions or use of third-parties.

Eighty-five percent of all organizations these days do *not* have personnel departments *(or, as they prefer to be called now, Human Resources Departments),* so when you go face-to-face to 85% of all places, you simply talk to the receptionist at the front office.

In the case of those 15% which *do* have personnel offices or departments - - and that includes *all* really large organizations - - when you go face-to-face you talk to the personnel people there.

Whether with receptionist or personnel department, you will probably be asked to fill out a job application. Job applications are forms which have such simple questions as: Name, Address, Age, Places of Previous Employment, etc. Such applications vary greatly in their complexity, from ones used by fast-food chains, to those used by, say, engineering firms. If you've never seen one in your life, you should familiarize yourself with them. One way to do this without jeopardy is to go to visit some fast-food place or any large organization that has a personnel department, and simply *ask* for a job application, then take it home with you. There you can study it, and take a stab at filling it out, just for practice. File it in the waste basket, after you've learned what you need to know. Now you know what an application form looks like, and how to fill it out. I hope you never need to.

This method of going face-to-face at an organization, when used with a number of organizations, and not just one, has an effectiveness rate that's basically half that of the one above: only 47.7% get an interview and job by using this approach.

The reason for this drop in effectiveness, so far as you the job-hunter is concerned, is due to the fact that receptionists or personnel departments hardly ever have the power to hire, except for entry-level positions. They exist primarily to screen you before passing you on, if they ever do, to some person 'upstairs' - - namely, the person–who–has–the–power–to–hire–you. So, your hope is that, after the application, and perhaps an interview, they will pass you on to said person. In such a case, you end up where you would have directly with approach #1, above, except that here an extra step has been introduced - - an extra step where you may *unnecessarily* get screened out, I might add. It happens often enough to make one cry.

However, notwithstanding the mere 47.7% effectiveness rate I quoted above, it should be noted that in their pioneering study of the job-hunt some years ago, *The Job Hunt: Job-Seeking Behavior of Unemployed Workers in a Local Economy,* Harvey Belitsky and Harold A. Sheppard discovered that going face-to-face at a workplace was *the* most effective job-hunting method for blue-collar workers.

3. *The Next Most Ineffective.* (Yes, that means 'next to the worst.') With this approach, you contact the organization first of all through the mail, by sending them your resume or some covering letter, and hoping *they* will invite *you* in. Your resume or covering letter serves in lieu of a job application, and functions as a kind of extended calling-card - - one that you *hope* will pique the employer's interest.

This is job-hunters' favorite way of approaching an organization for a job-interview. Unjustifiably so. True, when it works, it works well enough, *but* you can approach eight hundred organizations by mail (as millions of job-hunters have) and get not one invitation to come in for an interview. Effectiveness rate, in that case, zero.

Taken overall, though, it has an 8% effectiveness rate in getting an interview and subsequently a job, when used with a number of organizations, and not just one. That is to say, this method - - approaching large organizations first of all through the mail - - has an effectiveness rate that is only one-sixth that of the method above.

If you don't know why, you may have skipped Chapter 3, or read it three months ago. To refresh your memory, the reason in a nutshell is this: this 'mail approach' enables employers to screen you out *real fast*, without ever 'wasting time' on an interview.

Most employers, or their subordinates, can *screen you out* on the basis of your resume in approximately thirty seconds, if it sits in a stack of fifty, say, on their desk. And if it sits in a stack of several hundred resumes, the person who is doing the screening picks up speed, and your resume may get as little as eight seconds, by actual count. So, in eight to thirty seconds, *you're gone.*

The organizations which have the time and the budget for it will subsequently send you a nice polite acknowledgement and turn-down. (Job-hunters seem to place an inordinate amount of hope upon the fact that they got a letter - - any letter - - from an organization they've applied to. Believe me, even when they say, *However, we will keep your resume on file and should anything...*it's a turndown.) Those organizations which have neither the time nor the budget will not even send you a letter. You'll have to guess whether they ever even saw your resume.

4. *The Most Ineffective.* Going to some centralized place (such as a Job Fair) where employers come to hire people - - and getting an interview with the representative there. If you are in college, the analog of this is a recruiter *from the organization that interests you* coming to your campus, when you are a junior or senior, to interview you. If you're lucky.

This method *looks as though* it should have a 100% effectiveness rate in getting an interview. This is, however, an illusion, for two reasons.

First of all, there's no assurance that the large organzation you are particularly interested in will even be there. If it's not there, the effectiveness of this particular approach to getting an interview is zero.

Secondly, even assuming it is there, your concern is not merely to get an interview with those people -- *that's* easy. You could go by their personnel department and get *that*.

No, your concern *has to be* to get an interview with one particular person: namely *(all together now)* the actual person–who–has–the–power–to–hire–you, for the job you want. In the case of these centralized job fairs or recruiter visits to campuses, you *can* be talking to the actual employer, but *in most cases* you are talking instead to a representative -- who must *pass you on,* if they are impressed with you. In other words, that representative has a function similar if not identical to that of their personnel department, and in many cases they *are* from their personnel department.

Because of this, the effectiveness of this approach in getting you an interview with the actual person–who–has–the–power–to–hire–you, then leading to a job, at the organization of your choice is *somewhere* between 8% and zero, whether used with a number of organizations, or just one.

Okay, these are the four ways to approach the large organization of your choice for a job-interview.

Now, you choose: which approach do you want to use? One that gets you a job-interview with the organization you have targeted:

- ☐ Zero percent of the time
- ☐ 8% of the time
- ☐ 47.7% of the time
- ☐ 86% of the time

It's your *call*. Personally, I vote for the 86% approach.

AN EMPLOYER'S LIFE
IS NOT AN 'APPY ONE

While *you* are bemoaning the difficulty of getting in to see an employer of your choice - - for a job-interview - - employers are having an equally difficult time getting interviews with the person *they* are looking for: namely, you.

We can illustrate this with Personnel Departments, or Human Resources Departments. In those relatively few organizations which have them, you would think they would make an employer's life a lot easier, when hiring time has come. Surely they keep the person–who–has–the–power–to–hire from being inundated with masses of job-hunters, while passing on up to him (or her) the cream of the crop - - after sifting through hundreds of resumes, if need be, from eager candidates.

Au contraire, mon ami. In practice, the departments often unwittingly work against the employer's best interests. More people get screened out *downstairs* than is necessary, because no personnel employee wants some *upstairs* executive screaming, "You're sending me too many people." Therefore, Personnel tends to live by the motto: *"When in doubt, screen them out."* Because of Personnel's over-zealous screening, the very people the employer was looking for, never make it to the job-interview, because they were *screened out* in the early stages of that organization's own process. It's like a second-seeded player at Wimbledon being knocked out of the tennis tournament by an unseeded player, in the very first round.

In addition, the hiring executive is sometimes *dismayed* to have to see people who should have gotten screened out by Personnel, but didn't. That's because Personnel is not always clear about what is wanted *upstairs*. People–who–have–the–power–to–hire sometimes don't define exactly what they're looking for, so Personnel is often left to guess. Consequently, they often send *upstairs* people who are not what the job requires, *thinking* they've found a gorgeous match.

The moral of this tale has three parts:

(1) Many times, employers don't get to see candidates who match the job, but do get to see candidates who don't match the job. And this, in spite of a mechanism that is supposed to keep

this from happening. *It is to tear out the hair.*

(2) Employers have just as much trouble getting interviews with *qualified* candidates, as *you* have getting interviews with *qualified* employers -- i.e., with those employers who have the power to hire you for the job that you want and can do best.

(3) Obviously, as we have seen throughout our journey together, the whole job-hunting process in this country is Neanderthal. But, this "Neanderthal-ness" doesn't just hurt you, the job-hunter. *It hurts the employer* as much as it does you.

HOW TO BE THE ANSWER
TO AN EMPLOYER'S PRAYERS

I cannot tell you the number of employers I know who can't figure out how to find the right employee. It is absolutely mind-boggling.

But, if you took the trouble to do Chapters 9, 10, and 11, then you are the right employee for whatever place or places you thoughtfully choose to approach --

because you took the trouble to figure out what your favorite and best skills are, and

because you took the trouble to figure out what your favorite and best subjects are, and

because you took the trouble to figure out what places have such jobs, and

because you took the trouble to figure out which of these offered a match between what they need and what you have to offer, and

because you took the trouble to figure out who there has the power to hire you.

If you, the right employee, now present yourself directly to the person–who–has–the–power–to–hire–you, you are not only answering your own prayers. You are answering the employer's, as well.

You are *just* what the employer is looking for, but didn't know how to find -- until *you* took the trouble to do this matching-up *for* him -- or her.

The only questions that will still be left open, during the job-interview, will be whether or not the employer can *perceive* that you are the right employee; *and* whether or not your *personalities* match. For in the end, as Nathan Azrin says, the hiring process is much more like *dating* than it is like *buying a used car.*

HOW DO I FIND OUT WHO IS
THE PERSON WHO HAS
THE POWER TO HIRE ME?

As I said before, in a small organization with 25 or less employees, this is an easy problem. Calling the place and asking for the name of the boss, should do it. It's what we call *The One-Minute Research Project.*

But if the place where you are dying to work is a much larger organization, then the answer is: "Through the research you already did, and through your contacts."

CONTACTS, CONTACTS,
WHO'S GOT CONTACTS?

We need to begin with some definitions, since this subject is commonly misunderstood by many job-hunters.

Every person you know, is a contact.

Every member of your family.

Every friend of yours.

Every person in your address book.

Every person on your Christmas-card list.

Every merchant or salesperson you ever deal with.

Every person who comes to your apartment or house to do any kind of repairs or maintenance work.

Every check-out clerk you know.

Every gas station attendant you know.

Every leisure partner you have, as for walking, exercising, swimming, or whatever.

Every doctor, or medical professional you know,

Every professor, teacher, etc. you once knew or maybe still know how to get ahold of.

Every clergyperson, rabbi, or religious leader you know.

Every person in your church, synagogue, mosque, or religious assembly.

Everyone you know in Rotary, Kiwanis, Lions, or other service organizations.

Every person you are newly introduced to.

Every person you meet, stumble across, or blunder into, during your job-hunt, whose name, address, and phone number you have the grace to ask for.

Got the picture?

Some job-hunters have written to tell me they cultivate new contacts wherever they go. For example, if they go to hear a speaker on some subject that interests them, they make it a point to join the crowd that gathers 'round the speaker at the end of the talk, and - - with notepad poised - - ask such questions as: "Is there anything special that people with my expertise can do?" And here they mention their specialty: computer scientist, health professional, chemist, writer, or whatever. Very useful information has thus been turned up. You can also ask if you can contact the speaker for further information - - "and at what address?"

Conventions, likewise, afford rich opportunities to make contacts.

Another way people have cultivated contacts, is to leave a message on their telephone answering machine which tells everyone who calls, what information they are looking for. One job-hunter used the following message: "This is the recently laid off John Smith. I'm not home right now because I'm out looking for a good job as a computer trouble-shooter in the telecommunications field; if you have any leads or just want to leave a message, please leave it after the tone."

You may also cultivate contacts by studying the *things* that you like to work with, and then writing to the manufacturer of that *thing* to ask them for a list of organizations in your geographical area which use that *thing*. For example, if you like to work on a particular machine, you would write to the manufacturer of that machine, and ask for names of organizations in your geographical area which use that machine. Some manufacturers will not be at all responsive to such an inquiry; but others will, and may give you some very helpful leads.

GET OUT THE FILE CARDS

Now, because your memory is going to be overloaded during your job-hunt or career-change, it is useful, as you begin your job-hunt, to put each of the above names on a 3 × 5 card, with addresses, phone numbers, and anything about where they work or who they know that may be of use at a later date. Go back over those cards frequently.

Yes, of course that adds up to *a lot* of file cards. You've got *a lot* of contacts. That's the whole point.

You may need every one of them.

Whenever a job-hunter writes me and tells me they've run into a brick wall, as far as finding out names of organizations or names of the person–who–has–the–power–to–hire is concerned, the problem *always* turns out to be: they aren't making sufficient use of their contacts.

The more people you know, the more people you meet, the more people you talk to, the more people you enlist as part of your own personal job-hunting network, the better your job-finding success is likely to be.

It takes about eighty pairs of eyes, and ears, to help find the career, the workplace, the job that you are looking for.

Your contacts are those eyes and ears.

They are what will help you get the ideal job you are looking for.

HOW DO YOU USE
YOUR CONTACTS?

Well, let's say it is a mythical organization called *Mythical Corporation* that interests you.

You know the kind of job you'd like to get there, but first you want to find out the name of the person–who–has–the–power–to–hire–you there. What do you do?

If it's a large organization, you go to your local public library, and search the directories there that I listed at the end of the previous chapter. Hopefully that search will yield the name of the person you want.

If it doesn't, which will particularly be the case with smaller organizations, *then you turn to your contacts.*

You approach as many people as necessary, among all those you know, and you ask each of them, "Do you know anyone who works, or used to work, at *Mythical Corporation?*"

You ask that question again and again of *everyone* who is on your file cards, until you find someone who says, *"Yes, I do."*

Then you ask them:

• "What is the name of the person you know who works, or used to work, at *Mythical Corporation?* Do you have their phone number and/or address?"

• "Do you think it would be worth my while to go see them?"

• "May I tell them it was you who recommended that I talk with them?"

• "Would you be willing to call ahead, to set up an appointment for me, and tell them who I am?"

You may then want to conduct the appointment over the phone, at an agreed-upon time, or you may want to go see them face-to-face, away from their worksite.

If you do go see them, you do *not* try to travel across town so as to arrive there right on time - - because this makes no allowance for the normal unpredictable things that happen to delay us all, when we least expect it. No, you always leave for the appointment with about double the time you think it will take to get there, which means you will usually arrive at the site ahead of time. Then you go get a cup of coffee nearby, or you walk around the block if you need to, until it's actually time for the appointment. Then you go in the front door right on time.

(When a reporter arrived late, once, for an appointment with a very famous person, that person replied, "How dare you keep me waiting? Are you that stupid?" You may wince at the put-down, *but* that's how a lot of people *feel* about people who are late for appointments, even if they would *never* say it, or at any rate not so strongly. You *don't* want anyone thinking that about *you* - - and especially not, when you are coming to them to ask for their help.)

After the usual polite chit-chat, you ask them the question you are dying to know. Because they are *inside* the organization that interests you, they are usually able to give you the exact answer to your question: "Who would have the power to hire me here, for this kind of position *(which you then describe)?*"

Then you further ask them what they can tell you about that person's job, that person's interests, and anything about their style of interviewing.

You also ask them about the organization, in general, for any information that they might think useful for you to know.

Finally, you ask them if they could help you get an appointment with that person.

GETTING IN

If the contact you are talking to, doesn't know the person–who–has–the–power–to–hire well enough to get you an interview, then you thank them for their time and help -- get their exact name and address, so you can send a thank-you note that night.

And then, you go back to your contacts -- now armed with the name of the person you are trying to get in to see -- and pose a new question. Approaching as many of your contacts as necessary, you ask each of them, "Do you know Ms. or Mr. See, at *Mythical Corporation* or do you know someone who does?"

You ask that question again and again of *everyone* who is on your file cards, until you find someone who says, *"Yes, I do."*

Then of course, over the phone or -- better -- in person, you ask them the same familiar questions:

- "What can you tell me about him -- or her?"
- "Given the kind of job I am looking for *(which you here describe)*, do you think it would be worth my while to go see them?"
- "May I tell them you recommended that I talk with them?"
- "Do you have their phone number and/or address?"
- "Would you be willing to call ahead, to set up an appointment for me, and tell them who I am?"

Getting in to see someone, even for the purpose of a job-interview, is not that difficult. Everyone has friends, including this person–who–has–the–power–to–hire–you. You are simply approaching them through their friends. And you are doing this, not as one who is coming to ask a favor. You are doing it as one who is coming to offer a gift. You are coming not as 'job-beggar,' but as 'resource person.'

CONCLUSION

I close this chapter with my favorite (true) story about approaching an organization. This concerns a job-hunter in Virginia. He decided he wanted to work for a particular health-care organization in that State, and not knowing any better, he approached them by visiting their Personnel department. After dutifully filling out a job-application, and talking to someone there in that department, he was told there were no jobs available. Stop. Period. End of story.

Approximately three months later he learned about the technique of approaching your favorite organization by using contacts. He did the kind of work described above, and succeeded in getting an interview with the person–who–had–the–power–to–hire–him for the position he was interested in. The two of them hit it off, immediately. The appointment went swimmingly. "You're hired," said the person–who–had–the–power–to–hire–him. "I'll call Personnel and tell them you're hired, and that you'll be down to fill out the necessary stuff."

Our job-hunter never once mentioned that he had previously approached that same organization through that same Personnel department, and been turned down.

*Well, yes, you do have
great big teeth; but, never mind
that. You were great to at
least grant me this interview.*

Little Red Riding Hood

CHAPTER THIRTEEN

Conducting
The
Interview

Chapter 13

IS THIS ANY WAY
TO RUN A BUSINESS

To begin with, the job-interview is not a very reliable way of choosing an employee. In a survey conducted among a dozen top United Kingdom employers, and reported in the *Financial Times Career Guide 1989* there, it was discovered that the chances of an employer finding a good employee through the hiring interview was only 3% better than if they had picked a name out of a hat. In a further ironic finding, it was discovered that if the interview were conducted by someone who would be working directly with the candidate, the success rate dropped to 2% below that of picking a name out of a hat. And if the interview were conducted by a personnel expert, the success rate dropped to 10% below that of picking a name out of a hat.

No, I don't know how they came up with this comparison. But it is more than amusing; it strikes me as probably true. I have watched so-called personnel experts make wretchedly bad choices about hiring for their own office, and when they would morosely confess this some months later, over lunch, I would puzzle out loud, "If we don't even know how to hire well, ourselves, how do you keep a straight face when you're called in as consultant to another organization?" And they would ruefully reply, "We treat it as though it were a science."

The job-interview is not a science, it is a very very hazy art, done badly by most of its employer-practitioners, in spite of their best intentions and goodwill.

Moreover, it requires you as job-hunter to do something that runs against the grain, for many people. You are required to *compete* with others, and show the employer why you are *better* than the other people competing for the same job. Many job-hunters *hate* this aspect of job-interviewing.

I once met an eighty-year-old woman who was telling me about a different culture altogether. Back in the early thirties, she said, there was a small mine up in the hills above the town where she lived. One day, the news in the town was that the mine was hiring, at a little shack up in the hills. The men in the town, many of whom were out of work, lined up early outside the hiring shack, to try to get those jobs. The men were called in, one at a time. Her father was in the line, she said, and while waiting, he struck up a conversation with the man in the line behind him. That conversation was interrupted when it was her father's turn to go into the shack. The man who was hiring there, said to him, "Well, you're lucky. This is the last job I have to give out, today." "Well, in that case," replied her father, "give it to the next man out there. He has five children depending on him to feed them, while I have only three. I'll find another job, I'm sure."

I'm sure this nobility of spirit was not *universal* in that Age. But that it existed at all, compared to the current popular *rule* of life -- *every man for himself,* or *every woman for herself* -- seems stirring and inspiring. The homeless, the 1992 L.A. riots and other urban revolts, all tell us how badly we need to rediscover this kind of generosity, this perception that all mankind is a family, in which those who are less in need must protect those who are more in need. By comparison, the sometimes cut-throat competition of our Day is *extremely* depressing, and even obscene. More to the point, the job-interview process in our country, and elsewhere in the world, *contributes* to this continuing fragmentation of the human family.

Nonetheless, the job-interview, with all its *required* competition, and unscientific nature, is the doorway -- the *only* doorway -- to getting a job in today's world of work, if you would work for another. So, you're going to have to participate in the whole ritual, no matter how dumb and Neanderthal it may seem to your simple common sense.

The only refuge from it is to go into business for yourself (see Chapter 7). Even then, it is likely that eventually you will have to hire someone else, in which case you'll be back into the job-interview process -- only, this time, on the other side of the table. *(Remember to bring the hat, to put the names in!)*

THE ELEVEN MOST IMPORTANT TRUTHS ABOUT A JOB-INTERVIEW

Whole books have been written about the job-interview, so obviously there's a lot that can be said.

But over the years it has seemed to me that there are eleven really important, basic truths about interviewing, which stand out above all the rest. I list those eleven -- with titles -- on the file cards which follow, along with some brief commentary:

BEFORE THE INTERVIEW: PRACTICE

1. Before you go on job-interviews, be sure to practice the PIE process first (see page 268) until you are so used to talking with people about mutual interests, that interviewing has lost all of its terrors for you.

If you have several organizations to interview at, you should probably save the interview you care the most about until last, so you can make all your mistakes at the interviews you don't care about as much.

The manner in which you do your interviews -- and the manner in which you would do the job you are seeking -- are not assumed by most employers to be two unrelated subjects, but one and the same. A

slipshod half-hearted interview is taken as a warning that you might do a slipshod half-hearted job, were they foolish enough to hire you. Therefore, prepare thoroughly for each interview; know a lot about the place, before you walk in.

INTERVIEWING IS A TWO-WAY STREET

2. Your natural question to yourself, as you approach any job-interview, will be, "How do I convince this employer to hire me?" Wrong question. It implies that you have already made up your mind that this would be a grand person to work for, so all that remains is for you to sell yourself. That is rarely the case. In most cases, you don't know enough yet, to say that -- despite all your research. You have to use the job-interview as a chance to gather further information about this organization, and this boss, before you can decide, "Do I really want to work here?" That's the nature of the job-interview: each of you has to gather information, and if you both like what you see, then each has to 'sell' the other on the idea of working there.

If you understand *this* about an interview, you will be ahead of 98% of all other job-hunters - - who all too often go to the job-interview as a lamb goes to the slaughter. You *are* on trial, of course, in the employer's eyes. *But,* so is the employer and that organization, in *your* eyes. This is what makes the job-interview tolerable or sometimes *borderline* enjoyable: you are studying everything about this employer, at the same time that they are studying everything about you.

Two people, both sizing each other up. You know what that reminds you of. Dating. Well, the job-interview is indeed every bit like 'the dating game.' Both of you have to like each other, before you can even discuss the question of *'going steady,'* i.e., a job.

The importance of your actively weighing this organization and this job, during the job-interview, cannot be overstated. The tradition in our country is to find a job, take it, and then try to figure out, after you're in it, whether it is a good job or not.

You're trying to go against that tradition, as any sensible job-hunter or career-changer should, by finding out whether or not you'd like to work there, *before* you accept a job there. In so doing, you're saving *them* grief as well as *yourself*.

Books on interviewing, of which there are many,[1] often publish lists of up to eighty-nine questions that an employer may ask you. They list things like:

- Tell me about yourself.
- Why are you applying for this job?
- What do you know about this job or company?
- How would you describe yourself?
- What are your major strengths?
- What is your greatest weakness?
- What type of work do you like to do best?
- What are your interests outside of work?
- What accomplishment gave you the greatest satisfaction?
- What was your worst mistake?
- Why did you leave your last job?
- Why were you fired (if you were)?
- How does your education or experience relate to this job?
- Where do you see yourself five years from now?
- What are your goals in life?
- How much did you make at your last job?

But they all boil down, in essence, to the five basic questions on the file card on the next page. And this is the case, even if the interview begins and ends with these five questions never once being uttered aloud. They're there, beneath the surface of the conversation, all the time.

1. Martin John Yate, *Knock 'Em Dead with Great Answers to Tough Interview Questions*. Bob Adams, Inc., 260 Center St., Holbrook, MA 02343. 1992.

H. Anthony Medley, *Sweaty Palms: The Neglected Art of Being Interviewed*. Ten Speed Press, Box 7123, Berkeley, CA 94707. 1992, revised.

David Krause, *Get the Best Jobs in DP: The Computer Professional's Technical Interview Guide*. Mind Management, 24304 100th Ave. West, Edmonds, WA 98020. 1989. How to survive interviews that are essentially tests of your technical expertise.

Phillip G. Zimbardo, *Shyness, What It Is, What to Do About It*. Jove Publications, 757 Third Ave., New York, NY 10017. 1977.

David Bowman and Ronald Kweskin, *Q: How Do I Find the Right Job? A: Ask the Experts*. John Wiley & Sons, Inc., Professional and Trade Division, 605 Third Ave., New York, NY 10158-0012. 1990.

John Caple, *The Ultimate Interview*. Doubleday, 666 Fifth Ave., New York, NY 10103. 1991.

WHAT THE EMPLOYER IS TRYING TO FIND OUT

3. Beneath the dozens of Possible Questions that employers may ask in a job-interview, there are really only five basic ones:

1. "Why are you here?" They mean by this, why did you pick out our organization to seek a job at?

2. "What can you do for us?" They mean by this, what are your skills and your fields of knowledge?

3. "What kind of person are you?" They mean by this, do you have a personality that they will enjoy working with, or not? Do you get along with people? What are your values?

4. Assuming you can do the job, "what distinguishes you from nineteen other people who can do the same thing?"

5. "Can we afford you?" They mean by that, if they decide they want you, what will it take to get you, and are they willing and able to pay that amount?

The good news is that since there are really only five questions, there are really only five answers you need to know. But, you'd *better* know those five answers. Of course, if you did your homework (Chapters 9, 10, and 11) you will. If you didn't, you won't. Period. End of story.

WHAT YOU ARE TRYING TO FIND OUT

4. The most basic thing you are trying to figure out, as described above, is do you want to work there? (The answer is not necessarily Yes.)

If you have any kind of a real or imagined handicap -- age, inexperience, physical or mental disability, ethnic background, etc. -- you are also trying to find out which kind of employer you are talking to:

a) Those who are bothered by your handicap

b) Those who are not bothered by your handicap

If you discover you are talking to one who is bothered, you want to thank them for their time and quickly excuse yourself. If you discover this employer isn't bothered by your handicap, then you want to continue the discussion.

Now, you may think this aphorism about there being two kinds of employers is true, but *so what?* So, a lot. It means you can't say something like *'Employers' won't hire me.* There's no such thing as 'Employers,' because (let's all say it together, now):

> There are two kinds of employers *out there:*
>
> • those who *will* be put off by your handicaps, and therefore *won't* hire you;
>
> AND
>
> • those who will *not* be put off by your handicaps, and therefore *will* hire you, if you are qualified for the job.

You are only looking for the second kind of employer, who is *not* put off by your handicap, and therefore will hire you if you can do the job. The first kind of employer is of no interest to you, except as they may give you leads to the second -- and you must not allow yourself to become discouraged because you are running into a lot of *them,* and they are all rejecting you.

To take a 'worst case' scenario, if out of 100 employers, 90 would be bothered by your handicap or your history, but 10 wouldn't care about it in the slightest - - so long as you can do the work well - - your task is to make your way as quickly as you can through the 90, and find those other 10. They are the only ones you want to work for, anyway. You wouldn't *really* want to work for those who are prejudiced against you, now would you? We all want to work for an employer who's rootin' for us to succeed, not one who's just waiting for us to fall flat on our face.

"I'll tell you why I want this job. I thrive on challenges. I like being stretched to my full capacity. I like solving problems. Also, my car is about to be repossessed."

In reading all this, I'm sure you think *you've* got the one handicap that *all* employers would find bothersome. For example, that you're over 60 years old, and 'employers' wouldn't want someone that old. Okay, let's all repeat it again:

> "All employers divide into two groups: 1) those who would be put off by your age, and 2) those who would not be put off by your age, so long as you are a good worker. Your job is to find the second kind of employer, and not pay any attention to the first."

And so it goes. So it always goes.

> ## WHAT THE EMPLOYER DOES DURING THE INTERTERVIEW
>
> **5.** The employer observes everything about you and also asks questions. Most of those questions are about your past. But their intent is to find something in your past, that will predict the future -- because, in the end, all any employer can really be interested in is the future. You need to pay attention to the time frame of the employer's questions. For example, "Where did you go to high school?" is in the past. If the questions' time frame stays stuck in the past, you are not likely to be hired. As the employer's questions move, in their time frame, from being preoccupied with the distant past, to the near past, to the present, and then to the future, this is very favorable for you. It means they're thinking seriously about hiring you.

Distant past: *"Where did you grow up?"*

Near past: *"Tell me about your last job."*

Present: *"What kind of a job are you looking for?"*

Future: *"If you were offered this job, where would you see yourself five years from now?"*

I will have more to say about the employer's questions, at the end of this chapter.

Now -- about the employer observing you. It is likely that *nothing* will escape the scrutiny of the person across the desk from you. And I mean: your haircut or hairdo; your manner of dress; your posture; your use of your hands; your body odor or perfume; your breath (good or bad); your fingernails (dirty or clean, clipped or not); the sound of your voice; the way in which you do or don't interrupt; the hesitant or assured manner in which you ask your questions or give your answers; your values as evidenced by the things which impress you or don't impress you in the office, in your history, and so on; the carefulness with which you did or didn't research this company before you came in; the thoroughness with which you know your skills and strengths; your awareness of what you are willing to sacrifice in order to get this job *and* what you are *not* willing to sacrifice in order to get this job; your enthusiasm for your work; and blah, blah, blah. We can also throw in whether or not you smoke *(in a race between two equally qualified people, the nonsmoker will win out over the smoker 94% of the time, according to a study done by a professor of business at Seattle University);* whether, if at lunch, you order a drink or not; whether you show courtesy to the receptionist, secretary, waiter or waitress, or not; and so forth. *Everything* is grist for the mill, as the employer tries to divine "what kind of person is this?" What the employer will typically use to screen you *out,* are:

- any signs of dishonesty or lying;
- any signs of irresponsibility or tendency to goof off;
- any sign of arrogance or excessive aggressiveness;
- any sign of tardiness or failure to keep appointments and commitments on time, including the job-interview;
- any sign of not following instructions or obeying rules;
- any sign of constant complaining or blaming things on others;
- any sign of laziness or lack of motivation;
- any sign of a lack of enthusiasm for this organization and what it is trying to do;
- any sign of instability, inappropriate response, and the like.

Since the employer will probably end up having to fire anyone with these personality traits, the employer would like to find these things out *now* rather than later.

Beyond these tangibles, there are the intangibles of *making a good impression.* Study after study has confirmed that if you are a male, you will make a better impression if:

- your hair or beard are neatly trimmed;
- you have obviously freshly bathed, used a deodorant and mouthwash, and have clean fingernails;
- you have freshly laundered clothes on, and a suit rather than a sports outfit, and sit without slouching;
- your breath does not dispense gallons of garlic, onion, stale tobacco, or strong drink, into the enclosed office air;

- your shoes are neatly polished, and your pants have a sharp crease;
- you are not wafting tons of after-shave cologne fifteen feet ahead of you.

And, if you are a female, you will make a better impression if:

- your hair is newly 'permed' or 'coiffed';
- you have obviously freshly bathed, used a deodorant and mouthwash, and have clean or nicely manicured finger-nails;
- you wear a bra, freshly cleaned clothes, a suit or sophisti-cated-looking dress, and sit without slouching;
- your breath does not dispense gallons of garlic, onion, stale tobacco, or strong drink, into the enclosed office air;
- you wear shoes rather than sandals;
- you are not wafting tons of perfume fifteen feet ahead of you.

Now please, dear friend, do not send me mail telling me how asinine you think some of these 'requirements' are. I *know* that. I'm only reporting what study after study reveals affects whether or not you get hired. There are of course employers who care about none of these things, and will hire you if you can do the job. Period. Do remember, however, that where you have to work with other people, these things are often given a lot of weight. This employer already has other employees; he or she wants to know that you will not alienate them, or cause friction. You must, at least generally, 'fit in.'

If you don't want to 'fit in,' then you might want to consider forming your own (one-person) business, and - - particularly if it is a mail-order business - - you can then dress or conduct your-self just as you darn please, and no one will notice. If, however, you want to work for someone else, all the above factors are a part of what the employer is probably noticing, *and* evaluating.

WHAT YOU MUST DO
DURING THE INTERVIEW

6.   You are trying to find out the answers to five questions. Though they will rarely ever be said out loud, you must keep them in your head throughout the interview:

1. What does this job involve?

2. Do my skills truly match this job?

3. Are you the kind of people I would like to work with?

4. If we do match, can I persuade you that there is something unique about me, that makes me different from nineteen other people who can do the same thing I can do?

5. Can I persuade you to hire me, and at the salary I need or want?

Let's recapitulate. Your role during the interview is:

1) to find out the information that you need to know, in order to decide whether you want to work there or not; and,

2) to help the employer find out the information that he or she needs to know, in order to decide whether they want to hire you or not.

If you did the homework in Chapters 9, 10, 11, and 12 in this book, you might begin the interview by reporting to them just exactly how you've been conducting your job-hunt, and what impressed you so much about *their* organization during your research, that you decided to come in and talk to them about a job. Then you can devote your attention, during the remainder of the interview, to exploring the five questions on the file card above.

If you're not there about a job that already exists, but rather, you want them to *create* a job for you, then your five questions get changed into four statements:

1. What you like about this organization.

2. What sorts of needs you find intriguing in this field and in

this organization (don't ever use the word "problems," as most employers resent it - - unless you hear the word coming out of their mouth, first).

3. What skills seem to you to be needed in order to meet such needs.

4. What is unique about the way you perform those skills.

5. Your presentation of the evidence for your claim that you have the very skills in question, and that you perform them in the manner or style you claim.

As for what makes you different from nineteen other people who can do the same kind of work as you do, this is something you must devote some thought to, ahead of time. For example, if you analyze problems, how do you do that? *Painstakingly? Intuitively, in a flash? By consulting with greater authorities in the field?* You see the point. You are trying to put your finger on the 'style' or 'manner' in which you do your work, that is distinctive.

You will also show how you are different from others, by the very way in which you conduct yourself in the interview. Here are six ways in which you can make yourself look, and be, unique - - illustrated on the following file cards:

THE FIRST THING THAT MAKES YOU DIFFERENT FROM 'THE OTHERS' WHO ARE APPLYING FOR THE SAME JOB

YOU AS TIMEKEEPER

7. You want to come across as someone who knows the value of Time. For example, when you ask for an appointment with an employer, ask for twenty minutes only, of their time, and don't stay one minute longer, unless the employer begs you to. Watch your watch like a hawk. Tell them you like to honor agreements. That will almost always make a big impression.

You want to come across as someone who doesn't hog the Time. Whenever you are interviewing with an employer, talk one-half the time only, and let the employer talk the other half of the time. When the employer asks you a question, don't 'hold forth' for longer than two minutes, at any one time.

You want to come across as someone who values Timing, also. For example, the timing of salary negotiation should be the very last thing you two ever discuss, and only after they have definitely said they want you. Observe that timing, rigorously.

There are reasons for the above advice. For example, studies[2] have revealed that generally speaking the people who get hired are those who mix speaking and listening fifty-fifty in the interview. That is, half the time they spend letting the employer do the talking, half the time in the interview the job-hunter does the talking. People who didn't follow that mix, were the ones who didn't get hired, according to the study. I think the *reason* why this is so, is that if you talk too much about yourself, you come across as one who would ignore the needs of the organization; while if you talk too little, you come across as trying to hide something about your background.

Again, studies[3] have revealed that when it is your turn to speak, you should not speak any longer than two minutes at a time, if you want to make the best impression. In fact, a good answer to an employer's question sometimes only takes twenty seconds to give. This is useful information for you to know, in conducting a successful interview - - as you certainly want to do.

With regard to *Timing,* observe it rigorously, even if the employer doesn't. He or she may ask you *early on,* "What kind of a salary are you looking for?" You need to resist the question *at that time,* and gently insist that until *they* have said "We want you," and *you* have decided, "I want them," all discussion of salary is highly inappropriate. This is explained further, in the next chapter.

---

2. This one done by a researcher at Massachusetts Institute of Technology.

3. This one conducted by my colleague, Daniel Porot, in Geneva, Switzerland.

THE SECOND THING THAT MAKES YOU DIFFERENT FROM 'THE OTHERS' WHO ARE APPLYING FOR THE SAME JOB

YOU AS PROBLEM-SOLVER

8. You want to come across as focussed on what you can do for the employer, rather than on what the employer can do for you. You want the employer to see you as a Resource Person, rather than as a 'job-beggar,' to quote Daniel Porot. The major issue is not merely what skills you have, but also how you use them. You want to come across as a Problem-Solver there at work, rather than as one who simply 'keeps busy.' If you don't know what kind of problems, think of what a bad employee would do, in your position (come in late, take too much time off, not care about what the employer wants, etc.). Emphasize how much you do the opposite. You want them to know you will increase the organization's effectiveness, and (where applicable) their profits.

Every organization has two main topics for its continuing day-by-day preoccupation: the problems they are facing, and what the solutions might be.

The main thing the employer is trying to figure out during the job-interview, is - - if they hire you - - will you be part of the solution there, or just another part of their problems.

You will be part of the solution if you come to them as A Resource Person. And the secret of coming to them as A Resource Person is that you have previously tackled Chapters 9, 10, and 11 in this book, systematically and methodically, prior to the job-interview. The three questions there - - WHAT, WHERE, and HOW - - when thoughtfully and diligently answered, will identify you immediately as more than just a job-beggar.

During the course of the interview, you need to make it clear that you are there to see this employer, in order to make an oral proposal, followed hopefully by a written proposal, of what *you can do for them.* You will see immediately what a switch this is from the way most job-hunters approach an employer! *("How much do you pay, and how much time off will I have?")* Will he or she be glad to see you, with this different emphasis? In most cases, you bet they will. They *want* a resource person, and a problem-solver.

Toward this end, you need to find out as much about that organization as you possibly can, before you ever go in for an interview. Lay your hands on everything you can, that is in print about them. If this is a large organization, read as many of their brochures, annual reports, addresses of the chairman or boss - - whatever -- as you can. If they have a personnel or human relations department, or a public relations department, that's where you'll find that stuff. Also, go to your local library and ask the librarian or reference librarian to see every clipping they may have about that organization.

If it is a small organization, you can still find out if there is anything in print about their work or what they do. *(Even places that only have two employees often have something in print about what the organization is trying to achieve. Also, some local daily or weekly paper may have run an article about them.)* Be sure and talk to everybody you know, to find out anything they may know, about this organization.

This is not a matter of prying into their private life. It is a matter of knowing their history, so that you can understand their purposes and goals. Moreover, all organizations, be they large or small, profit or nonprofit, love to be loved. If you have gone to all this trouble, to learn so much about them - - before you ever walk in their doors, they will be impressed, believe me.

Most job-hunters never go to this trouble. They walk in knowing little or nothing about the organization. This drives employers *nuts.* One time, the first question an IBM college recruiter asked a graduating senior was, "What do the initials IBM stand for?" The senior didn't know, and the interview was over. Another time, an employer said to me, "I'm so tired of job-hunters who come in, and ask, 'Uh, what do you do here?' that the next time someone walks in who knows something about us, I'm going to hire him or her, on the spot."

Thus, if *you* come in, and have done your homework on the organization, this immediately makes you stand out from other job-hunters, and dramatically increases your chances of getting a job there. How much information should you gather? Well, in a nutshell, more than you are going to need -- at least during the hiring interview. The depth of your research will pay off in the quiet sense of knowledgeability that you exude.

THE THIRD THING THAT MAKES YOU DIFFERENT FROM 'THE OTHERS' WHO ARE APPLYING FOR THE SAME JOB

YOU AS PROOF-GIVER

9. The most important thing during the interview, regarding your skills, is that you not merely claim you have certain skills, but prove you have them. You must set yourself apart from other job-hunters by being a Proof-giver, not merely a Claimer. Often you do this by the way in which you conduct the interview.

If, for example, you say you are very thorough in all you do, but you haven't researched the organization you are presently interviewing at, your actions will contradict your claims.

If you are an artist, craftsperson, or other person who produces something, try to think of some way to show the employer what you are capable of doing -- through pictures, samples of things you have made or produced, videotape, or whatever -- during the interview.

THE FOURTH THING THAT MAKES YOU DIFFERENT FROM 'THE OTHERS' WHO ARE APPLYING FOR THE SAME JOB

YOU AS COURTEOUS AND KIND

10. Be courteous at all times. Employers are a fraternity. Or a sorority. The task of hiring makes them feel like they are members of the same tribe. During the interview, you want to be observed as one who has courtesy toward all members of that tribe, i.e., all employers. Don't ever bad-mouth a previous employer. Say something nice, or else keep quiet about them. You will immediately stand out from other job-hunters, because of your graciousness.

And, be courteous to this employer, even if they are obviously not going to hire you. During the following week, or two, they may be having lunch with another

employer, who says, "I'm looking for someone. Do you know of anybody?" If you were well-remembered for your courtesy, the employer who turned you down, may submit your name to this new employer.

THE FIFTH THING THAT MAKES YOU DIFFERENT FROM 'THE OTHERS' WHO ARE APPLYING FOR THE SAME JOB

Knowing how to negotiate for a fair salary. Most job-hunters don't know how. If you do, this will set you apart from the rest. However, the subject of negotiating deserves a chapter all by itself, and accordingly, is the subject of the next chapter.

THE SIXTH THING THAT MAKES YOU DIFFERENT FROM 'THE OTHERS' WHO ARE APPLYING FOR THE SAME JOB

YOU AS THANKS-GIVER

11. Every evening, after a job-interview, you must take time to sit down and write (with pen or type-writer) a brief thank-you note to each person you saw that day. That means, not only employers, but also their secretaries, receptionists, or anyone else who gave you a friendly welcome or a helping hand. (Be sure and ask for their names, or cards, while you are still there visiting that organization.) Don't make the note just a perfunctory 'Thanks very much for your time.' Add something individual about the way they treated you. Use the note to mention anything you forgot to mention while there, and -- with employers -- to under-line the main points you want them to remember about you. Mail the note promptly the very next morning, or even that night.

A job-hunter presented herself for a job-interview as public relations officer for a major-league baseball team. That evening, she wrote and mailed a thank-you note. She was eventually hired for the job, and when she asked why, they told her that they had decided to hire her because, out of thirty-five appli-cants, she was the only one who had written a thank-you note.

That's why every expert on interviewing will tell you two things: (1) thank-you notes are *crucial*, because they may be the one factor that gets you the job; and (2) most job-hunters ig-nore this advice. Indeed, it is safe to say that it is the most overlooked step in the entire job-hunting process.

If you want to stand out from the others applying for the same job, send thank-you notes -- to *everyone* you meet there, that day. If you need any additional encouragements (*besides the*

fact that it may get you the job), here are six additional reasons for sending a thank-you note -- particularly to the employer who interviewed you:

First, you are presenting yourself as one who has good skills with people. Your actions with respect to the job-interview must back this claim up. Sending a thank-you note does that. You *are* good with people; you remember to thank them.

Secondly, it helps the employer to remember you.

Thirdly, if a committee is involved in the hiring process, the one man or woman who interviewed you has something to show the committee.

Fourth, if the interview went rather well, and you are hopeful of being invited back, the thank-you letter can reiterate your interest in further talks.

Fifth, the thank-you note gives you an opportunity to correct any wrong impression you left behind you. You can add anything you forgot to tell them, that you want them to know. And from among all the things you two discussed, you can underline the main two or three points that you want to stand out in their minds.

Lastly, if the interview did not go well, and you lost all interest in working there, they may still hear of other openings, elsewhere, that might be of interest to you. In the thank-you note, you can mention this, and ask them to keep you in mind. Thus you may gain additional leads.

Should you include a resume with your thank-you note to the employer who interviewed you? Some experts will advise you to. Under the third canon above, it gives your interviewer something additional to show the other members of the hiring committee, if there is such.

However, infinitely preferred to a resume is a piece of paper that is, in essence, a *brief* written proposal *(one or two pages at most)* as to what it is you would like to be able to do at that organization, and what you hope you could accomplish for them.

As evidence of your ability to do that, you should cite relevant past accomplishments of yours, taking care in each case to cite:

a) what the problem was

b) what especial obstacle (timewise, or otherwise) you had to overcome

c) what means you used to overcome the obstacle, and solve the problem

d) what the results were, of your actions, stated as concretely as possible in terms of things accomplished, money saved, money earned, etc.

The virtue of such a written proposal is that it looks forward rather than (as the resume does) backward. And it 'puts into writing the essence of the hiring interview: you are not asking them merely to do something for you. More importantly, you are offering to do something for them.

CONCLUSION:
FEAR AND THE INTERVIEW

If the employment interview were simply two people, job-hunter and employer, trying to get answers to natural questions, the interview would be a snap. Unfortunately, this simple exchange is corrupted by the fact that both individuals sitting there are filled with a number of fears and anxieties, which they don't feel free to discuss openly. Yes, I said, *both of you.* You know *you* are sitting there with sweaty palms, but you will probably assume that the employer is sitting there enjoying this whole masochistic process. That is sometimes, but rarely, true.

The employer is a human-being just like you are. He or she may *never* have been hired to do *this. This* just got thrown in with all their other duties. And they may *know* they're not very good at it.

So, let's briefly catalog some of the employer's typical fears. You are sitting there. The employer is sitting there. This is what they are afraid of, as the job-interview begins:

a. That You Won't Be Able to Do the Job: That You Lack the Necessary Skills or Experience

b. That If Hired, You Won't Put In a Full Working Day

c. That If Hired, You'll Be Frequently "Out Sick," or Otherwise Absent Whole Days

d. That If Hired, You'll Only Stay Around for a Few Weeks or At Most a Few Months

e. That It Will Take You Too Long to Master the Job, and Thus Too Long Before You're Profitable to That Organization

f. That You Won't Get Along with the Other Workers There, or That You Will Develop a Personality Conflict with the Boss Himself (or Herself)

g. That You Will Do Only the Minimum That You Can Get Away With, Rather Than the Maximum That You Are Capable Of

h. That You Will Always Have to Be Told What to Do Next, Rather Than Displaying Initiative; That You Will Always Be in a Responding Rather Than an Initiating Mode (and Mood)

i. That You Will Have a Work-Disrupting Character Flaw, and Turn Out to Be: Dishonest, Totally Irresponsible, a Spreader of Dissension at Work, Lazy, an Embezzler, a Gossip, a Sexual Harasser, a Drug User or Substance Abuser, a Drunk, a Liar, Incompetent - - In a Word: Bad News

j. *(If This Is a Large Organization, and Your Would-Be Boss Is Not the Top Person)* That You Will Bring Discredit upon Them, and upon His or Her Department/Section/Division, etc., for Ever Hiring You in the First Place - - Making Them Lose Face, and Possibly Costing Your Would-Be Boss a Raise or Promotion

k. That You Will Cost a Lot of Money, If They Make a Mistake in Hiring

Incidentally, the cost of the interviewing time, plus the cost of relocation, moving, etc., added up *(as recently as 1988)* to an average cost of $6,076 for each new professional or managerial employee hired, according to the Employment Management Association. Therefore, that is also the minimum cost of a mistake. No wonder the employer is sweating.

Now, how are they going to find out the answers to these fears? Well, in the old days, an employer might have gotten useful information *outside* the job-interview, by obtaining references from your previous employers. No more. In the past decade, as job-hunters have started filing lawsuits left and right, alleging 'unlawful discharge,' or 'being deprived of an ability to make a living,' about half of all Previous Employers have adopted the policy of refusing to volunteer any information about Past Employees, except name, rank and serial number - - i.e., the person's job-title and dates of employment.

The interviewer is therefore completely on his own - - or her own - - in trying to figure out whether or not to hire you. The hiring interview is *everything*.

The most important thing for you to keep in mind during the interview, as I mentioned on an earlier file card, is that no employer cares about your past. The only thing any employer can possibly care about is your future. Therefore, the more a question *appears* to be about your past, the more certain you may be that some Fear is behind it. And that Fear is about your future - - i.e., what will you be like, *after* the employer decides to hire you, *if* they decide to hire you.

It will help you greatly in the interview if you simply remind yourself, "This guy is afraid," or "This woman is afraid." It will also help you if you can sense *what* fear lies beneath each question that employer asks you - - so that you can tacitly answer the fear, and not just the surface question.

Here are some *examples:*

Employer's Question	The Fear Behind The Question	The Point You Try to Get Across	Phrases You Might Use To Get This Across
"Tell me about yourself"	The employer is afraid he/she isn't going to conduct a very good interview, by failing to ask the right questions. Or is afraid there is something wrong with you, and is hoping you will blurt it out.	You are a good employee, as you have proved in the past at your other jobs. (Give the briefest history of who you are, where born, raised, interests, hobbies, and kind of work you have enjoyed the most to date.) *Keep it to two minutes, max.*	In describing your past work history, use any *honest* phrases you can about your work history, that are self-complimentary: "Hard worker" "Came in early, left late" "Always did more than was expected of me" etc.
"What kind of work are you looking for?"	The employer is afraid that you are looking for a different job than that which the employer is trying to fill. e.g., he/she wants a secretary, but you want to be an office manager, etc.	You are looking for precisely the kind of work the employer is offering (but don't say that, if it isn't true). Repeat back to the employer, in your own words, what he/she has said about the job, and emphasize the skills you have to do *that*.	If the employer hasn't described the job at all, say, "I'd be happy to answer that, but first I need to understand exactly what kind of work this job involves." *Then* answer, as at left.
"Have you ever done this kind of work before?"	The employer is afraid you don't possess the necessary skills and experience to do this job.	You have skills that are transferable, from whatever you used to do; and you did it well.	"I pick up stuff very quickly." "I have quickly mastered any job I have ever done."

Employer's Question	The Fear Behind The Question	The Point You Try to Get Across	Phrases You Might Use To Get This Across
"Why did you leave your last job?" *-- or* "How did you get along with your former boss and co-workers?"	The employer is afraid you don't get along well with people, especially bosses, and is just waiting for you to 'bad-mouth' your previous boss or co-workers, as proof of that.	Say whatever positive things you possibly can about your former boss and co-workers *(without telling lies)*. Emphasize you usually get along very well with people -- and then let your gracious attitude toward your previous boss(es) and co-workers prove it, right before this employer's very eyes (and ears).	If you left voluntarily: *"My boss and I* both felt I would be happier and more effective in a job where (here describe your strong points, such as) I would have more room to use my initiative and creativity." If you alone were fired: "Usually, I get along well with everyone, but in this particular case the boss and I just didn't get along with each other. Difficult to say why." *You don't need to say any more than that.* If you were laid off and your job wasn't filled after you left: "My *job* was terminated."
"How is your health?" *-- or* "How much were you absent from work during your last job?"	The employer is afraid you will be absent from work a lot, if they hire you.	You will not be absent. If you have a health problem, you want to emphasize that it is one which will not keep you from being at work, daily. Your productivity, compared to other workers', is excellent.	If you were *not* absent a lot at your last job: "I believe it's an employee's job to show up every work day. Period." If you *were* absent a lot, say why, and stress that it was due to a difficulty that is now *past*.

Employer's Question	The Fear Behind The Question	The Point You Try to Get Across	Phrases You Might Use To Get This Across
"Can you explain why you've been out of work so long?" -- *or* "Can you tell me why there are these gaps in your work history?" *(usually said after studying your resume)*	The employer is afraid that you are the kind of person who quits a job the minute he/she doesn't like something at it; in other words, that you have no 'stick-to-it-iveness.'	You love to work, and you regard times when things aren't going well as challenges, which you enjoy learning how to conquer.	"During the gaps in my work record, I was studying/doing volunteer work/doing some hard thinking about my mission in life/finding redirection." (Choose one)
"Wouldn't this job represent a step down for you?" -- *or* "I think this job would be way beneath your talents and experience." -- *or* "Don't you think you would be underemployed if you took this job?"	The employer is afraid you could command a bigger salary, somewhere else, and will therefore leave him/her as soon as something better turns up.	You will stick with this job so long as you and the employer agree this is where you should be.	"This job isn't a step down for me. It's a step up -- from welfare." "We have mutual fears: every employer is afraid a good employee will leave too soon, and every employee is afraid the employer might fire him/her, for no good reason." "I like to work, and I give my best to every job I've ever had."
And, lastly "Tell me, what is your greatest weakness?"	The employer is afraid you have some character flaw, and hopes you will now rashly blurt it out, or confess it.	You have limitations just like anyone else, but you work constantly to improve yourself and be a more and more effective worker.	Mention a weakness and then stress its positive aspect. e.g., "I don't like to be oversupervised, because I have a great deal of initiative, and I like to anticipate problems before they even arise."

*It has long been an axiom of mine
that the little things
are infinitely the most important.*
> Sir Arthur Conan Doyle

God is in the details.
> Mies van der Rohe

CHAPTER FOURTEEN

Salary
Negotiation

"Let's talk salary. How does 'astronomical' sound to you?"

Chapter 14

MEANWHILE, BACK AT
THE RANCH

While you are writing out your thank-you note, the employer you saw that day is very likely reflecting on the whole day's interviews -- mentally sifting through all the candidates they saw, trying to decide who stands out, so far. And -- if that includes you -- weighing whether to invite you back, for a second round of interviews. There usually *is* a second round. You, of course, want to be in that second round, and you are wondering how many days you should give them, before you contact them again.

It helps a lot if you established some kind of understanding about all of this, at the end of your *first* interview, by asking three questions: "When may I expect to hear from you?" (Wait for their answer.) "What would be the latest I can expect to hear from you?" (Wait for their answer.) "May I contact you after that date, if for any reason you haven't gotten back to me?" (Wait for their answer.) Then, after you leave, keep this covenant, and don't contact them (except with a thank-you note) until after the deadline agreed upon.

If they forget about you, and you do have to contact them after the agreed-upon date, and if they tell you things are still up in the air, you ask the same three questions all over again. And so on, and so forth.

Incidentally, it is entirely appropriate for you to insert a thank-you note into the running stream, after *each* interview or telephone contact. That will help them remember you.

WHEN EMPLOYERS NEVER
INVITE YOU BACK

There are many job-hunters who have no difficulty in getting a first interview at various places, but they *never* get invited back for a second interview, and hence never get a job. If this is happening to you, there may be something wrong with the way you are coming across during interviews. Unfortunately, employers will hardly ever tell you this. You will never hear them say something like, "You're too cocky and arrogant during the interview." You will always be left completely in the dark as to what it is you're doing wrong.

FRANK & ERNEST reprinted by permission of NEA, Inc.

One way around this deadly silence, is to ask for *generalized* feedback, from some friendly employer you saw back a while ago. You can try phoning them, reminding them of who you are, and then asking the following question -- deliberately kept generalized, vague, unrelated just to *that* place, and above all, *future-directed:* "You know, I've been on several interviews at several different places now, where I've gotten turned down. From what you've seen, is there something about me in an interview, that is causing me not to get hired at those places? If so, I'd really appreciate your giving me some pointers so I can do better in my future job-interviews."

Most of the time they'll *still* duck saying anything hurtful or helpful. (Said an old veteran to me once, "I used to think it was my duty to hit everyone with the truth. Now I only give it to those who can use it.") *Occasionally* you will run into an employer who is willing to risk giving you the truth, because they think you know how to use it.

In the absence of any help from employers, you might want to get a good business friend of yours to role-play a mock job-interview with you, in case they see something glaringly wrong with how you're 'coming across.' If from either friend or employer-on-the-phone, you do get feedback, no matter how painful it is, thank them from the bottom of your heart. Their advice, seriously heeded, can bring about just the changes in your interviewing strategy that you most need.

WHEN EMPLOYERS DO INVITE YOU BACK

But, assuming things went favorably in the first interview, you *will* be invited back for another interview, *or interviews* at that place - - with the person you saw before, and/or with a committee. Eventually, after a second, third, or fourth interview, if you like them and they increasingly like you, a job offer *will* be made.

Then, and only then, it is time to deal with the question that is inevitably on any employer's mind, as we saw in Chapter 13: *how much is this person going to cost me?* And the question that is on *your* mind: *how much does this job pay?*

It's time for salary negotiation.

Salary negotiation would never happen if *every* employer in *every* job-interview were to mention, right from the start, the top figure they are willing to pay for that position. *Some* employers do. And that's the end of any salary negotiation. But, of course, most of them don't. They start *lower,* hoping they'll be able to get you for less. This creates *a range.* And that range is what salary negotiation is all about.

For example, if the employer wants to hire somebody for no more than $10 an hour, they may start *the bidding* at $8 an hour. In which case, the range runs from $8 to $10 an hour. Or if they want to pay no more than $14 an hour, they may start the bidding at $11 an hour. In which case the range runs from $11 to $14 an hour.

If a range *is* involved, then you have every right to try to negotiate a higher salary *within that range.* The employer's goal, is to save money, if possible. Your goal is to bring home to your family, partner, or your own household, the best salary that you can, for the work you will be doing. Nothing's wrong with the goals of either of you. But it does mean that, where the employer starts lower, salary negotiation is proper, and expected.

1992 Statistics about Salaries

The average hourly wage in the U.S. currently is $10.50 per hour.[1] High school graduates earn, on average, $10.72 per hour. College graduates earn, on average, $16.69 an hour. These figures do not include 'perks,' such as health-care, retirement funds, etc., which often add considerably to the total wage.

The average annual income for all full-time workers in the U.S. for 1992 is $22,672. (*Average* means as many are above that figure as below it.) The average annual income for production or nonsupervisory workers is $18,946. Middle-income families are currently defined as people making $18,500–$74,000 per year.

Inflation is currently running about 3% a year. Pay raises in many cases are barely exceeding that (3.2%, on average).

THE FIVE KEYS TO SALARY NEGOTIATION

There are five basic keys to successful salary negotiation during a job-interview. They are:

1. *Never* discuss salary until the end of the interviewing process, when they have definitely said they want you.

2. *Never* be the first one to mention a salary figure.

3. Before you go to the interview, do homework on how much you need.

4. During the interview, try to determine whether the salary being offered is fixed or contains room for negotiation.

5. Before you go in, do research on salaries for your field and that organization.

The rest of this chapter is devoted to a discussion of these five keys.

---

1. This figure is as of May, 1992, and it is for production or nonsupervisory workers on non-farm payrolls.

1 Never discuss salary until the end of the interviewing process, and they have definitely said they want you.

IT'S WHAT I'VE ALWAYS HEARD.. TIMING IS EVERYTHING..

Every expert on salary negotiation will tell you this, but let's really press the point home:

When To Discuss Salary

Not until all of the following conditions have been fulfilled --

- Not until they've gotten to know you, at your best, so they can see how you stand out above the other applicants.
- Not until you've gotten to know them, as completely as you can, so you can tell when they're being firm, or when they're flexible.
- Not until you've found out exactly what the job entails.
- Not until they've had a chance to find out how well you match the job-requirements.
- Not until you're in the final interview at that place, for that job.
- Not until you've decided, "I'd really like to work here."
- Not until they've said, "We want you."
- Not until they've said, "We've *got* to have you."

-- do you even *mention* salary -- nor do you let *them* mention salary. Period. Exclamation point. End of story.

Until all the above has happened, any salary they mention will be too low. They don't yet understand what you're really worth.

If you'd prefer this to be put in the form of a diagram, here it is:[2]

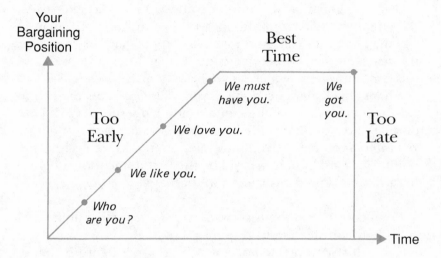

You may think to yourself, "But if they have a certain salary in mind for this position, what's the difference whether I find it out early or late?"

The difference is that if you really *shine* during the job-interview, they may -- at the end -- mention a higher salary than they originally had in mind, just because you stand out above all the other candidates -- and they're determined to have you.

Therefore, until they have made you a firm offer, try to postpone all discussion of salary. You have *nothing* to lose, and *everything* to gain.

If it is the employer who brings up the subject -- early in the job-interview -- with some question like "How much are you expecting to make?" you should simply, kindly, and firmly reply, "Until you've decided you definitely want me, and I've decided I want to work here, I feel any discussion of salary is premature."

---

2. Reprinted, by permission of the publisher, from *Ready, Aim, You're Hired,* by Paul Hellman, © 1986 Paul Hellman. Published by AMACOM, a division of American Management Association, New York. All rights reserved.

2   *Never* be the first one to mention a salary figure.

Salary negotiation *is* a kind of contest. As I indicated earlier, the employer wants to pay the least they can. You want them to pay the most they can. And what the experts have learned over the years, just from observing countless job-interviews, is that in this contest *whoever mentions a salary figure first, generally loses.*

That's why experienced employers will *always* toss the ball to you, with the following innocent-sounding question, "What kind of salary are you looking for?" *Well, how kind of them to ask what you want* - - you may be thinking. No, no, no. Kindness isn't the point. They are hoping *you* will be the first to mention a figure, because they know this rule well, that *whoever mentions a salary figure first, generally loses.*

So of course, you will *never* want to respond with a dollar and cents figure. Instead, your response should always be: "Well, you created this position, so you must have some figure in mind, and I'd be interested in knowing what that is."

3   Before you go to the interview, do homework on how much you need.

You cannot possibly do salary negotiation unless you know what is *the floor,* below which you simply cannot afford to go. And this is particularly important in these troubled '90s, since many employers have *a fixed ceiling* above which they simply cannot afford to go. When you're in the middle of salary nego-tiation, you've *got* to know instantly if *their* ceiling turns out to be beneath *your* floor.

That means knowing, beforehand, just how much it is you need to make, at a minimum. You can determine this in one of two ways: a) take a wild guess - - and risk finding out after you take the job that it's simply impossible for you to live on that salary *(America's favorite strategy)*; or, b) make out a firm, detailed outline of your estimated expenses *now*, listing what you need *monthly* in the following categories:[3]

Your Monthly Expenses

Housing
    Rent or mortgage payments .... $_____
    Electricity/gas .... $_____
    Water .... $_____
    Telephone .... $_____
    Garbage removal .... $_____
    Cleaning, maintenance, repairs[4] .... $_____
Food
    What you spend at the supermarket
    and/or meat market, etc. .... $_____
    Eating out .... $_____
Clothing
    Purchase of new or used clothing .... $_____
    Cleaning, drycleaning, laundry .... $_____
Automobile/transportation
    Car payments .... $_____
    Gas .... $_____
    Repairs .... $_____
    Public transportation *(bus, train, plane)* .... $_____
Insurance
    Car .... $_____
    Medical or healthcare .... $_____
    House and personal possessions .... $_____
    Life .... $_____

continued

---

3. If this kind of financial figuring is not your cup of tea, find a buddy, friend, relative, family member, or *anyone*, who can help you do this. If you don't know anyone who could do this, go to your local church, synagogue, religious centre, social club, gym, or wherever you hang out, and ask the leader or manager there, to help you find someone. If there's a bulletin board, put up a notice on the bulletin board.

4. If you have extra household expenses, such as a security system for example, be sure and include the quarterly (or whatever) expenses here, divided by three.

Medical expenses
 Doctors' visits .... $ _____
 Prescriptions .... $ _____
 Fitness costs .... $ _____
Support for other family members
 Child-care costs (if you have children) .... $ _____
 Child-support *(if you're paying that)* .... $ _____
 Support for your parents *(if you're helping out)* $ _____
Charity giving/tithe (to help others) .... $ _____
School/learning
 Children's costs *(if you have children in school)* .. $ _____
 Your learning costs *(adult education, job-
 hunting classes, etc.)* .... $ _____
Pet care *(if you have pets)* .... $ _____
Bills and debts *(Usual monthly payments)*
 Credit cards .... $ _____
 Local stores .... $ _____
 Other obligations you pay off monthly .... $ _____
Taxes
 Federal[5] *(next April's due, divided by months
 remaining until then)* .... $ _____
 State *(likewise)* .... $ _____
 Local/property *(next amount due, divided by
 months remaining until then)* .... $ _____
 Tax-help *(if you ever use an accountant, pay
 a friend to help you with taxes, etc.)* .... $ _____
Amusement/discretionary spending
 Movies, video rentals, etc. .... $ _____
 Other kinds of entertainment .... $ _____
 Reading, newspapers, magazines, books .... $ _____
 Gifts (birthday, Christmas, etc.) .... $ _____

Total Amount You Need Each Month .... $ _____

---

5. Incidentally, looking ahead to next April 15th, be sure and check with your local IRS office or a reputable accountant to find out if you can deduct the expenses of your job-hunt on your Federal (and State) income tax returns. At this writing, some job-hunters can, if - - big IF - - this is not your first job that you're looking for, if you haven't

Your checkbook stubs will tell you a lot of this stuff. But you may be vague about your cash or credit card expenditures. For example, you may not know how much you spend at the super-market, or how much you spend on gas, etc. But there is a simple way to find out. Just carry a little notepad and pen around with you for two weeks or more, and jot down *everything* you pay cash *(or use credit cards)* for - - *on the spot, right after you pay it.* At the end of those two weeks, you'll be able to take that notepad and make a realistic guess of what should be put down in these categories that now puzzle you. *(Multiply the two-weeks figure by two, and you'll have the monthly figure.)*

Parenthetically, you may want to prepare two different ver-sions of the above budget: one with the expenses you'd ideally like to make, and the other a minimum budget, which will determine the floor, below which you simply cannot afford to go.

4 Try to determine whether the salary being offered is fixed or contains room for negotiation.

Salary negotiation has become infinitely more complicated in the '90s. Many employers have fired or laid off experienced workers who have given years to the company, and they have done so for one reason and one reason only: those experi-enced, dedicated employees now cost too much. They can be

been unemployed too long, and if you aren't making a career-change. Do go find out what the latest "if"s are. If IRS tells you you are eligible, keep careful receipts of everything related to your job-hunt, as you go along: telephone calls, stationery, print-ing, postage, travel, etc.

replaced by new workers who may not have the experience, and may make a lot of mistakes. But these new employees have one sterling virtue: they cost *half* of what the previous employees cost.

Signs of the times: of the 12 million new jobs created in the last decade, more than half pay less than $7,000 a year.[6]

The emphasis in the '90s is on cutting costs. So, you are going to discover that at many organizations, if there are several candidates who seem to be equally qualified, the job-applicant who saves that organization the most money, is the one who is going to get hired.[7]

> It's an old game, played with new determination by employers in the '90s, called "*among a bunch of equally qualified candidates, the one who is willing to work for the lowest salary* wins."

This is particularly true if applicants for this position are 'a dime a dozen,' and you are viewed by the employer as *only one among many*. What you have to labor to do during the job-interview, of course, is to make clear that you stand out above all the rest. The key to doing this, is to do the careful homework and preparation of Chapter 9 in this book. That's in a section labeled *Career Change,* but it's actually essential homework for any job-hunter who wants to stand out.

As I said earlier, salary negotiation is still possible even in the belt-tightening '90s, anytime the employer does not open the discussion of salary by naming the top figure they have in mind, but starts instead at a lower figure.

Okay, so here is our $64,000 question: how can you tell whether the figure the employer first offers you is only their *starting bid,* or is their *final final offer?* The answer is: by doing some research first.

---

6. Time, 12/17/90.

7. If you want to ask for a higher salary, be prepared to show in what ways you will *make money* or in what ways you will *save money* for that organization, such as will justify your higher salary.

5 Before you go in, do research on salaries for your field and that organization.

You, of course, want to know if it's *really necessary* to do this kind of research. Trust me, salary research pays off *handsomely*.

Let's say it takes you from one to three days to run down this sort of information on the three or four organizations that interest you the most. And let us say that because you've done this research, when you finally go in for the job-interview you are able to ask for and obtain a salary that is $4,000 a year higher in range, than you would otherwise have gotten. In just the next three years, you will be earning $12,000 extra, because of your salary research. *Not bad pay, for one to three days' work!* And it can be even more.

If it is true that *information* is the key to a successful job-hunt and to successful salary-negotiation, it is equally true that there is a financial penalty exacted from those who are too lazy, or in too much of a hurry, to go gather that information.

Okay, let's look at the steps in doing this research:

1. You want, at the very least, to find out what the *ballpark* figures are for the kind of work you do, or want to do. I have listed below a sampling of the kind of information you can dig up at your local library, using the resources listed in Appendix B and elsewhere.[8] This is a summary of the 1991 *median* earnings, nationwide, for a *select* listing of jobs:

Table 1

Half of All The People Doing This Kind of Work Make More Than This, Half Make Less Than This

Job, Profession, Career	Nationwide Median Yearly Wage	Job, Profession, Career	Nationwide Median Yearly Wage
Child-care worker, in household	$ 6,864	Mechanic	$24,804
Garage and service station	11,648	Wholesale/retail buyer	25,116
Farm workers	12,428	Legal assistant	25,220
Gardeners and groundskeepers	13,988	Advertising and related sales	25,376
Bank teller	14,196	Science technician	25,896
Retail trade employee	14,300	Graphic designer	26,000
Dental assistant	15,600	Radiologic technician	26,000
Recreation worker	16,432	Sales representative	26,156
Telephone operator	16,588	Real estate salesperson	26,364
Butchers and meat cutters	16,796	Plumbers	26,468
Taxicab drivers and chauffeurs	17,628	Designer	26,624
Secretary	18,668	Drafting occupations	26,676
Roofers	19,552	Transportation worker	26,820
Bus drivers	19,656	Librarian, archivist, or curator	27,092
Automobile mechanics	20,020	Psychologist	27,872
Services worker	20,060	Teacher, elementary school	27,924
Food worker	20,080	Electricians	27,976
Typesetters and compositors	20,436	Construction worker	28,020
Travel agent	20,488	Mining worker	28,960
Practical nurse	20,592	Television news reporter	29,035
Finance, insurance, or real estate worker	21,640	Police or detective	29,068
Health technician or technologist	21,996	Postal clerk	29,068
Photographer	22,048	Therapist	29,276
Truck drivers, heavy equipment	22,308	Public relations executive	30,732
Manufacturing production worker	22,360	Teacher, secondary school	30,784
Religious worker	23,348	Reporter or editor	30,836
Crafts artist	23,400	Accountant	30,996
Painter, or printmaker artisan	23,400	Physical therapist	31,512
Sculptor	23,400	Firefighting	31,616
Dietitian	23,608	Social scientist, or urban planner	31,824
Durable goods production worker	23,800	Counselor, vocational/career	31,928
Clergy	23,868	Architect	32,396
Clinical lab technician	23,972	Tobacco products worker	32,920
Social worker	24,232	Registered nurse	32,968
		Telephone installers and repairers	33,540

Biologist	$33,852	Mechanical engineer	$43,472
Computer programmer	34,424	Auditor	43,500
Petroleum worker	35,520	Pharmacist	43,940
Chemist	35,724	Television sales account executive	44,565
Sales, securities and financial services	36,296	Advertising manager	44,600
Writer, technical	36,660	College admissions officer	45,000
Bank branch manager	37,000	Electrical and electronics engineer	45,292
Geologist	37,856	Chemical engineer	45,448
Economist	38,064	Aeronautical or aerospace engineer	46,176
College professor	38,844	Airline pilot	48,464
Personnel specialist	39,104	Physician	51,688
Systems analyst	39,260	Software engineer	54,200
Purchasing managers	40,768	Attorney or judge	54,340
Computer analysts and scientists	41,184	Broker, retail	79,169
Industrial engineer	41,652	Dentist	86,966
Advertising copywriter	41,700	Personnel executive	108,200
Tax accountant	42,000	Orthodontist	109,750
Civil engineer	42,068	Psychiatrist	113,750
		Surgeon	147,920

Source: The U.S. Government's *Employment and Earnings, January 1992.*

The yearly figures, above, are roughly convertible to hourly wages, if you so desire. (We assume a 40 hour week, and a 50 week year, which is less than some people work, and more than others -- but close enough.)

Take *however many* thousands the yearly figure is, and divide the number of thousands by two; that will give you the *approximate* hourly wage. Thus, with $30,000 a year, you take the 30, divide by two, and you find it equals (approximately) $15 an hour.

---

8. Places to look for your information include the Department of Labor's monthly *Employment and Earnings,* ("Household Data, Annual Averages, Median weekly earnings of full-time wage and salary workers by detailed occupation and sex") - - plus its annual *Supplement to Employment and Earnings; Area Wage Surveys* (covers office, professional, technical, maintenance, custodial, and material movement jobs in major metropolitan areas), and individual area bulletins which are available separately, and cover mainly production and non-supervisory workers. Order from the Bureau of Labor Statistics, Publications Sales Center, P.O. Box 2145, Chicago IL 60690. Areas covered include Alexandria–Leesville, Virginia; Ashville, North Carolina; Atlanta; Beaumont–Port Arthur and Lake Charles, Texas; Cedar Rapids, Iowa; Houston; Huntsville; Logansport–Peru, Indiana; Milwaukee; Minneapolis–St. Paul; Monmouth–Ocean and Newark, New Jersey; Norfolk–Virginia Beach–Newport News, Virginia; Northern New York; North-western Florida; Pittsburgh; Portsmouth–Chillicothe–Gallipolis, Ohio; Raleigh–Durham, North Carolina; St. Louis; Oakland, San Francisco, and San Jose, California; Washington DC–Maryland.

Also look in *The Occupational Outlook Handbook* - - it has ballpark figures for a *selected* list of jobs. The job you are interested in *may* be included.

Additional sources: Arsen Darnay, ed., *American Salaries & Wages Survey.* Gale Research, Inc., P.O. Box 33477, Detroit, MI 48232-5477. 1991. It's *expensive;* see your local library.

John W. Wright, *The American Almanac of Jobs and Salaries, revised and updated 1990–1991 edition.* Avon Books, Dept. FP, 1790 Broadway, New York, NY 10019. This book is revised periodically, but at this writing *this* is the most recent edition. It has a lot of interesting help, but *do* remember that the salary figures are all from 1987, sometimes 1988.

2. You want, if you can, to find more definitive information for your type of work in your geographical area. A lot of people make more than the median, particularly in large metropolitan areas. In fact, there are often *dramatic* fluctuations within regions, within industries, and between companies or organizations -- even in the same town or city. You'll have to find out through *further* research, along the lines of Chapter 11, just what the earnings are in your particular area. Here are some typical occupations as illustrations: [9]

Table 2

Occupation	Nationwide Median for All Workers	However The Top 10% Make *At Least*
Waiters and waitresses	$11,336 yr.	$18,304 yr.
Maids and housemen	11,856 yr.	17,264 yr.
General office clerks	17,628 yr.	26,832 yr.
Bookkeepers	17,940 yr.	26,104 yr.
Social workers	24,232 yr.	38,012 yr.
Precision production occupations	24,388 yr.	38,012 yr.
Registered nurses	32,968 yr.	42,796 yr.
Lawyers	52,416 yr.	95,160 yr.

Source: The U.S. Government's *Occupational Outlook Quarterly,* Fall 1990.

In doing your research, you *have* to keep in mind the lamentable fact that there are sex differences in salaries. In general, the *median* for women in any occupation will fall *below* the figure in Table 1, while the *median* for men will be *above* it. By way of illustration, here are the same occupations as in Table 2:[10]

---

9. If you want to know what the top 10% make, at the very least, for other occupations than are listed here, I refer you to this issue of the *Quarterly.* Keep in mind that the figures are for 1989, and have probably increased by about 15% by the time you read this *(more, if this is an old copy of* Parachute, *and you're reading it in the year 1998).*

Table 3

Occupation	Nationwide Median for Women	Nationwide Median for All	Nationwide Median for Men
Waiters and waitresses	$10,660 yr.	$11,336 yr.	$14,612 yr.
Maids and housemen	11,440 yr.	11,856 yr.	14,248 yr.
General office clerks	17,316 yr.	17,628 yr.	18,824 yr.
Bookkeepers	17,732 yr.	17,940 yr.	20,696 yr.
Social workers	23,140 yr.	24,232 yr.	26,364 yr.
Precision production occupations	16,484 yr.	24,388 yr.	26,416 yr.
Registered nurses	32,760 yr.	32,968 yr.	36,556 yr.
Lawyers	42,692 yr.	52,416 yr.	56,732 yr.

Source: The U.S. Government's *Employment and Earnings, January 1992.*

3. You want, if you can, to find more definitive information for the particular organizations you are approaching. This is of course the hairiest part of salary research, so it will help if we take some examples:

First Example: *Working at your first entry-level job, say at a fast-food place.*

You may not need to do any salary research. They pay what they pay. You can walk in, ask for a job application, and interview with the manager. He or she will usually tell you the pay, outright. It's usually *inflexible.* But at least you'll find it easy to

---

10. A special note to women job-hunters: the *cause* of the above disparity between men and women's salaries, needs to be better understood than it usually is. It is seen, by some women job-hunters, as further evidence of the conscious and unconscious sexism that pervades our male-dominated society, and workplace. This is certainly true. But, part of the problem also rests on the shoulders of women job-hunters, who compete *with one another* by *reducing* their salary demands. *You* may vow to hold your ground on this. But, the minute you have one other woman competing for that same job, who is equally as competent as you, but hungrier than you, and willing to work for less than you, then you have trouble - - right here in River City. Not only will *she* usually get the job, but, the salary average for women in that occupation will thus continue to be lower than that of men. The only way to change this situation is for each woman job-hunter to make such a compelling case during the job-interview for why she does her work *better* than any other worker - - man or woman - - that she can thus justify asking for a salary equal to that of a man. Not only will she thus raise her own salary, if successful, but she will also help bring the average that women make, in that occupation, closer to what men make.

discover what the pay is. (Incidentally, filling out an application, or having an interview there, doesn't commit you to take the job - - but you probably already know that. You can always decline an offer from *any place*. That's what makes this approach harmless.)

| | Second Example: *Working at a place where you can't discover what the pay is, say at a construction company.* |

If that construction company where you would *hope* to get a job is difficult to research, go visit a *different* construction company in the same town - - one that isn't of much interest to you - - and ask what they make *there*. Or, if you don't know who to talk to there, fill out one of their applications, and talk to the hiring person about what kinds of jobs they have (or might have in the future), at which time prospective wages is a legitimate subject of discussion. Then, having done this research on a place you don't care about, go back to the place that *really* interests you, and apply. You still don't know *exactly* what they pay, but you do know what their competitor pays - - which will usually be *close*.

| | Third Example: *Working in a one-person office, say as a secretary.* |

Here you can often find useful salary information by perusing the *Help Wanted* ads in the local paper for a week or two. Most of the ads probably won't mention a salary figure, but a few *may*. Among those that do, note what the lowest salary offering is, and what the highest is, and see if the ad reveals some reasons for the difference. It's interesting how much you can learn about salaries, with this approach. I know, because I was a secretary myself, once upon a time.

Another way to do salary research is to find a *Temporary Work Agency* that places secretaries, and let yourself be farmed out to various offices: the more, the merrier. It's relatively easy to do salary research when you're *inside* the place. (Study what that place pays *the agency*, not what the agency pays you.) If it's an office where the other workers like you, you'll be able to ask questions about a lot of things, *including* salary. It's like *summertime*, where the research is easy.

☐ Fourth Example: *Going into business for yourself, say cleaning private homes.*

You, of course, are new to this sort of a business, and you haven't a clue as to what to charge, or what homeowners are willing to pay *in your town or city.* However, there is a way out. When it is a familiar line of work, such as this, there often is some kind of outfit, or agency, that farms out such people -- not unlike the *Temporary Agencies* mentioned previously. These places are usually listed in your telephone book's *Yellow Pages.* However, it will often take some ingenuity on your part to discover *where* in the *Yellow Pages* they are listed. *Cleaning homes,* for example, may be listed not under "Cleaning" nor under "Homes," but under *House Cleaning.* If you're having trouble finding the kind of place you're looking for, remember the *Yellow Pages* usually has an index at the beginning. If all else fails, remember that agencies such as this often advertise in the Help Wanted section of your local newspaper,

The Going Rate

Estimated hourly wages for temporary workers in 1991.

Computer analyst	$23.40
Registered nurse	23.15
Computer programmer	20.40
Manager	15.70
Licensed practical nurse	14.85
Word processor	10.55
Secretary	9.85
Machinist	9.45
Bookkeeper	7.05
Typist	7.00
Data entry keyer	6.95
Telemarketer	6.85
Receptionist	6.80
General office clerk	6.35
Guard/hospital orderly janitor/kitchen worker	6.05
Laborer	5.15

Source: National Association of Temporary Services

in a section called "Services Offered" or "Domestic Services Offered." So, look for them there.

When you find an agency that you like the sound of, go sign up with them. When they send you out, you will quickly learn how much the homemaker pays for this service *(compared with how much of that the agency will let you keep!).* Then, when you are ready to strike out on your own, having quit that job, you will know what homeowners are willing to pay for the service you have to offer (not the lesser amount which you were allowed to keep, but the overall amount that the homeowners paid the agency). In setting your rates, then, you can choose to price your services lower, equal, or higher - - as you choose.

4. Finally, you want, if you can, to find out in the particular organizations you are approaching, what the person *who would be above you* makes, and what the person *who would be below you* makes. That *usually* determines what the range is, that the employer *has* to operate within, for *your* salary:

Table 4

If the Person Who Would Be Below You Makes	And The Person Who Would Be Above You Makes	Then The Range for Your Job Would Be
$22,000	$27,000	$23,000 – $26,000
$10,000	$13,500	$10,500 – $12,500
$ 6,240	$ 7,800	$ 6,400 – $ 7,600

One teensy-tiny little problem: *how* do you find out the salary of those who would be above and below you? Well, first you have to find out their *names* or the names of their *positions*. If it is a small organization you are going after - - one with twenty or less employees - - finding this information out should be *duck soup*. Any employee who works there is likely to know the answer, and you can usually get in touch with one of those employees, or even an ex-employee, through your contacts. Since two-thirds of all new jobs are created by companies of that size, that's the size organization you are likely to be researching, anyway.

If you are going after a larger organization, then you have our familiar life-preserver to fall back on, namely, every contact you have (family, friend, relative, business, or church acquaintance) who might know the company, and therefore, the information you seek. You are looking for Someone Who Knows Someone who either is working, or has worked, at the particular place or places that interest you, who therefore has or can get this information for you.

If you absolutely run into a blank wall on a particular organization (everyone who works there is pledged to secrecy, and they have shipped all their ex-employees to Siberia), then seek out information on their nearest *competitor* in the same geographic area. *For example,* let us say you were researching Bank X, and they were proving to be inscrutable about what they pay their managers. You would then try Bank Y as your research base, to see if the information were easier to come by, there. And if it were, you would then assume the two were similar in their pay scales, and that what you learned about Bank Y was applicable also to Bank X.

BACK TO THE INTERVIEW

With this research in your hip pocket, when you are in the actual job-interview and the employer mentions the figure *they* have in mind, you are then ready to respond: "I understand of course the constraints under which all organizations are operating in the '90s, but I believe my productivity is such that it would *justify* a salary in the range of"-- *and here you mention a figure near the top of their range.* Hopefully, this will succeed in getting you the salary you want.[11]

During your salary negotiation, do not forget to pay attention to so-called fringe benefits. 'Fringes' such as life insurance, health benefits or health plans, vacation or holiday plans, and retirement programs add another 25% to many workers' salaries. That is to say, if an employee receives $800 salary per month, the fringe benefits are worth another $200 per month. You should therefore remember to ask what benefits are offered, and negotiate if necessary for the benefits you want. Thinking this out ahead of time, of course, makes your negotiating easier, by far.

Once you have the job, you will want to remember that promotion and future raises will generally depend on:

a) getting your boss to like you; genuine compliments occasionally, will help. Brutal honesty -- 'you're the most difficult person I've ever had to work for' -- will not.

---

11. Daniel Porot, in Europe, suggests that if you and an employer really hit it off, and you're *dying* to work there, but they cannot afford the salary you need, consider offering them part of your time. If you need, and believe you deserve, say $25,000, but they can only afford $15,000, you might consider offering them three days a week of your time for that $15,000 (15/25 = 3/5). This leaves you free to take other work those other two days.

b) figuring out how the place *actually* works (not how they *claim* it works).

c) learning who to trust there, and who not to trust; beware of charming, but devious, people.

d) befriending people who always seem to know what's going on there, so that you are among the first to pick up the internal gossip at that place and not the last. You need *early warning* about what's going to happen next, there.

e) picking up challenging assignments, or originating them (once you've done all that was expected of you).

f) if it is a large place, accepting every chance that is offered you to work across departments or even outside the company, so that you are seen, seen, seen.

g) being always results-oriented, and never copping out by attempting to offer some lame excuse for why something didn't get done. (Though a brief, heartfelt, handwritten note of apology is *never* out of order.) Your job, in any organization, is not to *try* to do something, but to actually *accomplish* it. Last but not least:

h) keeping track of your accomplishments there, on a weekly basis -- jotting them down, every weekend, in your own private diary. Career experts, such as Bernard Haldane, recommend you do this without fail. You can then summarize these accomplishments annually on a one-page sheet, for your boss's eyes, when raise or promotion is a legitimate subject for you to bring up.[12]

You can prepare the ground for all this during your salary negotiation, by saying: *"If I accomplish this job to your satisfaction, as I fully expect to -- and more -- when could I expect to be in line for a raise?*

Once all salary negotiation is concluded to your satisfaction, do remember to ask to have it summed up in a letter of agreement -- or employment contract -- that they give to you. It may be you cannot get it in writing, but do try! The Road to Hell is

---

12. In any good-sized organization, you will often be amazed at how little attention your superiors pay to your noteworthy accomplishments, and how little they are aware at the end of the year that you really are *entitled* to a raise. Noteworthy your accomplishments may be, but no one is taking notes . . . unless *you* do.

paved with oral promises that went unwritten, and - - later - - unfulfilled.

Many executives unfortunately 'forget' what they told you during the job-interview, or even deny they ever said such a thing.

Also, many executives leave the company for another position and place, and their successor or the top boss may disown any *unwritten* promises: *"I don't know what caused them to say that to you, but they clearly exceeded their authority, and of course we can't be held to that."*

CONCLUSION

Job-hunting always involves luck, to some degree. But hopefully, with a little bit of luck, the techniques described in these chapters should work for you, even as they have worked for so many thousands before you.

Assuming they do, when you are in that next job - - hopefully your *ideal job* - - you will know the truth of something Dick Lathrop first said over twenty years ago, in his book *Who's Hiring Who:*

here may be others who applied there who could have done the job better than you. But it is true today, and it will ever be true: the person who gets hired is not necessarily the one who can do that job best; but, the one who knows the most about how to get hired.

The Pink Pages

Introduction

As I started writing this section on "Religion and Job-Hunting," I toyed at first with the idea of following what might be described as an "all-paths approach" to religion. But, after much thought, I decided not to try that. This, because I have read many other writers who tried, and I felt the approach failed miserably. An "all-paths" approach to religion ends up being a "no-paths" approach, even as a woman or man who tries to please everyone ends up pleasing no one. It is the old story of the "universal" vs. the "particular."

Those of us who do career counseling could predict, ahead of time, that trying to stay universal is not likely to be helpful, in writing about religion. We know well from our own field that truly helpful career counseling depends upon defining the **particularity** or uniqueness of each person we try to help. No employer wants to know only what you have in common with everyone else. He or she wants to know what makes you unique and individual. As I have argued throughout this book, the identification and inventory of your uniqueness or *particularity* is crucial if you are ever to find meaningful work.

This particularity invades and carries over to *everything* a person does; it is not suddenly "jettisonable" when he or she turns to religion. Therefore, when I or anyone else writes about religion I believe we **must** write out of our own particularity -- which *starts,* in my case, with the fact that I write, and think, and breathe as a Christian. So, this article speaks from my own personal Christian perspective. I want you to be forewarned.

I have always been acutely aware, however, that this is a pluralistic society in which we live, and that I owe a great deal of sensitivity to the readers of my books who may have convictions very different from my own. I rub up against these different convictions, daily. By accident and not design it has turned out that the people who work or have worked here in my office with me, over the years, have been predominantly Jewish, along with some non-religious and a smattering of Christians. Furthermore, **Parachute's** more than 4 million readers have included Christians of every variety and persuasion, Jews, members of the Baha'i faith, Hindus, Buddhists, adherents of Islam, and believers in 'new age' religions, as well as (of course) secularists, humanists, agnostics, atheists, and many others. Consequently, I have tried to be very courteous toward the feelings of all my readers who come from other persuasions or convictions than my own, *while at the same time* counting on them to translate my Christian thought forms into their own thought forms -- since this ability to thus translate is the indispensable *sine qua non* of anyone who aspires to communicate helpfully with others.

In the Judeo-Christian tradition from which I come, one of the indignant Biblical questions is, "Has God forgotten to be gracious?" The answer was a clear No. I think it is important *for all of us* also to seek the same goal. I have therefore labored to make this section gracious as well as helpful.

R. N. B.

The Epilogue

Religion
and
Job-Hunting:

How to Find Your Mission in Life

How I Came To Write This

Some time ago, a woman asked me how you go about finding out what your Mission in life is. She assumed I would know what she was talking about, because of a diagram which appears a number of times in one of my other books, The Three Boxes of Life:

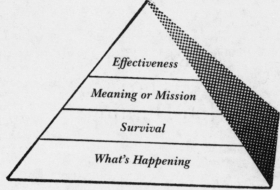

The Issues of the Job-Hunt

As this diagram asserts, the question of one's Mission in life arises naturally as a part of many people's job-hunt.

She told me that what she was looking for was not some careful, dispassionate, philosophical answer, where every statement is hedged about with cautions and caveats -- "It may be . . ." or "It seems to me . . ." Nor did she want to know why I thought what I did, or how I learned it, or what Scriptures support it. "I want you to just speak with passion and conviction," she said, "out of what you most truly feel and believe. For it is some vision that I want. I am hungry for a vision of what I can be. So, just speak to me of what you most truly feel and believe about our mission in life. I will know how to translate your vision into my own thought forms for my own life, when I reflect afterwards upon what you have said. But I want you to talk about this now with passion and conviction -- please."

And so, I did. And I will now tell you what I said to her.

The Motive for Finding
A Sense of Mission in Life

We begin with the fact that, according to fifty years of opinion polls conducted by the Gallup Organization, 94% of us believe in God, 90% of us pray, 88% of us believe God loves us, and 33% of us report we have had a life-changing religious experience (*The People's Religion: American Faith in the 90s. Macmillan & Co. 1989*).

It is hardly surprising therefore, that so many of us are searching these days for some sense of mission. Career counselors are often afraid to give help or guidance here, for fear they will be perceived as trying to talk people into religious belief. It is a groundless fear. Clearly, the overwhelming majority of U.S. job-hunters and career-changers already have their religious beliefs well in place.

But, we want some guidance and help in this area, because we want to *marry* our religious **beliefs** with our **work**, rather than leaving the two -- our religion and our work -- compartmentalized, as two areas of our life which never talk to each other. We *want* them to talk to each other and uplift each other.

This marriage takes the particular form of a search for a Sense of Mission because of our conviction that God has made each of us unique, even as our fingerprints attest. We feel that we are not just another grain of sand lying on the beach called humanity, unnumbered and lost in the 5 billion mass, but that God caused us to be born and put here for some unique reason: so that we might contribute to Life here on earth something no one else can contribute in quite the same way. At its very minimum, then, when we search for a sense of Mission we are searching for reassurance that the world is at least a little bit richer for our being here; and a little bit poorer after our going.

Every keen observer of human nature will know what I mean when I say that those who have found some sense of Mission have a very special joy, "which no one can take from them." It is wonderful to feel that beyond eating, sleeping, working, having pleasure and *it may be* marrying, having children, and growing older, you were set here on Earth for some special purpose, *and* that you can gain some idea of what that purpose is.

So, how does one go about this search?

I would emphasize, at the outset, two cautions. First of all, though I will explain the steps that seem to me to be involved in finding one's Mission -- based on the learnings I have accumulated over some sixty years, I want to caution you that these steps are not the only Way -- by any means. Many people have discovered their Mission by taking other paths. And you may, too. But hopefully what I have to say may shed some light upon whatever path you take.

My second caution is simply this: you would be wise not to try to approach this problem of "your Mission in life" as primarily an **intellectual** puzzle -- for the mind, and the mind alone, to solve. To paraphrase Kahlil Gibran, *Faith* is an oasis in the heart that is not reached merely by the journey of the mind. It is your will and your heart that must be involved in the search as well as your mind. To put it quite simply, it takes the total person to learn one's total Mission.

It also takes the total disciplines of the ages -- not only modern knowledge but also ancient thought, including the wisdom of religion, faith, and the spiritual matters. For, to put it quite bluntly, the question of Mission inevitably leads us to God.

The Main Obstacle in Finding Your Mission in Life: Job-Hunting Compartmentalized from Our Religion or Faith

Mission challenges us to see our job-hunt in relationship to our faith in God, because *Mission* is a religious concept, from beginning to end. It is defined by Webster's as "a continuing task or responsibility that one is destined or fitted to do or specially called upon to undertake," and historically has had two major synonyms: *Calling* and *Vocation*. These, of course, are the same word in two different languages, English and Latin. Regardless of which word is used, it is obvious upon reflection, that a Vocation or Calling implies *Someone who calls*, and that a destiny implies *Someone who determined the destination for us*. Thus, unless one opts for a military or governmental view of the matter, the concept of Mission with relationship to our whole life lands us inevitably in the lap of God, before we have even begun.

There is always the temptation to try to speak of this subject of *Mission* in a secular fashion, without reference to God, as though it might be simply "a purpose you choose for your own life, by identifying your enthusiasms, and then using the clues you find from that exercise to get some purpose you can choose for your life." The language of this temptation is ironic because the substitute word used for "Mission" -- *Enthusiasm* -- is derived from the Greek, *'en theos'*, and literally means "God in us."

It is no accident that so many of the leaders in the job-hunting field over the years -- the late John Crystal, Arthur Miller, Ralph Mattson, Tom and Ellie Jackson, Bernard Haldane, Arthur and Marie Kirn, and myself -- have been people of faith. If you would figure out your Mission in life, you must also be willing to think about God in connection with your job-hunt.

The Secret of Finding Your Mission in Life: Taking It in Stages

The puzzle of figuring out what your Mission in life is, will likely take some time. It is not a *problem* to be solved in a day and a night. It is a *learning process* which has steps to it, much like the process by which we all learned to eat. As a baby we did not tackle adult food right off. As we all recall, there were three stages: first there had to be the mother's milk or bottle, then strained baby foods, and finally -- after teeth and time -- the stuff that grown-ups chew. Three stages -- and the two earlier stages were not to be disparaged. It was all Eating, just different forms of Eating -- appropriate to our development at the time. But each stage had to be mastered, in turn, before the next could be approached.

The Three Stages of Mission: What We Need to Learn

By coincidence, there are usually three stages also to learning what your Mission in life is, and the two earlier stages are likewise not to be disparaged. It is all "Mission" -- just different forms of Mission, appropriate to your development at the time. But each stage has to be mastered, in turn, before the next can be approached. And so, you may say either of two things: You may say that you have *Three Missions in Life.* Or you may say that you have *One Mission in Life, with three parts to it.* But there is a sense in which you must discover what those three parts are, each in turn, before you can fully answer the question, "What is my Mission in life?" Of course, there is another sense in which you never master any of these stages, but are always growing in understanding and mastery of them, throughout your whole life here on Earth.

As it has been impressed on me by observing many people over the years (admittedly through *Christian spectacles*), it appears that the three parts to your Mission here on Earth can be defined generally as follows:

(1) *Your first Mission here on Earth* is one which you share with the rest of the human race, but it is no less your individual Mission for the fact that it is shared: and it is, **to seek to stand hour by hour in the conscious presence of God, the One from whom your Mission is derived.** *The Missioner before the Mission,* is the rule. In religious language, your Mission here is: *to know God, and enjoy Him forever, and to see His hand in all His works.*

(2) Secondly, once you have begun doing that in an earnest way, *your second Mission here on Earth* is also one which you share with the rest of the human race, but it is no less your individual mission for the fact that it is shared: and that is, **to do what you can, moment by moment, day by day, step by step, to make this world a better place, following the leading and guidance of God's Spirit within you and around you.**

(3) Thirdly, once you have begun doing that in a serious way, *your third Mission here on Earth* is one which is uniquely yours, and that is:
   a) **to exercise that Talent which you particularly came to Earth to use -- your greatest gift, which you most delight to use,**
   b) **in the place(s) or setting(s) which God has caused to appeal to you the most,**
   c) **and for those purposes which God most needs to have done in the world.**

When fleshed out, and spelled out, I think you will find that there you have the definition of your Mission in life. Or, to put it another way, these are the three Missions which you have in life.

The Two Rhythms of the Dance of Mission: Unlearning, Learning, Unlearning, Learning

The distinctive characteristic of these three stages is that in each we are forced to *let go* of some fundamental assumptions which the world has *falsely* taught us, about the nature of our Mission. In other words, throughout this quest and at each stage we find ourselves engaged not merely in a process of *Learning*. We are also engaged in a process of *Un*learning. Thus, we can restate the above three Learnings, in terms of what we also need to *un*learn at each stage:

• We need in the first Stage to *un*learn the idea that our Mission is primarily to keep busy *doing* something (here on Earth), and learn instead that our Mission is first of all to keep busy being something (here on Earth). In Christian language (and others as well), we might say that we were sent here to learn how *to be* sons of God, and daughters of God, before anything else. *"Our Father, who art in heaven . . ."*

• In the second stage, "Being" issues into "Doing." At this stage, we need to *un*learn the idea that everything about our Mission must be *unique* to us, and learn instead that some parts of our Mission here on Earth are *shared* by all human beings: e.g., we were all sent here to bring more gratitude, more kindness, more forgiveness, and more love, into the world. We share this Mission because the task is too large to be accomplished by just one individual.

• We need in the third stage to *un*learn the idea that that part of our Mission which is truly unique, and most truly ours, is something Our Creator just *orders* us to do, without any agreement from our spirit, mind, and heart. (On the other hand, neither is it something that each of us chooses and then merely asks God to bless.) We need to learn that God so honors our free will, that He has ordained our unique Mission be something which we have some part in choosing.

• In this third stage we need also to *un*learn the idea that our unique Mission must consist of some achievement which all the world will see, -- and learn instead that as the stone does not always know what ripples it has caused in the pond whose surface it impacts, so neither we nor those who watch our life will always know *what we have achieved* by our life and by our Mission. *It may be* that by the grace of God we helped bring about a profound change for the better in the lives of other souls around us, but it also may be that this takes place beyond our sight, or after we have gone on. And we may never know what we have accomplished, until we see Him face-to-face after this life is past.

• Most finally, we need to *un*learn the idea that what we have accomplished is our doing, and ours alone. It is God's Spirit breathing in us and through us which helps us to do whatever we do, and so the singular first person pronoun is never appropriate, but only the plural. Not "*I* accomplished this" but "*We* accomplished this, God and I, working together . . ."

That should give you a general overview. But I would like to add some random comments on my part about each of these three Missions of ours here on Earth.

> # Some Random Comments About
> # Your First Mission in Life

Your first Mission here on Earth is one which you share with the rest of the human race, but it is no less your individual Mission for the fact that it is shared: and that is, **to seek to stand hour by hour in the conscious presence of God, the One from whom your Mission is derived.** The Missioner before the Mission, is the rule. In religious language, your Mission is: to know God, and enjoy Him for ever, and to see His hand in all His works.

Comment 1: How We Might Think of God

Each of us has to go about this primary Mission according to the tenets of his or her own particular religion. But I will speak what I know out of the context of my own particular faith, and you may perhaps translate and apply it to yours. I will speak as a Christian, who believes (passionately) that Christ is the Way and the Truth and the Life. But I also believe, with St. Peter, "that God shows no partiality, but in every nation any one who fears him and does what is right is acceptable to him." (Acts 10:34-35)

Now, Jesus claimed many unique things about Himself and His Mission; but He also spoke of Himself as the great prototype for us all. He called himself "the Son of Man," and He said, "I assure you that the man who believes in me will do the same things that I have done, yes, and he will do even greater things than these . . ." (John 14:12)

Emboldened by His identification of us with His life and His Mission, we might want to remember how He spoke about His Life here on Earth. He put it in this context: **"I came from the Father and have come into the world; again, I am leaving the world and going to the Father."** (John 16:28)

If there is a sense in which this is, in even the faintest way, true also of our lives (and I shall say in a moment in what sense I think it is true), then instead of calling our great Creator "God" or "Father" right off, we might begin our approach to the subject of religion by referring to the One Who gave us our Mission and sent us to this planet not as "God" or "Father" but -- *just to help our thinking* -- as: **"The One From Whom We Came and The One To Whom We Shall Return,"** when this life is done.

If our life here on Earth be at all like Christ's, then this is a true way to think about the One who gave us our Mission. We are not some kind of eternal, pre-existent *being*. We are **creatures**, who once did not exist, and then came into Being, and continue to have our Being, only at the will of our great Creator. But as creatures we are both body and soul; and although we know our body was created in our mother's womb, our soul's origin is a great mystery. Where it came from, at what moment the Lord created it, is something we cannot know. It is not unreasonable to suppose, however, that the great God created our *soul* before it entered our body, and in that sense we did indeed stand before God before we were born; and He is indeed **"The One From Whom We Came and The One To Whom We Shall Return."**

Therefore, before we go searching for "what work was I sent here to do?" we need to establish or in a truer sense *reestablish* -- contact with this **"One From Whom We Came and The One To Whom We Shall Return."** Without this reaching out of the creature to the great Creator, without this reaching out of *the creature with a Mission* to *the One Who Gave Us That Mission*, the question **what** *is my Mission in life*? is void and null. The *what* is rooted in the *Who*; absent the Personal, one cannot meaningfully discuss The Thing. It is like the adult who cries, "I want to get married," without giving any consideration to *who* it is they want to marry.

Comment 2: How We Might Think of Religion or Faith

In light of this larger view of our creatureliness, we can see that *religion* or *faith* is not a question of whether or not we choose to (*as it is so commonly put*) "have a relationship with God." Looking at our life in a larger context than just our life here on Earth, it becomes apparent that some sort of relationship with God is a given for us, about which we have absolutely no choice. God and we **were and are** related, during the time of our soul's existence before our birth and in the time of our soul's continued existence after our death. The only choice we have is what to do about **The Time In Between,** i.e., what we want the nature of our relationship with God to be during our time here on Earth and how that will affect the *nature* of the relationship, then, after death.

One of the corollaries of all this is that by the very act of being born into a human body, it is an inevitable that we undergo a kind of *amnesia* -- an amnesia which typically embraces not only our nine months in the womb, our baby years, and almost one third of each day (sleeping), but more importantly any memory of our origin or our destiny. We wander on Earth as an amnesia victim. To seek after Faith, therefore, is to seek to climb back out of that amnesia. Religion or faith is **the hard reclaiming of knowledge we once knew as a certainty.**

Comment 3: The First Obstacle to Executing This Mission

This first Mission of ours here on Earth is not the easiest of Missions, simply because it is the first. Indeed, in many ways, it is the most difficult. All can see that our life here on Earth is a very physical life. We eat, we drink, we sleep, we long to be held, and to hold. We inherit a physical body, with very physical appetites, we walk on the physical earth, and we acquire physical possessions. It is the most alluring of temptations, *in our amnesia*, to come up with just a *Physical* interpretation of this life: to think that the Universe is merely interested in the survival of species. Given this interpretation, the story of our individual life could be simply told: we are born, grow up, procreate, and die.

But we are ever recalled to do what we came here to do: that without rejecting the joy of the Physicalness of this life, such as the love of the blue sky and the green grass, we are to reach out beyond all this to **recall** and recover a *Spiritual* interpretation of our life. *Beyond* the physical and *within* the physicalness of this life, to detect a Spirit and a Person from beyond this Earth who is with us and in us -- the very real and loving and awesome Presence of the great Creator from whom we came -- and the One to whom we once again shall go.

Comment 4: The Second Obstacle to Executing This Mission

It is one of the conditions of our earthly amnesia and our creatureliness that, sadly enough, some very *human* and very *rebellious* part of us *likes* the idea of living in a world where we can be our own god -- and therefore loves the purely Physical interpretation of life, and finds it *anguish* to relinquish it. Traditional Christian vocabulary calls this **"sin"** and has a lot to say about the difficulty it poses for this first part of our Mission. All who live a thoughtful life know that it is true: our greatest enemy in carrying out this first Mission of ours is indeed *our own* heart and our own rebellion.

Comment 5: Further Thoughts About What Makes Us Special and Unique

As I said earlier, many of us come to this issue of our Mission in life, because we want to feel that we are unique. And what we mean by that, is that we hope to discover some "specialness" intrinsic to us, which is our birthright, and which no one can take from us. What we, however, discover from a thorough exploration of this topic, is that we are indeed special -- but only because God thinks us so. Our specialness and uniqueness reside in Him, and His love, rather than in anything intrinsic to our own *being*. The proper appreciation of this distinction causes our feet to carry us in the end not to the City called Pride, but to the Temple called Gratitude.

What is religion? Religion is the service of God out of grateful love for what God has done for us. The Christian religion, more particularly, is the service of God out of grateful love for what God has done for us in Christ.

Phillips Brooks, author of
O Little Town of Bethlehem

Comment 6: The Unconscious Doing of The Work We Came To Do

You may have *already* wrestled with this first part of your Mission here on Earth. You may not have called it that. You may have called it simply "learning to believe in God." But if you ask what your Mission is in life, this one was and is the precondition of all else that you came here to do. Absent this Mission, and it is folly to talk about the rest. So, if you have been seeking faith, or seeking to strengthen your faith, you have -- willy nilly -- already been about *the doing of the Mission you were given.* Born into **This Time In Between,** you have found His hand again, and reclasped it. You are therefore ready to go on with His Spirit to tackle together what you came here to do -- the other parts of your Mission.

Some Random Comments About Your Second Mission in Life

Your second Mission here on Earth is also one which you share with the rest of the human race, but it is no less your individual mission for the fact that it is shared: and that is, **to do what you can moment by moment, day by day, step by step, to make this world a better place -- following the leading and guidance of God's Spirit within you and around you.**

Comment 1: The Uncomfortableness of One Step at a Time

Imagine yourself out walking in your neighborhood one night, and suddenly you find yourself surrounded by such a dense fog, that you have lost your bearings and cannot find your way. Suddenly, a friend appears out of the fog, and asks you to put your hand in theirs, and they will lead you home. And you, not being able to tell where you are going, trustingly follow them, even though you can only see one step at a time. Eventually you arrive safely home, filled with gratitude. But as you reflect upon the experience the next day, you realize how unsettling it was to have to keep walking when you could see only one step at a time, even though you had guidance in which you knew you could trust.

Now I have asked you to imagine all of this, because this is the essence of the second Mission to which *you* are called -- and *I* am called -- in this life. It is all very different than we had imagined. When the question,

"What is your Mission in life?" is first broached, and we have put our hand in God's, as it were, we imagine that we will be taken up to *some mountaintop,* from which we can see far into the distance. And that we will hear a voice in our ear, saying, "Look, look, see that distant city? That is the goal of your Mission; that is where everything is leading, every step of your way."

But instead of the mountaintop, we find ourself in *the valley* -- wandering often in a fog. And the voice in our ear says something quite different from what we thought we would hear. It says, **"Your Mission is to take one step at a time, even when you don't yet see where it all is leading, or what the Grand Plan is, or what your overall Mission in life is. Trust Me; I will lead you."**

Comment 2: The Nature of This Step-by-Step Mission

As I said, in every situation you find yourself, you have been sent here to do whatever you can -- moment by moment -- that will bring more gratitude, more kindness, more forgiveness, more honesty, and more love into this world.

There are dozens of such moments every day. Moments when you stand -- as it were -- at a spiritual crossroads, with two ways lying before you. Such moments are typically called **"moments of decision."** It does not matter what the frame or content of each particular decision is. It all devolves, in the end, into just two roads before you, *every time.* **The one** will lead to *less* gratitude, *less* kindness, *less* forgiveness, *less* honesty, or *less* love in the world. **The other** will lead to *more* gratitude, *more* kindness, *more* forgiveness, *more* honesty, or *more* love in the world. Your Mission, each moment, is to seek to choose the latter spiritual road, rather than the former, *every time.*

Comment 3: Some Examples of This Step-by-Step Mission

I will give a few examples, so that the nature of this part of your Mission may be unmistakably clear.

You are out on the freeway, in your car. Someone has gotten into the wrong lane, to the right of *your* lane, and needs to move over into the lane you are in. You *see* their need to cut in, ahead of you. **Decision time.** In your mind's eye you see two spiritual roads lying before you: the one leading to less kindness in the world (you speed up, to shut this driver out, and don't let them move over), the other leading to more kindness in the world (you let the driver cut in). **Since you know this is part of your Mission, part of the reason why you came to Earth, your calling is clear. You know which road to take, which decision to make.**

You are hard at work at your desk, when suddenly an interruption comes. The phone rings, or someone is at the door. They need something from you, a question of some of your time and attention. **Decision time.**

In your mind's eye you see two spiritual roads lying before you: the one leading to less love in the world (you tell them you're just too busy to be bothered), the other leading to more love in the world (you put aside your work, decide that God may have sent this person to you, and say, "Yes, what can I do to help you?"). **Since you know this is part of your Mission, part of the reason why you came to Earth, your calling is clear. You know which road to take, which decision to make.**

Your mate does something that hurts your feelings. **Decision time.** In your mind's eye you see two spiritual roads lying before you: the one leading to less forgiveness in the world (you institute an icy silence between the two of you, and think of how you can punish them or otherwise get

even), the other leading to more forgiveness in the world (you go over and take them in your arms, speak the truth about your hurt feelings, and assure them of your love). **Since you know this is part of your Mission, part of the reason why you came to Earth, your calling is clear. You know which road to take, which decision to make.**

You have not behaved at your most noble, recently. And now you are face-to-face with someone who asks you a question about what happened. **Decision time.** In your mind's eye you see two spiritual roads lying before you: the one leading to less honesty in the world (you lie about what happened, or what you were feeling, because you fear losing their respect or their love), the other leading to more honesty in the world (you tell the truth, together with how you feel about it, in retrospect). **Since you know this is part of your Mission, part of the reason why you came to Earth, your calling is clear. You know which road to take, which decision to make.**

Comment 4: The Spectacle Which Makes the Angels Laugh

It is necessary to explain this part of our Mission in some detail, because so many times you will see people wringing their hands, and saying, *"I want to know what my Mission in life is,"* all the while they are cutting people off on the highway, refusing to give time to people, punishing their mate for having hurt their feelings, and lying about what they did. And it will seem to you that the angels must laugh to see this spectacle. *For these people wringing their hands,* their Mission was right there, on the freeway, in the interruption, in the hurt, and at the confrontation.

Comment 5: The Valley vs. The Mountaintop

At some point in your life your Mission may involve some grand *mountaintop experience,* where you say to yourself, "This, this, is why I came into the world. I know it. I know it." *But until then,* your Mission is here in *the valley,* and the fog, and the little callings moment by moment, day by day. More to the point, it is likely you cannot ever get to your mountaintop Mission unless you have first exercised your stewardship faithfully in the valley.

It is an ancient principle, to which Jesus alluded often, that if you don't use the information the Universe has already given you, you cannot expect it will give you any more. If you aren't being faithful in small things, how can you expect to be given charge over larger things? (Luke 16:10,11,12; 19:11-24) If you aren't trying to bring more gratitude, kindness, forgiveness, honesty, and love into the world each day, you can hardly expect that you will be entrusted with the Mission to help bring peace into the world or anything else large and important. If we do not live out our day-by-day Mission in the valley, we cannot expect we are yet ready for a larger *mountaintop* Mission.

Comment 6: The Importance of Not Thinking of This Mission As 'Just A Training Camp'

The valley is not just a kind of "training camp." There is in your imagination even now an invisible *spiritual* mountaintop to which you may go, if you wish to see where all this is leading. And what will you see there, in the imagination of your heart, but the goal toward which all this is pointed: **that Earth might be more like heaven. That human's life might be more like God's.** That is the large achievement toward which all our day by day Missions *in the valley* are moving. This is a *large* order, but it is accomplished by faithful attention to the doing of our great Creator's **will** in little things as well as in large. It is much like the building of the pyramids in Egypt, which was accomplished by the dragging of a lot of individual pieces of stone by a lot of individual men.

The valley, the fog, the going step-by-step, is no mere training camp. The goal is real, however large. **"Thy Kingdom come, Thy will be done, on Earth, as it is in heaven."**

Some Random Comments
About Your Third Mission
in Life

Your third Mission here on Earth is one which is uniquely yours, and that is:

a) **to exercise that Talent which you particularly came to Earth to use -- your greatest gift which you most delight to use**

b) **in those place(s) or setting(s) which God has caused to appeal to you the most,**

c) **and for those purposes which God most needs to have done in the world.**

Comment 1: Our Mission Is Already Written, "in Our Members"

It is customary in trying to identify this part of our Mission, to advise that we should ask God, in prayer, to speak to us -- and **tell us** plainly what our Mission is. We look for a voice in the air, a thought in our head, a dream in the night, a sign in the events of the day, to reveal this thing which is otherwise *(it is said)* completely hidden. Sometimes, from just such answered prayer, people do indeed discover what their Mission is, beyond all doubt and uncertainty.

But having to wait for the voice of God to reveal what our Mission is, is not the truest picture of our situation. St. Paul, in Romans, speaks of a law "written in our members," -- and this phrase has a telling application to the question of **how** God reveals to each of us our unique Mission in life. Read again the definition of our third Mission (above) and you will see: the clear implication of the definition is that God has **already** revealed His will to us concerning our vocation and Mission, by causing it to be **"written in our members."** We are to begin deciphering our unique Mission by studying our talents and skills, and more particularly which ones (or One) we most rejoice to use.

God actually has written His will *twice* in our members: *first in the talents* which He lodged there, and secondly *in His guidance of our heart*, as to which talent gives us the greatest pleasure from its exercise (**it is usually the one which, when we use it, causes us to lose all sense of time).**

Even as the anthropologist can examine ancient inscriptions, and divine from them the daily life of a long lost people, so we by examining **our talents** and **our heart** can *more often than we dream* divine the Will of the Living God. For true it is, our Mission is not something He **will** reveal; it is something He **has already** revealed. It is not to be found written in the sky; it is to be found written in our members.

Comment 2: Career Counseling: We Need You

Arguably, our first two Missions in life could be learned from religion alone -- without any reference whatsoever to career counseling, the subject of this book. Why then should career counseling claim that this question about our Mission in life is its proper concern, *in any way?*

It is when we come to this third Mission, which hinges so crucially on the question of our Talents, skills, and gifts, that we see the answer. If you've read the body of this book, before turning to this Epilogue, you know without my even saying it, how much the identification of Talents, gifts, or skills is the province of career counseling. Its expertise, indeed its *raison d'etre*, lies precisely in the identification, classification, and (forgive me) "prioritization" of Talents, skills, and gifts. To put the matter quite simply, career counseling knows how to do this better than any other discipline -- **including** traditional religion. This is not a defect of religion, but the fulfillment of something Jesus promised: "When the Spirit of truth comes, He will guide you into all truth." (John 16:12) Career counseling is part (we may hope) of that promised late-coming truth. It can therefore be of inestimable help to the pilgrim who is trying to figure out what their greatest, and most enjoyable, talent is, as a step toward identifying their unique Mission in life.

If career counseling needs religion as its helpmate in the first two stages of identifying our Mission in life, religion repays the compliment by clearly needing career counseling as **its** helpmate here in the third stage.

And this place where you are in your life right now -- facing the job-hunt and all its anxiety -- is the perfect time to seek the union within your own mind and heart of both career counseling (as in the pages of this book) and your faith in God.

Comment 3: How Our Mission Got Chosen: A Scenario for the Romantic

It is a mystery which we cannot fathom, in this life at least, as to why one of us has this talent, and the other one has that; why God chose to give one gift -- and Mission -- to one person, and a different gift -- and Mission -- to another. Since we do not know, and in some degree cannot know, we are certainly left free to speculate, and imagine.

We may imagine that before we came to Earth, our souls, *our Breath, our Light*, stood before the great Creator and volunteered for this Mission. And God and we, together, chose what that Mission would be and what particular gifts would be needed, which He then agreed to give us, after our birth. Thus, our Mission was not a command given peremptorily by an unloving Creator to a reluctant slave without a vote, but was a task jointly designed by us both, in which as fast as the great Creator said, **"I wish"** our hearts responded, **"Oh, yes."** As mentioned in an earlier Comment, it may be helpful to think of the condition of our becoming human as that we became amnesiac about any consciousness our soul had before birth -- and therefore amnesiac about the nature or manner in which our Mission was designed.

Our searching for our Mission now is therefore a searching to recover the memory of something we ourselves had a part in designing.

I am admittedly a hopeless romantic, so of course I like this picture. If you also are a hopeless romantic, you may like it too. There's also the chance that it just may be true. We will not know until we see Him face-to-face.

Comment 4: Mission As Intersection

> There are all different kinds of voices calling you to all different kinds of work, and the problem is to find out which is the voice of God rather than that of society, say, or the superego, or self-interest. By and large a good rule for finding out is this: the kind of work God usually calls you to is the kind of work (a) that you need most to do and (b) the world most needs to have done. If you really get a kick out of your work, you've presumably met requirement (a), but if your work is writing TV deodorant commercials, the chances are you've missed requirement (b). On the other hand, if your work is being a doctor in a leper colony, you have probably met (b), but if most of the time you're bored and depressed by it, the chances are you haven't only bypassed (a) but probably aren't helping your patients much either. Neither the hair shirt nor the soft birth will do. The place God calls you to is the place where your deep gladness and the world's deep hunger meet.
>
> Frederick Buechner
> *Wishful Thinking -- A Theological ABC*
>
> Excerpted from *Wishful Thinking -- A Theological ABC* by Frederick Buechner. Copyright © 1973 by Frederick Buechner. Reprinted with permission of HarperCollins, Inc.

Comment 5: Examples of Mission As Intersection

Your unique and individual mission will most likely turn out to be a mission of Love, acted out in one or all of three arenas: either in the Kingdom of the Mind, whose goal is to bring more Truth into the world; or in the Kingdom of the Heart, whose goal is to bring more beauty into the world; or in the Kingdom of the Will, whose goal is to bring more Perfection into the world, through Service.

Here are some examples:

"My mission is, out of the rich reservoir of love which God seems to have given me, to nurture and show love to others -- most particularly to those who are suffering from incurable diseases."

"My mission is to draw maps for people to show them how to get to God."

"My mission is to create the purest foods I can, to help people's bodies not get in the way of their spiritual growth."

"My mission is to make the finest harps I can so that people can hear the voice of God in the wind."

"My mission is to make people laugh, so that the travail of this earthly life doesn't seem quite so hard to them."

"My mission is to help people know the truth, in love, about what is happening out in the world, so that there will be more honesty in the world."

"My mission is to weep with those who weep, so that in my arms they may feel themselves in the arms of that Eternal Love which sent me and which created them."

"My mission is to create beautiful gardens, so that in the lilies of the field people may behold the Beauty of God and be reminded of the Beauty of Holiness."

Comment 6: Life As Long As Your Mission Requires

Knowing that you came to Earth for a reason, and knowing what that Mission is, throws an entirely different light upon your life from now on. You are, generally speaking, delivered from any further fear about how long you have to live. You may settle it in your heart that you are here until God chooses to think that you have accomplished your Mission, or until God has a greater Mission for you in another Realm. You need to be a good steward of what He has given you, while you are here; but you do not need to be an anxious steward or stewardess.

You need to attend to your health, *but you do not need to constantly worry about it*. You need to meditate on your death, *but you do not need to be constantly preoccupied with it*. To paraphrase the glorious words of G. K. Chesterton: **"We now have a strong desire for living combined with a strange carelessness about dying. We desire life like water and yet are ready to drink death like wine."** We know that we are here to do what we came to do, and we need not worry about anything else.

Final Comment: A Job-Hunt Done Well

If you approach your job-hunt as an opportunity to work on this issue as well as the issue of how you will keep body and soul together, then hopefully your job-hunt will end with your being able to say: "Life has deep meaning to me, now. I have discovered more than my ideal job; I have found my Mission, and the reason why I am here on Earth."

For Further Reading

The following resources are written primarily from a Christian orientation, but they should be suggestive and helpful for people of any faith, as you mentally translate these texts into your own thought-forms and concepts of your faith:

Mattson, Ralph, and Miller, Arthur, *Finding a Job You Can Love.* Thomas Nelson Publishers, Nelson Place at Elm Hill Pike, Nashville, TN 37214. 1982. The most useful, I think, of all the books in this section.

Lewis, Roy, *Choosing Your Career, Finding Your Vocation: A Step by Step Guide for Adults and Counselors.* Integration Books, Paulist Press, 997 Macarthur Blvd., Mahwah, NJ 07430. 1989.

Blanchard, Tim, *A Practical Guide to Finding and Using Your Spiritual Gifts.* Tyndale House Publishers, Inc., Wheaton, Illinois.

Moran, Pamela J., *The Christian Job Hunter.* Servant Publications, 840 Airport Blvd., Box 8617, Ann Arbor, MI 48107. 1984.

Edwards, Lloyd, *Discerning Your Spiritual Gifts.* Cowley Publications, 980 Memorial Drive, Cambridge, MA 02138. 1988.

Moore, Christopher Chamberlin, *What I Really Want To Do . . . : How to Discover The Right Job.* CBP Press, Box 179, St. Louis, MO 63166. 1989.

Staub, Dick; Trautman, Jeff; and Cutshall, Mark, eds., *Intercristo's CAREER KIT: A Christian's Guide to Career Building.* Intercristo, 19303 Fremont Ave. N., Seattle WA 98133. 1985. Booklets (6) and cassette tapes (3) enclosed in binder.

Wehrheim, Carol and Cole-Turner, Ronald S., *Vocation and Calling. Introduction/Hearing God's Call/Sharing Gifts: An Intergenerational Study Guide.* United Church Press, 475 Riverside Dr., 10th fl., New York, NY 10115. 1985.

Lewis, Roy, *Choosing Your Career, Finding Your Vocation: A Step by Step Guide for Adults and Counselors.* Paulist Press. 1990. Particularly helpful for mid-life issues.

Rinker, Richard N., and Eisentrout, Virginia, *Called to Be Gifted and Giving: An Adult Resource for Vocation and Calling.* United Church Press, 475 Riverside Dr., 10th fl., New York, NY 10115. 1985.

For Counseling

All counselors in these centers are sincere; many are also very skilled. If you run into a clerical counselor who is sincere but inept, you will probably discover that the ineptness consists in an inadequate understanding of the distinction between career **assessment** -- roughly comparable to taking a snapshot of people as they are in one frozen moment of time -- vs. career **development** -- which is roughly comparable to teaching people how to take their own motion pictures of themselves, from here on out.

Having issued this caution, however, I will go on to add that at some of these centers, listed below, are some simply *excellent* counselors who fully understand this distinction, and are well trained in that empowering of the client, which is what career *development* is all about.

We begin with counseling centers founded primarily to help **clergy** (though in most cases not restricted just to them). No profession has developed, or had developed for it, so many resources to aid in career assessment as has this profession.

THE OFFICIAL INTERDENOMINATIONAL CAREER DEVELOPMENT CENTERS

The Career and Personal
Counseling Service
St. Andrew's Presbyterian College
Laurinburg, NC 28352
919-276-3162
Also at: 4108 Park Rd., Suite 200
Charlotte, NC 28209
704-523-7751
Elbert R. Patton, Director

The Career and Personal
Counseling Center
Eckerd College
St. Petersburg, FL 33733
813-864-8356, Ext. 356
John R. Sims, Director

The Center for Ministry
8393 Capwell Dr., Suite 220
Oakland, CA 94621-2123
510-635-4246
Robert L. Charpentier, Director

Lancaster Career
Development Center
561 College Ave.
Lancaster, PA 17603
717-397-7451
L. Guy Mehl, Director

North Central Career
Development Center
3000 Fifth St. NW
New Brighton, MN 55112
612-636-5120
John Davis, Director

Northeast Career Center
407 Nassau Street
Princeton, NJ 08540
609-924-9408
Roy Lewis, Director

Career Development Center
of the Southeast
531 Kirk Rd.
Decatur, GA 30030
404-371-0336
Robert M. Urie, Director

Midwest Career
Development Service
1840 Westchester Blvd.
Westchester, IL 60154
708-343-6268
Also at: 2501 North Star Rd.
Columbus, OH 43221
614-486-0469
Also at: 754 N. 31st St.
Kansas City, KS 66110
Ronald Brushwyler, Director

Southwest Career
Development Center
Box 5923
Arlington, TX 76011
817-640-5181
William M. Gould, Jr.,
Director-Counselor

Center for Career
Development and Ministry
70 Chase St.
Newton Center, MA 02159
617-969-7750
Stephen Ott, Director.

Clergy wishing to stay within the parish ministry, but wanting help with the search, will want to know about:

Mead, Loren B., and Miller, Arthur F., and Ayers, Russell C., and Bolles, Richard N., *Your Next Pastorate: Starting the Search*. Order #AL122 from The Alban Institute, Inc., 4125 Nebraska Ave., N.W., Washington, DC 20016.

And now, on to centers which are open to anyone, and do career counseling from a spiritual point of view:

ALSO DOING CAREER COUNSELING FROM A RELIGIOUS POINT OF VIEW

Bernard Haldane, Wellness Education Council, 4502 54th NW, Seattle, WA 98105, 206-525-2205. A pioneer in the clergy career management and assessment field, Bernard teaches *(totally independently of the agency which bears his name)* seminars and training of volunteers (particularly in churches) to do job-search counseling.

Career and Personal Counseling Center, 1904 Mt. Vernon St., Waynesboro, VA 22980, 703-943-9997. Lillian Pennell, Director.

CareerConcepts, 1451 Elm Hill Pike, Suite 314, Nashville, TN 37210, 615-367-5000. Robert H. McKown.

CareerWorks -- a division of Intercristo. 19303 Fremont Ave. N., Seattle, WA 98133, 206-546-7395. Jeff Trautman, Director.

Enablement Information Service, Inc., 14 Beacon St., Rm. 707, Boston, MA 02108, 617-742-1460. James L. Lowery, Jr., Executive Director.

Life/Career Planning Center for Religious, 10526 W. Cermak Rd., Suite 111, Westchester, IL 60153, 708-531-9228. Dolores Linhart, Director. Doing work with Roman Catholics.

Life Stewardship Associates, 6918 Glen Creek Dr., SE, Dutton, MI 49316, 616-698-3125. Ken Soper, M.Div., M.A., Director.

Lifework Design, 448 S. Marengo Ave., Pasadena, CA 91106, 818-577-2705. Kevin Brennfleck, M.A., and Kay Marie Breenfleck, M.A., Directors.

Mid-South Career Development Center, 2315 Fisher Place, Knoxville, TN 37920, 615-573-1340. W. Scott Root, Director.

Ministry of Counseling and Enrichment, 1333 N. 2nd St., Abilene, TX 79601, 915-675-8131. Mary Stedham, Director.

New Life Institute, Box 1666, Austin, TX 78767, 512-469-9447. Bob Breihan, Director.

Olson Counseling Services, 8720 Frederick, Suite 105, Omaha, NE 68124, 402-390-2342. Gail A. Olson, P.A.C.

People Management Group International, P.O. Box 33608, Seattle, WA 98133, 206-443-1107. Arthur F. Miller, Jr., Chairman. Dick Staub, President.

Two are better than one;
  for if they fall,
the one will lift up his fellow;

but woe to him that is alone when he falleth,
and hath not another to lift him up.

    Ecclesiastes

Appendix A

When Books Are Not Enough
and
You Want A Live Person
To Help You:

Career Counselors and Other Resources

LOOK BEFORE YOU LEAP:
How to Choose a Career Counselor,
If You Decide You Need One

It would be nice if the matter of finding a career counselor were relatively simple: look up in the phone book, choose a name, and go see
them. But you don't just want a career counselor, of course. You want a
good career counselor. And that's no more easy a task to find than is a *good*
doctor or a *good* dentist or a *good* lawyer.

You are, unfortunately, going to have to *work* at this. But there are some
things I can tell you that will hopefully make your task simpler and easier.

TYPES OF CAREER COUNSELORS
BY SUBJECT MATTER

If you are seeking help with the job-hunt, you need to be aware that
career counselors divide essentially into two types. The first type of counselor is the one whose *primary* expertise is in the area called 'career development' or 'career assessment.' They help people figure out what they
want to do with their lives, by way of career choice, etc. They *may* know
very little about the actual job-hunt process, so if that's the kind of help
you're looking for, this is not the counselor for you.

The second type of counselor is the one whose primary expertise is in
the area called 'job-search.' They almost always also know something about
'career development' or 'career assessment,' as above, but their *primary* expertise is in the job-search process.

This latter group of counselors divides, yet again, into two groups.
There are those whose primary expertise in the job-search process concerns the *traditional* approach: resumes and interviewing, as described in
Chapters 3 and 13 in this book. If you have already given up on that traditional approach, then this is not the counselor for you.

And then there are those career counselors whose primary expertise is
in the *creative* process of job-hunting, described in Chapters 9, 10, 11, and
12, as well as 4, in this book. This is the one you want.

TYPES OF CAREER COUNSELORS
BY METHOD OF PAYMENT

There is another way of thinking about career counselors. This concerns the method of payment they require. There are those who charge
a lump-sum fee *in advance* for 'their program.' And then there are those
who charge by the hour, only. This is of great significance in choosing a
career counselor, however silly that may sound. Most of the mischief that
occurs in the career counseling field is founded on the cornerstone of
method of payment. I'll try to explain why.

Think about these two methods in terms of *manageable risk.* You will
realize immediately that there is *a lot* more risk in your signing up for a
lump-sum-fee-in-advance program, than there is in your signing up for a
pay-as-you-go-by-the-hour program.

To illustrate: let us say it's your third hourly session with a counselor who charges by the hour, and you decide you just aren't getting what you wanted. What do you do? You quit after that third hour, with no hard feelings. How much do you still owe them? Nothing. Since you've paid session by session, you're all paid up. And that is that.

However, in contrast to this, let us say it's your third hourly session with a counseling firm that charged you a lump-sum fee up front, and you decide you just aren't getting what you wanted. What do you do? You protest, of course. It falls on deaf ears, usually. Then you decide to quit the program after that third hour. How much do you still owe them? Nothing. You're all paid up. In fact, you're *more* than paid up. *They* owe you money: sometimes *a whole lot*. (Fees for lump-sum programs range from $2,000 up to $10,000 or more.) Are you going to be able to get your money back, minus the three sessions you've had? No, you aren't. No matter *what* they told you to the contrary, before you first signed up, based on *actual experience of previous job-hunters* the odds are about 90–1 that you *won't* get your money back. And I guarantee you, you *will* have many hard feelings.

I have received hundreds of letters, over the years, from job-hunters who were 'taken' by either an inept or fraudulent career-counseling firm. (From heaven's point of view, I'm sure there is a vast difference between 'inept' and 'fraudulent.' It concerns their heart. But, from your point of view, as a job-hunter, there is no difference between an 'inept' and 'fraudulent' career counselor. The end result is the same in either case: you're poorer -- literally -- for knowing them, and you still have no job.)

The Better Business Bureaus, the Consumer Fraud division of your state or city Attorney General's office, not to mention the Federal Trade Commission, also get similar letters. The complaints almost never concern career counselors who charge by the hour, as you go. No, they concern firms who ask for a lump sum up front.

If you had a chance to read these letters, as I have, you would discover that they have a common thread -- or threads: *the career counselor or career counseling firm being complained about,* they all say, *demanded its fee up front, sometimes on a very brief 'payment plan,' rather than allowing the client to pay "as you go" by the hour; the fee was excessive, ranging on up to $10,000; there was a contract, that they required be signed before the program started; the firm did not do what they verbally promised they would do for that fee; did not have exclusive lists of job openings as they had claimed to have, nor the success rate they originally claimed, nor did they give the amount of time to the client they verbally promised in advance (sometimes it turned out to be as few as six hours); 'job campaigns' for the clients were slow to start, usually not until the full advance fee was paid; promised lists were slow in being provided and often were outdated and full of errors; the friendly person they had met when they first went there was actually a salesperson, and was never seen again once the contract was signed; and, whereas they may have liked that original contact (the salesperson), they did not like the actual career counselor they were blindly assigned to; moreover that counselor was often difficult (or impossible) to get ahold of after a certain period of time (sometimes coinciding with the final payment by the client of the advance fee); the job-hunting 'plan' was often no news at all to the client; the promised contact with employers on the client's* *behalf was not forthcoming; subsequent phone calls or letters of complaint to the firm by the client were ignored or treated with indignation; and the fee was not refunded in whole or in part, when the client was dissatisfied, despite implicit (or explicit) promises to the contrary back at the beginning, when the client first signed up,* and *despite repeated complaints or threatened law-suits on the part of the dissatisfied customer.* And that's just for starters!

Now, these complaints -- numerous though they are -- do **not** mean that *every* firm which charges a lump sum up front for their program is necessarily bad. Some are okay. *But* the problem is: you have no way of telling which is which, *until* they've got all your money. And by then, it's too late. *Way* too late.

It is better, and safer by far, for you to choose a firm which charges you by the hour, and requires you to sign no contract. *That* risk is manageable. You will find, these days, that the best career counselors *(and some of the worst, too)* will charge you whatever the going rate is for a comparable hour with a really good therapist, in your geographical area. Currently, in large metropolitan areas, that runs around $100 an hour. In suburbia or rural areas, it may be *much* less. That fee is for *individual* time with the career counselor. If you can't afford that fee, ask whether they run *groups*. If they do, the fee will be much less. And, in one of those delightful ironies of life, since you get a chance to listen to problems which other job-hunters in your group are having, similar to yours, the group will *often* give you more help than an individual session would. Not *always*; but *often*. It's always ironic when *cheaper* and *more helpful* run hand in hand.

If the career counselor in question does offer groups, the charge should again be *payable each session*, and you should be able to drop out at any time, without further cost, if you decide you are not getting the help you want.

You may at that point want to explore the question of whether or not you would get more of the help you need from individual sessions, with that same counselor -- or with a different counselor. Many job-hunters do need individual attention. But expect the cost to be higher, than it is for groups.

There are, incidentally, some career counselors who run *free* (or almost free) job-hunting workshops through local churches, synagogues, chambers of commerce, community colleges, adult education programs, and the like, as their community service, or *pro bonum* work (as it is technically called). I have had reports of such workshops from Idaho, California, and Canada, thus far. They surely exist in other places as well. If money is a big problem for you, in getting help with your job-hunt, ask around to see if such workshops as these exist in *your* community.

'THE PARACHUTE SEAL OF APPROVAL'

Okay, there's a basic overview of the kinds of career counselors. You want a career counselor whose expertise is in the job-search process, and the creative job-search process at that, and who charges by the hour. Well, and good.

Of course, what you're hoping I will offer you at this point is some sort of "authorized list" of names nationwide: people who understand this whole job-hunting process thoroughly, know how to do all the exercises in this book, have been through some kind of careful credentialing process, and received the Parachute Seal of Approval.

Ah, dear reader, how I wish it were so. But, unhappily, there is no such list. First of all, while I do train people once a year, I have only trained 3,000 over the years -- which is *a drop in the bucket*, compared to the number of career counselors that are out there. Moreover, I can't *guarantee* that simply because they've been through my hands, they truly understand. So, publishing a list of *their* names wouldn't answer your problem.

Secondly, there are lots of people out there who understand the whole job-hunting process thoroughly and well, even though they've never been trained by me and may not even (necessarily) have read this book. In most cases, of course, I've never met them, and consequently I don't know who they are or where they are. I simply know *that* they are.

What this adds up to, you've already guessed. You've got to do your own homework, here. Hunting for a decent career counselor is just like hunting for a job. You've got to do your own research, and your own interviewing, in your own geographical area, or you will deserve what you get.

DOING YOUR OWN RESEARCH
IN YOUR COMMUNITY OR NEARBY

What do you want? Let's rehearse what you're looking for. The three things you absolutely want from anyone you're paying good money to, are:
a) a firm grasp of the whole job-hunting process, at its most creative and effective level;
b) the ability on their part to communicate that information lucidly and clearly to you;
c) rapport with you.

This last is the killer. Without that, you can forget the first two. That's why you have to do your own research. No one but you knows whether or not you're going to get along with a particular career counselor. Maybe he's a wonderful man, but unhappily he reminds you of your Uncle Harry. You've always **hated** your Uncle Harry. No one knows that, but you. Or maybe the counselor is a wonderful woman, but unhappily. . .*well, you get the point.*

No one can do this research for you. Because the real question is not "Who is best?" but "Who is best **for you**?" Those last two words demand that it be you who 'makes the call.'

Now, what do you want? Well, you want to find the names of at least three career counselors in your community, you want to go talk with them, and decide which of the three (if any) you want to hook up with.

Where do you look? Where do you find names? Well, the phone book is always a good place to start. They may be listed under a wide variety of titles: career counselors, executive career counselors, executive career consultants, career management teams, vocational psychologists, executive consulting counselors, career guidance counselors, executive advisors, executive development specialists, executive job counselors, manpower experts, career advisors, employment specialists, executive recruitment consultants, management consultants, placement specialists, executive search specialists, vocational counselors, life/work planners, etc. You're going to have to do some hunting.

Outside the phone book, you ask among your friends if any of them have ever used a career counselor. And if so, what did they think of them. If that doesn't turn up any leads, you look at the Sampler toward the rear of this Appendix, to see if there are any names near you, *with which to start*. They may know how you find out the other names in your community.

One way or another, you want to obtain, as I said, at least three names. Why? Because you're going to be doing comparison shopping.

Of course, you're tempted to skip over that little requirement. *"Well, I'll just call up one place, and if I like the sound of them, I'll sign up. I'm a pretty good judge of character."* Right. I hear many a sad tale from people who adopted that attitude, and all that I can say when it's too late is, "I'm sorry indeed to hear that you had a very disappointing experience; that is very unfortunate, I know, I've been through it myself. But -- as the Scots would say -- "Ya dinna do your homework."[1] Often you could easily have discovered whether a particular counselor was competent or not, before you *ever* gave them any of your money, simply by asking the right questions during this comparison shopping which I'm pleading with you to regard as *essential*.

How do you ask? **You visit in person each of the three places you have chosen.** Don't try to do this over the telephone, *please!* There is so much more you can tell, when you're looking the person straight in the eyes. Remember, these are exploratory visits only. For that reason, be sure and leave your wallet and checkbook at home, please! You are only comparison shopping or information-gathering at this point. You are *not* ready yet to reach a decision. *Please* make this unmistakably clear, when you are setting up the appointment for the interview. And should they ask you to bring in your partner or spouse with you, *beware*. That is a well-known tactic of some of the slickest salespeople in the world, who *want* your spouse or partner there so they can manipulate one *or* the other of you to reach a decision on the spot, while they have you in their 'grasp.'

---

1. If you are reading this too late, did pay some firm's fee all in advance, and feel you were ripped off, you will want to know about Mr. Stuart Alan Rado. Mr. Rado was a victim of one of the career counseling agencies, and ever since, he has been waging a sort of "one-man crusade" against career counseling firms which take advantage of the job-hunter. Send Mr. Rado your story, together with a self-addressed stamped envelope, and he will send you a one-page sheet of some actions you can take. It may not get your money back, but at least you'll feel better for having done something. His address is: 1500 23rd St., Sunset Island #3, Miami Beach, FL 33140. 305-532-2607.

What do you ask? When you go (by yourself) on this exploratory visit, you ask *each* of the three places you go to, the same questions. Keep a little pad or notebook with you that looks something like this:

MY SEARCH FOR A GOOD CAREER COUNSELOR

Questions I Will Ask Them	Answer from counselor #1	Answer from counselor #2	Answer from counselor #3
1. What is your program?			
2. Who will be doing it?			
3. What is your success rate?			
4. How much time will you give me?			
5. What is the cost of your services?			

As you ask the questions at each place, take time to write down direct quotes of their answers, *as* they are answering, please! *Don't* trust your memory. Good counselors will not mind your doing this, in the least. Bad counselors will: *"Do you have to do all that writing as we talk? I find it very distracting."* Too bad. You need to be able to compare, later, *exactly* what each of the three places said.

SOME QUESTIONS, BY MEANS OF WHICH YOU MAY BE ABLE TO SEPARATE THE SHEEP FROM THE GOATS

You can see from the diagram above, that the questions you need to ask *each* place are these:

1. *What is your program?* Sometimes, their answers to this question will bedazzle you: *we will give you help*, say they, *with evaluating your career history, in-depth analysis of your background, establishment of your job objective, in-depth analysis of your capabilities, writing an effective resume, names of companies, preparing the covering letter, background materials on companies, interviewing techniques, video playback of mock interviews between you and a pretend-employer, help you rehearse for interviews on closed circuit TV, use videotape or cassettes to record*

your skills or your resume, coach you on salary negotiations, filling out forms, answering ads, aptitude tests, special problems -- unemployment, age, too broad a background, too narrow a background, too many job changes, too few job changes, poor references, etc. We will, they say, open doors for you, tell you which companies are hiring, and so forth and so on.

But, when all the jargon and the gimmicks are set aside, what are they offering: is it basically "the numbers game" (see Chapter 3 in this book) **or** is it some variation of the creative minority's prescription (see Chapters 9, 10, 11, and 12). If it's the latter, three cheers.

Also, if they give you the feeling that you must do most of the program, with their basically assuming the role of coach, give three more cheers. On the other hand, if you get the feeling that everything (including tests, interpretation of the tests, and decision making about what this means you should do, or where you should do it) will be done *for you* in this program, three warning bells should go off in your head.

2. Who will be doing it? Ask the man or woman you are facing if *they* will be the counselor who works with you throughout the program. If they say *No*, ask to meet the person who will be. If they deny you access to that person, thank them politely for their time, and *walk out*.

Assuming you do get to meet the person whom you will actually be working with, there are a couple of considerations you should weigh:

(a) *Do you like the counselor?* I don't care what their expertise is, if you don't like them, you're going to have a rough time getting what you want. I guarantee it. Rapport is *everything*.

(b) *How long has the counselor been doing this?* It's perfectly legitimate to ask this, and also to ask what training they have had for career counseling. If they get huffy, or try to dodge the questions, politely thank them for their time, and take your leave gently *but firmly*. You might be interested to know that some executive or career counseling firms hire yesterday's clients as today's new staff. Such new staff are sometimes given training only after they're "on-the-job." They are practicing on you. No matter how small or large the fee you would be paying, you have a right to *expertise already acquired*. Incidentally, beware of their summing up their experience in terms of double phrases, such as "I've had eighteen years' experience in the business and career counseling world." What that may mean is: seventeen and a half years as a fertilizer salesman, and one half year doing career counseling. Persist. *"How long have you been with this firm, and how long have you been doing* **formal career counseling**, *as you are here?"*

3. What's their success rate? If they make it clear that they have had a good success rate, but if you fail to work hard at the whole process, then there is no guarantee you are going to find a job, give them three stars. On the other hand, if they practically guarantee you a job, and say they have never had a client that failed to find a job, no matter what, **watch out.** They're *lying*. I have studied career counseling programs for over twenty years, have attended many, have studied records at State and Federal offices, and I have *never* seen a program that placed more than 86% of their clients *in*

their best years. And it goes downhill from there. A prominent executive counseling firm was reported by the Attorney General's Office of New York State to have placed only 38 out of 550 clients (a 93% failure rate).[2]

4. How much time will they give you? At a minimum? At a maximum? This is only a major consideration when you're dealing with *lump-sum-in-advance* firms, who require you to sign a contract (about which, more later).

Anyway, answers like, *"Hey, we work with you until you get a job, no matter how long that takes,"* should basically be distrusted. Try again: "What's the most hours you've ever had to give to a client, in the past?" Believe me, there's got to be a maximum, no matter what they may at first try to tell you. Why? Because every career counselor has, in the past, run into extremely dependent types as clients, who would be visiting them an hour every day of the week, including Saturdays and Sundays, if the counselor or the firm didn't have some policy about time limits. **Press** to find out what that policy is, just so you'll know. How much time *will* they give you? And, **will they put this in writing?** Ah, there's the test that separates the men from the boys, and the women from the girls, in the counseling profession.

5. What is the cost of their services? Is it paid hourly, as you go along, or must it all be paid "up front" before you even start? I've already hammered this one to death. Anyway, *now* is the time for you to ask it, at each place.

To elaborate on what I said earlier, with my rich skills at overkill, when you are dealing with counselors who charge by the hour, there is a *set* rate. Each time you keep an appointment, you pay them at the end of that hour for their help, according to that rate. There is no written contract. You signed nothing. You can stop seeing them at any time, if you feel you are not getting the help you wish.

On the other hand, with those who have a policy of requiring you to pay for the entire "program" before you start -- or shortly after you start -- there is **always** a written contract. You **must** sign it. (Often, your partner or spouse will be asked to sign it, too.) The fee normally ranges on up to $10,000.

I didn't use to be so direct about this, but the years have taught me a great lesson. So, now I say, uncategorically, if there is a contract involved, don't sign it. I have had to listen to grown men and women *cry* over the telephone, all because they signed a contract. Most often they were executives, or senior managers, who never had to go job-hunting before, and unknowingly signed up with some executive counseling firm that was fraudulent, or at least on the *edge* of legality.

If you want to avoid their tears in your own job-search, I can tell you what they told me they learned. As I lay this out for you, you may *think* I

---

2. For further details, go to your local library and look up "Career Counselors: Will They Lead You Down The Primrose Path?" by Lee Guthrie, in the December 1981 issue of *Savvy Magazine,* pp. 60ff.

am exaggerating: I mean, can there possibly be such *mean* men and women, who would *prey* on job-hunters, when they're down and out. Yes, ma'am, and yes, sir, there are.[3] That's why you have to do this preliminary research so thoroughly.

Anyway, here's what the hundreds of people who've gotten *taken*, learned too late: You may *think* the purpose of that firm's contract is that *they* are promising *you* something, that they can be held to. Uh-uh! More often, the main purpose of the contract is to get *you* to promise *them* something. Like, money. Don't. . . . do. . . .it.

Further, don't let your defenses be lulled by the fact that the contract may allow you to pay the up-front fee *in installments*. If you sign that contract, you **are** obligated to pay the full sum, one way or the other.

You will sometimes be told that, *"Of course*, you can get your money back, or a portion of it, at any time, should you be dissatisfied with the career counselor's services." Nine times out of ten, however, you are told this *verbally*, and it is not in the written contract. Verbal promises, without witnesses, are difficult if not impossible for you to later enforce. The written contract is binding.

Sometimes the written contract will claim to provide for a partial refund, at any time, *until* you reach a cut-off date in the program, which the contract specifies. Unfortunately, as many job-hunters have found out *way* too late, and to their sorrow, the cut-off date is often calculated by the counselor or agency in a very different way than you or I would calculate it. Consequently, you are often beyond that cut-off date, and the possibility of any refund, long before *your* calculations tell you you should be.

To make matters worse, many *crafty* fraudulent firms bend over backwards to be extra nice, extra available, and extra helpful to you *until* that cut-off point is reached. So, when the cut-off point for getting a refund has been reached, you let it pass because you are very satisfied with their

---

3. If you are **dying** to know more, and your local library has back files of magazines and newspapers (on microfiche, or otherwise) there was a period when bad firms and counselors came under heavy fire (1978-1982) and you can look up some of the articles of that period, as well as those articles which have appeared more recently, to wit:

"A Consumer Guide to Retail Job-Hunting Services," Special Report, reprinted from the *National Business Employment Weekly*; available from Dow Jones Reprint Service, P.O. Box 300, Princeton, NJ 08543-0300. A *very* thorough series of articles on the industry, which names *names,* and gives the addresses of Consumer protection agencies in each state, to whom you may complain. **Required reading**, for anyone who wants to avoid getting 'burned.'

"'Employment counselors' costly, target of gripes," *The Arizona Republic,* October 8, 1989.

"Career-Counseling Industry Accused of Misrepresentation," *New York Times*, Sept. 30, 1982, p. C1.

"Consumer Law: Career Counselors and Employment Agencies" by Reed Brody, *New York Law Journal*, Feb. 26, 1982, p. 1. Reed was Assistant Attorney General of the State of New York, and more recently Deputy Chief of the Labor Bureau within that State's Department of Law; in this capacity he became the leading legal expert in the country, on career counseling malpractices, though unfortunately (for us) he now works overseas in Europe, in another profession.

"Career Counselors: Will They Lead You Down the Primrose Path?" by Lee Guthrie, *Savvy Magazine,* Dec. 1981, p. 60ff.

"Franklin Career Search Is Accused of Fraud In New York State Suit," *Wall Street Journal*, Jan. 29, 1981, p. 50.

"Job Counseling Firms Under Fire For Promising Much, Giving Little," *Wall Street Journal,* Jan. 27, 1981, p. 33.

past services, and believe there will be many more weeks of the same. Only, there aren't. *At fraudulent firms*, once the cut-off point is passed, the career counselor becomes virtually impossible for you to get ahold of. Call after call will *not* be returned. You will say to yourself *"What happened?"* Well, what happened, my friend, is that you paid up in full, they have all the money they're ever going to get out of you, and now they don't want to give you any more time.

And so, the moral of this tale is:

Avoid places which require you to sign a contract, and in particular avoid any contract that commits you to pay an amount of money that you really can't afford to lose.

WHEN YOU'VE FINISHED YOUR COMPARISON SHOPPING

Having gotten the information *you* want, and therefore having accomplished your purpose for your visit, politely thank them for their time and trouble, and depart.

You then go on to the other two places, and ask the very same questions. Carefully write down their answers in your notebook, *as* they are saying them, please! There should be no charge for such comparison shopping visits as this. Make this clear when you set up the original appointment. If they subsequently bill you, phone them and inquire politely whether or not a mistake has been made by their billing department (good thinking). If they persist in billing you, pay a visit to your local friendly Better Business Bureau, and lodge a nice unfriendly complaint against the firm in question. You'd be surprised at how many firms experience **instant repentance** when the Better Business Bureau phones them. *(They don't want a complaint on their BBB record.)*

Back home now, after visiting the three places you chose for your comparison shopping, you have to decide: a) whether you want none of the three, or b) one of the three and if so, which one.

Look over your notes on all three places. Compare those places. It's time for thought, maybe using some others as a sounding board: partner, spouse, business friend, consultant friend, placement center, buddy, primary other or anyone whose judgment you trust.

But remember also to listen to your own intuition, and to your own heart. You don't have to choose **any** of the three counselors, if you didn't really care for any of them. If that is the case, then choose three new counselors, dust off the notebook, and go out again.

It may take a few more hours to find what you want. But remember: the wallet, the purse, the job-hunt, the life, that you save will be your own.

A Sampler

This is not a complete directory of anything. It is exactly what its name implies: a Sampler. Countless good people, agencies, and places exist, which will not be found in this Sampler. *Also, countless bad people, places, and agencies will not be found in this Sampler.* To list all the career counselors *out there*, would require an encyclopedia. Some states, in fact, have *encyclopedic* lists of counselors and businesses, in various books or directories, and your local bookstore or library should have these, under such titles as "How to Get A Job in. . . ."

The listing of an organization, agency or person here is NOT a recommendation or endorsement of that organization, agency or person by me, nor are they allowed to advertise or imply that it is. *(If they do, in their brochures or otherwise, we reluctantly remove them.)* Most of the places listed here are listed at their own request, and the listing is without charge of any kind. We, of course, ask them some questions, before listing them, since the listing is restricted to those counselors and places which claim some expertise in helping readers use *Parachute* -- but obviously we are in no position to make any final judgment as to their expertise, from this distance. So, it may be that some unhelpful places *got* included, even as many good places are *not* included here.

When counselors disappear from this Sampler, over the years, it is for a number of reasons. Sometimes, as I just said, it's because they've used their listing here as part of their promotion, claiming we have recommended them thereby, when it doesn't mean *that*, and the *condition* of their being listed is that they don't claim it does. Sometimes it's because they've folded, without a trace. Sometimes it's because of space considerations, here. Sometimes it's because readers have complained about them. *(We are not in a position to evaluate the justice of such complaints, but we are advocates for the job-hunter, so rather than risk continuing to list a place that* may *be unhelpful, we simply remove it. Such places survived before we listed them, and they will survive quite nicely in the future, whether we list them or not.)* Incidentally, if you find a place that is no longer in existence, or impossible to get ahold of, or is -- in your opinion -- totally unhelpful, you could be of great service to our other readers by dropping us a line and telling us so. P.O. Box 379, Walnut Creek, CA 94597.

As we go to press, this Sampler is as accurate and up-to-date as we can make it. *Unfortunately*, however, there is no way any Sampler can remain up-to-date and accurate, for more than about two days, and six hours. Staff changes. Phone numbers change. Places move, or fold, almost weekly in this field. I apologize for any information or listing that proves to be inaccurate by the time you get to use it. Again, please let me know.

If you have a favorite place that is not listed below, send us the pertinent information. We will then ask them some intelligent questions about their familiarity (or lack of familiarity) with this book, and if they sound as though they would be helpful to our readers we will list them in the next edition. *Don't, however, bother to send us college services which are available only to the students and alumni or alumnae of that college. After many complaints from readers, it is now our policy that we no longer list places that thus restrict their clientele. If you discover that we have inadvertently included a place that only serves Their Own, please let us know immediately, and we'll gently remove them from the next edition.*

If the listings here aren't helpful for the geographical location where you are, ask everyone you know -- family, friends, and even people you've just met -- if they know any really helpful career counselors in your area.

Try also your telephone book's local Yellow Pages, under the headings (in the index) of Personnel & Employment, under Business and Financial Services. This index will likely refer you to such entries in the body of the Yellow Pages as: *Aptitude and Employment Testing, Career and Vocational Counseling, Personnel Consultants* and (if you are a woman) *Women's Organizations and Services.* You will discover, however, that even the Yellow Pages can't keep up with the additional groups that spring up daily, weekly, and monthly -- including job clubs and other group activities. Fortunately, many of these *are* listed in the *National Business Employment Weekly*, on its pages called "Calendar of Career Events." Available on newsstands, $3.95 per issue; or, order an issue directly from: National Business Employment Weekly, 420 Lexington Ave., New York, NY 10170. 212-808-6792, or 800-JOB HUNT. Among all the listings below, as well as those that you turn up on your own, you will have to pick and choose very carefully.

I repeat: you must do your own comparison shopping, and do your own sharp questioning before you decide to go with anyone. If you don't, you will deserve whatever you get (or, more to the point, *don't* get). The purse or wallet you save, will be your own.

The listings below are alphabetical within each state, except that counselors listed by their name are in alphabetical order according to their *last* name. To make this clear, only their last name is in **bold** type.

You will discover a veritable alphabet-soup of initials after some of the counselors' names. B.A., M.A. and Ph.D. you know. Do *not* assume their degree is in career counseling. Ask. N.C.C. means "Nationally certified counselor." There are about 20,000 such in the U.S. N.C.C.C. means "Nationally certified career counselor." There are currently about 850 in the U.S. Other initials, such as L.P.C. -- "Licensed professional counselor" -- and the like, often refer to State licensing. There are a number of States, now, that have some sort of regulation of career counselors. In some States it is mandatory, in others it is optional. Much as you might *think* these degrees mean something about the expertise of the counselor in the job-hunt, often they don't. It's much more useful for you to ask, "How many times have you had to go job-hunting yourself, and how many of those times did you use *Parachute?*" That'll tell you more, though again it doesn't always define how expert the counselor is, in the job-search process. The simple fact is: there is no definitive way for you to determine a career counselor's expertise. It's something you'll have to *smell* out, as you go along. That's another reason you want to pay them by the hour, and not pay them all up front.

Generally speaking, the places, and counselors, below counsel *anybody*. A few, however, take only women as clients. Ask. If they aren't able to help you, your phone call wasn't wasted, *so long as* you then go on to ask them "who else in the area can you tell me about, who helps with job-search, and are there any among them that you would particularly recommend?"

> *Incidentally, if you are looking for places which specialize in doing career counseling from a religious point of view, these are listed at the end of The Epilogue, "How To Find Your Mission in Life," on page 355.*

ALABAMA

Enterprise State Junior College, P.O. Box 1300, Enterprise, AL 36331, 205-347-2623 or 393-ESJC. Nancy Smith, Director of Guidance Services.

ALASKA

Alaska Professional Career Counselors, 310 K St., Suite 404, Anchorage, Alaska 99501, 907-337-0200. Pat Reeves, Director.

Career Transitions, 2221 East Northern Lights Boulevard, Suite 207, Anchorage, AL 99508, 907-278-7350. Deeta Lonergan, Director.

ARIZONA

College PLUS Career Connections, 4540 S. Rural Rd., #P-8, Tempe, AZ 85282, 602-730-5246. Dr. Warren D. Robb, Director.

Lou Ann S. **Dickson,** Ph.D., 2131 E. Southern Ave., Tempe, AZ 85282, 602-820-1599.

Southwest Institute of Life Management, 11122 E. Gunshot Circle, Tucson, AZ 85749, 602-749-2290. Theodore Donald Risch, Director.

ARKANSAS

Donald **McKinney,** Ed.D., Career Counselor, Rt. 1, Box 351-A, DeQueen, AR 71832, 501-642-5628.

CALIFORNIA

Alumnae Resources, 120 Montgomery St., Suite 1080, San Francisco, CA 94104, 415-274-4700.

Jill **Andreoni,** 1451 East Chevy Chase Dr., Suite 203, Glendale, CA 91206, 818-247-4062.

Judy Kaplan **Baron Associates,** 6046 Cornerstone Ct. West, Suite 208, San Diego, CA 92121, 619-558-7400. Judy Kaplan Baron, Director.

Beverly **Brown,** M.A., 809 So. Bundy Drive, #105, Los Angeles, CA 90049, 310-447-7093.

Career Action Center, 445 Sherman Ave., Palo Alto, CA 94306, 415-324-1710.

Career Development Institute, 690 Market St., Suite 404, San Francisco, CA 94104, 415-982-2636.

Career Development Life Planning, 3585 Maple St., Suite 237, Ventura, CA 93003, 805-656-6220. Norma Zuber, N.C.C.C., M.S.C., & Associates.

Career Dimensions, Box 7402, Stockton, CA 95267, 209-473-8255. Fran Abbott.

Career Directions, 952 Sandcastle Drive, Cardiff-by-the-Sea, CA 92007, 619-436-3994. Virginia Byrd, M.Ed., Career Consultant.

Careerpath Guidance, 1050 University Ave., San Diego, CA 92103, 619-296-1055. Carla Grindle.

Career Planning Center/Business Action Center, 1623 S. La Cienega Blvd., Los Angeles, CA 90035, 213-273-6633.

Career Strategy Associates, Koll Center Newport, 5000 Birch St., Suite 3000, Newport Beach, CA 92660, 714-476-3652. Betty Fisher.

The **Center for Life & Career Development,** 655 University Ave., Suite 127, Sacramento, CA 95825, 916-646-3414. Dr. Fran A. Epstein.

The **Center for Life and Work Planning,** 1133 Second St., Encinitas, CA 92024, 619-943-0747. Mary C. McIsaac, Executive Director.

Civic Center Volunteers. Marin County Personnel Office, Administration Bldg., Civic Center, San Rafael, CA 94903, 415-499-6104.

Constructive Leisure, Patsy B. Edwards, 511 N. La Cienega Blvd., Los Angeles, CA 90048, 213-652-7389.

Consultants in Career Development, 2017 Palo Verde Ave., Suite 201B, Long Beach, CA 90815, 213-598-6412. Dean Porter, Senior Partner.

Criket Consultants, 502 Natoma St., P.O. Box 6191, Folsom, CA 95630, 916-985-3211.

Cypress College, Career Planning Center, 9200 Valley View St., Cypress, CA 90630, 714-826-2220, Ext. 120.

Margaret L. **Eadie,** M.A., A.M.Ed., WHAT NEXT Education and Career Consultant, 1000 Sage Pl., Pacific Grove, CA 93050, 408-373-7400.

Experience Unlimited Job Club, Mr. Herman L. Leopold, Coordinator, Employment Development Dept., 1225 4th Ave., Oakland, CA 94606, 415-464-1259/464-0659. There are 21 other Experience Unlimited Centers in California, found at the Employment Development Department in Chula Vista, El Cajon, Escondido, Fremont, Fullerton, Hollywood, Lancaster, Monterey, North Hollywood, Ontario, Pasadena, Pleasant Hill, Sacramento, San Bernardino, San Diego, San Francisco, Santa Ana, Santa Maria, Simi Valley, Sunnyvale, and West Covina. For further information about E.U., you may contact: Ms. Michael Clark, P.O. Box 1131, 480 North Mountain View Ave., San Bernardino, CA 92402.

Mary Alice **Floyd,** M.A., N.C.C. and Gerald L. **Floyd,** M.A., N.C.C., Career Counselor/Consultant, 3233 Lucinda Lane, Santa Barbara, CA 93105, 805-687-5462.

Marvin F. **Galper,** Ph.D., 4024 Ibis St., Suite A, San Diego, CA 92103, 619 -295-4450.

Judith **Grutter,** M.S., N.C.C., Career Development Counselor/Consultant, Webb, Grutter, Helander & Associates, 130 S. Euclid Ave., Suite #5, Pasadena, CA 91101, 818-795-3883.

Life's Decisions, 2701 Cottage Way, #1, Sacramento, CA 95825, 916-481-1246. Joan E. Belshin, M.S., N.C.C.

Lifework Design, 448 S. Marengo Ave., Pasadena, CA 91106, 818-577-2705. Kevin Brennfleck, M.A., and Kay Marie Breenfleck, M.A., Directors.

Susan W. **Miller,** M.A., 6363 Wilshire Blvd., Suite 210, Los Angeles CA 90048, 213-837-7768/651-5514.

Modern Career Decisions, 7547 Homewood Ct., Pleasanton, CA 94588, 510-846-9071. Rod Meyer, CPC, Executive Director.

Sacramento Women's Center, Women's Employment Services and Training (WEST) for low-income women, 2306 "J" St., Suite 200, Sacramento, CA 95816, 916-441-4207.

Saddleback College, Counseling Services and Special Programs, 28000 Marguerite Pkwy., Mission Viejo, CA 92692, 714-582-4571. Jan Fritsen, Counselor.

Santa Rosa Career Management Services, 1100 Coddingtown Center, Suite A, Santa Rosa, CA 95402, 707-525-1955. Jack Geary, M.A., President.

Marion Bass **Stevens,** Ph.D., Career & Employment Counseling, The Peninsula Regent, One Baldwin Ave., #208, San Mateo, CA 94401, 415-344-0809.

Stoodley & Associates, 1434 Willowmont Ave., San Jose, CA 95118, 408-448-3691. Martha Stoodley, M.S., M.F.C.C., President.

The **Successful Job Search Center,** 1700 N. Broadway, Suite 407, Walnut Creek, CA 94596, 800-874-JOBS. Marston Watson, President.

Transitions Counseling Center, 171 N. Van Ness, Fresno, CA 93701, 209-233-7250. Margot E. Tepperman, L.C.S.W.

Turning Point Career Center, University YWCA, 2600 Bancroft Way, Berkeley, CA 94704, 510-848-6370. Winnie Froehlich, M.S., Director.

Caroline **Voorsanger,** Career Counselor for Women, 2000 Broadway, Suite 1108, San Francisco, CA 94115, 415-567-0890.

Patti **Wilson,** 15880 Rose Ave., Los Gatos, CA 95030, 408-354-1964.

Women at Work, 78 N. Marengo Ave., Pasadena, CA 91101, 818-796-6870.

COLORADO

Resource Center, Arapahoe Community College, 2500 West College Dr., P.O. Box 9002, Littleton, CO 80160-9002, 303-794-1550.

CRS Consulting, 425 W. Mulberry, Suite 108, Ft. Collins, CO 80521, 303-484-9810. Contact Marilyn Pultz.

Human Resource Innovations, 425 W. Mulberry, Suite 108, Ft. Collins, CO 80521, 303-224-9473. Contact: Lorie Smith.

Samuel **Kirk and Associates,** Central Office, 1418 S. Race, Denver, CO 80210, 303-722-0717.

Patricia **O'Keefe,** M.A., 350 Cook St., Denver, CO 80206, 303-393-8747.

Women's Resource Agency, 1011 N. Weber St., #C, Colorado Springs, CO 80903, 719-471-3170.

CONNECTICUT

Accord Consultants, Inc., The Exchange, Suite 305, 270 Farmington Ave., Farmington, CT 06032, 203-674-9654. J. Tod Gerardo, President and Director.

Associated Counseling Professionals, Career Development Division, 38 Barker St., Hartford, CT 06114-1815, 203-296-5523 or toll-free in CT, 1-800-654-4320. John H. Widenheft, M.A., Clinical Director.

C. Jackson **Blair,** Life Management Programs, 75 Gray Rock Rd., Southport, CT 06490, 203-259-8762.

Career Choices, Oak Park, Madison, CT 06443, 203-245-4123.

Career Services, 94 Rambling Rd., Vernon, CT 06066, 203-871-7832. Jim Cohen, Ph.D., President.

Fairfield Adult Career & Educational Services, Fairfield University, Dolan House, Fairfield, CT 06430, 203-254-4110.

Gillespie Associates, 9 Berkeley St., Norwalk, CT 06850, 203-838-8464. Jonathan B. Horwitz, Ed.D.

Gold and Robert Associates (formerly Ilise Gold Associates), Career and Life Planning Specialists, 164 Kings Highway N., Westport, CT 06880, 203-222-9223. Ilise Gold and Tracey Robert.

People Management, Inc., See the listing under *Washington State.*

The Offerjost-Westcott Group, 263 Main St., Old Saybrook, CT 06475, 203-388-6094. George W. Offerjost, Chairman.

Vocational and Academic Counseling for Adults (VOCA), 115 Berrian Rd., Stamford, CT 06905, 203-329-1955.

DELAWARE

Life/Career Planning, 2413 Brickton Rd., Wilmington, DE 19803, 302-478-7186. Minh-Nhat Tran, Consultant.

YWCA of New Castle County, Women's Center, 233 King St., Wilmington, DE 19801, 302-658-7161. Mona B. Bayard, Program Coordinator.

DISTRICT OF COLUMBIA

Community Vocational Counseling Service, The George Washington University Counseling Center, 718 21st St. NW, Washington, DC 20052, 202-994-4860. Robert J. Wilson, M.S., Coordinator.

Comptex Associates, Inc., Melwood Shopping Center, 9402 Pennsylvania Ave., Upper Marlboro, MD 20772, 301-599-9222. Mary H. Johnson, President, and Eugene Williams, Sr., Executive Vice President.

George Washington University, Continuing Education for Women, 801 22nd St. NW, Suite T409, Washington, DC 20052, 202-994-5762, or -8164, or -8165.

FLORIDA

The **Career and Personal Counseling Center,** Eckerd College, Box 12560, St. Petersburg, FL 33733, 813-864-8356. John R. Sims.

Career Consultants of America, Inc., 2701 W. Busch Blvd., Suite 270, Tampa, FL 33618, 813-933-4088. Michael Shahnasarian, Ph.D., Executive Director.

Center for Career Decisions, 980 N. Federal Hwy., Suite 203, Boca Raton, FL 33432, 407-394-3399. Linda Friedman, M.A., Director.

The Women's Center, Valencia Community College, 1010 N. Orlando Ave., Winter Park, FL 32789, 407-628-1976.

Centre for Women, 305 S. Hyde Park Ave., Tampa, FL 33606, 813-251-8437. Beth Ficquette, Executive Director.

Chabon & Associates, 2090 Palm Beach Lakes Blvd., Suite 1000, West Palm Beach, FL 33409, 407-640-8443. Toby G. Chabon, M.Ed., N.C.C., President.

Challenge: The Displaced Homemaker, Florida Community College at Jacksonville, 101 W. State St., Jacksonville, FL 32202, 904-633-8316. Joan Putnam, Project Coordinator.

Crossroads, Palm Beach Community College, 4200 Congress Ave., Lake Worth, FL 33461-4796, 407-433-5995. Pat Jablonski, Program Manager.

Larry **Harmon,** Ph.D., Career Counseling Center, Inc., 2000 South Dixie Highway, Suite 103, Miami, FL 33133, 305-858-8557.

Ellen O. **Jonassen**, Ph.D., Harbor Oak Medical Center, 1106 Druid Rd. S., Suite 201, Clearwater FL 34616, 813-442-6007.

Life Designs, Inc., 7860 SW 55th Ave. #A, South Miami, FL 33143, 305-665-3212 or 665-9393. Dulce Muccio and Deborah Tyson, co-founders.

New Beginnings, 1108 E. Memorial Blvd., Lakeland Mall, #60, Lakeland, FL 33801, 813-683-6444. Laurie Krosney, Employment and Training Specialist.

Resource Center for Women, formerly FACE Learning Center, Inc., 12945 Seminole Blvd., Bldg. II, Suite 8, Largo, FL 34648, 813-585-8155 or 586-1110.

GEORGIA

Career and Education Information Center, Lenox Square Professional Concourse, Suite 103, 3393 Peachtree Rd. NE, Atlanta, GA 30326, 404-233-7497. Barbara Buchanan, Executive Director.

Career Pursuit, 2971 Flowers Rd. S., Suite 101, Atlanta, GA 30341, 404-457-9636. Estelle Ford-Williamson, M.A., Career and Management Development Specialist.

Charles W. **Cates,** Ph.D., 1485 N. Decatur Rd., Atlanta, GA 30306, 404-373-0336.

Jennifer B. **Kahnweiler**, Ph.D., 7445 Brandonshire Rd., Dunwoody, GA 30350, 404-399-6868.

St. Jude's Job Network Club, St. Jude's Catholic Church, 7171 Glenridge Dr., Sandy Springs, GA 30328.

Mark **Satterfield,** 5262 Walker Rd., Stone Mountain, GA 30088, 404-469-3462.

HAWAII

No listings

ILLINOIS

Abbot Services, 6057 W. Eddy St., Chicago, IL 60634, 312-545-5892. Richard Gans, Career Counselor.

Applied Potential, Box 585, Highland Park, IL 60035, 708-234-2130.

Career Directions, Inc., 5005 Newport Dr., Suite 404, Rolling Meadows, IL 60008, 312-870-1290. Peggy Simonsen, Director. Also at 25 E. Washington St., #1500, Chicago, IL 60602.

Career Path, 3033 Ogden Ave., Suite 203, Lisle, IL 60532, 312-369-3390. Donna Sandberg, M.A., Owner/Counselor.

Career Workshops, 5431 W. Roscoe St., Chicago, IL 60641, 312-282-6859. Patricia Dietze.

Jean **Davis,** Career Counseling, 1405 Elmwood Ave., Evanston, IL 60201, 708-492-1002

Harper College Community Counseling Center, Palatine, IL 60067, 708-397-3000, ext. 2577.

David P. **Helfand**, Ed.D., N.C.C., 250 Ridge, Evanston, IL 60202, 708-328-2787.

Illinois Vocational Student Services Network, 145 Fisk St., Dekalb, IL 60115, 815-758-8597. Olive Poliks, Career Guidance Consultant. The Network also has offices in Springfield, Addison, Macomb, Rantoul, Grayslake, Belleville, and Olney.

Lansky Career Consultants, 233 E. Erie # 611, Chicago, IL 60611, 312-642-5738.

McFadden & Associates, 1510 W. Sunnyview Dr., Peoria, IL 61614, 309-691-3312. Mary F. McFadden, President.

Midwest Women's Center, 828 S. Wabash, Suite 200, Chicago, IL 60605, 312-922-8530.

Moraine Valley Community College, Job Placement Center, 10900 S. 88th Ave., Palos Hills, IL 60465, 708-974-5737.

The **Professional Career Counselors & Consultants Network (PCCN),** 307 N. Michigan #2001, Chicago, IL 60601, 312-332-4516. For $5, PCCN will send you a directory of their members who offer consulting to the public. Eleanor Margulis, President.

Right Livelyhood$, 23 W. 402 Green Briar Drive, Naperville, IL 60540, 708-369-9066. Marti Beddoe, Career/Life Counselor.

Jane **Shuman,** Career Management Consultant, 122 Circle Dr., Springfield, IL 62703, 217-529-7220.

INDIANA

Career Consultants, 107 N. Pennsylvania St., Suite 404, Indianapolis, IN 46204, 317-639-5601. Mike Kenney, Senior Partner.

Sally **Jones,** Program Coordinator/Developer, Indiana University, School of Continuing Studies, Owen Hall, Room 202, Bloomington IN 47405.

John D. **King & Associates,** Career Counseling and Consulting, 205 N. College, Suite 614, Bloomington, IN 47404, 812-332-3888.

William R. **Lesch**, M.S., Career & Life Planning, Health Associates, 9240 N. Meridian St., Suite 292, Indianapolis, IN 46260, 317-844-7489.

IOWA

LifeWorks, 2010 South Ankeny Blvd., Ankeny, IA 50021, 515-964-6710. Michael Anderson, Dennis Mullin, Dr. Ray Martin.

University of Iowa, Business and Liberal Arts Placement/Career Information Services, IMU, Iowa City, IA 52242, 319-335-3201.

KANSAS

No listings.

KENTUCKY

Ol/Ronniger, Career Consultants, The Summit II, 4360 Brownsboro Rd., Louisville, KY 40207, 502-894-9400. Phillip Ronniger.

LOUISIANA

Career Planning and Assessment Center, Metropolitan College, University of New Orleans, New Orleans, LA 70148, 504-286-7100.

MAINE

Women's Worth Career Counseling, 18 Woodland Rd., Gorham, ME 04038, 207-892-0000. Jacqueline Murphy, Counselor.

MARYLAND

Careerscope, Inc., Suite 219, Harper's Choice Village Center, 5485 Harper's Farm Rd., Columbia, MD 21044, 410-992-5042/596-1866. Ann Sim, Executive Director.

Career Transition Services, 3126 Berkshire Rd., Baltimore MD 21214-3404, 410-444-5857. Michael Bryant.

College of Notre Dame of Maryland, Continuing Education Center, 4701 N. Charles St., Baltimore, MD 21210, 301-532-5303.

Goucher College, Goucher Center for Continuing Studies, Towson, Baltimore, MD 21204, 301-337-6200.

Maryland New Directions, Inc., 2220 N. Charles St., Baltimore, MD 21218, 301-235-8800. Rose Marie Coughlin, Director.

Prince George's Community College, Career Assessment and Planning Center, 301 Largo Rd., Largo, MD 20772, 301-322-0886. David C. Borchard, Director.

MASSACHUSETTS

Affordable Counseling, 104 Sanborn Ave., West Roxbury, MA 02132, 617-327-5343. Carl Schneider.

Alewife Counseling Associates, 18 Palmer St., Arlington, MA 02174, 617-643-2988. Jane Hynes.

Career Management Associates, 19 Damon Road/Minot, Scituate, MA 02066, 617-545-7070. Kent Wampler and Marci Mahoney.

Career Management Consultants, Thirty Park Ave., Worcester, MA 01605, 617-853-8669. Patricia M. Stepanski, President.

Career Resource Center, Worcester YWCA, 1 Salem Square, Worcester, MA 01608, 617-791-3181.

Center for Career Development & Ministry, 70 Chase St., Newton Center, MA 02159. Sr. Violet Grennan, OSF, Associate Director.

Center for Careers, Jewish Vocational Service, 105 Chauncy St., 6th Fl., Boston, MA 02111, 617-451-8147.

David J. **Giber,** Ph.D., 80 Waverley St., Arlington, MA 02174. 617-648-5732.

Jewish Vocational Service, Mature Worker Programs, 333 Nahanton St., Newton, MA 02159.

Wynne W. **Miller,** 785 Centre St., Newton, MA 02158-2599, 617-527-4848.

Murray Associates, 555 Washington St., Wellesley, MA 02181, 617-235-8896. Robert Murray, Ed.D., Licensed Psychologist.

Neville Associates, Inc., 10 Tower Office Park, Suite 416, Woburn, MA 01801, 617-938-7870. Dr. Joseph Neville, Career Development Consultant.

Radcliffe Career Services (open to the general public), 77 Brattle St., Cambridge MA 02138, 617-495-8631.

Suit Yourself, Inc., 115 Shade St., Lexington, MA 02173, 617-862-6006 or 508-358-4567. Debra Spencer.

Women's Educational & Industrial Union, Career Services, 356 Boylston St., Boston, MA 02116, 617-536-5657.

MICHIGAN

Ellman & Associates, Suite 220-B, 7001 Orchard Lake Rd., West Bloomfield, MI 48322, 313-737-7252. Barbara Kabcenell Ellman, M.A., N.C.C., Career Management Professional.

Donald D. **Fink,** Ed.D., Career Consultant, Psychology Associates, 1000 Parchment Dr., S.E., Grand Rapids, MI 49546, 616-957-9112.

New Options: Counseling for Women in Transition, 2311 E. Stadium, Suite B-2, Ann Arbor, MI 48104, 313-973-0003. Phyllis Perry, M.S.W.

Oakland University, Continuum Center for Adult Counseling and Leadership Training, Rochester, MI 48063, 313-370-3033.

University of Michigan, Center for the Education of Women, 330 East Liberty, Ann Arbor, MI 48104, 313-998-7080.

Women's Resource Center, 252 State St. SE, Grand Rapids, MI 49503.

MINNESOTA

Associated Career Services, 1611 West County Road B, Suite 120, Roseville, MN 55113, 612-631-9115. Stanley J. Sizen, Career Counselor.

Career Dynamics, Inc., 8300 Norman Center Dr., #240, Bloomington, MN 55437, 612-921-2378. Joan Strewler, Psychologist.

Human Dynamics, 3036 Ontario Rd., Little Canada, MN 55117, 612-484-8299. Greg J. Cylkowski, M.A., founder.

Leider, Inc., 7101 York Ave. S., Minneapolis, MN 55435, 612-921-3334. Richard J. Leider, Executive & Professional Career Consultant.

Working Opportunities for Women, 2700 University Ave., #120, St. Paul, MN 55114, 612-647-9961.

MISSISSIPPI

Mississippi State University, Career Services Center, P.O. Box 3814, Colvard Union, Suite 316, Mississippi State, MS 39762, 601-325-3344.

MISSOURI

Career Planning and Placement Center, Adult Evening Program, 110 Noyes Hall, University of Missouri, Columbia, MO 65211, 314-882-6803.

Women's Center, University of Missouri-Kansas City, 5100 Rockhill Rd., 104 Scofield Hall, Kansas City, MO 64110, 816-235-1638.

MONTANA

No listings.

NEBRASKA

Career Planning Center, Central Community College, Hastings Campus, Hastings, NE 68901, 402-461-2456.

Olson Counseling Services, 8720 Frederick, Suite 105, Omaha, NE 68124, 402-390-2342. Gail A. Olson, P.A.C.

NEW JERSEY

Adult Advisory Services, Kean College of New Jersey, Administration Bldg., Union, NJ 07083, 201-527-2210.

Adult Resource Center, 100 Horseneck Road, Montville, NJ 07045, 201-335-6910.

Arista Concepts Career Development Service, P.O. Box 2436, Princeton, NJ 08540, 609-921-0308. Kera Greene, M.Ed.

Career Options Center, YWCA Tribute to Women and Industry (TWIN) Program, 232 E. Front St., Plainfield, NJ 07060, 908-756-3836, or 908-273-4242. Janet M. Korba, Program Director.

Loree **Collins,** 3 Beechwood Rd., Summit, NJ 07901, 201-273-9219.

Douglass College, Douglass Advisory Services for Women, Rutgers Women's Center, 132 George St., New Brunswick, NJ 08903, 201-932-9603.

Sandra **Grundfest,** Ed.D., Princeton Professional Park, 601 Ewing St., Suite C-1, Princeton, NJ 08540, 609-921-8401.

Minsuk, Macklin, Stein & Associates, 14 Washington Rd., Princeton Junction, NJ 08550-1028, 609-275-5800. Also: 115 Rt. 46, Bldg. F, Mountain Lakes, NJ 07045. 201-402-4294.

W.L. Nikel & Associates, Career Development and Outplacement, 28 Harper Terrace, Cedar Grove, NJ 07009, 201-575-5700. William L. Nikel, M.B.A., Founder.

The **Professional Roster,** 171 Broadmead, Princeton, NJ 08540, 609-921-9561.

Women's Center, Princeton University, 201 Aaron Burr Hall, Princeton, NJ 08544, 609-452-5565.

NEW MEXICO

Young Women's Christian Association, YWCA Career Services Center, 7201 Paseo Del Norte NE, Albuquerque, NM 87113, 505-822-9922.

NEW YORK

Academic Advisory Center for Adults, Turf Ave., Rye, NY 10580, 914-967-1653.

Alan B. **Bernstein** CSW, PC, 122 East 82nd St., N.Y.,NY 10028, 212-288-4881.

Career Agenda, Inc., 560 West 43rd St., Suite 40B, New York, NY 10036, 212-268-0564. Carol Allen, President.

The **Career Center,** 1525 Western Ave., Albany, NY 12203, 518-869-1311. Thomas J. McKenna, Director.

Career Development Services, 14 Franklin St., Temple Bldg., Suite 1200, Rochester, NY 14604, 716-325-2274.

Career Services Center, Long Island University, C.W. Post Campus, Brookville, NY 11548, 516-299-2251. Mince Kohler, Director.

The John C. **Crystal Center**, 152 Madison Ave., 23rd fl., New York, NY 10016, 212-889-8500, or 1-800-333-9003. Nella G. Barkley, President. (*John died in 1988; Nella was his business partner, for many years preceding his death, and now carries on his work. The Center also has offices in Chicago and Los Angeles, run under the aegis of The Crystal-Barkley Corporation. The 800 number above will work for reaching all three centers.*)

Susan **Hadley,** Career and Life/Work Planning Consultant, 59 Jefferson St., Nyack, NY 10960, 914-353-0579.

Hofstra University, Career Counseling Center, 240 Student Center, Hempstead, NY 11550, 516-463-6788.

Kingsborough Community College, Office of Career Counseling and Placement, 2001 Oriental Blvd., Rm. C102, Brooklyn, NY 11235, 718-368-5115.

Janice **La Rouche** Assoc., Workshops for Women, 333 Central Park W., New York, NY 10025, 212-663-0970.

Miriam J. **Mennin**, M.A., N.C.C., 33 Andrea Lane, Scarsdale, NY 10583, 914-725-5501.

Network Resumes & Career Services, 60 E. 42nd St., Rm. 2901, New York, NY 10165, 212-687-2411. John Aigner, Counselor.

New Options, 960 Park Ave., New York, NY 10028, 212-535-1444.

Orange County Community College, Counseling Center, South St., Middletown, NY 10940, 914-341-4070.

Celia **Paul Associates,** 200 Madison Ave., New York, NY 10016, 212-873-3588.

Personnel Sciences Center/Aptitude Testing Corporation, 41 E. 42nd St., Suite 805, New York, NY 10017, 212-661-1870.

Regional Learning Service of Central New York, 405 Oak St., Syracuse, NY 13203, 315-425-5252.

Ruth Shapiro Associates, 200 E. 30th St., New York, NY 10016, 212-889-4284.

L. Michelle **Tullier,** Ph.D., Career Counselor. Virginia J. Bush & Associates, 444 E. 86th St., New York, NY 10028, 212-447-5178.

WIN Workshops (Women in Networking), Emily Koltnow, 730 Fifth Ave., New York, NY 10019, 212-333-8788.

Women's Center for Continuing Education, Syracuse University College, 610 E. Fayette St., Syracuse, NY 13244, 315-423-4116. Phyllis R. Chase, Director.

NORTH CAROLINA

Career Consulting Associates of Raleigh, P.O. Box 17653, Raleigh, NC 27619, 919 782 3252. Susan W. Simonds, President.

Career, Educational, Psychological Evaluations, 2915 Providence Rd., Suite 300, Charlotte, NC 28211, 704-362-1942. Nancy Cook.

Career Management Center, 3203 Woman's Club Drive, Suite 217, Raleigh, NC 27612, 919-787-1222. Temple G. Porter, Director.

Sally **Kochendofer,** Ph.D., 20109K Henderson Rd., Davidson, NC 28036, 704-892-4975.

Diane E. **Lambeth,** M.S.W., Career Consultant. 512 Hertford St., Raleigh, NC 27609, 919-571-7423.

Life Management Services, Crossroads Bldg. 1, 5625 Dillard Rd., Suite 105, Cary, NC 27511, 919-859-4822.

Joyce **Richman & Associates, Ltd.,** 2911 Shady Lawn Dr., Greensboro, NC 27408, 919-288-1799

Women's Center of Raleigh, 315 E. Jones St., Raleigh, NC 27601, 919-829-3711.

OHIO

Adult Resource Center, The University of Akron, Buckingham Center for Continuing Education, Akron, OH 44325-3102, 216-972-7448.

Cuyahoga County Public Library Info-PLACE Service, Career, Education & Community Information Service, 5225 Library Lane, Maple Heights, OH 44137-1291, 216-475-2225.

Hill & Hill Consulting, Inc., 393 Hawthorne Lane N.E., Warren, OH 44484, 216-856-4440. Barbara H. Hill, President.

J & K Associates, 607 Otterbein, Dayton, OH 45406-4507, 513-274-3630. Pat Kenney, Ph.D., President.

New Career, 328 Race St., Dover, OH 44622, 216-364-5557. Marshall Karp, M.A., N.C.C., L.P.C., Owner.

Pyramid Career Services, Inc., 1642 Cleveland Ave., NW, Canton, OH 44703, 216-453-3767. Zandra Bloom, Director.

OKLAHOMA

Career Development Services, 4823 S. Sheridan, Suite 304, Tulsa, OK 74145, 918-665-1161/1162. William D. Young, Ed.D., L.P.C.

Career Development, PO Box 5099, Beaverton, OR 97006, 503-649-0996. Edward H. Hosley, Ph.D., Director.

Joseph A. **Dubay,** 2153 S.W. Main Street, Portland, OR 97205, 503-224-3600.

Verk, Life Work, 1441 Oak St., #7, Eugene, OR 97440, 503-687-9170. Larry H. Malmgren, M.S., President.

Career Management Consultants, Inc., 3207 N. Front St., Harrisburg, PA 17110, 717-233-2272. Louis F. Persico, Career Consultant.

Cedar Crest College, Women's Center, Allentown, PA 18104, 215-437-4471.

Center for Adults in Transition, Bucks County Community College, Newtown, PA 18940, 215-968-8188. Patricia Sharer, Assistant Director.

Henry D. **Landes Associates,** 1011 Cathill Rd., Sellersville, PA 18960, 215-256-3011, 723-8413.

Options, Inc., 215 S. Broad St., Philadelphia, PA 19107, 215-735-2202. Marcia P. Kleiman, Director.

Priority Two, Rm. 208, Pittsburgh National Bank Bldg., Beaver & Blackburn Rds., Sewickley, PA 15143, 412-741-8368. Five locations in the Pittsburgh area.

Resources for Excellence, P.O. Box 8989, 726 South Ave., Pittsburgh, PA 15221, 412-242-3001. David R. Johnson, Director.

Terence Duniho, 120 Moore St., Providence, RI 02907, 401-273-9183.

Career Counselor Services, Inc., 25 Woods Lake Road, Suite 324, Greenville, SC 29607, 803-370-9453. Al A. Hafer, Ed.D., NCCC, NCC, LPC.

Converse College, Office of Career Services, 580 E. Main St., Spartanburg, SC 29302-0006, 803-596-9027. Ms. Kathy McKinzie, Associate Director of Career Services.

Greenville Technical College, Career Advancement Center, Greenville, SC 29606, 803-250-8281. Larry A. Hudson, Counselor.

Career Concepts Planning Center, Inc., Centennial Square Plaza, 2100 S. 7th St., Rapid City, SD 57701, 605-394-5783, toll free: 1-800-456-0832. Melvin M. Tuggle, Jr., President.

Sioux Falls College, The Center for Women, Clidden Hall, Sioux Falls, SD 57105, 605-331-6697.

Career Resources, 2323 Hillsboro Rd., Suite 300, Nashville, TN 37212, 615-297-0404. Jane C. Hardy, Principal/Career Counselor.

Mid-South Career Development Center, 2315 Fisher Place, Knoxville, TN 37920, 615-573-1340. W. Scott Root, President/Counselor.

S.O.S. (Secretarial Office Services), 314 N. White St., Athens, TN 37303, 615-745-4513. Adelia Wyner, Consultant.

Austin Women's Center, 1700 S. Lamar Blvd., Suite 203, Austin, TX 78704, 512-447-9666.

Career Action Associates, First Interstate Bank Plaza, Suite 512, 12655 N. Central Expressway, Dallas, TX 75243, 214-392-7337. Office also in Fort Worth, 817-763-9528. Rebecca Hayes, Licensed Professional Counselor.

Catalyst Career Consultants, 2520 Longview, Suite 112, Austin, TX 78705, 512-474-7773. Joia Jitahidi, Senior Consultant.

Richard S. **Citrin,** Ph.D., Psychologist, Iatreia Institute, 1152 Country Club Ln., Ft. Worth, TX 76112, 817-654-9600.

Counseling Services of Houston, 1964 W. Gray, Suite 204, Houston, TX 77019, 713-521-9391. Rosemary C. Vienot, M.S., Licensed Professional Counselor, Director.

Employment/Career Information Resource Center, Corpus Christi Public Library, 805 Comanche, Corpus Christi, TX 78401, 512-880-7004. Lynda F. Whitton, Career Information Specialist.

New Directions Counseling Center, 8140 North Mopac, Bldg. II, Suite 230, Austin, TX 78759, 512-343-9496. Jeanne Quereau, M.A., Licensed Professional Counselor.

New Life Institute, Box 1666, Austin, TX 78767, 512-469-9447. Bob Breihan, Director.

San Antonio Psychological Services, 6800 Park Ten Blvd., Suite 208 North, San Antonio, TX 78213, 512-737-2039.

Mary **Stedham,** Counseling/Consulting Services, 2434 S. 10th, Abilene, TX 79605, 915-672-4044.

UTAH

University of Utah, Center for Adult Transitions, 1195 Annex Bldg., Salt Lake City, UT 84112, 801-581-3228.

VIRGINIA

Career Development Center for Women, 5501 Backlick Rd., #110, Springfield, VA 22151, 703-750-0633.

Educational Opportunity Center, 7010-M Auburn Ave., Norfolk, VA 23513, 804-855-7468. Agatha A. Peterson, Director.

Golden Handshakes, Church of the Epiphany, 11000 Smoketree Dr., Richmond, VA 23236, 804-794-0222. Diane Smith, Chairperson; also at Winfree Memorial Baptist Church, P.O. Box 244, Midlothian, VA 23113, 804-794-5031. Steve Davis, Volunteer Coordinator.

Hollins College, Career Counseling Center, Roanoke, VA 24020, 703-362-6364. Peggy Ann Neumann, Director.

Life Management Services, Inc., 6849 Old Dominion Drive, Suite 219, McLean, VA 22101, 703-356-2630. Hal and Marilyn Shook, President and Vice President.

Mary Baldwin College, Rosemarie Sena Center for Career and Life Planning, Staunton, VA 24401, 703-887-7221.

Psychological Consultants, Inc., 6724 Patterson Ave., Richmond, VA 23226, 804-288-4125.

Swenholt Associates, Inc., 6308 Crosswoods Circle, Falls Church, VA 22044, 703-256-2383. Frankie P. Swenholt, President.

Virginia Commonwealth University, University Advising Center, Box 2002, 827 W. Franklin St., Rm. 101, Richmond, VA 23284-2002, 804-367-1580 or 367-0200. Marcia F. Zwicker, Director.

The **Women's Center,** 133 Park St., NE, Vienna, VA 22180, 703-281-2657. Virginia C. Marshall, Director of Program Development.

WASHINGTON

Career Management Institute, 8404 27th St. West, Tacoma, WA 98466, 206-565-8818. Ruthann Reim, M.A., N.C.C., President.

The **Individual Development Center, Inc. (I.D. Center),** 1020 E. John, Seattle, WA 98102, 206-329-0600. Mary Lou Hunt, N.C.C., M.A., President.

People Management Group International, P.O. Box 33608, Seattle, WA 98133, 206-443-1107. Arthur F. Miller, Jr., Chairman. Dick Staub, President.

University Extension GH-21, Career Development Services, Seattle, WA 98195, 206-543-2300.

Vecchio & Associates, Career Consultants. 624 Skinner Bldg., 1326 Fifth Ave., Seattle, WA 98101, 206-622-8070. Carol Vecchio, President.

WISCONSIN

Career Connections Center, Career Counseling for Career Changers, Alverno College, 3401 S. 39th St., Milwaukee, WI 53215, 414-382-6010.

David Swanson, Career Seminars and Workshops, 1033 N. Mayfair Rd., Suite 200, Milwaukee, WI 53226, 414-259-0265.

WYOMING

Lifetime Career Consultants, P.O. Box 912, Jackson, WY 83001, 307-733-6544. Barbara Gray. Also P.O. Box 1867, Jackson, WY 83001, 307-733-4471. Caryn Haman.

National Education Service Center, P.O. Box 1279, Riverton, WY 82501-1279, 307-856-0170.

University of Wyoming, Center for Career Planning & Placement, PO Box 3195/Knight Hall 228, Laramie, WY 82071, 307-766-2398. Dr. Pat McGinley.

U.S.A. -- NATIONWIDE

Forty Plus Clubs. A nationwide network of voluntary, autonomous nonprofit clubs, manned by its unemployed members, paying no salaries, supported by initiation fees and monthly dues. At this writing, there are clubs in the following cities: Buffalo, Chicago, Columbus, Colorado Springs, Dallas, Denver, Fort Collins, Honolulu, Houston, Los Angeles, New York, Oakland (California), Philadelphia, Salt Lake City, Toronto, and Washington, D. C. If you live in one of these cities, you can check the white pages of your Phone Book; also you can call Forty Plus of New York, 15 Park Row, New York, NY 10038, 212-233-6086 to get current information about any of the nationwide locations -- to see if the club is still there, and what their current address and phone number are.

Des Roches, Wallace, Bond Inc., 360 Albert St., Suite 1701, Ottawa, Ontario K1R 7X7. 613-238-7636. Kenneth Des Roches.

Robin T. **Hazell** & Associates, 60 St. Clair Ave., E., Toronto, Ontario M4T 1N5, 416-961-3700.

The Institute for Career Management, 390 Bay St., Suite 2000, Toronto M5H 2&2, Canada, 416-861-0426.

Job-Finding Club, 305-280 Smith St., Winnipeg, Manitoba R3C 1K2, 947-1948, 947-1996. Connie LeBlanc, Project Manager.

Peat Marwick Stevenson & Kellogg, 130 Dufferin, 12th Floor, London, Ontario N6A 5R2, 519-663-2660. W. Allan Methven.

Susan Steinberg, M.Ed., 74 Denlow Blvd., Don Mills, Ontario M3B 1P9, 416-449-6936.

YMCA Career Planning & Development, 15 Breadalbane St., Toronto, Canada M4Y 2V5, 416-324-4123.

Cabinet Daniel Porot, 1, rue Verdaine, CH-1204 Geneve, Switzerland, phone 0114122 21 04 38. Daniel Porot, Founder.

Castle Consultants International, Thames House, 140 Battersea Park Rd., London SW11 4NB, England, phone 071 622 7011. Walt Hopkins, Founder and Director.

The **Chaney Partnership,** Hillier House, 509 Upper Richmond Rd. West, London SW14 7EE, phone 081-878-3227. Isabel Chaney, B.A.

Peter **Kessler,** Haus zur Pyramide, Dorfstrasse 55, CH-8715 Bollingen SG, bei Jona-Rapperswil, Switzerland, phone 055 28 22 80.

Raadgevend Bureau Claessens, B.V., Head Office Breda, De Bijster, Bijster 16, 4817 HX Breda, Netherlands. This organization has many branch offices throughout Germany, France, Belgium and the Netherlands. Write to the head office for the additional locations. Frans Claessens, Founder and Director.

Robert J. **Bisdee** & Associates, 22 Allenby Ave., Malvern E., Victoria, Australia 3145, phone 613-885-4716. Dr. Bob Bisdee, Director.

All of the overseas counselors listed above have attended my two-week workshop.

Centre for WorkLife Counselling, P.O. Box 407, Spit Junction, Australia 2088, phone 02-969-4548. Paul Stevens, Director.

Judy **Feierstein,** M.A., 46/2 Derech Bet Lechem, Jerusalem 93504, Israel, phone 02 710673.

Addendum:
IF YOU ARE A CAREER COUNSELOR, OR WANT TO BE ONE

If you liked the subject matter of this book a lot (and, even more, another book of mine called *The Three Boxes of Life and How to Get Out of Them*), you will of course be thinking about the possibility of becoming a career counselor yourself. Those just getting started in the field of career counseling (inside or outside academia) will, of course, want to read this current edition of *Parachute* from cover to cover, and then **do** all the exercises within it, before they inflict them on their helpless students or clients. *Teaching is Sharing, and Sharing should only follow Experiencing.*

Career-counseling, as you will recall from the beginning of this Appendix, may deal with career-development, or with career-change, or with job-hunting -- or any combination of those three. The focus of this book is on career-change and job-hunting, therefore below I have only listed resources dealing with those subjects, not the much broader field of career development -- which would go on for pages and pages.

Periodicals or Newsletters:

Career Planning & Adult Development Newsletter, published monthly by the Career Planning and Adult Development Network, 4965 Sierra Rd., San Jose, CA 95132. Richard L. Knowdell, Editor.

CNews: Career Opportunities News, Garrett Park Press, Box 190, Garrett Park, MD 20896. Useful news for counselors (and job-hunters) about employment fields, fellowships, new books, etc.

Careers Guidance Index: *Sources of Free and Inexpensive Career Guidance Materials.* Careers, Inc., P.O. Box 135, Largo, FL 34649-0135. Published monthly. They also have "Occu-Labels," which are over 550 labels addressed to places which have free or inexpensive career and educational materials. Ask them for current prices.

The Journal of Employment Counseling, a professional journal concerned with research, theory, and new and improved job counseling techniques and tools. It does not, in my experience, deal so much with the job-hunt, as with counseling; and the counseling is pretty much along the traditional job-hunting lines. This is the official publication of the National Employment Counseling Association, a division of the American Counseling Association (ACA)[4], 5999 Stevenson Ave., Alexandria, VA 22304. $20/yr.

The Damn Good Resume Writer©, A National Newsletter for Professionals, Exploring and Promoting Excellence in Resume Writing. Published quarterly. P.O. Box 3289, Berkeley, CA 94703. Yana Parker, Editor.

All the above periodicals or newsletters have a subscription fee.
We recommend that you ask them for subscription information
and a sample issue, before subscribing.

Books:

Stevens, Nancy Duncan, *Dynamics of Job-Seeking Behavior.* Charles C Thomas, Publisher, 2600 S. First St., Springfield, IL 62717. 1986. Uses various frameworks (such as Holland's RIASEC theories) to analyze three different job-seeking behavioral patterns.

Azrin, Nathan H., and Besalel, Victoria A., *Job Club Counselor's Manual: A Behavioral Approach to Vocational Counseling.* Pro-Ed, 8700 Shoal Creek Blvd., Austin, TX 78758, 512-451-3246. For any counselor interested in working with job-hunters more than one at a time, this work is *mandatory* reading. Nathan invented the job club idea, and when followed *faithfully* it has a very high success rate (around 86%). Problem is: every technique described in Nathan's book was designed to eliminate some difficulty or obstacle to your client's job-hunt, and each time you try to take short-cuts with his program and cut out *this* technique or *that* (as counselors are *very* wont to do), you *re-introduce* into your client's job-hunt the problem that the technique was designed to eliminate. Therefore, if you're going to use this manual, use it *faithfully.*

The Guide to Basic Skills Jobs, Vol. 1. RPM Press, Inc., Verndale, MN 56481. 1986. A catalog of viable jobs for individuals with only basic work

---

4. Previously known as the American Association for Counseling and Development (AACD), and -- before that -- as the American Personnel and Guidance Association (APGA).

skills. This volume identifies 5,000 major occupations within the U.S. economy which require no more than an eighth grade level of education, and no more than one year of specific vocational preparation. Immensely useful book if you counsel that kind of job-hunter.

Career & Job Search Instruction Made Easy, JIST Works, Inc., The Job Search People, 720 North Park Ave., Indianapolis, IN 46202. 1-800-648-JIST.

Job Information and Seeking Training Program Instructor's Guide and Job Seekers Workbook. 1980. JIST Works, Inc., 720 North Park Ave., Indianapolis, IN 46202. 1-800-648-JIST.

Porot, Daniel, *Comment Trouver Une Situation.* Les Editions d'Organisations, 5, rue Rousselet, F-75007 Paris. 1985. If you read French, this is Daniel's approach to the job-hunt. Since he is *the* expert in Europe, this is well worth reading.

Lathrop, Richard, *The Job Market.* The National Center for Job-Market Studies, Box 3651, Washington, DC 20007. *What would happen if we decreased the length of the job-hunt in America,* and other iconoclastic ideas which are also eminently sensible.

See also the bibliography in Appendix B, for information on books that are related to particular client populations that you desire to counsel.

Instruments:

This, of course, is a wide world. There are a *million* instruments out there: the Strong-Campbell Interest Inventory, the Holland SDS, the Myers-Briggs, and a host of others -- including my own *Quick Job-Hunting (and Career-Changing) Map: How to Create A Picture of Your Ideal Job or Next Career.*

If you want to know about other instruments available to you, see: Kapes, Jerome T., and Mastie, Marjorie Moran, eds., *A Counselor's Guide to Career Assessment Instruments.* 1988 ed. Published by the National Career Development Association, a division of AGA, 5999 Stevenson Ave., Alexandria, VA 22304.

Film, Audiotape, Videotape:

Sladey, Pat, *Find the job you want...and get it!* A four- **audiocassette** program, on the subjects: Find the Hidden Job Market; Sell Yourself in the Interview; Prepare Winning Resumes & Letters; and Stay Motivated During the Search. Available from: Pat Sladey & Associates, P.O. Box 440352, Aurora, CO 80044. *There is also a **videotape** version of this program, on four videocassettes.*

For other videos dealing with the job-hunt, see the 1992 Catalog. Wintergreen Software, Inc., P.O. Box 1229, Madison, WI 53701.

Computer Software:

The computer is a wonderful tool. I use one all day long, every day that I work *(for the curious, a Macintosh IIci with color screen)*. Nonetheless, my personal opinion is that computer software *for career counselors or job-hunters* is mostly still in the Dark Ages. What help computer software does give with choosing careers is *simplistic*; what help it gives with the actual job-hunt is *elementary* -- except perhaps in the area of resumes, and you know what I think about the effectiveness of resumes. (See Chapter 3.) *However,* for those who wish to explore this arena further, I list here two directories and some *examples* of what is 'out there,' most of which costs less than $150, sometimes much less. **Their listing here is not, however, to be construed as a recommendation, in any sense of the word. Reread the lines above.**

Directories

The Personnel Software Census. Advanced Personnel Systems, P.O. Box 1438, Roseville, CA 95661. Has sections on 'Career Management' and 'Job Search/Resume Writing.' Lists about 20 programs in those two categories. An even more up-to-date listing is available on disk.

1992 Catalog. Wintergreen Software, Inc., P.O. Box 1229, Madison, WI 53701. Lists software not found in any other catalog; also videotapes.

Examples of Programs

Jackson, Tom, *The Perfect Resume Computer Kit.* Permax Systems Inc., P.O. Box 6455, Madison, WI 53716-0455. Assists in preparing resumes, based on Tom's very popular book. Enables the user to prepare customized, target resumes. There is both a Personal Version and a Counselor's Version. For IBM computers and compatibles.

Parker, Yana, *ReadyToGo Resumes (Self-Teaching Resume Templates).* Damn Good Resume Service, P.O. Box 3289, Berkeley, CA 94703. 1993. This is a computer disk, and manual, for both Macintosh and IBM computers and compatibles. It is based on her very popular book, *Damn Good Resume Guide.*

Resume Writer. Schonberg Associates, Inc., 2368 Victory Pkwy., Cincinnati OH 45206. A book plus software. Comes in business or student editions. For IBM computers and compatibles.

BetterWorking: The Resume Kit™. Spinnaker Software Corporation, One Kendall Square, Cambridge, MA 02139. 1990. Written for Macintosh computers, as well as for IBM computers and compatibles. This program has an *excellent* manual, including a long, helpful, and realistic section called *"Beyond Resumes,"* -- obviously written by someone who knows what she is talking about, and who is wise and witty to boot.

Career Navigator. Drake Beam Morin, Inc., 100 Park Ave., New York, NY 10017. Computer-based training and guidance during one's job-search. For IBM computers and compatibles.

Studner, Peter K., *The Super-Search™ System.* Jamenair Ltd., P.O. Box 241957, Los Angeles, CA 90024. A book plus software. The software has the book's resumes on disk, plus databases of contacts, and computerizes one's job-hunt journey. For IBM computers and compatibles.

Training:

By Others: There are countless training opportunities for career counselors in the U.S. and abroad. *Career Planning & Adult Development Newsletter,* mentioned earlier (published monthly by the Career Planning and

Adult Development Network, 4965 Sierra Rd., San Jose, CA 95132) maintains a *very good* calendar of these events, and anyone interested in further training would be well advised to be receiving this *Newsletter*.

By Me: Whenever the subject of training comes up, I am asked (endlessly) whether or not *I* do any teaching. We receive hundreds of letters each year asking this. Since I would like to cut down on the mail and also save *you* some trouble, I will give you the desired information, right here.

I do not do any training anymore, or speaking, except in August of each year, when I teach nonstop for fifteen days along with my esteemed colleague from Europe, Daniel Porot, whose insights you have seen frequently in the main body of this book. We call it:

Fifteen Days of
LIFE/Work Planning
with Vacation
at the Inn of the Seventh Mountain

This is not, as its name would suggest, held in the Orient. The Inn of the Seventh Mountain is a beautiful and popular resort on the outskirts of **Bend, Oregon**, which -- as everyone knows -- is in the center of the United States (Honolulu is 3,000 miles to the West, New York City is 3,000 miles to the East).

The workshop is now fifteen days in length. In 1993, the dates are July 30--Aug.14. In 1994, the dates are August 5--20. Since fifteen days is a long time, and people who attend usually do so in lieu of their regular summer vacation, we have deliberately put this workshop at a first-class vacation resort, which past participants have absolutely delighted in -- as they can 'have their cake and eat it, too.' The Inn has two swimming pools, waterslide, hot baths/saunas, hiking trails, tennis, whitewater rafting, horseback riding, moped rental, bicycle rental, roller-skating, ski-lifts to the top of Mount Bachelor, and other vacation amenities, outdoor eating -- with *wonderful* food -- all in a lovely pine-forest setting near the foot of a large mountain topped with snow even in the summertime. In fairness you should be told that if you come, you won't have *a lot* of time to enjoy these amenities, as you will be working *very* hard during the fifteen days. But every day from 12--3 is free time for you, and lunch can be very brief.

The workshop is led, from beginning to end, by Daniel and myself; we teach as a team. Daniel's expertise and teaching skills are really dazzling. The total training at this workshop exceeds 100 hours.

The workshop is limited to the first 60 people who apply, each year. In age participants have ranged from 17--74, have embraced all ethnic groups, and have come from all parts of the world. In 1990, for example, participants came from Denmark, Germany, Switzerland, Gabon (Africa), Jamaica, Brazil, Canada, New Zealand, and Australia -- as well as the U.S. (obviously). In 1991, they were from England, Canada, New Zealand, Australia, and the U.S.

We have been told by the hundreds of counselors who have attended since 1974 that they find this to be the most thoroughgoing training in the art of career counseling and life/work planning that is available anywhere in the world today. Maybe it is, and maybe it isn't. But one thing it is, for sure. **It is fun.** Year after year people say that this was close to the most enjoyable fifteen days of their entire life. *Be sure to bring your playful self.*

The cost of the entire workshop -- the tuition -- is $1,000 if you register before November 30th, for the following summer; or $1,500 if you register after November 30th. This includes all materials and sessions.

The cost of the room and board at the Inn, with all its facilities, is **additional**, and will run you (*or your institution*) around $125 a day *for your room, breakfast, lunch, dinner, and three refreshment breaks each day* -- though this sum can vary, depending on the type of accommodations you want.

If you wish more information about the workshop, and/or a registration blank, you should write to:

The Registrar
Fifteen-Day Workshop
What Color Is Your Parachute?
P.O. Box 379
Walnut Creek, CA 94597

Phone 1-510-935-1865 (10 a.m.– 4:30 p.m. Monday thru Friday,
Pacific Coast Time).
Fax No.: 1-510-932-4864 (twenty-four hours a day).

If you are interested in attending in a particular year, you are required to register by June 1st of that year, since the Inn releases all its rooms to the general public at that time. We *have* squeezed people in as late as July 15th *if the rooms at the Inn weren't fully booked by then (they often are -- as it is a **very** popular resort)*.

I should mention that this workshop is open to **people who are not career counselors;** and each year many 'non-counselors' attend -- job-hunters of all ages, career-changers, homemakers, union organizers, CEOs, teachers, people facing a move, people facing retirement, the recently divorced, college students, clergy and so forth. It is also attended by people from all over the world. Our methodology at this workshop is to have you master the principles of life/work planning by rigorously applying them to *your own life* during the two weeks, rather than discussing the problems of clients or their case histories, etc., as is often the fashion these days. Because of this methodology, **the workshop is useful to anyone.**

My son, be admonished:
of making many books there is no end;
and much study is a weariness of the flesh.

Ecclesiastes

Appendix B
Bibliography:

*Books and Notes
for Job-Hunters
and Career-Changers*

```
A SAMPLER
OF INFORMATION SOURCES
for You, as Job-Hunter and Career-Changer,
To Use
```

Here is a list of *some* of the books which -- from the experience of career-changers and job-hunters before you -- will likely prove useful *at one time or another* during the research phase of your career-search.

Since many of these resources are much too expensive for the average job-hunter to purchase, be grateful for your local public library, or business library, or local college library.

You don't need to use *all* of the books listed below. Just those that will help you with the particular question you're trying to find answers to, at any given moment. Incidentally, the surest way to make certain your trip to the library is a total waste of time, is to be *hazy* about what you're trying to find out. So, please, before you go to the library, each time, write out on a piece of paper, for your own use, "This is the information I am trying to find out *today:* _____." Be specific. Be clear.

Now, let's look at books that may help you with whatever question you come up with, about organizations:

American Men and Women of Science.

American Society of Training and Development Directory: Who's Who in Training and Development, 1640 King St., Box 1443, Alexandria, VA 22313-2043.

Better Business Bureau report on a particular organization that you may be interested in (call the BBB in the city where the organization is located).

Business Information Sources, by Lorna M. Daniels. University of California Press, Berkeley, CA 94720. Annotated guide to business books and reference sources.

Career Guide to Professional Associations. Garrett Park Press, Garrett Park, MD 20896.

The Career Guide: Dun's Employment Opportunities Directory. Covers more than 5,000 major U.S. companies that have indicated they plan to recruit during the publication year. Primarily for college graduates.

Chamber of Commerce data on an organization or field that interests you (visit the Chamber in the appropriate city or town).

Company/college/association/agency/foundation Annual Reports. Get these directly from the personnel department or publicity person at the company, etc., or from the Chamber or your local library.

Consultants and Consulting Organizations Directory 1992, 12th ed. Gale Research, Inc., Box 33477, Detroit, MI 48232-5477. Lists over 15,000 firms, individuals and organizations engaged in consulting work. Consultants are usually experts in their particular field, and hence may be useful to you in your information search about that job or career-change that you are contemplating.

Contacts Influential: Commerce and Industry Directory. Businesses in particular market area listed by name, type of business, key personnel, etc. Contacts Influential, Market Research and Development Services, 321 Bush St., Suite 203, San Francisco, CA 94104, if your library doesn't have it.

Corporate and Industry Research Reports. Published by R.R. Bowker/ Martindale-Hubbell, 121 Chanlon Rd., New Providence, NJ 07974. Can be very helpful.

Corporate Technology Directory. 1990, 5th ed. Lists companies by the products they make or the technologies they use. Corporate Technology Information Services, Inc., 12 Alfred St., Suite 200, Woburn, MA 01801-9998.

Dictionary of Holland Occupational Codes.

Dictionary of Occupational Titles.

Directory of American Research and Technology: Organizations Active in Product Development for Business. R.R. Bowker/Martindale-Hubbell, 121 Chanlon Rd., New Providence, NJ 07974.

Directory of Corporate Affiliations. National Register Publishing Co., Inc.

Directory of Information Resources in the United States. (Physical Sciences, Engineering, Biological Sciences) Washington, DC., Library of Congress.

Directory of Special Libraries and Information Centers 1993, 16th ed. Gale Research, Inc., Box 33477, Detroit, MI 48232-5477. Lists 22,000 research facilities, on various subjects, maintained by libraries, research libraries, businesses, nonprofit organizations, governmental agencies, etc. Detailed subject index, using over 3,500 key words.

Dun & Bradstreet's Million Dollar Directory. Very helpful.

Dun & Bradstreet's Million Dollar Directory — Top 50,000 Companies. Very helpful. An abridged version of Dun's *Million Dollar Directory Series.*

Dun & Bradstreet's Reference Book of Corporate Managements.

Encyclopedia of Associations 1993. Vol. 1, National Organizations of the U.S.; Vol. 2, Geographic and Executive Indexes; Vol. 3, New Associations and Projects. Gale Research, Inc., Box 33477, Detroit, MI 48232-5477. Lists 25,000 organizations, associations, clubs and other nonprofit membership groups that are in the business of giving out information. There is a companion series of books: *Regional, State and Local Organizations 1992–1993,* a five-volume set, which lists over 50,000 similar organizations on a regional, state, or local level. There is another companion volume, also: *International Organizations 1993.* This lists 4,000 international organizations, concerned with various subjects. There was still another companion volume, *Association Periodicals,* 1st ed., which listed 12,000 newsletters, periodicals, and journals put out by national associations in particular. It is still available, but no longer updated.

Encyclopedia of Business Information Sources, 9th ed. Gale Research, Inc., Box 33477, Detroit, MI 48232-5477. Identifies electronic, print, and live resources dealing with 1,500 business subjects. Their companion volume is entitled *Business Organizations, Agencies and Publications Directory,* 6th ed., listing over 24,000 entries, such as federal government advisory organizations, newsletters, research services, etc.

F & S Indexes (recent articles on firms).

F & S Index of Corporations and Industries. Lists "published articles" by industry and by company name. Updated weekly.

Fitch Corporation Manuals.

Fortune Magazine's 500.

The Foundation Directory.

Hoover's Handbook: Profiles of Over 500 Major Corporations, ed. by Gary Hoover, Alta Campbell, and Patrick J. Spain. Publishers Group West, 4065 Hollis, Emeryville, CA 94608.

How to Reach Anyone Who's Anyone, by Michael Levine Price/Stern/Sloan, 360 N. La Cienega Blvd., Los Angeles, CA 90048.

How To Read A Financial Report: Wringing Cash Flow and Other Vital Signs Out of the Numbers, 3rd ed., by John A. Tracy, CPA. John Wiley & Sons, Business Law/General Books Division, 605 Third Ave., New York, NY 10158-0012. Also Chichester, Brisbane, Toronto, and Singapore.

Information Industry Directory 1993. 13th ed. Gale Research, Inc., Box 33477, Detroit, MI 48232-5477. Lists 30,000 computer-based information systems and services, here and abroad. Their companion volume, *Computers and Computing Information Resources Directory,* 1st ed., lists trade shows, conventions, users' groups, associations, consultants, etc., worldwide.

International Business Travel and Relocation Directory, 6th ed. Gale Research, Inc., Box 33477, Detroit, MI 48232-5477. It presents all the relevant details for every country in the world.

Investor, Banker, Broker Almanac.

Macmillan's Directory of Leading Private Companies.

MacRae's Blue Book.

Moody's Industrial Manual (and other Moody manuals).

National Business Telephone Directory. Used to be published by Gale Research, Inc., Box 33477, Detroit, MI 48232-5477. In one single alphabetical listing, contains phone numbers, address, and city for over 350,000 business and industrial establishments that have more than 20 employees. Particularly useful when you know the name of an organization, but not what city or state it is located in. Since this is technically out of print, see if your library has a back copy.

National Directory of Addresses and Telephone Numbers. Concord Reference Books, 240 Fenel Lane, Hillside, IL 60162.

National Recreational Sporting and Hobby Organizations of the U.S. Columbia Books, Inc., 777 14th St. NW, Washington, DC 20005.

National Trade and Professional Associations of the United States and Canada and Labor Unions. Garrett Park Press, Garrett Park, MD 20896.

Newsletters Directory, 6th ed. Gale Research, Inc., Box 33477, Detroit, MI 48232-5477. Detailed entry on 10,000 newsletters in various subject fields, or categories. It includes newsletters that are available only on-line, through a computer and modem.

Occupational Outlook Handbook. Superintendent of Documents, U.S. Government.

Occupational Outlook Handbook for College Graduates. Superintendent of Documents, U.S. Government.

Petras, Kathryn and Ross, *Jobs '93: By Career, By Industry, By Region.* Covers thousands of careers, companies, and associations. Prentice Hall Press, 15 Columbus Circle, New York, NY 10023. 1993.

Professional's Job Finder. This is a wonderful book by Daniel Lauber which lists job-sources such as trade magazines, journals, computerized job-listings, job-matching services, etc., for all the mainline industries and professional occupations. He has done a very thorough research job. Caveat: *some* of the "leads" given here are hideously expensive, so pray your local library has them. Further caveat: in hard times, these places may be as bereft of job leads as anyone else, but they are certainly worth trying. There are companion volumes entitled *Government Job Finder, Non-Profits' Job Finder* among others. If your library doesn't have them, try your local bookstore. If neither has them, write to Planning/Communications, 7215 Oak Ave., River Forest, IL 60305.

Register of manufacturers for your state or area (e.g., *California Manufacturers Register*).

Research Centers Directory 1993, 17th ed. Gale Research, Inc., Box 33477, Detroit, MI 48232-5477. Also: *Research Services Directory,* 5th ed. The two volumes together cover some 13,000 services, facilities, and companies that do research into various subjects, such as feasibility studies, private and public policy, social studies and studies of various cultures, etc.

Standard and Poor's Corporation Records.

Standard and Poor's Industrial Index.

Standard and Poor's Industry Surveys. Good basic introduction, history, and overview of any industry you may be interested in.

Standard and Poor's Listed Stock Reports (at some brokers' offices).

Standard and Poor's Register of Corporations, Directors and Executives. Key executives in 32,000 leading companies, plus 75,000 directors.

Standard Industrial Classification Manual, 1985. Published by the U.S. Government Printing Office. Gives the Standard Industrial Classification code number for any field or industry -- which is the number used by most business references in their indices.

Statistics Sources 1993, 16th ed. Gale Research, Inc., Box 33477, Detroit, MI 48232-5477. Tells you where to find statistics on more than 20,000 specific topics. Key live sources are also featured.

Telecommunications Systems and Services Directory, 1992–1993, 4th ed. Gale Research, Inc., Box 33477, Detroit, MI 48232-5477. Lists over 2,000 national and international firms dealing with communications systems, teleconferencing, videotext, electronic mail, fax services, etc.

Telephone Contacts for Data Users. Customer Services Branch, Bureau of the Census, 1-301-449-1600, for statistical information on any subject.

Thomas' Register of American Manufacturers. Thomas Publishing Co.

Trade association periodicals.

Trade journals.

Training and Development Organizations Directory, 5th ed. Gale Research, Inc., Box 33477, Detroit, MI 48232-5477. For those of you interested in teaching or training, it lists over 2,500 firms and their areas of interest and expertise.

United States Government Manual.

U.S. Industrial Outlook. Published by the U.S. Department of Commerce. Covers 350 manufacturing and service industries. Gives the trends and outlooks for each industry that you may be interested in.

Value Line Investment Survey, from Arnold Bernhard and Co., 5 E. 44th St., New York, NY 10017. (Most libraries have a set.)

Walker's Manual of Far Western Corporations and Securities.

Ward's Business Directory, 3 vols. (Vol. 1, Largest U.S. Companies; Vol. 2, Major U.S. Private Companies; Vol. 3, Major International Companies). Information Access Company, 1201 Davis Dr., Belmont, CA 94002. Updated yearly. Despite the titles, helpful in identifying smaller companies, as well as large.

Who's Who in Finance and Industry, and all the other Who's Who books. Useful once you have the name of someone-who-has-the-power-to-hire, and you want to know more about them.

Besides these reference books, some periodicals are worth perusing: *Business Week, Dun's Review, Forbes, Fortune,* and the *Wall Street Journal.*

Many public libraries have very efficient database search capabilities, through their computers, and can dig up, copy, and mail to you copies of reports on local companies (for a modest cost). For example, one Pennsylvania job-hunter got the Cleveland (Ohio) Library to send him copies of annual reports on a Cleveland-based company. So, when you get to the point where you're researching organizations, if there's an organization or company that particularly interests you, you might want to try contacting the nearest large public library to their home base, and see what that library can turn up for you.

For help on a question no one seems to know the answer to, try the National Referral Center at the Library of Congress, 1-202-287-5670. Also, you can call the Federal Information Center of the General Services Administration at 1-202-755-8660 to find the names of experts in any field.

Additional Reading

Parachute is designed to give you all that you need for figuring out what you want to do, and then going about the job-hunt successfully. But no one book *(including this one)* can reach every reader's every need. If you find *Parachute* isn't giving you all that you need or want, there are other books that may succeed for you. They are listed immediately below.

It may also be that while *Parachute* is helping, you feel you have special needs in your situation *(your age, sex, background, etc.)* where you need or want more light shed. That section begins on page 416.

RECOMMENDED

Wegmann, Robert and Chapman, Robert, *The Right Place at the Right Time: Finding a Job in the 1990s.* Ten Speed Press, Box 7123, Berkeley, CA 94707. 1987, revised and updated, 1990. Highly highly recommended. Bob Wegmann, who died January 2, 1991 after a long illness, knew more about what was going on in the world of work than anyone else in the country. His death is a *great* loss, but here are his insights for us to still profit by.

Wegmann, Robert, and Chapman, Robert, and Johnson, Miriam, *Work in the New Economy: Careers and Job Seeking into the 21st Century.* JIST Works, 720 North Park Ave., Indianapolis, Indiana 46202. 1989. Updated. Highly recommended, of course. Bob Wegmann's insights in another form.

Sher, Barbara, *Wishcraft: How to Get What You Really Want.* Ballantine Books, 201 E. 50th St., New York, NY 10022. 1983. A very helpful book; our readers love it.

LeCompte, Michelle, ed., *JOB HUNTER'S SOURCEBOOK: Where to find employment leads and other job search resources.* Gale Research, Inc., P.O. Box 33477, Detroit, MI 48232-5477. 1991. This is a new resource which I think is exceptional, as it tells you how to find sources of information and job-leads for a whole variety of occupations (155, in all). Somebody did their homework well.

Jackson, Tom, *Guerrilla Tactics in the New Job Market* (2nd ed.). Bantam Books, 666 Fifth Ave., New York, NY 10103. 1991. A very popular and useful book, now revised for the '90s. Tom has some great ideas and insights found in no other authors'.

Jackson, Tom, *Not Just Another Job: How to Invent a Career That Works for You—Now and in the Future.* Times Books, a division of Random House, Inc., 201 E. 50th St., New York, NY 10022. 1992.

Figler, Howard E., *The Complete Job-Search Handbook: All the Skills You Need to Get Any Job and Have a Good Time Doing It.* Henry Holt & Co., Inc., 115 W. 18th St., New York, NY 10011. 1988, Revised and Expanded Edition. Identifies the twenty skills the job-hunter needs in order to pull off a job hunt *successfully*. A very unusual approach to the subject of skills, as well as to the subject of the job-hunt.

Germann, Richard, and Arnold, Peter, *Bernard Haldane Associates' Job and Career Building*. Ten Speed Press, Box 7123, Berkeley, CA 94707. 1981, 1980. A detailed description of how to find a job, *once you know what it is you want to do;* very detailed, and helpful, particularly for executives. Adapted from the well-known program of Bernard Haldane Associates.

Haldane, Bernard, *Career Satisfaction and Success: How to Know and Manage Your Strengths*. Insights from the master himself. Bernard has been in this field longer than anyone I know of. Published by Wellness Behavior, 4502 54th Ave., NE, Seattle, WA 98105. 1988.

Miller, Arthur F., and Mattson, Ralph T., *The Truth About You: Discover What You Should Be Doing with Your Life*. Ten Speed Press, Box 7123, Berkeley CA 94707. 1977, 1989. I like this book a lot. I know of no other book that sets out to do what my friend Arthur has done here: look for *overall patterns* in your choice of jobs -- within the overarching context of *faith*. The process is still an art, not a science, and some readers will be frustrated by that. But the rest will find it suggestive and thought-provoking.

Hirsch, Arlene S., *VGM's Careers Checklists: 89 Proven Checklists to Help You Plan Your Career and Get Great Jobs*. VGM Career Horizons, 4255 West Touhy Ave., Lincolnwood, IL 60646-1975. 1991. Clever format. Primarily a book of job-hunting notes, put in the form of lists. Those who find the previous book too undefined will probably like this book. It should appeal to anyone who likes to be organized, and likes to check things off.

Wallach, Ellen J., and Arnold, Peter, *The Job Search Companion: The Organizer for Job Seekers*. The Harvard Common Press, 535 Albany St., Boston, MA 02118. 1984. Also a book for those who like to get organized. Primarily a book of very useful "forms" for keeping track of your job-search. Intended as a supplement to other job-hunting books.

Irish, Richard K., *Go Hire Yourself an Employer*. Anchor Press, Doubleday, New York, NY. 1987, third ed. An old and popular classic, now reissued.

Campbell, David P., *If You Don't Know Where You're Going, You'll Probably End Up Somewhere Else*. Argus Communications, Niles, IL. 1974. Useful for those who need to be convinced of the need for career planning.

Kojm, Kurt Barnaby, *The Changing Job Jungle: How to Find Your Almost Perfect Career*. About Face Press, 1833 Kensington Ave., Buffalo NY 14215. 1991. A potpouri of traditional ideas about job-hunting, but some readers will find it suggestive and helpful.

OTHER RESOURCES FOR THE JOB-HUNTER OR CAREER-CHANGER BY RICHARD BOLLES

Bolles, Richard N., *How to Create A Picture of Your Ideal Job or Next Career, Advanced Version* (revised) *of the Quick Job-Hunting (and Career-Changing) Map*. Ten Speed Press, Box 7123, Berkeley, CA 94707. 1991, revised. An 8 ½ x 11-inch 48–page workbook, which expands upon Chapters 9, 10, and 11 in this book; in color. $5.95.

Bolles, Richard N., *The Quick Job-Hunting Map for Beginners*. Ten Speed Press, Box 7123, Berkeley, CA 94707. 1990. A workbook version of the Map for high school students just entering the labor force, and those other job-hunters who may prefer a simpler alternative to the Map above. $1.25.

Bolles, Richard N., "The Anatomy of a Job." A 24 x 36 inch poster, designed as a worksheet to be used with *How to Create A Picture* (above). It lists the families of skills on one side, and has a flower-diagram on the other, that can be filled in. 1991. $4.95.

Bolles, Richard N., *How to Find Your Mission in Life*. Ten Speed Press, Box 7123, Berkeley, CA 94707. 1991. A gift-book edition of the Epilogue in this book. $5.95.

Bolles, Richard N., *Job-Hunting Tips For The So-Called Handicapped or People Who Have Disabilities. A Supplement to What Color Is Your Parachute*. Ten Speed Press, Box 7123, Berkeley, CA 94707. 1991. 61 pp. $4.95.

Bolles, Richard N., *The Three Boxes of Life, and How To Get Out of Them*. 480 pages. Ten Speed Press, Box 7123, Berkeley, CA 94707. 1978. $14.95. 350,000 copies in print.

With other co-authors:

Crystal, John C., and Bolles, Richard N., *Where Do I Go From Here With My Life?* 272 pages. Ten Speed Press, Box 7123, Berkeley, CA 94707. 1974. $11.95. 150,000 copies in print.

OTHER VERSIONS OF PARACHUTE

German: Bolles, Richard N., *Tausend geniale Bewerbungstips: Stellensuche richtig vorbereiten*. Goldmann Verlag, Neumarkterstrasse 18, 8000 München. 1987.

Spanish: Bolles, Richard, N., *'cODe Qué Color Es Su Paracaidas?* Editorial Diana, S.A., Roberto Gayol 1219, Mexico, D.F. 1983.

French: Bolles, Richard N., *Chercheurs d'emploi, n'oubliez pas votre parachute*. Translated by Daniel Porot. Sylvie Messinger, éditrice, 31 rue de l'Abbé-Grégoire, Paris 6e, France. 1983. Also: Bolles, Richard N., *Chercheurs d'emploi, n'oubliez pas votre parachute*. Translated by Daniel Porot. Guy Saint-Jean Editeur Inc. 674 Place Publique, Laval, Quebec H7X 1G1, Canada. 1983.

Dutch: Bolles, Richard N., *Werk zoeken-een vak apart, Een professionele aanpak voor het vinden van een (nieuwe) baan*. Translated by F.J.M. Claessens. Uitgeverij Intermediair, Amsterdam/Brussels. 1983.

Japanese: Bolles, Richard N., *'87 What Color Is Your Parachute?* (In Japanese) Japan UNI Agency, Inc., Ten Speed Press and Writers House, Inc., NY. 1986.

Italian: currently being translated.

CAREER BOOKS IN OTHER COUNTRIES AND LANGUAGES

French: Porot, Daniel, *Votre entretien d'embauche: 107 conseils pour le Reussir.* Premiere edition. Les Editions d'organisation, 26, avenue Emile-Zola, F -- 75015 Paris. Tel: 45-78-61-81. 1990. Highly, highly recommended, for those who read French.

Danish: Lausten, Torben, *Kan vingerne bære? Håndbog i JOBJAGT og karriereudvikling.* Udgivet af Forlaget Thorsgaard ApS, Frederikssund, Denmark. 1989.

Japanese: Brockman, Terra, *The Job Hunter's Guide to Japan.* Kodansha International/USA Ltd., 114 Fifth Ave., New York, NY 10011. 1990.

Special Situations

Most of you will find that the main body of *Parachute* tells you all you need to know, in order to successfully conduct your job-hunt. However, *if* you are in one of the groups listed below, and you want additional guidance or information, I have made further comments,and listed some additional resources for you, in the remainder of this Appendix.

Job-Hunting Notes

1. ELEMENTARY SCHOOL STUDENTS, HIGH SCHOOL STUDENTS, AND SUMMER JOBS

If you are a high school student looking for work, you already know that you face especial difficulties during your job-hunt. You can overcome these difficulties. But you do need to be aware of what they are.

Employers currently are turning down, on average, 5 out of every 6 young people who apply for a job, and some companies report that fewer than 1 in 10 applicants meet *their* skills-needs. What's the problem? In a 1991 Harris Poll,[1] 78% of employers said graduates do not have discipline in their work habits. 90% of all employers felt that high school graduates "do not know how to solve complex problems."

Many also feel high school graduates lack basic skills, like **reading**, **writing**, **math** *or* **typing** (as, on a computer keyboard). In 1945, the written vocabulary of a 6- to 14- year-old American child was 25,000 words. Today it is only 10,000. The average young adult in this country is reading at only a 2.6 level of English proficiency, while current jobs require a proficiency, on the average, of 3.0 (*going up to 3.6 by the year 2000, experts say*).

If you are still in high-school, **get those skills --** in reading, writing, math, and typing -- while you are there. If you are *out* of high school, but lack these skills, consider seriously going to night school at your local high school or community college, to make up for lost time.

In spite of the difficulties reported above, any high school student who is willing to diligently follow the job-hunting strategies in this book, particularly Chapters 9, 10, 11, as well as 3 and 4, should be able to put themselves well ahead of the pack. The rules are: *Know your skills. Know what you want to do. Talk to people who have done it. Find out how they did it. Do the homework, on yourself and the companies, thoroughly. Seek out the person who actually has the power to hire; use contacts to get in to see him or her. Show them how you can help them with their problems.* Cut no corners, take no shortcuts.

Below are some books that you or your parents and counselors may find additionally helpful (I have begun this listing with some resources proper for elementary school, since some teachers and counselors want to at least broach the subject of *What do you want to do, when you grow up?* during *those* years):

Otto, Luther B., *How to Help Your Child Choose a Career.* M. Evans & Co., 216 E. 49th St., New York, NY 10017. l984.

Hummel, Dean L., and McDaniels, Carl, *How to Help Your Child Plan a Career.* Acropolis Books, Ltd., Colortone Bldg., 2400 17th St., NW, Washington, DC 20009. l979.

Litvin, Jay, and Salk, Dr. Lee, *How To Be A Super Sitter™*. VGM Career Horizons,4255 West Touhy Ave., Lincolnwood (Chicago), IL 60646-1975.

---

1. Reported in the *San Francisco Chronicle* 9/30/91.

1991. Gives advice to young babysitters about getting jobs, keeping a business going, and how to go about the job.

Mosenfelder, Donn, *Vocabulary for the World of Work*. Educational Design, Inc., 47 W. 13th St., New York, NY 10014. 1985. The 300 words that people entering the work force most need to know.

Kimeldorf, Martin, *Job Search Education*. Educational Design, Inc., 47 W. 13th St., New York, NY 10011. 1985. Worksheets for the young job-hunter. Educational Design puts out a number of different books for elementary and high school students, in addition to the ones listed here, and they have a catalog of such materials, which you can ask for.

The Guide to Basic Skills Jobs, Vol. 1. RPM Press, Inc., Verndale, MN. 1986. A catalog of viable jobs for individuals with only basic work skills. This volume identifies 5,000 major occupations within the U.S. economy which require no more than an eighth grade level of education, and no more than one year of specific vocational preparation.

Henderson, Douglass, *Get Ready: Job-Hunters Kit* (for high school students). This package includes: *Get Ready, Teachers Manual; Get Ready, Students Manual;* and cassette. Done in 'rap' style, with music. Very popular. Get Ready, Inc., a subsidiary of Educational Motivation, Inc., Box 18865, Philadelphia, PA 19119. 1980.

Haldane, Bernard, and Haldane, Jean, and Martin, Lowell, *Job Power: The Young People's Job Finding Guide*. Acropolis Books Ltd., 2400 17th St. NW, Washington, DC 20009. 1980. Undoubtedly the best job-hunting book available for high school students.

Farr, J. Michael, *A Young Person's Guide to Getting and Keeping a Job*. JIST Works, 720 N. Park Ave., Indianapolis, IN 46202. 1990.

Kimeldorf, Martin, *Write Into A Job: Resumes and More*. Meridian Education Corporation, 236 E. Front St., Bloomington, IL 61701. 1990. Written particularly for entry-level or high school job-seekers. Teaches them how best to describe their marketable skills, in resumes or in other forms.

Kennedy, Joyce Lain, and Laramore, Dr. Darryl, *Joyce Lain Kennedy's Career Book*. VGM Career Books, 4255 W. Touhy Ave., Lincolnwood, IL 60646-1975. 1988. Joyce is a very popular and knowledgeable syndicated writer on the subject of careers, while Darryl has written other books on youth and jobs.

As for **summer jobs,** whether for high school or college students, here are the best-known directories. Most of them are annually updated, and the year of their revision often appears in their title:

Beusterien, Pat, ed., *Summer Employment Directory of the United States*. Peterson's Guides, P.O. Box 2123, Princeton, NJ 08543. Issued in annual revisions. The year of the revision appears in the title of the book.

Woodworth, David, ed., *Directory of Overseas Summer Jobs*. Peterson's Guides, P.O. Box 2123, Princeton, NJ 08543. Issued in annual revisions.

Hatchwell, Emily, ed., *Directory of Summer Jobs in Britain*. Peterson's Guides, P.O. Box 2123, Princeton, NJ 08543. Issued in annual revisions.

2. COLLEGE STUDENTS

If you are a college graduate or student looking for work, you already know that you face especial difficulties during your job-hunt. You can overcome these difficulties. But you do need to be aware of what they are.

The major problem is the illusion we have that there is a job that goes with the degree. *Don't corporate recruiters just come on campus during your senior year, and clamor for you to come work for them?* Well, no, they don't. In 1991 June, only one in three graduates had jobs waiting for them at graduation time. At some colleges or universities, that figure is reduced to only one in ten, when times are hard.[2] The rest have to hunt -- hard -- after they are out. The situation is likely to improve *some* during the rest of the 1990's, but in most cases it is *you* who is going to have to take charge of your job-hunt. You can no longer rely on corporate recruiters coming to campus (if you ever could). The race for the best jobs belongs not to the strong, but to those who take initiative and know how to conduct their job-hunt themselves.

That leads us to the second problem, which is that job-hunting isn't taught in most colleges, even though it has today become a necessary survival skill. So, you'll have to pick it up on your own -- as you already know, or you wouldn't be looking at this book.

The rules are easy to learn, since they are the same for you as they are for everyone: *Know your skills. Know what you want to do. Talk to people who have done it. Find out how they did it. Do the homework, on yourself and the companies, thoroughly. Seek out the person who actually has the power to hire; use contacts to get in to see him or her. Show them how you can help them with their problems.*

Memorize Chapters 8, 9, 10, 11, 12, 13, and 14 in this book, as well as Chapters 3 and 4, please. And *do* the exercises therein. Cut no corners, take no shortcuts.

If you want further reading, here it is:

Shingleton, Jack, *Which Niche? Answers to the most common questions about careers and job hunting.* Bob Adams, Inc., 260 Center St., Holbrook, MA 02343. 1989, 1969. A little book, marvelous for its brevity, and its humor. Has many cartoons by well-known San Francisco cartoonist Phil Frank.

Phifer, Paul, *College Majors and Careers: A Resource Guide for Effective Life Planning.* Garrett Park Press, Box 190, Garrett Park, MD 20896. 1987.

Phifer, Paul, *Career Planning Q's & A's: A Handbook for Students, Parents, and Professionals.* Garrett Park Press, Box 190, Garrett Park, MD 20896. 1990.

Moore, Richard W., Ph.D., *Winning the Ph.D. Game: How to Get Into and Out of Graduate School with a Ph.D. and a Job.* Dodd, Mead & Co., 79 Madison Ave., New York, NY 10016. 1985. This seems to me to be an unusually helpful and well-researched book for Ph.D. graduates.

Books on summer jobs are listed at the end of Section 1.

---

2. *USA Today*, 5/1/92

3. IMMIGRANTS TO THE U.S.

If you are newly arrived in this country, and are looking for work, you already know that you face especial difficulties during your job-hunt. You can overcome these difficulties. But you do need to be aware of what they are. And, how to overcome them.

Most of what you need to know, on both counts, can be learned in two ways. First of all, by talking to other immigrants, who have been here longer than you have, and have already 'learned the ropes.' And secondly, by reading this book you are holding in your hands, especially Chapters 3 and 4.

The rules are the same for you as they are for everyone else: *Know your skills. Know what you want to do. Talk to people who have done it. Find out how they did it. Do the homework, on yourself and the companies, thoroughly. Seek out the person who actually has the power to hire; use contacts to get in to see him or her. Show them how you can help them with their problems.* Pay particular attention to Chapters 9, 10, and 11. Also study Chapters 3, 4, 12, 13, and 14. Cut no corners, take no shortcuts.

If you want further reading, there is:

Friedenberg, Joan E., Ph.D., and Bradley, Curtis H., Ph.D., *Finding a Job in the United States.* NTC Publishing Group, 4255 W. Touhy Ave., Lincolnwood, IL 60646-1975. 1988, 1986. A guide for immigrants, refugees, limited-English-proficient job-seekers, foreign-born professionals -- anyone who is seeking work in the United States. It contains job information based on the successful experience of job-seekers, plus advice from the U.S. Department of Labor. Includes information about American job customs and laws related to immigration, as well as a systematic plan for job-hunting.

4. WOMEN

Approximately 74% of all women aged 20 to 44 years of age -- that totals over 57 million women -- are in the workforce, currently employed or looking for work.

When women first started coming into the world of work in droves, which was in the early 1970s, there was a widespread feeling that they needed special job-hunting· techniques -- and that they needed career counselors who catered particularly to women job-hunters. Consequently, books for women job-hunters came out in those days by the bushel basket, and counselors catering just to women *thrived*. That day has passed, and now it is widely recognized that the advice for women who go job-hunting is the same as it is for men: *Know your skills. Know what you want to do. Talk to people who have done it. Find out how they did it. Do the homework, on yourself and the companies, thoroughly. Seek out the person who actually has the power to hire; use contacts to get in to see him or her. Show them how you can help them with their problems. Cut no corners, take no shortcuts.*

Since this realization dawned, there has been a great decline in the number of *women's* job-hunting books -- though a few do still appear each year. In spite of this trend, it is foolish to claim that there are no unique

problems to women who are job-hunting. There are. You *can* overcome these problems, but you need to be aware of what they are.

Some problems reside within the myths that still dance in the heads of *some* employers, particularly *male* employers. Some *still* believe, for example, that if they hire a woman, she will be out sick more than a man. (As my mother always used to say when she couldn't believe the ideas some people had: *Honestly, what is the world coming to?*) Well, anyway, if you are a woman going job-hunting, it will be useful to have some statistics at your fingertips. In this instance, the statistics (from the National Center for Health Statistics) are: women average 5.5 lost work days per year while men miss 4.3 days. In other words, women take only one more sick day *per year* than men do. Next?

There are problems that women face *as* they get the job, or *after* they get the job. Salary is a major one. Single women are notoriously underpaid, whether with children or without. The number of single parents in America currently -- most of them women -- is 10.1 million; of these, 2.1 million live in households headed by someone else -- most often, their parents.[3] The reason they do this is overwhelmingly because they can't afford to live on their own. Said one, "I'd have to earn twice my present salary in order to be able to live on my own." Married women don't fare much better, salarywise. True, in roughly one out of every five marriages, the wife is out-earning her mate; but then there are the other four. On average, working wives earned $13,250 in a recent year[4] compared to working husbands who averaged $29,150 that same year. Part of the inequity is due to the fact that 50% of all working wives only work part-time. Wives working full-time averaged $18,930 in a recent year[5] which is better than the $13,250 cited above -- but still far below husbands' average

3. Reported in the *San Francisco Chronicle,* 4/28/92.
4. 1987, the last year for which statistics were available as we went to press.
5. 1987, again.

salary of $29,150. In general, men get paid more than women of equal experience and training, for the same positions. You *can* increase the salary offered you, *if* you know something about salary negotiation, before you go in for the job interview. Be *sure* and study Chapter 14, in this book. Related to salary is the problem of childcare. In a recent year[6] it was found, about one third of the nation's 18.2 working mothers had to pay for childcare -- and this cost them between $2,000 and $6,000 annually; the average was $2,305. That has certainly increased, as you read this. For the working poor, childcare costs represented one fifth of their income. Needless to say, these costs reduce the *net* amount of their already-low paycheck, considerably.

Another problem, as the Anita Hill/Clarence Thomas hearings on Capitol Hill drove home to the nation, is that of sexual harassment or abuse in the workplace. While harassment in this crazy topsy-turvy world can sometimes be inflicted by women managers on the men or women they work with, or by males to males, the vast majority of harassment is done by males to females: and the harassment ranges from subtle to gross. The crux of the problem lies in *some* men's egos, insecurity, insensitivity, and in their assumption that women probably think like they do. *Wrong!* One survey, for example, found that 75% of men in the workplace found sexual advances from the opposite sex *flattering*, while 75% of women in the workplace found them *offensive*. When women are asked why they put up with it, often silently, their universal reply is: "I need the job."

The idea of not putting up with it, but instead filing a sexual harassment suit, winning it, thus getting rid of your nemesis, and then being able to continue working in that same organization, is a wonderful vision. But do count the cost. Jobs are not just a series of tasks. They are people environments. Much depends on your having *good* rapport with the rest of the staff. Absent that rapport -- if you are shunned by your co-workers or superiors, in the aftermath of winning your sexual harassment suit -- your *wonderful* job can turn into *a nightmare* very quickly.

Moreover, future male employers are often reluctant to hire you if you are (unfairly) viewed as 'a trouble-maker,' based on your having filed this harassment suit; I have had to counsel three women to whom this has happened. Of course, if you limit your future job-hunting to firms run by women, this may not be a factor; on the contrary, they may regard you as a heroine. However, the accent is on the word *may*.

My advice is simple: if you think that filing a harassment suit is not going to fundamentally harm your rapport with the people you have to work with (let us say *everyone* dislikes the person who is your nemesis), *and you are not worried about what it will do to your future employability, then seek out some good advice (I mean, from a lawyer), and if it is agreed that a suit is a good idea, by all means go ahead with it.*

On the other hand, if you think that filing such a suit *is* going to irreparably damage the people environment for you at that job, and in the

---

6. And again.

future, and you therefore decide not to file it, *don't* just decide to stay at that place and continue to take the abuse. Don't 'knuckle under.' Don't let anyone -- even your best friend, partner or spouse -- tell you *"Well, hey, if it's a good job and you like everything else about it, just put up with the sexual innuendos."* A good job, with sexual harassment present, is now by definition a bad job.

What keeps people in bad jobs *(most often)* is lack of confidence in their ability to go find another job, of equal merit. So, take command of your life. Sharpen up your job-hunting skills, *now.* Devour this book. Do all the exercises. When you're confident about your ability to go find another job, go find it. *Then* quit this one. You *don't* need to lose your self-esteem for a paycheck.

It's obvious the workplace is still a pretty chauvinist place, despite some limited improvement over the years. This is reflected not merely in sexual harassment, but also in another problem: that of the invisible *'glass ceiling.'* This now well-known phrase refers to the difficulty women have, in getting promoted beyond a certain point. At lower levels, women are doing better than they used to. They now represent 40% of all managers.[7] But when you get to higher levels, it's a different story. *Oops! The glass ceiling!* In organizations in general, women hold fewer than 5% of senior management jobs.[8] In the Fortune 500 companies in particular, the percentage is 3%.[9]

This explains why so many women are gravitating instead to small organizations, or forming their own companies. The number of women-owned businesses totaled almost 5.4 million in 1990.[10] They provide jobs for 10% of all U.S. workers, or close to 11 million people. This is almost as many people as the Fortune 500 firms employ. 40% of women-owned businesses have been in business twelve years or longer. If the idea of following in their footsteps interests you, be *sure* and study Chapter 6.

Due partly to the obstacles cited above, partly to the hard times we are in, partly to many mothers' desire to be with their children while they may, partly to women concluding they want more time to smell the flowers, some women are dropping out of the workplace and taking on the role of homemaker. In 1990, the percentage of women in the work-force did not increase over the previous year, for the first time since 1948. In fact, it dropped. So, if you're contemplating dropping out of the workforce, for any of the above reasons, don't feel lonely, as though you were going against the trend. You've got lots of company. Even though this means you will not be going job-hunting, I would still advise you to do Chapters 9, and 10, in order to be clear about how you want to use your energies and skills, in the home and community.

If you're moving in the other direction, from the house to the marketplace, there are some *very* helpful resources you may want to get your

7. Reported in *USA Today,* 4/24/92.
8. *Ibid.*
9. According to a study by the Feminist Majority Foundation, released in August of 1991.
10. See: *Women Owned Businesses: The New Economic Force,* the 1992 Data Report of the National Foundation for Women Business Owners, available from them at 1377 K St., N.W., Suite 637, Washington, D.C. 20005.

hands on. The first listing is for either male or female homemakers:

Ekstrom, Ruth B., Harris, Abigail M., and Lockheed, Marlaine E., *How to Get College Credit for What You Have Learned as a Homemaker and Volunteer*. 1977. Project HAVE SKILLS, Education Testing Service, Princeton, NJ 08541. They also publish the: *HAVE SKILLS Women's Workbook, HAVE SKILLS Counselor's Guide*, and *HAVE SKILLS Employer's Guide*. All of these include the famous "I CAN" lists, based upon the pioneering work, in the assessment of volunteer skills and knowledge, of the Council of National Organizations for Adult Education. The preeminent resource for women coming out of the home into the marketplace, who wonder what they can claim about their home experience. It applies to all homemakers returning to the marketplace, regardless of whether or not they wish college credit for what they have learned so far in life. It should also be useful to *househusbands* who want to now return to the marketplace. These workbooks classify the homemaker's skills under the various roles of: administrator/manager, financial manager, personnel manager, trainer, advocate/change agent, public relations/ communicator, problem surveyor, researcher, fund-raiser, counselor, youth group leader, group leader for a serving organization, museum staff assistant (docent), tutor/teacher's aide, manager of home finances, home nutritionist, home child caretaker, home designer and maintainer, home clothing and textile specialist, and home horticulturist. *Very* helpful book, with accompanying aids.

Nivens, Beatryce, *Careers for Women without College Degrees*. McGraw-Hill Book Company, 11 West 19th St., New York, NY 10011. 1988. Has some useful information about the skills required for some typical occupations that a woman might be considering.

Doss, Martha Merrill, *Women's Organizations: A National Directory*. Lists over 2,000 women's organizations nationwide as well as locally, plus much more. Garrett Park Press, Box 190, Garrett Park, MD 20896. 1986.

If you are interested in sales positions, you will want to know about the National Association for Professional Saleswomen, P.O. Box 2606, Novato, CA 94948. They have chapters across the country, and they publish a newsletter, called *Successful Saleswoman*.

If it's daycare that concerns you, there are directories beginning to come out now, such as:

The New York Daycare Directory (Includes northern New Jersey and southwestern Connecticut). Bob Adams, Inc., 260 Center St., Holbrook, MA 02343. 1989.

The Boston Daycare Directory. Bob Adams, Inc., 260 Center St., Holbrook, MA 02343. 1989.

5. MINORITIES (BLACK, HISPANIC, NATIVE AMERICANS, OR ASIAN)

Minorities comprise the coming workforce of the year 2000. Already, one out of every three *new* workers is either Black, Hispanic or Asian, according to the Bureau of Labor Statistics. One out of every five workers, new or experienced, was from one of these minorities in 1986.

In spite of this, if you are a member of one of the minorities, you already know that you face especial difficulties in looking for a job. You can overcome these difficulties. But you need to be aware of what they are.

The principal one is the mental view that others have of the world. I call this *tribalism*, and it is the root of so many troubles throughout the world: in the Persian gulf region, the Middle East, Yugoslavia, Russia, Africa, and -- *of course* -- *here. So long as whites remain dominant among employers here, tribalism* and its bastard offspring, *prejudice*, will be something you have to take into account.

Everyone is familiar with the consequences that this tribalism has had for **blacks**: while the number of affluent black households (a yearly income of $50,000 or more) doubled between 1982 and 1987, nonetheless 33% of the nation's 30.2 million blacks still live in poverty; black unemployment in 1988 averaged 11.7%, versus 5.5% for the nation; the median 1987 income of black families was only 56% of that of white families.

Other minorities run into the same tribalism. Minorities hold fewer than 1% of senior management jobs in this country.[11] So, if you're a member of a minority, that's what you're up against. Now, what can you do about it -- what will help you compete more successfully in the job-market? **Answer:** *Know your skills. Know what you want to do. Talk to people who have done it. Find out how they did it. Do the homework, on yourself and the companies, thoroughly. Seek out the person who actually has the power to hire; use contacts to get in to see him or her. Show them how you can help them with their problems.* Pay particular attention to Chapters 3, 4, 9, 10, and 11. Also study Chapters 12, 13, and 14. *as though your life depended on it.* Cut no corners, take no shortcuts.

When it comes time to look for sources of information, or contacts, the following may be of help, in your local library, or direct from the publisher:

Cole, Katherine W., ed., *Minority Organizations: A National Directory.* 3rd ed. Garrett Park Press, Box 190, Garrett Park, MD 20896. 1987. An annotated directory of 7,700 Black, Hispanic, Native American, and Asian American organizations.

The Black Resource Guide. Black Resource Guide, Inc., 501 Oneida Pl., NW, Washington, DC 20111. 1987. A comprehensive list of over 3,000 black resources or organizations in the U.S.

Johnson, Willis L., ed., *Directory of Special Programs for Minority Group Members: Career Information Services, Employment Skills Banks, Financial Aid Sources,* 5th ed. Garrett Park Press, Box 190, Garrett Park, MD 20896. 1990.

---

11. Reported in *USA Today,* 4/24/92.

6. EXECUTIVES, THE BUSINESS WORLD AND CORPORATE JOBS

If you are an executive looking for work, you already know that you face especial difficulties during your job-hunt. You *can* overcome these difficulties. But you do need to be aware of what they are. And, how to overcome them.

The first is, there are a lot of other executives out there, job-hunting at the same time you are. This most recent recession hit white collar workers *hard*. In other words, you've got a lot of stiff competition. That's why the average job search period for executives was 6.8 months recently.[12] Secondly, the length of your job-search will likely be related to your age, and the amount of salary that you are seeking. One large outplacement firm kept records and discovered that if an executive was 25–34 years of age, the average length of their job-hunt was about 20 weeks, but if over 55 years in age, it took almost 30 weeks. They further discovered that for those seeking an annual salary of $40,000 to $75,000, the average length of their job-hunt was about 25 weeks, while for those seeking more than $100,000, the average length of their job-hunt was almost 30 weeks.[13] That's what you're up against.

However, these statistics reflect not only a difficult job-market, but *more importantly* the method of job-hunting that executives traditionally depend upon. Chapter 3, in this book, describes executives' traditional method of job-hunting, mostly because they don't know any better. Avoid that method, like the plague.

Your salvation depends on the same creative job-hunting methods as anyone else: *Know your skills. Know what you want to do. Talk to people who have done it. Find out how they did it. Do the homework, on yourself and the companies, thoroughly. Seek out the person who actually has the power to hire; use contacts to get in to see him or her. Show them how you can help them with their problems.* Pay particular attention to Chapters 3, 4, 9, 10, and 11, *as though your life depended on it*. Also study Chapters 12, 13, and 14. Cut no corners, take no shortcuts.

If you aren't yet an executive, but think you would like to be one, know what you are walking into. According to a 1990 survey by Accountemps, it ain't all glamor: the average business executive reports that he or she spends on average 60 hours a year *on hold* on the phone, and 128 hours a year reading or writing unnecessary memos, and 288 hours a year attending unnecessary meetings. To get a more precise fix on the kind of executive that you'd like to be, in the kind of company that you'd like to work for, go talk to executives who are already there, and ask them what their week is like.

For would-be executive, and experienced executive alike, there are the following additional helps:

---

12. According to Drake Beam Morin Inc., for the year 1990.
13. Reported in the *National Business Employment Weekly,* in the 8/27/89 edition. Statistics were for the year 1989.

Boll, Carl R., *Executive Jobs Unlimited.* Updated edition. Macmillan Publishing Co., Inc., 866 Third Ave., New York, NY 10022. 1979, 1965. One of the two classics in the executive job-hunting field.

Drucker, Peter, *Management: Tasks, Responsibilities, Practices.* HarperCollins, 10 E. 53rd St., New York, NY 10022. 1973. The other classic in this field. Should be absolutely required reading for anyone contemplating entering, changing to, or becoming a professional within any organization in the business world.

Burton, Mary Lindley, and Wedemeyer, Richard A., *In Transition: From the Harvard Business School Club of New York Personal Seminar in Career Management.* HarperBusiness, a division of HarperCollins Publishers, 10 E. 53rd St., New York, NY 10022. 1991.

Corporate Jobs Outlook, "The Key to America's Top Employers," P.O. Drawer 100, Boerne, Texas 78006, is a newsletter published bi-monthly, with detailed information about current situations at top corporate employers. Your library may have it, and it is also available online, for those of you who have a computer and subscribe (or want to subscribe) to **NewsNet** (the telephone number is 800-345-1301, except in Pennsylvania or outside the U.S., where it is 215-527-8030). They emphasize that the seven keys to look for in your research of any corporate employer are: financial stability; growth plans; research and development programs; product development or manufacturing -- emerging products, services, or use of new technologies; marketing and distribution methods; employee benefits; and quality of work factors -- continuing training, health programs, childcare, promote-from-within, performance reviews.

Cole, Kenneth J., *The Head-hunter Strategy.* John Wiley & Sons, Inc., 605 Third Ave., New York, NY 10158. 1985.

"I used to ask myself, 'What can I do to help my fellow man?' but I couldn't think of anything that wouldn't have put me to considerable inconvenience."

7. 'RECOVERING PEOPLE' (FROM ALCOHOLISM, DRUGS, OTHER CHEMICAL DEPENDENCIES, CO-DEPENDENCIES), AND OTHER '12-STEP PROGRAM PEOPLE'

You know what I'm going to say: if you are 'in recovery' and looking for work, you may face especial difficulties during the hiring interviews. You *can* overcome these difficulties. But you do need to be aware of what they are. And, how to overcome them.

Any prejudice about your history can be overcome if you: *Know your skills. Know what you want to do. Talk to people who have done it. Find out how they did it. Do the homework, on yourself and the companies, thoroughly. Seek out the person who actually has the power to hire; use contacts to get in to see him or her. Show them how you can help them with their problems.* Pay particular attention to Chapters 3, 4, 9, 10, and 11, *as though your life depended on it.* Also study Chapters 12, 13, and 14. Cut no corners, take no shortcuts.

If you want additional help, there are the following resources:

Tanenbaum, Nat, and Eric A., *The Career Seekers: A Program for Career Recovery.* The Working Press, a division of The Career Center, Inc., P.O. Box 49631, Atlanta, GA 30359. 1988. This book is for people who are actively practicing any 12-step program, or are in counseling for co-dependency; but its principles apply to all who see themselves as 'recovering people.' Very useful supplement to *Parachute.*

Whitfield, M.D., Charles L., *A Gift to Myself.* Health Communications, Inc., Deerfield Beach, FL. 1990. Deals with root emotional issues often blocking job-hunters in recovery.

8. EX-MILITARY

If you are an ex-military person who has decided to look for work outside the military, in the general workplace, you already know that you will have some problems convincing the world you know *anything* except how to wage war. You *can* convince them, but it will take work.

Your major problem is that you speak a different language from those out there in the world. You have been living in a sub-culture within our general culture, and this sub-culture is in many respects like the general job-market, *except* that it has its own unique vocabulary. It is *crucial* that you sit down and inventory the skills you have been using during your time in the military (Chapters 9, 10, and 11 in this book are *mandatory* for you to *do*). Take especial care to take your skills and fields of knowledge out of the military *jargon*, and translate them into language that is understood in the general marketplace.

There are three aids to help you do this: (1) Each service's personnel manuals has a section where military jobs and tasks are cross-coded to the civilian *Dictionary of Occupational Titles.* (2) There is also a two-volume Military Occupation Training Data series, available from Defense Manpower Data Center, 1600 Wilson Blvd., Suite 400, Arlington VA 22209, which does the same thing. (3) Militran, Inc, Box 490, Southeastern, PA 19399-0490, 1-800-426-9954, has a *Militran Guide to Career Opportunities,* published monthly in three editions: one for Army personnel, one for Navy-Marine Corps personnel, and one for Air Force Personnel, which not only list what civilian job title is equivalent to your former military job title, but also list a considerable number of ads which they have culled from various newspapers around the country, *indexed by those same civilian job titles.*

Militran also operates a free computerized resume database for all military personnel. In any profession, such databases typically are more used by job-seekers than they are by employers, but you may want to try this one, anyway. For information about the database, write to Militran, 1255 Drummers Lane, Suite 306, Wayne, PA 19087.

If you are or were an officer, you should know that the Retired Officers Association (TROA), 201 North Washington Street, Alexandria, VA 22314-2529, 703-838-8117 has an Officer Placement Service which maintains a comprehensive job-search library, computerized placement service, and resume critique. It is, however, open only to officers who become members of TROA.

Officer or not, your salvation depends on the same creative job-hunting -- and career-changing -- methods as anyone else: *Know your skills. Know what you want to do. Talk to people who have done it. Find out how they did it. Do the homework, on yourself and the companies, thoroughly. Seek out the person who actually has the power to hire; use contacts to get in to see him or her. Show them how you can help them with their problems.* Pay particular attention to Chapters 3, 4, 9, 10, and 11, *as though your life depended on it.* Also study Chapters 12, 13, and 14. Cut no corners, take no shortcuts.

An additional book:

Schlachter, Gail Ann, and Weber, R. David, *Financial Aid for Veterans, Military Personnel, and Their Dependents 1990-1991.* Reference Service Press, 1100 Industrial Road, Suite 9, San Carlos, CA 94070. 1990. Outlines over 1,000 programs open to veterans and their dependents.

9. CLERGY AND RELIGIOUS

If you are an ordained person who has decided to look for work outside the church, in the general workplace, you already know that you will have some problems convincing the world you know *anything* except theology. As a matter of fact, you *can* convince them, but it will take work.

Your major problem is that you speak a different language from those out there in the world. Like the military (above) you have been living in a sub-culture within our general culture, which describes your skills and work-experience in its own unique vocabulary. It is *crucial* that you sit down and inventory the skills you have been using during your time in the clergy (Chapters 9, 10, and 11 in this book are *mandatory* for you to do), and that you take especial care to *translate* your skills and fields of knowledge out of the clerical *jargon* and into language that is understood in the general marketplace.

The rules for *your* job-hunt, or career-change, are the same as they are for everyone: *Know your skills. Know what you want to do. Talk to people who have done it. Find out how they did it. Do the homework, on yourself and the companies, thoroughly. Seek out the person who actually has the power to hire; use contacts to get in to see him or her. Show them how you can help them with their problems.* Pay particular attention to Chapters 3, 4, 9, 10, and 11, *as though your life depended on it.* Also study Chapters 12, 13, and 14. Cut no corners, take no shortcuts.

In case you want further reading, or counseling, the books and counselors who look at job-hunting and career-changing particularly from a religious point of view are to be found at the end of The Epilogue, on page 373.

10. EX-OFFENDERS

If you are an ex-offender, and are looking for work, *of course* you are going to face especial difficulties during the hiring interviews, because of your history. You *can* deal with this problem, if you remember this above all: all employers divide into two groups: those who will be bothered by your incarceration, and those who won't be. Your job is to find the second group of employers, and just thank the first very politely for their time.

With the second, your case will be helped immeasurably if you: *Know your skills. Know what you want to do. Talk to people who have done it. Find out how they did it. Do the homework, on yourself and the companies, thoroughly. Seek out the person who actually has the power to hire; use contacts to get in to see him or her. Show them how you can help them with their problems. Cut no corners, take no shortcuts.*

If you want to start working on this while you are still in prison, devour *this* book. Pay particular attention to Chapters 3, 4, 9, 10, and 11, *as though your life depended on it.* Do all the pertinent exercises therein. Also study Chapters 12, 13, and 14. Cut no corners, take no shortcuts.

You can also obtain a "Pre-Employment Curriculum" from the American Correctional Association, 4321 Hartwick Rd., College Park, MD 20740.

If you decide you want to work on a college degree program while you are in prison, it can be done. See the Appendix entitled,

"Advice for People in Prison," in Bear, John, *College Degrees by Mail: 100 Good Schools that Offer Bachelor's, Master's, Doctorates and Law Degrees by Home Study.* Ten Speed Press, Box 7123, Berkeley, CA 94707. 1991.

Once you're out, and you are job-hunting, Federal/State Employment Offices can often be of particular assistance to ex-offenders. All offices can provide for bonding of ex-offenders, if needed to obtain employment. They also have information on tax-breaks for employers who hire ex-offenders. The larger offices even have Ex-Offender Specialists.

For further reading: *A Survival Source Book for Offenders,* from Contacts, Inc., Box 81826, Lincoln, NE 68501.

11. PEOPLE WITH DISABILITIES OR HANDICAPS

If you have a physical, mental, emotional, or other disability, and are looking for work, *of course* you are going to face especial difficulties during the hiring interviews, because of your disability. You *can* deal with this problem, if you remember this above all: all employers divide into two groups: those who will be bothered by your disability, and those who won't be. Your job is to find the second group of employers, and just thank the first very politely for their time.

With the second, your case will be helped immeasurably if you: *Know your skills. Know what you want to do. Talk to people who have done it. Find out how they did it. Do the homework, on yourself and the companies, thoroughly. Seek out the person who actually has the power to hire; use contacts to get in to see him or her. Show them how you can help them with their problems.* Cut no corners, take no shortcuts.

Beyond this, there is much more to be said that is helpful, but unfortunately this requires more space than we have here. I have, therefore, produced a lengthy booklet on this subject, intended to be used with *Parachute*, available in your bookstore, or directly from Ten Speed Press, Box 7123, Berkeley, CA 94707. Its title is *Job-Hunting Tips For The So-Called Handicapped or People Who Have Disabilities. A Supplement to What Color Is Your Parachute.* 1991. 61 pp. $4.95.

If you wish to save this money, you can consult your local library to see if it has a copy of the booklet, *or* a copy of the 1990 or 1991 editions of *Parachute*, since this stuff first appeared as an Appendix in the back of those editions.

12. PEOPLE FACING RETIREMENT OR ALREADY RETIRED

Now, a word or two about **retirement**: if you work in a company with 20 or more employees, they cannot since 1986 force you to retire just because you reach a specified age, though they can force you to retire for unsatisfactory performance of your job at any age. Does this mean there are a lot more 'older workers' now than there used to be? No, strangely enough, it does not. In 1950, 46% of men over 65 were still in the labor force; and now that percentage is less than 17%. Most women now leave the work-force before they turn 60, and most men before they turn 63. In fact, one third of all career jobs now end by age 55.

What happens **after** retirement? The percentages, according to a relatively recent study,[14] are that half of the elderly who are out of the work-force are satisfied with their situation, one quarter are simply *unable* to work (presumably because of health), and one quarter are very unhappy with the fact that they aren't working. The numbers underlying those percentages are these:[15] 21.5 million Americans are between ages 50 and 64,

---

14. Reported in *The New York Times*, 4/22/90.
15. Reported in *National Business Employment Weekly*, 2/18/90.

of whom 13.3 million are working, and 8.2 million are not. Of the latter, 4.7 million don't want to work, 1.6 million are unable to, and almost 2 million would like to be back at work. In fact, one out of three retired **men** does return to the labor force, usually within two years.[16]

If you are retired, and would like to return to work, *of course* you are going to face especial difficulties during the hiring interviews, because of your age. You *can* deal with this problem, if you remember this above all: all employers divide into two groups: those who will be bothered by your age, and those who won't be. Your job is to find the second group of employers, and just thank the first very politely for their time.

With the second, your case will be helped immeasurably if you: *Know your skills. Know what you want to do. Talk to people who have done it. Find out how they did it. Do the homework, on yourself and the companies, thoroughly. Seek out the person who actually has the power to hire; use contacts to get in to see him or her. Show them how you can help them with their problems.* Cut no corners, take no shortcuts.

As you probably already know, your desire to work will be complicated by Social Security requirements, which amount basically to a disincentive to work: in order to continue to receive full benefits, *as of 1992,* you must not earn more than $7,440 a year if you are under 65. You will lose $1 in benefits for every $2 that you earn above that limit. If you are 65 to 69, you must not earn more than $10,200. You will lose $1 in benefits for every $3 that you earn above that limit. After you reach 70, however, there is no limit. Check with your local Social Security office to find out if the limits have been raised, by the time you read this.

If you want to work primarily (or solely) to supplement your retirement income, the foregoing is a serious disincentive, indeed. On the other hand, if you want to work for the pure joy of working, the economic disincentive will probably not faze you. You can always volunteer your time (see Chapter 6), without cost to the place where you serve. Now, to further reading:

If you want to prepare for your final ten years in the world of work, before retirement, there is:

Bolles, Richard N., "The decade of decisions," in *Modern Maturity* magazine, February-March 1990 issue (see your local library). Discusses the six options you can choose between, during the final ten years of your life in the world of work.

If you're trying to plan what your retirement will be like, even if you don't work, there is:

Chapman, Elwood N., *Comfort Zones: Planning Your Future.* Crisp Publications, Inc., 95 First St., Los Altos, CA 94022, or from Career Research & Testing, 2005 Hamilton Ave., Suite 250, San Jose, CA 95125-9872. 1990, second ed. A very popular and practical guide for retirement planning.

T. Rowe Price Retirees Financial Guide. A very useful and detailed financial planning guide put out by T. Rowe Price, possessing one other sterling

---

16. Reported in *American Demographics*, 12/90. Statistics for women in retirement are not yet available.

virtue: it is free. 1 800 541 5790. Their address is T. Rowe Price Investment Services, Inc., 100 E. Pratt St., Baltimore, MD 21202. *Naturally*, they hope you'll invest in some funds they list, so you might get some follow-up mail (I did). But it's a fine guide.

How to Plan Your Successful Retirement, AARP Book Publication. AARP, 1909 K St., NW, Washington, DC 20049. 1988.

If you want some guidance about possible places to retire to, in the U.S., there are:

Boyer, Richard, and Savageau, David, *Places Rated a·l·m·a·n·a·c*. Prentice Hall Press, A division of Simon & Schuster, Inc., 15 Columbus Circle, New York, NY 10023. 1989. All 333 metropolitan areas ranked and compared for living costs, job outlook, crime, health, transportation, education, the arts, recreation, and climate. Highly recommended. A knockout of a book. They update it periodically.

Savageau, David, *Retirement Places ra·t·e·d*. Prentice Hall Press, A division of Simon & Schuster, Inc., 15 Columbus Circle, New York, NY 10023. 1990. 151 top retirement areas ranked and compared for costs of living, housing, climate, personal safety, services, work opportunities, and leisure living. Highly recommended. Tremendously useful. He updates it periodically.

Best-Rated Retirement Cities & Towns, Consumer Guide Publications International, Ltd., 7373 N. Cicero Ave., Lincolnwood, IL 60646. 1988. A review of 100 of the most attractive retirement locations across America.

If you want to know what retired people do, by way of work, after retirement, the classic on this subject is:

Bird, Caroline, *Second Careers: New Ways to Work After 50*. Little, Brown and Company, Boston, Toronto, London. 1992. The subject of this book is not what 'seniors' ought to do after age 50, but what in fact they *do* do.....and why. This book is her 'report to the nation' of her analysis of some 36,000 questionnaires sent in by readers of *Modern Maturity* Magazine. Highly recommended.

If your aging is an issue for you, you might want to take out of your local library (or bookstore):

Dychtwald, Ken, and Flower, Joe, *Age Wave: The Challenges and Opportunities of an Aging America*. Bantam Books, 666 Fifth Ave., New York, NY 10103. 1990. The most important book out yet on all the implications of aging.

There's also a book which describes how old some people were, when they did their great achievement. Designed, of course, to inspire you to go and do likewise. It begins with actual achievements, like learning classical Greek, at age three. (Talk about over-achievers!) You'll probably be especially interested in what people did between ages 50–96:

Bierlein, J.F., *The Book of Ages*. Ballantine Books, a division of Random House, Inc., 201 E. 50th St., New York, NY 10022. 1992.

Addendum
OTHER CAREER BOOKS

If there's some career-related, or job-hunting, problem that you're dying to find out more about, and none of the above books will do, there are three alternative routes open to you.

(1) Your local public library, or nearby community college library. You will of course fly over there and see if they can shed some light. If they have a friendly reference librarian by all means ask to see him or her. They can be worth their weight in gold to you. Tell them your problem or interest, and see what they can dig up. They often know of hidden treasures, buried in articles and clippings, as well as books, which could be the answer to your prayers.

(2) Your local bookstores -- go there, browse, and see what they have.

(3) Mail order. There are a number of places which specialize in career books. Below is a *sampling* (only) of some of their catalogs, which you can write and ask for:

Career Development Resources Catalog. Career Research & Testing, 2005 Hamilton Ave., San Jose, CA 95125.

Career Planning and Job Search Catalog. JIST Works, Inc., 720 North Park Avenue, Indianapolis, IN 46202.

Careers, Inc. Catalog, Careers, Inc., 1211 10th St., S.W., P.O. Box 135, Largo, FL 34649-0135.

Catalog of job-quest books, Planning/Communications, 7215 Oak Ave., River Forest, IL 60305.

Garrett Park Press Catalog, Garrett Park Press, Box 190, Garrett Park, MD 20896.

Job & Career Library. Consultants Bookstore, Templeton Road, Fitzwilliam, NH 03447.

Peterson's Guides, P.O. Box 2123, Princeton, NJ 08543.

Ten Speed Press Catalog, Ten Speed Press, Box 7123, Berkeley, CA 94707. They often have a listing of just their career-related books. (As I write, it is called *The 1992 Career-Planning, Business Know-How and Skills for Personal Growth List*). Ask.

VGM *Career Books.* NTC Publishing Group, 4255 West Touhy Ave., Lincolnwood, IL 60646-1975.

The Whole Work Catalog: Career Resources. The New Careers Center, Inc., 1515 23rd Street, P.O. Box 339, Boulder, CO 80306.

Writer's Digest Catalog. Writer's Digest Books, 1507 Dana Ave., Cincinnati, OH 45207.

Books and periodicals designed particularly for career-counselors, are listed at the end of Appendix A, beginning on page 400. *Some job-hunters or career-changers looking for further insights, may want to browse there, to see if there is anything of interest to them.*

Index

Author Index

Other Resources

Additional materials by Richard N. Bolles to help you with your job-hunt:

HOW TO CREATE A PICTURE OF YOUR IDEAL JOB OR NEXT CAREER

This workbook (8½ by 11 inches) is designed to lead the reader through a series of detailed exercises, expanding upon Chapters 9 and 10 in *Parachute*. $5.95

THE ANATOMY OF A JOB

This 24 by 36 inch poster serves as a worksheet to supplement the workbook above *(How to Create A Picture . . .)*. The 'Skills Keys' are on one side, and the 'Flower' is on the other side. $4.95

HOW TO FIND YOUR MISSION IN LIFE

This is a gift book version of the current Epilogue in *Parachute*. Judging by the mail Dick Bolles receives, this is a favorite of readers who want their work to fulfill a purpose and bring more than simply money to their lives. $5.95

THE MISSION POSTER

This colorful 24 by 36 inch poster summarizes the main ideas in the booklet above *(How to Find Your Mission in Life)*. $4.95

JOB-HUNTING TIPS FOR THE SO-CALLED "HANDICAPPED" OR PEOPLE WHO HAVE DISABILITIES

Originally published as an appendix in *Parachute,* this popular material is now only available as a separate booklet. In this work, Dick Bolles uses his unique perspective on job-hunting and career-change to address the experiences of the disabled in doing these tasks. $4.95

To: Ten Speed Press
P. O. Box 7123
Berkeley, CA 94707

I would like to order:

_____ copies of **HOW TO CREATE A PICTURE OF YOUR IDEAL JOB OR NEXT CAREER** @ $5.95 each. _____

_____ copies of the poster **THE ANATOMY OF A JOB** @ $4.95 each. _____

_____ copies of **HOW TO FIND YOUR MISSION IN LIFE** @ $5.95 each. _____

_____ copies of **THE MISSION POSTER** @ $4.95 each. _____

_____ copies of **JOB-HUNTING TIPS FOR THE SO-CALLED "HANDICAPPED" OR PEOPLE WHO HAVE DISABILITIES** @ $4.95 each. _____

Subtotal $ _____

Postage is $2.50 for the first item ordered and 50¢ for each additonal item.

Postage $ _____

Total $ _____

Check or money order only, please, made out to Ten Speed Press.

Send to: (please print)

Name _____

Organization _____

Mailing Address _____

City, State, Zip _____

Update for 1994

TO: PARACHUTE
P.O. Box 379
Walnut Creek, CA 94597

I think that the information in the '93 edition needs to be changed, in your next revision, regarding (or, the following resource should be added):

_____

_____

_____

_____

_____

_____

I cannot find the following resource, listed on page _____:

_____

_____

_____

_____

_____

_____

Name _____

Address _____

Please make a copy.

Submit this so as to reach us by February 1, 1993. Thank you.

Notes

Notes